Net Crimes & Misdemeanors

For Pete,

Stay safe online!

J Hitchcock

Net Crimes & Misdemeanors

Outmaneuvering Web Spammers, Stalkers, and Con Artists

Second Edition

By J. A. Hitchcock

Edited by Loraine Page

Information Today, Inc.

Medford, New Jersey

First printing, 2006

Net Crimes & Misdemeanors: Outmaneuvering Web Spammers, Stalkers, and Con Artists, Second Edition

Library of Congress Cataloging-in-Publication Data

Hitchcock, Jayne A.
  Net crimes & misdemeanors : outmaneuvering web spammers, stalkers, and con artists / J. A. Hitchcock ; edited by Loraine Page.-- 2nd ed.
    p. cm.
  Includes bibliographical references and index.
    ISBN 0-910965-72-2
  1. Computer crimes. 2. Computer crimes--Prevention. I. Page, Loraine, 1952-
II. Title.

  HV6773 .H575 2002
  364.16'8--dc22

                                                              2006006218

Printed and bound in the United States of America.

President and CEO: Thomas H. Hogan, Sr.
Editor-in-Chief and Publisher: John B. Bryans
Managing Editor: Amy M. Reeve
Cover Design: Michele Quinn
Book Design: Kara Mia Jalkowski
Copy Editor: Dorothy Pike
Proofreader: Pat Hadley-Miller
Indexer: Sharon Hughes

Dedication

To my husband, Chris, who has never wavered in his support for me during the ups and downs of my cyberstalking case, who has been my biggest cheerleader when the going got tough, who has put up with my getting laws passed, traveling the world training law enforcement and doing speaking engagements, being interviewed by the media many, many times, and who has endured my writing of this book past dinnertime more often than not. You're the best, hon!

Table of Contents

Figures

Sidebars

Acknowledgments

Thank you's go to many people, and I know I'll probably forget someone.

My "Internet Posse"—especially the ones who stuck it out to the end, namely Cyber-Sheriff Chris Lewis, Jack Mingo, Stan Kid, Curt Akin, James Charles Rau, Mary Kay Klim, Bob Pastorio, Dick Harper, Erin Barrett, Colin Hatcher, Wayne Lutz, Crusader Rabbit, and Mary Jo Place, aka "Kiki"; also Marty, Sal, Bjorn, Ellie, Marjike, Kye and Katy Munger; and the newsgroup misc.writing. Without all of you, I never would have learned so much about the Net and how to educate others about it.

My lawyer, John Young. He took my cyberstalking case on contingency—you truly are a blessing.

My "big brother" Raymond E. Feist. He kept me sane when I was depressed about my cyberstalking case and encouraged me to keep at it when my book proposal was rejected numerous times.

My editor Loraine Page. When I groused to her that my book proposal was rejected by just about every publisher and I'd gone through three literary agents, she suggested sending the proposal to the book division of the publishing company that produces *Link-Up,* a print Internet magazine to which I contribute and she edits. I slapped myself on the forehead for not thinking of it myself. If it hadn't been for Loraine, this book might never have come to fruition—and she's one of the best editors I've ever worked with.

All the people interviewed for this book—victims and experts. There are too many to mention by name, but you know who you are and you were all wonderful to share your experiences and expertise.

My fellow volunteers at WHOA (Working to Halt Online Abuse) and WHOA-KTD (Kids/Teen Division). I couldn't ask for a better group of people to work with, and a special thank you to Lynda Hinkle, who founded WHOA in 1997 and handed over the reins to me in 1999.

The University of Maryland University College and my boss (and friend) Art Huseonica. UMUC became one of the first universities to deal with a cyberstalking case—mine—and they handled it well (especially Rocky). I'm glad I didn't "quit teachering" after all!

Finally, thank you to my family and my in-laws, who all stood behind me as I fought my cyberstalkers. Never once did you ask me to quit. You cheered me on and I will never forget it.

Foreword

If you are reading this book or thinking about acquiring it, you have taken an important step toward increasing your awareness of the ways in which the Internet may be abused. J. A. Hitchcock has prepared a second edition of her popular book, *Net Crimes and Misdemeanors*, reflecting new ways in which you may encounter the dark side of global networking. Her personal experiences lend credibility to the text and her concrete examples help readers formulate defenses to avoid becoming victims.

The Internet has much to offer that is positive and constructive. It started as an academic research exercise and the community that used it, 20 years ago, was largely homogeneous in its interests. As the Internet became better known and as the World Wide Web opened up the Internet to consumer use 10 years ago, the user population began to resemble the general population. Today, users cover the same gamut as drivers on the highway, and then some, considering there are many users who are not yet old enough to drive, but are old enough to cause online trouble.

This book is intended to provide readers with insights into some of the ways in which predators and troublemakers may abuse the Internet, causing direct harm or at least psychological damage on other unsuspecting users. A new vocabulary has evolved as some of these abuses have come to light. "Cyberstalking" and "phishing" are examples. Indeed, many of the abuses we see are in principle no different than those carried out with older technology (e.g., telephone, postal service). All of these media are global in scope. All can potentially be used anonymously. But the Internet has the distinguishing feature of having millions of computers connected to it. When a computer is invaded by software that turns it into a "cyberzombie"

XXVI Net Crimes & Misdemeanors

(another neologism!), it can be used as a weapon in the same way that a joy rider in a car might abuse control over the vehicle.

Hitchcock has added some new chapters to this edition and updated various examples to reflect changes in the networked landscape. While it is not possible to guarantee that all forms of abusive behavior can be stymied simply by personal action, it is valuable to be able to recognize the signature of such attacks—to know that if you are a victim, you are not alone, and to know where you can turn for help.

Identity theft is among the most serious of Net crimes. This is an increasingly common problem and one that needs the help of law enforcement, the credit card industry, and others to defend against or to recover from it. My impression from various accounts I have heard is that recovery from this problem is *not* easy and takes significant effort and persistence. It can take a long time to repair the damage to credit ratings, and sometimes your financial accounts may be frozen in such a way that you are severely hampered in the conduct of your daily affairs. The CEO of a prominent high-tech company had this happen to him. He had substantial cash in various accounts and was unable to access these for months, imposing serious hardships and in some cases very serious risks of damage to his investments and to obligations requiring funds for their satisfaction. The victim was no naïve newbie on the Net. He was a pioneer in high-tech networking but his expertise and knowledge were only partly helpful in recovering from this form of attack.

Hitchcock offers some first-class advice about ways to protect personal information and detect various kinds of fraud. Spam continues to plague the network but it is more dangerous now than ever. HTML or XML encoded e-mail can have executable code embedded in the e-mail or its attachments. Various forms of monitoring, including keyboard monitoring (capturing passwords, account numbers, and the like), are technically possible. The software makers, in their zeal to increase the flexibility of the Internet's services, have also increased the vulnerability of its users to these kinds of threats.

"Social engineering" is a term that refers to people who send e-mail or post Web pages or engage in instant messaging with the intention of misleading the recipient into thinking the party communicating is legitimate. One way they do this is by asking important questions you should supposedly answer to protect yourself. For example, you might receive an urgent e-mail that appears to come from your bank asking for your account number and password saying that it needs to check your account. You would think only an idiot would respond to such a request, but the e-mail may be accompanied by the familiar logo of the company that is (mis)represented and be couched in such urgent terms that you feel compelled to reply. This is sometimes called a "phishing" expedition because the images and hyperlinks in the e-mail or Web page appear to point to the bank or company with which you normally do business, but, in fact, the hyperlinks actually point to a computer that is pretending to be the legitimate server. Most legitimate businesses warn their users that under no circumstances will they ever ask online for your account number and password. (Except, of course, to log into the service—that's where the risk lies: How do you know whether you are connected to the real Web site or a fake?)

Technology is emerging that will help to solve some of these problems by allowing the serving hosts to verify, using digital signatures, that they are registered with legitimate certificate authorities. Software can automatically check these signatures to help users distinguish the real from the fake. But it won't hurt to become much more knowledgeable about how these attacks can happen, what they look like, and how to detect them.

Reading this book is a first step toward increasing your ability to stay safe in a cyberworld that has its dark side as well as its sunny one. *We can all thank J. A. Hitchcock for taking the time and effort* to produce this work and encourage her to carry on the effort as the Internet continues to evolve.

Vint Cerf
Internet Pioneer,
Vice President & Chief Internet
Evangelist of Google.com
March 2005
McLean, VA

Vint Cerf was awarded the prestigious Presidential Medal of Freedom,
the U.S.'s highest civilian honor, in November 2005.

About the Web Site:

www.netcrimes.net

The world of online information changes with each blink of the eye, and the limitations of any print volume covering Internet resources are obvious: New sites and resources appear every day, other sites are expanded to include new or enhanced features, and still other sites disappear without a trace.

At www.netcrimes.net, the author maintains a regularly updated directory of key Internet resources—including, wherever possible, active links to sites. This directory is designed to help you pinpoint sites offering specific types of help and information, and to keep you up-to-date on the trends and issues. It is being made available as a bonus to readers of *Net Crimes & Misdemeanors, Second Edition.* Please take advantage of the feedback feature at the site to let us know what you think, and to recommend additional sites that readers may find useful.

Safe surfing!

Disclaimer

Neither publisher nor author make any claim as to the results that may be obtained through the use of the above mentioned links to Internet sites and resources, which are maintained by third parties. Neither publisher nor author will be held liable for any results, or lack thereof, obtained by the use of any links, for any third party charges, or for any hardware, software, or other problems that may occur as a result of using www.netcrimes.net. This program of Internet resources and links is subject to change or discontinuation without notice at the discretion of the publisher.

Introduction: You Can Be Safe Online

You wouldn't walk down a dark street in an unfamiliar neighborhood alone, would you? You wouldn't divulge where you live or work to a stranger in an elevator, would you? Surprisingly, many otherwise sensible people throw caution to the wind when they're online, assuming, apparently, that they're completely safe. They're not, no matter how computer savvy they think they are.

Danger lurks on the Internet.

Consider these scenarios:

- You purchase bath products from an online shopping site. When you receive your credit card bill, you find there are several more charges on it ... and you didn't buy anything else.

- You go to an online auction, bid on a photograph "signed" by a celebrity, and win. You send in your payment and wait. And wait some more. You do some investigating and find that not only are you not going to get the photograph you paid for, but there are serious doubts about the authenticity of the autograph.

- You receive phone calls and knocks on your door from strangers—all in response to a message "you" placed online. Only you don't own a computer.

- You're on a newsgroup called alt.business.home and someone gets angry at an innocent question you've asked. Messages begin to appear from "you" insulting other people in the group. This results in a barrage of e-mails to you from the people "you" offended. Your e-mail account is canceled, and your employer receives phone calls from people complaining that "you" are harassing them online.

You may think you know better than to get caught up in a scam or a harassment situation. But I will show that it can happen to even the most experienced online user. It happened to me. In 1996, I thought I knew everything about the Internet. I'd already been online a number of years, was a teaching assistant for basic and advanced Internet courses at a university, wrote hardware and software reviews for magazines, participated in newsgroups and forums, and surfed like a pro. Then I unwittingly became the victim of Internet harassment so threatening that it changed my life. Read my story in Chapter 1.

Net crimes and misdemeanors are committed against more than 200,000 people a year, and the number is growing every day, according to statistics from the FBI and victim advocate organizations. It is estimated there are more than 1 billion people online worldwide. If only 1 percent become online victims, that is still more than 10 million people—a drop in the bucket as more people go online for the first time every day.

When my harassment occurred, I didn't know where to go for help. There certainly was no book available to explain things to me, and there were no laws to protect me. Because what happened to me was so extreme, and because I saw such a lack of understanding of cybercrime, I have since become one of the nation's leading cybercrimes experts, giving lectures nationwide and appearing on TV programs to get the word out about Internet crimes. I serve as president of Working to Halt Online Abuse (WHOA) and WHOA-KTD (Kids/Teen Division), online organizations that work with up to 100 online victims a week.

The media has given some coverage to this growing problem, but not enough. It tends to emphasize sensational cases without imparting safety information to the public. I give lectures and training workshops to law enforcement personnel around the country, and am always surprised at how few of those in attendance are up-to-date on online harassment and cyberstalking issues. I've been told time and again that a book explaining what can occur and offering preventative measures would be welcome.

That's why I decided to write this book.

Net Crimes & Misdemeanors, Second Edition is written in language that is easy to understand if you are not familiar with the online world, but it is not written so simply that experienced Internet users will find it too basic. Each chapter begins with an explanation of the chapter's focus—and sometimes a definition or two of online harassment terms—and includes one sample case or more to show that even smart folks can have bad experiences. This is followed by tips and advice from experts. If, as you're reading, you come across a computer term you're unfamiliar with, check the Glossary in the back of the book. If you see an organization or a product you want to know more about, check Appendix B, Resources, for the Web site address. In this second edition, two new chapters have been added, and information has been updated throughout so that you should be able to handle just about anything that can happen to you online. In addition, there is an official Web site for the book at www.netcrimes.net, where you will find an updated list of links from the book and other links that may be of interest.

This book is only a first step in learning how to be safe online. To be truly Net-savvy, you'll have to keep vigilant long after you've read these chapters. Although I am known as a cybercrimes expert, I always keep an eye open for the latest developments in the world of online safety. If you and I don't remain alert, danger could strike. I don't know about you, but I don't intend to let it happen to me—not again.

A note on the case histories: Some of the victims I describe are actually composites of people from cases I've worked on through WHOA; I have done this to keep those victims anonymous. Some victims allowed me to use their real names, and others allowed me to use their stories verbatim but asked me to use pseudonyms. When recounting case histories, sample e-mail messages, posts, or chat room transcripts, they are exactly as they appeared online—with grammatical and spelling errors intact. Profanities are not spelled out, however, because I wanted parents to be able to share the information in this book with their children.

Don't let trolls, spoofers, spammers, e-mail bombers, cyberstalkers, and other online miscreants make you live in fear or give up the many advantages of Internet use. In reading this book, you've already taken the first step to arm yourself.

You're on your way toward becoming safe online.

Cyberstalking Happened to Me

We'd been living in Maryland for just over a year in a nice, quiet neighborhood near Annapolis. On Saturday, December 21, 1996, a nasty cold I had quickly developed into bronchitis. We canceled plans to visit relatives on Christmas, had no tree or decorations up, and I was miserable. That night I went to bed early after taking some nighttime cold medicine. My husband, Chris, went upstairs to his office about 10 P.M. to get our e-mail. All of a sudden I heard his voice—very angry.

"What the hell?" he yelled.

I bolted upright, got out of bed, and went upstairs.

"What's the matter?"

"Who do you know named Sfon@aol.com?" Chris was furiously pounding keys on the keyboard.

"I don't know anyone by that name." I walked over to his desk and looked at the computer monitor.

Our e-mail messages were being downloaded. Hundreds of them. We usually averaged 30 messages a day.

"Can you stop it?"

"I'm trying." Chris repeatedly clicked the Cancel button and the messages finally stopped downloading.

Chris opened one message. Then another. And another. They were all the same. Someone had taken my reply to a message that had been posted on the "misc.writing" newsgroup and added an extra-long "Happy New Yearrrrrrrrrrrrrrrrrrrrrr" at the end of my signature file.[1] The "rrrrrrr's" went on for two pages when we printed out the message.

I was stunned. I had no idea who did this. Maybe someone didn't like my reply, which was intended to be humorous. No one I knew on misc.writing would stoop to something this low.

Chris downloaded the rest of the messages, weeded through the e-mail bombs to get our real messages, then deleted all but a couple of the e-mail bombs — just in case we needed them. For the rest of the time he was online that night no more e-mail bombs arrived.

The next night at about the same time, it happened again. Chris yelled again. I raced upstairs. His face was red.

"I can't believe this jerk," he muttered angrily, jabbing his finger in the direction of the computer monitor.

Hundreds of messages were being downloaded. This time it was a different message, but the same return address: Sfon@aol.com.

I hadn't told Chris that earlier in the day I went online and posted a message to the misc.writing newsgroup. I asked if anyone else had been e-mail bombed. No one had, but some of the people on the newsgroup asked me to send them one of the e-mail bombs we'd received. We discovered that the e-mails were coming from an ISP called IDT out of New York and not AOL.[2] Just about everyone on misc.writing knew one particular group of people in New York who were the most likely candidates for the e-mail bombs — the Woodside Literary Agency.

• • •

Earlier that year, I had read a post on Usenet from the Woodside Literary Agency:

```
Subject: WRITERS SEEKING PUBLICATION
From: CFSQ98A@prodigy.com (James Leonard)
Date: 1996/01/24
Newsgroups: rec.arts.books.childrens
```

```
The Woodside Literary Agency is now
accepting new authors, re: fiction and non-
fiction: children's books. Advances from
publishers can be high. You must have a
completed manuscript. We have offices from
New York to Florida. E-mail for informa-
tion: CFSQ98A@prodigy.com. If you respond
during the month of February, call my new
```

Florida agency at: 813-642-9660. I will be
there in February.

James

I called the phone number listed and spoke with James Leonard. He sounded professional and courteous and answered all of my questions. Then he asked me to submit a book proposal. Shortly after I mailed the proposal to Woodside, I received a letter from the company claiming it was the most professional proposal they'd ever read and they wanted to see the full manuscript. One paragraph down was a request for a $75 reading fee. Since I'd already published six books, I knew the majority of agents don't charge reading or editing fees. Red warning flags appeared in my mind.

I visited a discussion group called misc.writing and asked if anyone had heard of Woodside, and then I recounted my experience. I soon found that Woodside was infamous for spamming[3] its "Writers Wanted" message ad in any newsgroup it could find. It was obvious that Woodside hoped to entice aspiring writers or others unfamiliar with the business of writing and hit them with a reading fee. Woodside could find a lot of prey; wannabe writers are desperate to see their work published. Along with several writer friends, I began to search for Woodside's posts in various newsgroups. We left warnings about the agency as an act of kindness.

I began to receive e-mail from people who had sent Woodside their manuscripts or proposals and paid the requested reading fee. Some paid more than that—a contract fee and other miscellaneous fees—but never received anything in return except requests for more money. One woman lost about $1,000. Some of these people asked me for help. I contacted the New York State Attorney Generals (NYSAG) office. I was told if I could find more victims, it would begin an investigation into Woodside's activities. So I posted messages on writing newsgroups asking if anyone who had given money to Woodside would be willing to join this investigation.

What I considered a helpful warning to fellow writers was seen by Woodside as a call to war.

• • •

Chris waited while the messages downloaded. He deleted all but one—again, just in case it was needed later—and there were no more e-mail bombs for the rest of the night.

Although I was pretty sure this was the work of Woodside, I had to be positive before making accusations.

The next day I began receiving e-mail messages from mailing lists[4] claiming I had subscribed to them. I hadn't. Luckily, most of the lists asked for confirmation before adding me, so I was able to stop most of the subscriptions before they got started. For the others, I had to make the effort to contact them and get the subscriptions canceled.

I found out that the University of Maryland University College (UMUC), where I was employed, was also e-mail bombed with messages from "me." It was obvious that this was an attempt to get me fired. Here is one of the messages, dated December 29, 1996, verbatim:

```
I'm an assistant teacher at UMUC and I
think you and the whole of UMUC are a bunch
of morons insidiously festering away your
small brains. I may or I may not resign. I
may stay to awaken you idiots. I'm an
international author and I know what I'm
talking about. I am also very powerful and
wealthy, so don't even think of messing
with me.
    J.A.Hitchcock—Teaching computer cources
at stinking UMUC.
```

• • •

The next night, at 10 P.M., the e-mail bombs hit again. Chris had installed kill filters[5] so that this time any e-mail from Sfon@aol.com would be deleted automatically. But our e-mail inbox began to fill up anyway. It was Sfon@aol.com again, but with a new twist—he or she had added the letter "a" or "b" so that the return e-mail addresses read either Sfona@aol.com or Sfonb@aol.com. The kill filters Chris created were useless.

"That's it!" Chris yelled. "Call Netcom." Netcom was our ISP.

By this time it was midnight. Not only was I still sick, I was ready to burst into tears. If it was Woodside, why was I being targeted and not the other writers from misc.writing?

I called Netcom. The tech support representative who answered was very understanding and quickly gave us a new e-mail address and proceeded to weed out our real e-mail from the e-mail bombs.

Chris decided it was time to separate our e-mail into "his" and "mine." We had a free e-mail account with Geocities,[6] where our personal Web pages were located. Chris began using the hitchcocks@ geocities.com e-mail address and I used our new e-mail address from Netcom. Even with the new address, I knew I couldn't take the chance of posting messages on newsgroups for fear of being e-mail bombed again. I contented myself with just reading the messages even though I longed to join in on many of the discussions.

The change in e-mail addresses didn't stop the cyberharasser.

Messages forged in my name began appearing on newsgroups—hundreds of newsgroups, from alt.fan.harrison-ford to rec.climbing to alt.abortion. Some of the messages used my old e-mail address, latakia@ix.netcom.com, while others used sock puppets.[7] One message appeared in all caps on the alt.atheism newsgroup:

> ATHEISTS ARE MORONS:
> AS A DAILY SPOKESPERSON FOR THE NEWSGROUP MISC.WRITING, I FIND THAT ATHEISM IS FOR UNINFORMED BRAINDEAD IMBECILS. TO LEARN ABOUT CREATIVE THINKING CONTACT ME AT MISC.WRITING AND MAYBE I WILL SEND YOU ONE OF MY BOOKS. AFTER ALL, I AM AN INTERNATIONAL AUTHOR AND KNOW WHAT I AM TALKING ABOUT. HITCHCOCK.

Another appeared, also in all caps, on the alt.beer newsgroup with the subject heading "Beer drinkers are morons."

> BEER DRINKERS ARE MORONS:
> BEER DRINKING MOST CERTAINLY CREATS AN ENORMOUS POPULATION OF DRUNKS WHO NEVER CONTRIBUTE ANYTHING TO SOCIETY, THEIR FAMILIES OR ANYTHING LIVING. I AM AN INTERNATIONAL AUTHOR AND KNOW WHAT I AM TALKING ABOUT AND CAN BE REACHED AT MISC.WRITING. I'LL BE HAPPY TO GIVE YOU ONE OF MY BOOKS TO GET ALL YOU DRUNKS ON THE RIGHT PATH

WHERE IT IS ONLY AN ARM'S REACH AWAY.
HITCHCOCK.

Online friends from the misc.writing newsgroup went about canceling these messages whenever and wherever they popped up.

Then the cyberharasser discovered Chris's Geocities e-mail address and began e-mail bombing it with a vengeance. One of the e-mail bombs consisted of a single word repeated over and over—the name of our dog, Bandit. Chris was very upset at this new blow, and I was at a loss as to how to handle the whole thing.

Just when I thought it couldn't get worse, more forged posts appeared in newsgroups. The messages were still on the same "morons" theme but had a new twist: They now included my home phone number and dared the "morons" to call me. No one did, thankfully.

As if this weren't enough, problems began to appear in my offline life as well. Magazines I hadn't subscribed to arrived in my mailbox, as did memberships to music and book clubs I hadn't ordered. And I received notification of pending deliveries of porcelain figurines I never ordered. I had to call to cancel all of these. I realized someone was subscribing me to everything and anything.

We had company for dinner a week later, just after New Year's Day. We sat in the living room eating appetizers and chatting. Chris finished cooking dinner and I helped him serve it. It was a nice, relaxed evening with good friends, a relief after all the problems online.

A phone call came at the end of dinner. Chris answered and handed the receiver to me with a quizzical look on his face.

"It's some woman from California. She says it's about the Internet."

I shrugged my shoulders and took the phone from him.

"Hello?"

"Hi, my name is Cindy. I saw those posts on the newsgroups. I had the same thing happen to me and I thought you might want to know about them."

"I already know about the 'morons' posts and I have some people helping me cancel them," I replied.

She paused. "I don't think you've seen these. They're new messages posted on sex-related newsgroups."

"What?"

Everyone at the dining room table stopped talking.

"It's something called Hot For Lovebites," Cindy went on. "Your home phone number and address are in it. You'd better get online and see what I'm talking about. Then you might want to call the police."

"Thank you," I said and hung up the phone.

I excused myself from my guests, ran into my office, and turned on the computer. I quickly got online and discovered "I" had posted messages to hundreds of newsgroups—all of them sex-related or controversial, such as alt.skinheads or alt.sex.bestiality, and most of them with the subject heading Hot For Lovebites. I cringed as I read this post, which is verbatim except that I have substituted XXX's for my real address and phone number at that time:

```
From: Jayne Hitchcock
      <FunGirl@netcom.com>
Newsgroups: alt.sex.bondage
Subject: Hot Lovebites
Date: Sat, 04 Jan 1997 22:59:13 -0800


Female International Author, no limits to
imagination and fantasies, prefers group
macho/sadistic interaction, including love-
bites and indiscriminate scratches. Invites
you to write or call to exchange exciting
phantasies with her which will be the topic
of her next book. No fee for talented
University of Maryland students. Contact me
at misc.writing or stop by my house at XXX
XXXXX Lane, XXXXXX, MD. Will take your
calls day or night at (410) XXX-XXXX. I
promise you everything you've ever dreamt
about. Serious responses only.
```

Not only was the fungirl@netcom.com address fake, but my employer, UMUC, was being dragged into this. And I was scared to death because the harasser and untold others now had my address and phone number.

I swallowed hard, fired off a quick e-mail to my cyberfriends asking for help again, then went back to my dinner guests and very calmly told them what was happening. They were appalled.

The phone rang continually after the first call. I answered it only once—when I received a collect call. I thought it was from my mother or sister. But when the prompt came for the caller to identify himself, a man's guttural voice announced, "It's Loverboy."

I didn't get much sleep that night. I was online most of the time and kept finding more and more of the Hot For Lovebites posts. Every time the phone rang, I cringed.

The next morning I checked the answering machine for messages. There was only one. I heaved a sigh of relief. I played the message and a man's scary-sounding voice said, "This is a serious phone call. Do you know your phone number is on the Internet at Fungirl dot-com? I live nearby and you should go to the police before someone knocks on your door."

I knew this, and inwardly thanked him for being nice enough to warn me even though I felt it was a somewhat crude phone call.

I called the local police and they told me they weren't computer literate—they didn't know what a newsgroup was. They said they'd be happy to send a patrol car over, but I told them that if they didn't understand what I was talking about, they couldn't help me. They referred me to the police commissioner's office in Annapolis. When speaking with a representative there, the dismissal was swift: "I don't know what to tell ya, lady."

Frustrated and afraid, and not knowing how far the harassment would go, I contacted the FBI Computer Crimes Unit in Baltimore, Maryland. I was informed that unless a death threat or threat of physical harm had been directed at me or I'd actually been physically assaulted, there wasn't much they could do. But they said they would send an agent to look into it. When an agent finally arrived to interview me it was almost a month later.

The phone calls continued. One came from Germany, and the message that was left lasted for five minutes. This caller assured me I could call or fax him 24 hours a day if I was interested; he left both numbers with the country code. Another person who'd seen a Hot For Lovebites post left this message for me online:

```
You must be one DIM writer. I'm about 20
miles away from you {along with a goodly
amount of rapists, murderers, & crack-
heads} Good Luck, you are going to NEED it.
By the way, if you don't already own a gun;
I suggest you go down to West street in
Parole and buy one.
```

I began to fear that someone would actually come to the door looking for sex. I feared for my life. We bought a gun. I learned how to use it, and I learned well.

In cyberspace I had to fend for myself. So I did the only thing I could think of: I turned again to my fellow writers on the misc. writing newsgroup. Angered by the harassment and lack of help from law enforcement, we, as a group, decided to take control of the situation ourselves. I dubbed them my Internet Posse.

Control it we did. We dug into old files and records online. We made phone calls, took photos, and e-mailed anyone we thought would be able to help.

We finally found the proof we needed that the harasser was indeed the Woodside Literary Agency. It posted the "Writers Wanted" ad (similar to the one I had replied to) to several newsgroups on January 5, 1997. But it forgot to remove my name and fake e-mail address from the "From:" line on the message. This same fake e-mail address had been used earlier that day to forge the Hot For Lovebites posts and e-mail bombs in my name. This, along with other important information discovered soon after, encouraged me to file a civil suit against Woodside et al. in January 1997 in Eastern District Court, New York, for $10 million.

In the civil suit, my lawyer named the Woodside Literary Agency and any of the names attributed to it, plus 10 John Does and Richard Roes[8] in case we missed anyone.

Two of the people named in the suit, Ursula Sprachman and James Leonard, soon came forward with a lawyer. A third, John Lawrence, made himself known to my lawyer a week after I appeared on the TV program *Unsolved Mysteries* in May 1997. He filed a countersuit, claiming I was the person harassing and stalking him.

The ISP used for the harassment, IDT, cooperated fully with my lawyer. We soon found there were several accounts opened at IDT by the Woodside Literary Agency, but with different credit card numbers and different names so that when one account was canceled Woodside would jump to a new one and continue the harassment. IDT notified us that it found all of the accounts and canceled them. I began to breathe easier.

But the people at Woodside weren't done with me yet. My lawyer received a death threat over the phone. An employee of one of the ISPs Woodside spammed from also received a death threat. Woodside continued to harass me, online and off, including going to a great deal of trouble to find our new unpublished phone number. Woodside went so far as to call neighbors I'd never met and ask if they knew our phone number. One neighbor was so rattled he knocked on our door to tell us about it.

Fellow writers formed a legal fund for me called H.E.L.P. (Hitchcock Expenses for Legal Proceedings). Contributions were put in a savings account and used for any legal expenses I incurred for my case against Woodside. I soon found out that Ursula Sprachman called and wrote the Maryland State Police, Maryland State Attorney General, and the FBI in Baltimore to file a complaint about me, claiming that the H.E.L.P. fund was illegal and something should be done to stop me. I was notified of the complaint by each organization, which added it to their files on me. I'm pretty sure Ursula wanted me arrested. That was very disturbing and it frightened me.

A year to the day after the harassment began, December 21, 1997, the phone rang at 7:15 A.M. I sleepily picked it up, heard someone breathing on the other end, and said hello a few times. No answer, so I hung up. When I awoke an hour later, I remembered the phone call and dialed *69. The phone call had come from the Woodside Literary Agency. I called the police to file a report and then called the telephone company to install Caller ID. I wondered what would happen next.

I didn't have to wait long. It came in the form of a letter titled "For Employment Purposes," which was sent to UMUC inquiring about my position there, how much money I made, what I did, and so on. The letter made it look like the company was planning to hire me and was doing a background check. It wasn't signed but the letterhead said WILA, which are the initials for Woodside International Literary Agency—the company's "new" name. The scariest thing was that my social security number was given in the letter. What else did Woodside know about me?

A secretary at UMUC told me she called the phone number listed and was yelled at by a woman with a German accent. This woman, who gave her name as Rita Maldonado, was angry that the secretary refused to give out any information about me. Ursula Sprachman, one of the known defendants, has a German accent. The letter was sent to my lawyer as evidence.

At a speaking engagement soon after this latest incident, a car followed me in the parking lot. The security guard on duty chased after the car but couldn't get the license plate number. Although I can't prove that the Woodside people were in that car, I felt that this incident was too much of a coincidence.

It seemed as though Woodside et al. had become obsessed with me. Every time I turned around, they did something else. Much of what they did made no sense, and at times was actually humorous. But it seemed they were determined to make my life so miserable that I would drop the suit against them.

I became so paranoid at one point that I would get down on the ground and check under my car before going anywhere. If anyone drove too closely behind me or seemed to be following me, I changed directions, changed lanes, or took a different exit—whatever it took to make sure I wasn't being followed.

I got a cell phone and carried it with me everywhere. The mental stress of the whole thing got to be too much and I began to see a psychotherapist. She helped me put things in perspective, calmed me down, and gave me a chance to talk it out. If I hadn't gone to see her, I don't know how I would have coped. I know I was on the verge of a mental collapse.

I came to realize that I should turn the "negative" of this situation into a "positive." So I got busy. I contacted the writers who'd been scammed by Woodside, got copies of letters and cashed checks from them, and then sent all of it to NYSAG. On November 14, 1997, NYSAG filed a civil suit against the Woodside Literary Agency et al. on four counts: false advertising, deceptive business practices, fraud, and harassment (the last for what they did to me). On February 17, 1999, NYSAG won a default judgment against Woodside. In July and August 2001, victims who paid Woodside money received restitution checks as part of that judgment.

After I testified before three Maryland legislative sessions, a bill that would make e-mail harassment a crime passed in April 1998. It is now a misdemeanor to harass anyone via e-mail in the state of Maryland, with penalties of $500 and/or jail time.

I provided written testimony to the California legislature for a proposed cyberstalking bill. An amendment of the civil and penal codes related to stalking, this bill added the Internet and other forms of electronic communication as another method of harassment and stalking. It passed and became a law on January 1, 1999.

New Hampshire quickly approved a bill that made Internet harassment a Class A misdemeanor, punishable by up to one year in jail and/or up to a $2,500 fine. I testified before the State House, helped amend the bill, then testified before the State Senate, where the bill was unanimously passed and put into law immediately after Governor Jeanne Shaheen signed it on June 25, 1999. Other states soon followed, with either written or in-person testimony from me. Maine, Rhode Island, Minnesota, and Illinois were among them. Since the publication of the first edition of this book, 45 states have adopted cyberstalking or related laws. I'm working on similar legislation for the remaining states and then will approach a sponsor for a federal cyberstalking law. I don't want to see anyone else go through what I've gone through.

I volunteer my services to various organizations and law enforcement agencies nationwide, including the Department of Justice Victims of Crime, National Center for Victims of Crimes, various other law enforcement agencies, and Working to Halt Online Abuse (WHOA) and WHOA-KTD (Kids/Teen Division), of which I'm president.

I've become known as a cybercrimes expert, specializing in cyberstalking but also covering online identity theft, auction fraud, scams, and more. I speak about cybercrimes nationwide, appear on TV and radio, and am mentioned in magazine and newspaper articles. I travel the world to train law enforcement professionals on how to track down cybercriminals and work with victims. I've expanded my training sessions to include educational institutions, librarian conferences, corporations, and the general public. I want to get the word out to the public as much as possible to make them as cyber-streetsmart as I am now.

As a result of everything that's happened, my husband and I moved to an undisclosed location in New England and have taken extreme caution to keep our new residence private. Although it's worked to a certain degree, we know we're never going to be safe and that scares me. The good news is that in January 2000, I received a phone call from the U.S. Postal Inspection Service. They arrested Ursula Sprachman and James Leonard on federal charges of mail fraud and perjury. It turns out the third person, John Lawrence, was fictitious. James Leonard made up this persona, complete with social security number, driver's license, credit cards, bank accounts, and more, to do the majority of the harassment and cyberstalking. That they had become so obsessed with me as to go as far as creating this fictional persona scared me more than anything else they'd done so far.

Instead of facing a trial, the two decided to plead guilty. The federal sentencing hearing concluded on December 6, 2001. James Leonard received eight months in prison, which is the maximum sentence, and three years probation; Ursula Sprachman received three years probation, as she had no prior criminal record and because of her age and poor health (she succumbed to illness in 2003). My lawyer made a handshake agreement for a settlement in my civil suit, the amount of which I cannot disclose. The most important thing to me was that the writers who had been scammed got their money back.

I saw this situation to the end, and I prevailed and won—not only for me, but for all writers and for all online victims.

There is justice, after all.

Endnotes

1. Signature File: A line or two of words, usually a user's name and contact information or favorite Web site URL, automatically added to the end of every e-mail or Usenet message sent out.
2. AOL: America Online, a popular Internet service provider.
3. Spamming: When someone posts a message to more than 20 newsgroups at a time.
4. Mailing List: Similar to a newsgroup except that all messages and replies are sent to your e-mail inbox. Most mailing lists are moderated; someone reads the messages before sending them to the list, eliminating most of the spam and unwanted clutter. However, some mailing lists are so busy that members can receive 100 or more messages per day.
5. Kill Filter: Many e-mail programs offer this feature so that the e-mail program can automatically delete any e-mail the user doesn't want. Most people use this for spam.
6. Geocities: An online "homestead" where people can get free Web page space, free e-mail, and other online extras. Located at www.geocities.com.
7. Sock Puppet: An e-mail address that goes nowhere when someone tries to send a message to it.
8. John Does and Richard Roes are often used in cases where the plaintiff does not know all the names of the defendants.

Words Can Hurt

E-Mail Bomb

When hundreds of e-mail messages are sent to one e-mail address in an effort to overload the account and shut that e-mail inbox down.

E-Mail Threats

Threats and/or harassment sent via e-mail.

Springtime for Stalkers

In April 2004 James Speedy of Seattle, Washington, was arrested by local police for allegedly stalking singer Avril Lavigne. The 30-year-old was accused of sending the 19-year-old pop star harassing letters, gifts, and e-mail messages. The day he was arrested was the same day Lavigne performed at a free concert in Seattle, so the timing was perfect. Who knows if Speedy would have tried to approach the singer at the concert—or something worse?

Seattle Detective Jerry Reiner said the content of the letters and e-mails was enough to put Lavigne and her family in fear for their lives. Speedy wanted to become part of Lavigne's family even though he was married and had a child of his own. He was released on $5,000 bail and voluntarily went into counseling for his obsession with Lavigne.

April 2004 was a busy month for apprehending online stalkers. An Indiana man was arrested for continuing to harass a local news anchorwoman after he had been ordered to undergo mental health counseling. Tamron Hall, the anchorwoman, received e-mails, postal letters, and phone messages at WFLD-TV, a Chicago Fox affiliate, from Tonny Horne in 2003. He was arrested in June 2003, pled guilty to cyberstalking in October 2003, and was subsequently sentenced to two and a half years of mental health probation, which meant he had to attend counseling.

Horne failed to do so and almost a year later began barraging Hall with more e-mails and postal letters, all of them obscene in nature. This time when he was arrested prosecutors asked to have his probation revoked. He was sentenced to three years in prison in May 2004.

An interesting side note: Horne was the first person in Illinois to be convicted of cyberstalking.

Other celebrities and famous names in politics and Hollywood have also been targets of e-mail bombs and threats. The incidents were reported in the media and the perpetrators were dealt with swiftly and severely. But what happens when you're not a celebrity or well known? When the police won't help, you have to rely on your own resources, as one Florida woman discovered.

I Am Not a Terrorist

When Katrina Gordon opened her e-mail inbox in February 2004 she found angry responses to a message that had been forged in her name. Then came phone calls and postal letters filled with death threats. Forty-eight hours later she found her dog dead in her backyard. She panicked and approached the local media, hoping the coverage would discourage anyone from really harming her or her family and show that she was not the person behind the e-mails.

It didn't take long for her to discover who was pretending to be her. This person e-mail-bombed message boards and newsgroups with thousands of messages all made to look like they came from Gordon.

"My name, address, and phone number were sent to thousands of people all over the world to collect donations for Sami Al-Aryan, a former college professor here in Florida who had been arrested for alleged terrorist ties," Gordon said. "It even had my private non-published home phone number so that people could call and donate money for Sami Al-Aryan's defense with a credit card. It also stated that the U.S. government and CIA were the 'real' terrorists."

The forged message also promoted a pro-government Web site — which was owned by her ex-boyfriend. Aha!

The media coverage helped and the messages stopped. Katrina learned of a cyberstalking bill that had been introduced in the Florida Statehouse in 2003. She was more than happy to provide testimony by reading the forged e-mail message. The bill subsequently passed unanimously and the cyberstalking law went into effect October 1, 2004. It passed too late to affect Katrina's situation but other Florida victims now have a way to fight back.

"I discovered that terrorism and assault through the Internet can become real," Gordon noted. "Just because it's on the Internet doesn't mean it can't hurt you."

How They Do It

How do e-mail-bombers send so many messages out at once? It's not as difficult as you'd think. There are many programs that are available for free or for a small fee. Most have offbeat names such as Yet Another E-mail Bomber, Unabomber, KaBoom, Avalanche, Up Yours, and Voodoo. The good news is that these are detectable by many firewall or other programs that specialize in this type of potential threat:

Pest Patrol
www.pestpatrol.com
Free trial, $39.95

Pest Patrol has more information on the various e-mail bomb programs out there and also offers manual removal instructions.

The Killer
www.soft411.com/company/RD-Technologies/
The-Killer.htm
$45

Also helps reduce intake of spam as well as handling e-mail bombs and viruses.

MailShield
www.mailshield.com
Free trial, $60
Also reduces spam using a "quarantine" formula, holding messages until you approve them.

These programs work by detecting multiple e-mail messages with the same subject line downloading into your inbox, then blocking further messages.

Before you buy one of these or a similar product remember that firewall and anti-virus software properly installed on your computer and regularly updated should help prevent most e-mail-bombs.

Another measure you can take (it's free) is to create a filter in your e-mail program so that any message coming in from a certain e-mail address or domain or having a specific subject line is refused (also called "bounced"). Not all e-mail programs have this capability, so check your HELP files to see if yours does. This won't guarantee you'll never get e-mail-bombed but it helps if you can stop the situation before it gets out of hand.

If you are already being e-mail-bombed and don't have filtering capability, call your ISP immediately and let the people there know what is happening. They can block the IP address or domain that the messages are coming from.

Many ISPs have included in their Acceptable Usage Policy the promise that they will cancel any account that is being used for e-mail-bombings. This is good news for you.

Nina's Story

Nina lives in Australia. Overweight, she found solace in visiting a newsgroup called soc.support.fat-acceptance. But someone calling himself "Mike" took a distinct dislike to her newsgroup messages and began filling her e-mail inbox with harassment and threats using all capital letters, such as the following (note: the expletives were fully spelled out in his message):

YOU'RE A REVOLTING FREAK WHO SHOULD BE
TAKEN OUT BACK AND SHOT.
    ALL YOU FAT HIDEOUS BITCHES HAVE NO REA-
SON TO LIVE! END IT ALL!
    THE SOONER THE BETTER, FAT MESS! F---
OFF, FATS!"
    STOP EATING YOU FAT C--T SMEAR!

Some of his e-mails had a forged[1] return address of FAT_
BITCHES_MUST_DIE@JENNYCRAIG.COM. Others seemed to
come from a Yahoo! e-mail address. Nina did the right thing and contacted Yahoo! and the other online mail services she thought Mike
was using for his messages.

"But I was getting absolutely no response," said Nina, recalling the
unpleasant incident. "I even brought it to the notice of the local branch
of the Australian Federal Police, who basically said there wasn't much
they could do. The system administrator at my ISP was a friend of
mine and dealt swiftly with the one and only threat of an
e-mail bombing I received."

Even though the e-mail bombs never made it to her inbox and she
stopped posting to the newsgroup, Mike kept sending her e-mail messages. She tried to filter them out but he would just change the return
e-mail address to something else and the messages would come
through, getting worse each time.

Nina began to wonder where Mike was located. Because the Web
is international, he could be on another continent and just trying to
scare her into thinking she was in imminent danger—or he could be
in Australia living near her.

With no help from the local police or online mail services, she
turned to Working to Halt Online Abuse (WHOA). After examining
the full headers (explained later in this chapter) of the e-mail messages, the staff at WHOA found that the messages were going
through several remailers[2] but originated from an ISP in Chicago.
WHOA sent complaints to the appropriate ISP and remailers on
Nina's behalf. Within three hours, all the parties involved, including
his ISP, had canceled Mike's accounts.

"WHOA not only got a response, but solid results," Nina said. "It's
nice to know that I can now open my e-mail inbox without having to
worry."

Some Tips for Contacting the Police, DA, or AG

- Use the telephone; do not e-mail them. Better yet, go in person. Provide them with copies of the most harassing messages you have received, not everything you've kept—remember to have full headers (discussed later in this chapter). Give them as much information as possible. If you've traced the messages back to a certain ISP, let them know. Anything you can provide will only make it easier for them. Be as clear, concise, and calm as possible.

- Do not contact the FBI, Secret Service, CIA, ATF, or other federal agencies unless there has been a death threat directed at you, you have been physically harmed, or there is a threat of physical harm. They will refer you to your local police or state attorney general's office if you contact them for any other reason.

Andy's Houseguest

Male victims of e-mail harassment are often embarrassed to go to the police or an ISP with complaints and usually wait until something really scares them before doing anything.

That's how it went with Andy from California.

"Someone set up a Yahoo! e-mail account using my name," Andy explained. "They created the account so that when anyone replied to an e-mail from the Yahoo! account, a copy would be sent to my real AOL e-mail address."

When Andy got an acknowledgment from Yahoo! for the e-mail address "he" set up, he followed the procedures for canceling it. Two days later, he found another account had been created but this time an e-mail had been sent to everyone listed in his personal AOL address book. The message was titled "The Biggest Clown" and it contained no text. The same message was sent several times and each time Andy got a copy of it.

Some of the people listed as recipients e-mailed or called Andy to ask what was going on, and some thought it was funny. Andy found it disturbing and definitely not funny, but he decided to ignore it. Then a message titled "Meatloaf" was sent out. This time a photo was attached: a naked, obese man with Andy's head. It was an obvious forgery but the people receiving this were the employees and managers he worked with at a Hollywood film studio. This was not good.

Andy got more reaction this time, with recipients asking if the photo was a joke. He was humiliated. He didn't want to go to the police. He was a man, after all, and could take care of this himself. Besides, they'd probably just laugh at him. So he did some digging and discovered that the messages originated from Spain. Then it clicked. About six months earlier, he'd let a male friend, Antonio, from Spain, stay with him. Antonio had brought along a friend, Marcel. The three men got along fine, along with Andy's roommate and dog.

One day, Marcel asked Andy if he could check his e-mail. Andy agreed and signed onto his AOL account. Although Andy noticed later that Marcel had forwarded a message with all the addresses from his address book, Andy dismissed it as a mistake since Marcel didn't speak English very well.

Then he remembered something that happened when Antonio and Marcel were visiting. Antonio had gone to the store and Andy took his dog for a walk. Marcel followed him out and began yelling at him for no reason.

"We were standing in front of my apartment building, so I said we need to walk to a quieter place," Andy said. "Marcel refused and when I started to walk away, he grabbed me by the shoulders, then put one hand over my mouth. Luckily, my roommate came out and Marcel pulled away. Marcel was crying later, saying he almost killed me and then said he had almost killed his sister once. I don't know if he was overdramatizing but it was scary at the time. It was at that point that I decided I did not want further contact with him when he went back to Spain. I just never put two and two together when the e-mails were sent to people in my address book."

Andy contacted Yahoo! again about the second e-mail account created in his name and Yahoo! canceled it. He also did some more investigative work and found the forged e-mail messages were routed through two remailers in Canada but originated in Spain. Andy sent an e-mail to the remailers and to the ISP in Spain explaining the situation. Although he didn't hear anything from any of them, he did receive a postcard from Marcel begging for forgiveness. He didn't reply to Marcel and hasn't heard from him since.

Andy feels vindicated, and he's much more careful online now.

"I pretty much stay away from e-mails from strangers since the incident," he said. "I only use the Internet to shop, do research for work, or do some selling on eBay. I also learned a valuable lesson: Do not let anyone have access to my e-mail account, even if all they want to do is check their e-mail. Now I send people to our local library."

"I'm Your Worst Nightmare"

A Minnesota teenager found she was the target of an e-mail harassment campaign that she couldn't stop. Taryn was 15 years old in May 1998 and a popular, straight-A student. Like many others at her school, she was "wired" and spent time after school e-mailing and IMing[3] friends. Then she began to receive messages from an e-mail address she didn't recognize. The first one read:

```
I'm your worst nightmare. Your troubles
are just beginning.
```

The messages got worse from there and eventually included pornography. They continued for three weeks.

"I locked all the windows and doors in the house, even if my whole family was home," Taryn recalled. "We were all so upset about it."

Taryn's grades began to fall and she spent more and more time at home. She did the right thing by going to her local police, but they told her they couldn't tell where the messages originated. They didn't have the online expertise to do this at the time. She turned to her ISP who then worked with the police and finally figured out that the perpetrator was a high school friend of Taryn's. He had sent the messages on a dare and promised to never do it again. His sentence was 100 hours of community service. If he'd been 18, he would have gone to prison.

"That was the most terrifying thing I had ever been through," said Taryn. "So I decided I needed to make others aware of what they could do if they got threatening e-mails."

Taryn put together an online safety brochure called *Shut the Door*. She hands this out when she speaks at schools and to law enforcement personnel throughout Minnesota; she has distributed over

200,000 copies since 1999. The brochure is available online at www.netcrimes.net/shutthedoor.html.

"When I hear from other people that they feel better because they learned from my experience, it makes all the work I've put into my brochure worthwhile," Taryn noted. She didn't stop there. Together with help from WHOA and Minnesota Senator LeRoy Stumpf (D), she helped introduce a bill in February 2000 that would amend the current harassment law and make online harassment like hers a crime in Minnesota.

"I was really, really nervous when I gave my testimony to the House of Representatives," Taryn recalled. "I've spoken to adults before but this was such a formal setting it made me really nervous. But it went well. They decided to take the bill and fold it into a larger Crime Prevention/Sex Offenders Act."

The bill passed and went into effect March 23, 2000, when Governor Jesse Ventura signed it.

Taryn has received many awards—the Minnesota Governor's Acts of Kindness Award and the Prudential Spirit of Community Award, to name just two. These honors have been bestowed on her in recognition of the work she's done in online safety. She truly turned a negative experience—her harassment—into a positive one.

What You Should Do

This section will tell you explicitly what to do if faced with an e-mail harassment or e-mail bombing situation.

Katrina, Nina, Andy, and Taryn were correct when they looked for help from their own ISP first and then from the ISPs of the person harassing them. But they might have been able to stop the unpleasantness even sooner if they had contacted their harassers directly.

An e-mail to your harasser stating you are uncomfortable with the communications and want an immediate end to them might work. It's worth a try. In your e-mail message to them, don't go into detail and don't act defensive. Keep it simple and clear. If the harassment continues after you've made this effort, then contact the ISP(s) involved.

What these victims also did correctly was approach the ISPs with the full headers of the messages they'd received. If you are the recipient of online harassment or spam, you have to find out first who sent the message and where it originated. More than likely, the return address will be forged or the sender used a free e-mail account. This is where full headers come in. Each e-mail program has a different way to show full headers. (See the end of this section for examples of programs or services that show full headers; also, a list of the more popular programs and instructions on showing full headers is available at www.haltabuse.org/help/headers.) If you don't use an e-mail program that has the ability to show full headers, it's highly recommended that you switch to one that does. Without full headers, there's not much you can do, legally or otherwise.

What to Do If You're Being Harassed Online

If you've determined that you are being harassed online, follow these steps:

1. *Clearly tell the harasser to stop.* Usually, it's unwise to communicate with a harasser. However, as soon as you determine you're truly being harassed, you must very clearly tell them to stop. Send an e-mail or chat/IM message with something simple, such as, "Do not contact me in any way in the future." You don't need to explain why, just state that you don't want the person to contact you. If you want, copy (cc) the message to the harasser's ISP or forward a copy to his or her ISP along with copies of the harassment you've been receiving (don't forget those full headers—learn how to find full headers later in this chapter). Do not respond to any further messages from the harasser. It is common for the harasser to claim you are harassing him. But if you aren't contacting the person after your initial request to stop, it's clear you aren't the harasser. This is valuable if you end up going to court or getting law enforcement involved.

2. *Save everything.* One of the first things many harassment victims want to do is delete all communications they've received, especially if vulgar or obscene language is involved. Don't. It's important to

save absolutely every communication you have had with the harasser—e-mail, chat logs, instant messaging histories, anything—no matter how embarrassing it is. If the harasser has created a Web site about you, save copies of it to your hard drive or on a disk and print it out. Have someone you trust, who would testify in court for you if necessary, do the same. If you receive telephone calls from the harasser, have them traced immediately (call your local phone company for help with this). If you receive any kind of postal mail or other offline communications, save them along with the envelopes, boxes, and so on. Do not destroy any evidence.

3. *Complain to the appropriate parties.* If you're harassed in a chat room, contact whoever runs the Web site or server you were on. If you're harassed on an instant messaging service, read the terms of service and harassment policies it has provided and use any contact e-mail address given there. If someone has created a Web page to harass you, complain to the owners who host that page. The best way to find out where to complain is to put the URL, such as disney.com, into SamSpade (more on this later in the chapter) and you'll find out who owns the site and who administrates it. That's the person you'll want to e-mail. Or look on the Web site for contact information. Many sites have e-mail addresses specifically for harassment and abuse complaints. If you're being harassed via e-mail, complain to the sender's ISP plus any e-mail service (like Hotmail) used to send the messages. If the ISP(s) involved won't handle the matter appropriately by either canceling the harasser's account or warning them to stop, your next step is to call your local or county police. Make sure you ask to speak to the Computer Crimes Unit or, if there is none, to an officer or detective who is Net-knowledgeable. If local officers can't help, call your state police—many have Computer Crimes Units. If they can't help you, call your county District Attorney (DA) or the state Attorney General's (AG) Office. If you feel you can't go to law enforcement

agencies, consider contacting online agencies, such as WHOA, SafetyEd International, Operation Blue Ridge Thunder, or Cybersnitch (descriptions of each can be found in Appendix A). Visit their Web sites and make sure they handle cases such as yours. Some specialize in handling online child pornography or pedophile cases, others only adult harassment or stalking cases, and others a combination.

4. *Determine your desired result.* You need to be realistic about the situation. It's reasonable to expect that you can get the harasser to stop contacting and harassing you. It's reasonable to expect that you can increase your safety online and offline and also the safety of your family. It's not realistic to expect an apology from the harasser or any kind of payback or revenge. If you want to file a lawsuit because of something the harasser said about you, find a lawyer who will take the suit. To do this, you need to locate a lawyer who specializes in Internet-related cases, or is Web-literate and willing to take you on as a client. You do have to be realistic about this avenue, though. You'll probably have to pay significant legal and court costs, the case could drag on for months or years, and you may never get any kind of satisfaction. Your goal should be to stop the harassment. If that means you need to change your username, e-mail address, or chat handle, or stop going to a certain newsgroup, forum, or chat room, then do it. Your safety should be your primary concern. Once things calm down, you can probably go back to your old haunts. And you'll go back a much wiser and more careful person.

Here is an example of what you usually see when receiving an e-mail. We'll look at one of the messages sent to Nina:

```
From: "-MIKE-" <-mike-@yahoo.com>
To: <nina@vom.tm>
Subject: Thank you all
Date: Sun, 23 Jan 2000 125551 -0600
```

In this instance, the "From:" address is not where it originated. How can you tell? After activating the full headers, the message will look like this:

```
Return-Path: <-mike-@yahoo.com>
Received: from dynamite.com.au  (m2.
dynamite.com.au
[203.17.154.20])
by m0.dynamite.com.au
(8.8.5/8.8.5) with ESMTP id
EAA04193 for <nina@m0.vom.tm>; Mon, 24
Jan 2000 045827 +1100
Received: from flyhmstr.vom.tm
(mail.vom.tm [212.32.5.2]) by
dynamite.com.au (8.9.3/8.9.3) with ESMTP
id EAA03011 for <nina@vom.tm>; Mon, 24 Jan
2000 045621 +1100
Received: from millenicom.millenicom.com
([209.150.128.197] ident=root) by flyhm-
str.vom.tm with esmtp (Exim 3.11 #1
(Debian)) id 12CRF6-0007CS-00 for
<nina@vom.tm>; Sun, 23 Jan 2000 175604
+0000
Received: from default (01-023.024.pop-
site.net [216.126.160.23]) by millenicom.
millenicom.com (8.8.5/8.8.5) with SMTP id
LAA16204 for <nina@vom.tm>; Sun, 23 Jan
2000 115437 -0600
  Message-ID: <00670cdd2a017a078@default>
  From: "-MIKE-" <-mike-@yahoo.com>
  To: <nina@vom.tm>
  Subject: Thank you all
  Date: Sun, 23 Jan 2000 125551 -0600
```

First, we know that dynamite.com.au is Nina's ISP, so we ignore it. We go down to the second "Received: from" line and find:

```
mail.vom.tm [212.32.5.2]
```

The group of four numbers in brackets makes up the Internet Protocol[4] (IP) address, the official address for vom.tm. You and I may "see" vom.tm if we went to that Web site, but its actual "computerese" address would be 212.32.5.2. In other words, this IP address is the numerical equivalent of a Web site URL (address).

An IP address is always made up of four sets of numbers with a dot (period) between them. Each set consists of one to three numerals. With this example, you can see the first set has three numerals, the second set has two, the third set has one, and the fourth set has one. No two IP addresses are alike.

How does an IP address work? Every time you visit a Web site, your computer has to go through a server—through your ISP—called a Domain Name System (DNS) server. So if you wanted to visit www.disney.com, your computer sends that information to the DNS, which translates it into computerese—an IP address—so that you're taken to the correct host (Web site).

An ISP will have one server (or more) that automatically assigns itself for customers to go through to get online. Every one of these servers has a similar IP address, except for the last set of numbers. The first three sets of numbers comprise the primary DNS info and the last set designates which server it came from. So, if you went online one day, you might be on server 208.14.24.176, and the next day you'd be on 208.14.24.12; it all depends on how many servers that ISP uses—the larger the ISP, the more servers it will have to accommodate its customers.

Steve Atkins, creator of SamSpade (a great resource when looking up IP addresses and other information at www.samspade.org) expands on this for us:

> Each server connected to an IP network—such as the Internet—is addressed using a unique 32-bit number, the IP address. Many servers will have more than one IP address. For example, a server running virtual Web sites will have an IP address for each Web site it hosts. Other times, a pool of IP addresses is shared between a number of servers. For example, on a dynamic-IP dialup connection your machine will be allocated a different IP address each time you connect.

This is why full headers are so important. They tell the ISP involved who was using that IP address, right down to the second, such as 11:05:35 (see the full headers example).

In this e-mail example, though, there is a free e-mail service, Yahoo!, and a remailer involved. A remailer is a service that takes a message you send, reroutes it so the message looks like it came from somewhere else, and sends it to the intended recipient. By using Yahoo! and a remailer, Mike was hoping to confuse Nina. The third "Received: from" line is the remailer IP address:

```
millenicom.millenicom.com
[209.150.128.197]
```

And the fourth "Received: from" line finds the originating ISP:

```
popsite.net [216.126.160.23]
```

Sometimes, as in these examples, you will get the name of the originating ISP/Web site along with the IP address. Sometimes you will get just the IP address. What do you do if the IP address is all you have? A good resource is called WHOIS (see Figure 2.1), available through Network Solutions at www.networksolutions.com/cgi-bin/whois/whois. WHOIS is a database of domain names and who registered that domain, with contact information that sometimes includes a mailing address, telephone and fax numbers, and e-mail addresses. SamSpade is also a good source (see Figure 2.2).

If we take the IP address of 216.126.160.23, put it in the WHOIS text box, and click on the search button, the result would be:

```
StarNet, Inc. (POPSITE5-DOM)
473 W. Northwest Hwy., Suite 1A
Palatine, IL 60067
Administrative Contact
Doe, Jane (IS168-ORG) janedoe@
STARNETUSA.NET (847)963-0116
Technical Contact, Zone Contact
Technical, Support (TS548-ORG)
postmaster@STARNETUSA.NET
(847) 963-0116
Fax: (847) 963-1302
```

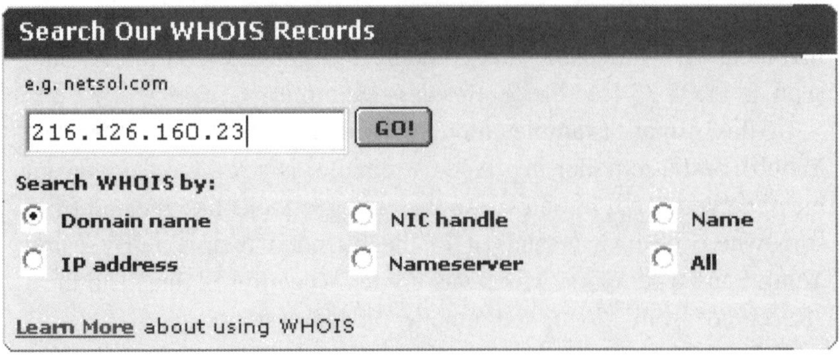

Figure 2.1   WHOIS

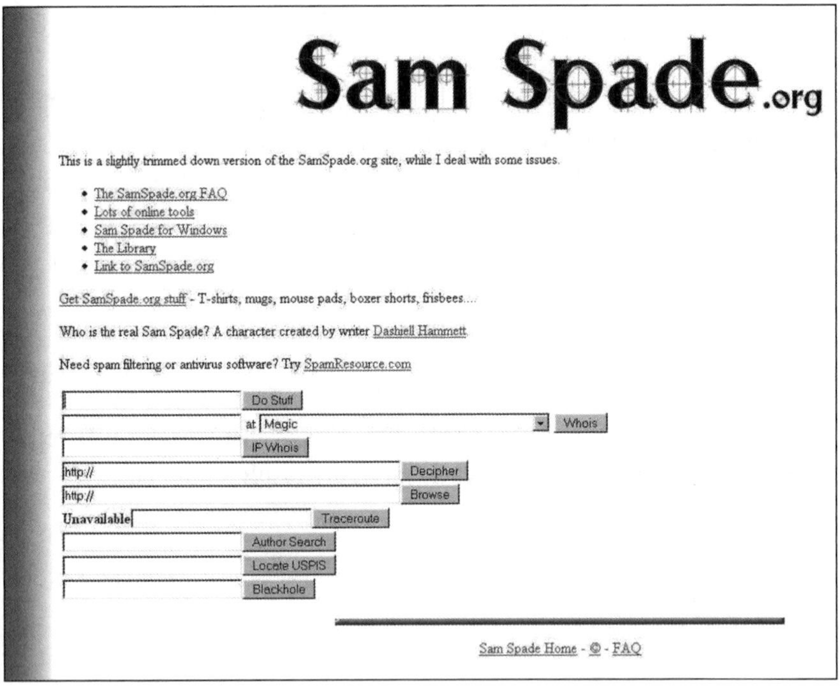

Figure 2.2   SamSpade

You would then forward the harassing e-mail message, with the full headers, to the technical contact. Before you forward the message, visit the Web site of the ISP/remailer/Web service involved and see if there is a specific e-mail address where you can send complaints (many services do have this). You might have to dig around on the site to find this e-mail; look for the site's guidelines[5] regarding harassing messages, perhaps under something like "Privacy Policy," "Terms and Conditions of Use," or "About Us." Most sites use the same e-mail username, such as abuse@yahoo.com, so if you don't find an e-mail address on WHOIS or the ISP's Web site, try abuse@ispname and also postmaster@ispname—the latter is the normal default e-mail address for most Web sites. Remember to send the complaint not only to the originating ISP, but also to any free e-mail services or remailers used.

For the e-mail Nina received, the full header message was sent to postmaster@starnetusa.net, castle@millenicom.com, and abuse@ yahoo.com.

Why wasn't the harassment complaint sent to the first IP address we found, vom.tm? If you look at Nina's e-mail address, you'll see she was using a free e-mail service (similar to Yahoo!) through vom.tm that then went through her ISP, dynamite.com.au.

How to Find Full Headers in E-Mail and Newsgroup Programs

Following are instructions for showing full headers in various e-mail and newsreader programs. Unless otherwise noted, forward or send the message with full headers to the ISP(s) involved. An updated list can be found at www.haltabuse.org/help/headers.

AOL E-Mail

Before you can forward the message, you need to save it with the full headers intact:

1. Open the e-mail message you want to save, as if you were reading it.

2. Click on File.

3. Click on Save as …

4. Identify which directory you would like to save the file in. This is done using the normal save function of Windows. If

you're not comfortable with directories, save the file in Desktop. This will have the file icon visible on your regular desktop screen and be very easy to find later on.

5. Provide a name for the file in the File Name box.

6. Select the "type" as "html" if possible. If your browser does not show "html" as a type, just select the type as "All Files" and add ".html" to the file name generated, such as e-mail.html. The dot before the html extension is important. The objective of this step is to have the extension of the file as an "html" type file.

7. Click Save.

To forward the file:

1. Click on Write.

2. Insert the e-mail address you want to forward the file to.

3. Type any information in the body of the message, if needed.

4. To add the html file you just generated in the previous steps, click on Attachments.

5. When the Attachments Window opens, click on Attach.

6. Find the file in the directory window and highlight the file name. If you followed the "Desktop" instructions, the directory name is c:\desktop. If there are too many files that appear, type "*.html" in the file name. The use of the asterisk (*) lists all files that are html.

7. Click on Open.

8. Click on OK.

9. Click on Send Now.

Please be aware that AOL only keeps messages in your inbox for seven days but offers an option in Preferences to automatically save every e-mail that you open, if you so choose. Additionally, a screen name of tose mail1 has been identified as a source of help for unacceptable e-mail in the AOL system. Just enter tose mail1 in the Send To screen. If you are outside of the AOL environment, the address is tose mail1@aol.com or simply click a button saying "Report spam."

CompuServe

1. Open the e-mail message.

2. On the line Received from Internet: click here for more information, click on the link.

3. This brings up a separate window with the full headers. You can do one of two things now:

    • Highlight, copy, then paste the headers into a blank e-mail message, then highlight, copy, and paste the original message text following the headers and send to the appropriate ISP(s) as a complaint.

    • Go back to the original message and forward to the ISP(s) involved. The default is that the full headers should appear to the recipient.

Eudora Pro

1. When reading an e-mail message, look at the toolbar just above the message itself. There should be a button that reads:

    BLAH

    BLAH

    BLAH

    in black and white. Click on this and the full headers will appear.

2. Select All, copy, and paste into a new message to send to the ISP, or click the forward button and the full headers will automatically be placed in the new e-mail message.

Excite Webmail

1. View the message.

2. Use the Save to Disk option.

3. Open the message's text file with your favorite text editor (notepad).

4. Copy the message from the text editor.

Free Agent/Agent (newsgroup program)

1. Click on Message, then Show Full Headers.

2. Go to the message, click inside the message pane.

3. Copy, then paste to a text file or forward the message.

Hotmail

1. Go to additional options.

2. Click on Mail Display Settings.

3. Click on Advanced Headers, then click OK.

4. Go back to the e-mail in question and open it.

5. Forward to the appropriate ISP(s).

Juno Version 4+

1. On the Options pull-down menu, select E-mail Options (or press ctrl-E).

2. Under Show Message Headers, select the Full option.

3. Click the OK button to save the setting.

Juno version 4+ can display MIME and HTML e-mail, but does not provide a way of viewing the HTML source for the message within Juno. To get the full source, including HTML codes:

1. Click File and then Save Message as Text File (or ctrl-T).

2. Give the file a name you'll remember.

3. Double-click on the resulting file.

4. Copy, then paste into an e-mail message and forward.

Lotus Notes 5x (Win 9x client)

1. Export the message as structured text to a file.

2. Copy/paste the entire message. You should get all the received fields with Received: already in place. You'll also get Reply-to: and other smtp headers.

Please note that some versions or installations of Lotus Notes do not comply with Internet standards and discard the headers. If that is the case, you should contact your system administrator to see if there are any logs of incoming mail that might assist you. You as the user will not be able to get the headers at all.

Microsoft Exchange

1. Open the message in Exchange to view it.

2. Choose File, then Properties, then Internet. The header will be visible and will be highlighted.

3. Right click, copy it, then paste into a new e-mail message.

Microsoft Internet Explorer

1. Choose Properties under File.

2. Click on the Details tab. This will show the full headers.

3. Right click and choose Select All, then copy the headers.

4. Start a new e-mail message, paste the headers into this new (and temporary) message.

5. Copy the header from the new message and paste it back onto the original, then send. The paste command doesn't work directly on the original message.

Microsoft Internet News

1. While viewing the message, click on File, Properties, then the Details tab.

2. Forward the message.

Microsoft Outlook 98 and Outlook 2000

1. Open the message and select View, then Options from the pull-down menu.

2. Near the bottom of the screen you'll see a section titled INTERNET HEADERS.

3. Copy the headers and paste them into a new e-mail message.

Microsoft Outlook Express 4, 5, & 6 for Windows

1. Right click on the message and select Properties.

2. Choose the Details tab and select the Message Source Button.

3. Select All and Copy.

4. Close the Message Source window and the Properties window.

5. Select New Mail and position your cursor in the body of the e-mail.

6. Paste the copied information.

Netscape Messenger

1. Select the message, then press Ctrl-U. A new window opens with the full message, including the complete header.

2. Copy, then paste into a new message.

Netscape News

1. Click View Document Source.

2. Copy and paste or forward the message.

Newswatcher

1. Go to File and choose Preferences.

2. Check the Show Article Headers box.

`Operamail`

1. Choose Options.

2. Enable [x] Show Message Headers in Body of Message.

`Pegasus`

1. Hit Ctrl-H (or the backspace key) while reading a message. Do this before hitting "F" (for Forward) so that the full headers are forwarded, too.

`Pine`

1. From the main Pine menu, type S for Setup, then C for Configure.

2. Use the spacebar and down arrow to scroll until you reach the option [] enable-full-header-cmd.

3. Type X in the box to toggle the option on.

4. Type E to exit Configure, and Y to save changes.

5. The next time you read a message, type H and the full headers will be displayed at the top of the message. Type H again to hide the headers.

`Unix`

There are two ways to show full headers in Unix:

1. Save the message in a directory.

2. Use the Type command or print it out.

Or:

1. Exit your current mail program and look at the mail message using mail or mailx.

2. Show a message with the Print or P command to display all of the header lines. Note the capital P—it's important.

3. Save the current message with the save-retain command to save all of the header lines (on some systems, Save or S does this too).

WebTV

1. While viewing the message, hit Forward on the sidebar.

2. Address the document to yourself.

3. Completely erase the subject line.

4. Put your cursor on the first line of the body (text area).

5. Hit Return (Enter) twice. Your cursor should now be on the third line of the text area.

6. Type any Alt character on this line; do not hit "return."

7. Cut and Paste the Alt character onto the subject line: (CMD+"A"), (CMD+"X"), (CMD+"V"). The Alt character should "jump" down to the message text area.

8. Hit Send. Open the Received Mail; full headers should appear.

Yahoo!

1. Click on Options.

2. Click on Mail Preferences.

3. Under Mail Viewing Preferences, click on Message Headers, then select ALL.

Will It Stop?

Usually, a complaint to the ISP/remailer/Web service is all it takes to get the e-mail harassment or e-mail bombing to stop. There's a good chance it won't happen again—many harassers are not typical criminals or hackers, but once they know they can't get away with the harassment, they usually stop.

Sometimes people harass because of a dare, like the teenager who threatened Taryn, or because of a simple disagreement that blew out of proportion. If ISPs cancel the accounts of the harassers or warn them to stop the harassment, they usually stop.

It's the harassers who aren't stopped at these beginning stages who are worrisome. They feel that if they can get away with e-mail harassment, how much further can they go?

The following chapters show what other kinds of online negatives there are, how other victims turned their experiences into positives as Taryn did, and how the harassers didn't get away with it—most of the time.

Endnotes

1. Forged: A term used when someone uses an e-mail address that is obviously a fake.
2. Remailer: An online service that allows you to send e-mail messages through its Web site instead of through your e-mail program so that you retain a bit of anonymity.
3. IMing: To send an instant message through a program such as AOL Instant Messenger, ICQ, or MSN Messenger; an instant message from the sender pops up on the recipient's computer screen. The two can then engage in live chat one-on-one as opposed to a regular chat room where many people can chat at once.
4. IP (Internet Protocol): How data is sent from one computer (aka "host") to another on the Internet. This is the most popular protocol on which the Internet is based. Each host has at least one IP address that uniquely identifies it from all other hosts on the Internet.
5. Guidelines: Many Web sites also call these their Terms of Service (TOS).

3

Spam Not in a Can

*I realize now that I was one of the first computer profes-
sionals to experience the feeling of dread evoked by a
flood of spam complaints.*

—Ray Everett-Church

Spam

Unsolicited electronic junk mail, usually advertisements or offers, and,
more often than not, unwanted by the receiver; sometimes used as a
revenge tactic by pretending to be someone, then spamming messages to hundreds, sometimes thousands of people.

In the early 1990s, as the Internet became accessible to more people, junk mail found its way online in the form of e-mail advertisements. Almost always unsolicited, these messages began appearing
in e-mail inboxes, mailing lists, and newsgroups a handful at a time,
and were seen as a minor annoyance more than anything.

But back in 1975 someone had seen the potential for a problem
with online junk mail. Jon Postel wrote in November 1975[1] that host
computers had to read every mail message coming in, but if there
was a malfunctioning host that began sending too many or unwanted
messages, there could be a problem. "It would be useful for a host to
be able to decline messages from sources it believes are misbehaving
or are simply annoying," he wrote.

Prophetic words.

What's in a Name?

Wait a minute, isn't SPAM the luncheon meat in the familiar blue can?

Meri Harris, spokesperson for Hormel Foods, the makers of SPAM, admits the company wasn't too thrilled when the term "spam" started being used to describe junk e-mail.

"But what can you do?" Harris says. "It's become so much a part of the Internet culture that as long as people don't come to us complaining about online spam and it's not spelled out in capital letters, like our trademark name, then we can live with it. We did get some people e-mailing us, thinking online spam came from us, and it got to a point where we put up a page on our site explaining the difference." Visit www.spam.com/ci/ci_in.htm.

So, why is the junk mail called spam? According to the narrative at the SPAM Web site, "Use of the term spam was adopted as a result of the Monty Python skit in which a group of Vikings sang a chorus of 'spam, spam, spam …' in an increasing crescendo, drowning out other conversation. Hence, the analogy applied because UCE was drowning out normal discourse on the Internet."

Although most people called it junk e-mail and promptly tossed it in their "trash,"[2] in 1994 a new term was coined for this problem: Unsolicited Commercial E-mail, or UCE. This was due to the following infamous story.

The Green Card Spam

Ray Everett-Church was working as an information specialist with the Washington-based American Immigration Lawyers Association (AILA). His job was to look for any news items related to U.S. government immigration policies. As their resident techno-geek, he began putting together an online newswire of the information he found. Occasionally, he also answered any technical questions.

"When I arrived in the office on the morning of April 13, 1994, the receptionist handed me a stack of angry faxes and forwarded a voice mailbox full of furious calls," he recalls. "By the time I stumbled to my cubicle, I had met the enemy. Their names were Laurence Canter and Martha Siegel."

A little background: In the early 1990s, Congress created the Green Card Lottery program. Although the program offered a great opportunity to immigrants, it also provided an opportunity for scammers to make money by charging hopeful immigrants high fees to file lottery entries when all that was required was a postcard, a stamp, and the person's name and address.

Canter and Siegel were a husband-and-wife law firm that saw dollar signs and wanted to jump on this potential moneymaking bandwagon. They were also technically savvy and began sending hundreds of messages to newsgroups.

"The faxes and phone calls I fielded asked what could be done to stop them and to sanction them for their activities," Everett-Church says. "As a voluntary association, AILA's only recourse was to throw them out of the association. However, when I went to AILA's senior staff to ask what that procedure entailed, a director of the organization said, 'Canter and Siegel? What did they do this time?' "

It turns out the pair was notorious for this sort of thing and had been disciplined many times. And now they were the initiators of the Green Card Spam, which is what the media termed it.

"They effectively were the ones that I consider 'the spam that started it all,'" says Everett-Church with a laugh. "I went on to get my license to practice law. They lost theirs. I realize now that I was one of the first computer professionals to experience the feeling of dread evoked by a flood of spam complaints. I've never quite forgotten that feeling, and it's part of the reason I've spent so much time combating Internet abuse."

As Counsel for the Coalition Against Unsolicited Commercial E-mail (CAUCE) at www.cauce.org (see Figure 3.1), Everett-Church now helps address legal problems related to spam and spammers.

"We're focused on legislation to combat spam," Everett-Church notes. "We're also educating companies on how to use e-mail for marketing in a responsible manner as well as working with state legislators to teach them about anti-spam laws—what makes good ones, how to avoid constitutional issues, and why not to accept marketers' whining at face value."

Figure 3.1   CAUCE

Federally, as well as in many states and in other countries, there are laws to combat spam. But the big problem is enforcing these laws. For more information on the latest spam statutes, visit www. spamlaws.com.

Spam I Am

Horror stories abound about jilted lovers signing up their exes for spam mailing lists. Angry consumers have been known to retaliate that way too. One woman made a lot of spam trouble for a company—an ISP, in fact—but didn't even know she was the cause of it.

"Nadine" is the name given to this particular woman in order to hide her identity. The full story of this inadvertent spam deluge can be found at www.honet.com/Nadine.

Basically, this is what happened. Nadine was a senior citizen who had taken to the Internet like a fish to water. One day in March 2000, she visited a Web site operated by delivere.com and signed up for a sweepstakes. She mistyped her address as nadine@honet.com. When a confirmation e-mail was sent to that e-mail address an automated "no such user" reply was sent immediately from the ISP honet.com to delivere.com.

But alas, e-mails started coming in to this wrong address. The unwanted e-mails came from Harris Polls, Ourhouse.com, Webstakes.com, and AT&T. Each time one of these came in, a reply was sent back by honet.com saying there was no such person using that e-mail address.

But spammers latched on. More and more e-mails arrived for that address and pretty soon the ISP was deluged. In fact, the e-mails haven't stopped even though honet.com jumped through hoops to stop them.

Michael Robinton is executive director of Insulin Pumpers, a non-profit organization in northern California that provides infrastructure support for people with diabetes. Part of what the organization does is provide a mailing list that includes users from all over the world. Robinton found that spam would sneak its way onto the mailing list as well as into his personal and business e-mail.

"At the beginning of 2003, the spam content of my incoming e-mail was approaching 500-plus messages a day, while legitimate mail was—and still is—in the neighborhood of 50 to 100 messages a day," he says.

Robinton searched online for software he could use to fight spam for his business Web site. When he didn't find anything, he took it upon himself to write to Spam Cannibal (www.spamcannibal.com), the makers of a sophisticated spam-filtering program specifically designed for businesses. It's a highly technical program but it works … for now.

On the Other Hand ...

If you want to receive some random spam, go to http://dustman.net/andy/randomspam and you'll see ... random spam. Hit your Reload/Refresh button on your Web browser and you'll see more random spam.

In Defense of Unsolicited Bulk E-mail (spam) at www.provider.com/framesbulke.html provides news and information from the spammers'—or to use a nicer word—marketing perspective.

A little humor goes a long way at www.satirewire.com/features/poetry_spam/poetryintro.shtml, Satirewire's Annual Poetry Slam, er, Spam. All of the poems were written using words from actual spam that the contestants had received in their e-mail inboxes. If this doesn't make you laugh, nothing will.

For more on the lighter side of spam, visit http://spam links.net/humor.htm. This site has anti-spam humor and spam cartoons.

Get all the latest news about spam at Petemoss.com SpamNews digest (www.petemoss.com). It's free.

Finally, 101 Things to Do with a Spammer is at http://computeme.tripod.com/spammer.html. Don't try these at home. My favorite is #32, "See how many spammers you can stuff into a phone booth."

Usenet Spammers

Usenet, also known as newsgroups, discussion groups, or forums, has a similar problem with spam. Because there are literally tens of thousands of newsgroups that cover any subject you can possibly think of (from Harrison Ford to writing to bicycling to sex), spammers have an easy way to send their messages. More likely than not, these spams contain fake return e-mail addresses, which makes it harder to track them down but not impossible. However, what's considered spam in e-mail isn't the same definition for spam on

Usenet. On Usenet, spam is when the same message is posted an unacceptably high number of times to one or more newsgroups, whether or not the content of the message is relevant to the newsgroup(s). Although no specific number has been agreed on, if the same message is posted 20 times to the same newsgroup or to 20 different newsgroups, it is considered spam. Some ISPs consider as few as five postings of the same message to be spam, and may cancel the offender's account. The message here is to be careful when posting messages to newsgroups.

Usenet spam is primarily aimed at lurkers—people who read newsgroups but rarely or never post or give out their e-mail addresses. The spammers are hoping one of the lurkers will actually read their spam and maybe even visit their Web site or reply to the spam (some people actually do). Usenet spam makes it difficult for regulars to navigate their favorite newsgroup(s). Some newsgroup members are sick and tired of spam, which leads this discussion to "spamhunters."

Spamhunters on Usenet eagerly send copies of spam to newsgroups devoted to spam, such as news.admin.net-abuse.sightings. Usenet management then makes sure the right ISPs are notified of the spammers. Sometimes the accounts of the spammers are canceled, but if they are persistent, they'll get a new account and begin spamming again.

If an ISP seems to be harboring spammers, a Usenet Death Penalty (UDP) will be set by Usenet administrators. A UDP effectively blocks all messages posted from the offending ISP, not just the spam. This means that a person who has a legitimate e-mail account with that ISP won't be able to post to any newsgroups. This usually gets a quick reaction from the ISP, which either works to identify the spammers or readjusts its services to prevent spamming.

Luckily, Microsoft Internet Explorer, Netscape Navigator/ Communicator, Forte Agent, and other newsreader programs offer a kill file feature, which can be used to filter out Usenet spam so that it almost never shows up when reading your newsgroups. Each program has a different way to set up kill files (which are also available in most e-mail programs), so it's best to consult the HELP files in your program(s) for instructions on how to use kill filing.

When setting up a kill file, you can input an e-mail address or specific words found in the subject line of common spam, such as Make Money Fast, Free Software, Lose Pounds Quickly, and so forth. Some people put dollar signs ($$$) in a kill file, as many spams include them in the subject line to try to entice you to read the spam. Other commonalities includes sexx (with two x's), penis (because the subject line usually reads Grow Your Penis Larger or Bigger Penis Guaranteed), two or more exclamation marks (!!!!), or question marks. Once the kill files are set, you'll see a dramatic drop in Usenet spam.

How to Tell If It's Spam

Sometimes a quick read of the message text is enough to convince you that it is spam. But if you're still not sure, here are some tips on how to tell if it is or not.

1. If the TO: line consists of someone else's e-mail address and not yours, it's probably spam.

2. If the TO: line has "undisclosed recipients," "undisclosed@," or something similar, or no e-mail address—yep, it's probably spam.

3. If the TO: line has your e-mail address and many others that are similar, such as helpfund@yahoo.com, helpme@yahoo.com, helppeople@yahoo.com, helping hands@yahoo.com, and so forth, it's more than likely spam. Spammers use software programs to create e-mail addresses, not knowing if they are real or not, so they send out their spam to all of the created e-mail addresses hoping someone will respond. This is also called a "dictionary attack" (see Glossary).

4. If the CC: line contains a lot of e-mail addresses and you weren't expecting the e-mail, it's probably spam.

5. If the subject line consists of an offer you didn't request, it's usually spam.

6. If the content of the e-mail is a big discount on an item, a low-interest loan, Russian mail order brides, making a body part grow larger (or smaller), low-cost medication/drugs, how to make money online, free pornography, or an announcement that you've won something … it's spam.

The Difference Between Spam and Harassment

You've received an e-mail message that surprises or disturbs you. The subject line is something like "I Missed You Last Night" or "You

Are So Hot." You open the message and find sexually explicit text. Is it spam? Is it harassment? If the message doesn't have your e-mail address in the TO: line or if there are other e-mail addresses in the TO: line in addition to yours, then it's probably spam (see "How to Tell If It's Spam" on page 52). If the e-mail has your address in the TO: and/or FROM: lines, the SUBJECT: line is usually a good give-away. If the message was sent only to your e-mail address, you need to determine whether it's harassment.

It is considered harassment if:

- The message contains any kind of threat
- The sender claims he or she will post your personal info online
- The sender claims he or she wants to harm or kill you
- You receive e-mail from people responding to an ad or message "you" supposedly posted

It is not considered harassment if someone:

- Disagrees with something you said online, however strongly or unpleasantly
- Sends you a single e-mail message that isn't overtly threatening

It's important to remember that spam is annoying, but it is not harassment. Messages posted to any open venue, such as a news-group, a Web-based board, a discussion forum, chat room, or even posted on someone else's Web site, are seldom truly harassing unless they're forged to appear to come from you or contain direct threats or libelous statements.

Harassment involves repeated communications via e-mail, instant messaging, newsgroups, or other forums after the harasser has clearly been told to go away. The legal definition of harassment, according to *Black's Law Dictionary*,[3] is "a course of conduct directed at a specific person that causes substantial emotional distress in such person and serves no legitimate purpose; words, gestures, and actions which tend to annoy, alarm, and abuse (verbally) another person." This is a broad definition, which state and federal legislation and common law have narrowed and refined in various ways. You may want to check your local laws to see if they specify harassment in another way. To learn how to deal with harassment, see Chapter 2, "Words Can Hurt."

How to Avoid Spam

You can't avoid it entirely, just like the junk mail that comes to your mailbox at home. But there are some things you can do to combat it. (Thanks go to Ray Everett-Church for some of these tips).

1. Know where your e-mail address can be found (online white pages, Web pages). Do you know who has your e-mail address? Do you participate in chat rooms? Message boards? Newsgroups? Do you have your e-mail address posted on your Web page? Spammers look for legitimate e-mail addresses everywhere on the Web and "harvest" these addresses for sending their spam out.

2. Guard your primary e-mail address. When some-body asks for it, think twice before giving it out.

3. Choose an ISP that actively blocks spam.

4. Learn to filter your e-mail. Some e-mail software has pretty decent filtering features that, if you take the time to read the instructions, can be useful in helping you manage your mailbox, and may even help you filter spam into the trash. It won't save you money, but it might save your sanity.

5. Don't hit Reply! Most of the return addresses in spam are false in order to deflect complaints. However, some spammers use real addresses because they really do want to hear from you. Why would they want to hear your angry diatribe? Because then they know that your e-mail address is functioning and that there's a real live body on the other end of that connection. By replying, you wave a big red flag that says, "Spam me some more!" Not only that, but the spammer will then sell your e-mail address to other spammers. You will see a big increase in the amount of spam you receive. So, don't hit Reply. And never, ever click on a link in the

message text that claims you will be unsubscribed if you go to their Web site.

6. In newsgroups or forums where spam appears, again, don't reply to a spam. If you want a good laugh, read some of the responses to spam on various newsgroups; they can be quite humorous. (For example, someone posted the following reply in response to an "enlarge your penis" spam: "Hey, I'm a woman—if it works, I can get rich!").

7. Establish secondary "screen names" for chat rooms/boards, which are among the most appealing places for spammers to gather e-mail addresses. Many ISPs, such as AOL, AT&T, and CompuServe, allow you to create secondary screen names or additional e-mail addresses at little or no cost, shielding your main address from the flood.

8. Give/use false e-mail addresses. Many people know that spammers troll through chat rooms and message boards looking for e-mail addresses, so they use fake or altered (sometimes called "munged") e-mail addresses. For example, "JohnDoe123@hotmail.com" might give out his address as "JohnDoe123@I-hate-spam.hotmail. com" and then give instructions to remove the "I-hate-spam" part before sending him e-mail. This tends to confound many spammers, particularly those who use automated e-mail "harvesting" programs that gather anything with an @ sign in the middle. Spammers are usually too lazy to sort the millions of addresses by hand, so they end up sending spam to the altered address.

9. Establish valid secondary e-mail accounts at free e-mail services (such as Hotmail or Yahoo!). This is useful if your ISP doesn't let you create secondary accounts easily or cheaply. Also, these e-mail services now offer their own spam combat. Many of these services filter known spam into bulk e-mail or spam folders that you can empty or schedule to

empty within a certain amount of time. This cuts down tremendously on the amount of spam that ends up in your inbox. These free e-mail services also allow you to report any additional spam. This helps them to increase their spam filtering.

10. Use unique e-mail account names not found in a dictionary. A growing number of spammers are grabbing names out of dictionaries, randomly sticking numbers in there, and then pasting on an ISP suffix such as @hotmail.com or @aol.com, or @wherever.com. This way they don't have to gather addresses. Thus was born the "dictionary" spamming attack, and this is why you might want to pick an e-mail address that is less predictable.

11. Learn how and where to complain to get spammers shut down, such as using SpamCop, SpamArrest, Vanquish, Mailwasher, Antispam, or other programs or Web sites listed in the Resources section at the back of this book.

Even with the best precautions, sometimes there is nothing you can do. In June 2004, an AOL employee was arrested for selling 92 million AOL e-mail addresses to a spammer who then resold the addresses to other spammers. The result was that many AOL users either changed their e-mail address username or switched to another ISP.

Fighting Spam

CAUCE is an ad hoc, all-volunteer organization created by Netizens[4] and is a good first stop for everything you want to know about online spam, anti-spam legislation, and what to do about spam (go to www.cauce.org). It costs nothing to join CAUCE, and each person who joins makes CAUCE's "voice" stronger on Capitol Hill (Washington, DC) and in member states—and better able to get anti-spam legislation passed and enforced.

SpamCop puts you in control of the spam you receive. Register for free at www.spamcop.net. When you receive spam, activate the full headers and copy and paste the spam into the text box at

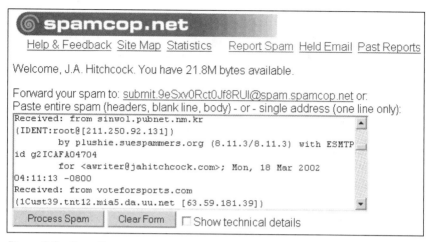

Figure 3.2   SpamCop

SpamCop's site and click on the Process Spam button (see Figure 3.2). SpamCop then does the work. You'll then get a "results" page (see Figure 3.3), on which SpamCop has determined whether it is really spam, and if so, shows you which ISP(s) the complaint will go to. Then all you do is click on the Send Spam Report(s) Now button. SpamCop takes care of sending the e-mails for you.

Julian Haight created SpamCop in 1998 to deal with spam he was getting in his personal e-mail inbox. Haight's first SpamCop program was a simple, 100-line script he put up on his personal Web page. "When it was released, there was a lot of skepticism in the spam-fighting community," says Haight. "I received a lot of criticism but also a lot of feedback, which helped make it what it is today."

SpamCop works by using a combination of Unix utilities such as nslookup[5] and finger[6] to crosscheck all the information in an e-mail header to find the correct e-mail address of the administrator on the network where the message originated. It then formulates a polite request for discipline, including all the information needed to track down the user responsible for the spam. Sometimes the person reporting the spam through SpamCop will receive a reply from the ISP involved thanking them for reporting the spam, and sometimes the account involved is canceled.

"SpamCop gets about 200,000 reports a day, if that gives you an idea of the scope of the problem with spam," says Haight. "There are some spammers who aren't too happy with the site. Someone once

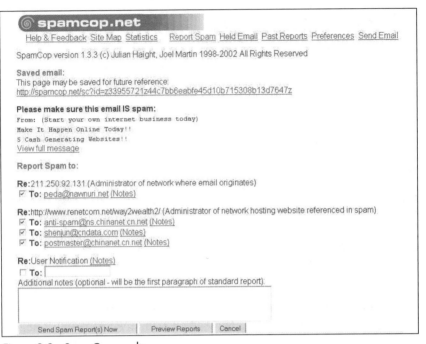

Figure 3.3   SpamCop results

sent out a spam 'advertising' SpamCop, which caused a problem. We've been sued and hacked. Thankfully, Ironport Systems purchased Spamcop, so there has never been a real threat of getting it shut down and I still run the day-to-day activities."

The SpamCon Foundation (www.spamcon.org, see Figure 3.4), founded by Tom Geller in January 1999, is for those who have been damaged by spam, or "e-mail vandalism," as Geller calls it. This site provides a list of states with anti-spam laws, the status of any state or federal legislation, information on how to sue spammers in states where there are current laws, a forum to discuss spam and spammers, and resources.

The Future of Spam

What will the spam situation be like in 5, 10, 20 years or more? Doug Muth, an adviser to CAUCE, feels it's hard to say.

"The anti-spam community continues to come up with new techniques to prevent spam, and spammers keep finding ways around them," he notes. "However, with the passage of the CAN-SPAM law,

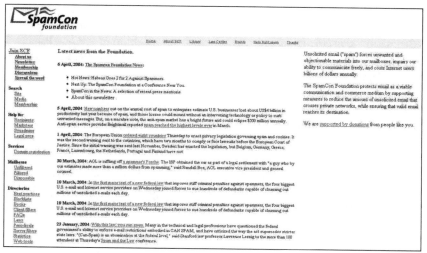

Figure 3.4 SpamCon Foundation

the federal government has begun taking a more active role than ever in dealing with spammers and making it more difficult to send spam and get away with it. The only thing for certain is that there is no clear answer right now as to what the future holds."

Robinton concurs. "I think spam will increase exponentially until the feds eliminate the current law so that states can use more punitive measures or until a federal law is enacted that allows consumers to go after spammers directly for damages," Robinton comments. "My suggestion would be $500 to $1,000 per unsolicited message."

You can bet spammers would "get the message." Pun intended.

If you're really angry about spam, go to www.spamhaus.org and find out how Spamhaus is working to protect Internet networks worldwide.

If you want all the technical details of spam, go to http://spam.abuse.net, where you'll find tutorials on filtering, blocking, and more.

Sometimes the war against spam can be won, if you take the initiative to fight it.

Endnotes

1. Full comments on this can be found at www.ietf.org/rfc/rfc0706.txt.

2. Trash: Usually a function in e-mail programs that allows the user to delete unwanted e-mail, thus putting it in the trash; usually the trash empties when the user exits or ends use of the e-mail program.

3. *Black's Law Dictionary* (8th ed. 2004), ISBN 0314151990, West Publishing Group.

4. Netizens: Common nickname for online users.

5. NSLookup: A software program where you enter a host name (for example, "disney.com") and see the corresponding IP address. NSLookup also does reverse name lookup to find the host name for an IP address you specify.

6. Finger: A program that reports the name associated with an e-mail address and may also show the most recent logon information or even whether the person is currently connected to the Internet.

Urban Legends and Hoaxes: Can They Possibly Be True?

Urban Legends

Online, they're much like the ones you've heard offline—stories so incredibly unreal they're, well, unreal. Online legends keep popping up in e-mail, on Web sites, in newsgroups, and in chat rooms even after they've been debunked.

Hoaxes

Similar to urban legends, hoaxes are the messages and posts that try to convince people they can get something for nothing, or that a bad virus is coming their way, or some other nonsense. P. T. Barnum supposedly said, "There's a sucker born every minute"—online, there's no shortage of hoaxes aimed at proving the point.

You've seen them in your e-mail inbox or heard about them in newsgroups, message boards, and forums. Sometimes you've even wondered if they could be true. Your friends e-mail you warnings about viruses, and this time it's a REALLY BAD VIRUS. Or you get a message stating that if you forward the message to eight of your friends, you'll have good luck, good health, or something else (but never money).

A boy sends you an e-mail about his quest to add as many business cards to his collection as he can, and he's dying of cancer.

Another boy writes that if you forward your message, a $1 donation will be sent to him, and if he can get 50,000 people to do this, his operation will be paid for.

The list goes on and on.

These are Web urban legends and hoaxes, the modern version of myths and chain letters. Rumors come and go depending upon our state of anxiety about the world. But some are perennials and stay with us seemingly forever. There are so many that I can't list them all here. Instead, I'll mention the more common ones, explain how to tell if it's a hoax, and advise what to do if you get one.

The David Allen Legend

This started off as a real mission. David actually did ask friends to send e-mail prayers for him in 1997 when he thought he was dying. Here he recounts his experience:

> On 5 March 1997, we began our home leave, flying from Chiang Mai in northern Thailand to Los Angeles in the USA. In the plane, I suddenly started having such strong stomach pains that I seriously doubted that I would make it to Los Angeles. It was an unidentified infection: I lost weight, and it was clear that I was suffering from an infestation of microscopic parasites and was possibly in danger of dying.
>
> The American doctors could not discover the exact source of the illness. In May 1997 I had to be fed intravenously. Shortly before my admission to hospital, I wrote an e-mail message to a mission team in Thailand, telling them that I did not yet feel ready to die. The thought of leaving my wife, newborn baby, and the new church in Thailand behind was unbearable.
>
> The reaction to my message was almost unbelievable, with Christians throughout the world praying, some so fervently that they cried, some fasted, others throwing themselves on the floor before God. I received over 7,000 e-mails from around 80 countries, often from whole churches united in prayer for me.
>
> One church even called me and said that they had been divided before hearing of my illness, but decided to put their small differences aside when they received the news,

and started to pray. My family received telephone calls from morning until evening for months. I must admit that I was overwhelmed.

Parasitologists from Washington's Walter Reed military hospital, doctors from England, Canada, Africa, Brazil, Mexico, Thailand, and other countries called to offer their help and advice. Then suddenly, probably in answer to prayer, the doctors were no longer needed. The tests became negative, the parasites had vanished and have not reappeared since.

People around the world began receiving requests in their e-mail inboxes to pray for David. Here is one such request:

Dear Friends and Family,

    The prayer for this Southern Baptist Missionary needs to be forwarded to everyone you know that can pray. Pray diligently and then send it along today!!!! Ezekiel David Allen is a young missionary on the Chiang Mai, Thailand mission team. He is critically ill with an unknown parasite and apparently WILL DIE WITHIN TWO MONTHS unless there is an intervention by the Lord. Please help create a global blanket of prayer for David, Michelle, and their four-month old daughter, Brianna.

From: David Allen

David's original e-mail to his mission team asking for prayers was pasted in this spot, followed by:

    We are encouraging everyone we know to lift up David and his family before the Lord of Lords. Please forward this message to those you think will join us in this global chain of prayer.

```
Thanks,
          INTERNATIONAL MISSION BOARD, SBC
          Southern Africa Regional Office
          PO Box A-614, Avondale
          Life is good because God IS.

P.S. Please send this out to all your
friends, sisters, brothers, and other
relatives.
```

Nice sentiments. It worked, but as David noted, he recovered and is fine these days, even though this legend seems to pop up every few months. Then the cycle begins all over again with thousands of people forwarding the original message to everyone they know. Just do a search on his name and you'll find over 10,000 Web sites that mention this common legend as if it were happening right now.

The E-Mail Tax

This appears here and there, sometimes worded differently, but it's the same old message. Online users will be charged five cents for every e-mail they send. Each time this appears, the U.S. Postal Service and U.S. Government have to announce that it is a hoax. But many people fall for it and end up forwarding the message to not only everyone they know, but to newsgroups and forums as if it's new news.

An interesting fact: Congress was so upset that it did pass a law — to stop the hoax. This is a sample of one of the hoax messages:

```
Dear Internet Subscriber:

    Please read the following carefully if
you intend to stay online and continue
using email: The last few months have
revealed an alarming trend in the
Government of the United States attempting
to quietly push through legislation that
will affect your use of the Internet. Under
proposed legislation the U.S. Postal
Service will be attempting to bilk email
users out of "alternate postage fees". Bill
602P will permit the Federal Govt to charge
```

a 5 cent surcharge on every email delivered, by billing Internet Service Providers at source. The consumer would then be billed in turn by the ISP. Washington D.C. lawyer Richard Stepp is working without pay to prevent this legislation from becoming law.

The U.S. Postal Service is claiming that lost revenue due to the proliferation of email is costing nearly $230,000,000 in revenue per year. You may have noticed their recent ad campaign "There is nothing like a letter". Since the average citizen received about 10 pieces of email per day in 1998, the cost to the typical individual would be an additional 50 cents per day, or over $180 dollars per year, above and beyond their regular Internet costs. Note that this would be money paid directly to the U.S. Postal Service for a service they do not even provide. The whole point of the Internet is democracy and non-interference. If the federal government is permitted to tamper with our liberties by adding a surcharge to email, who knows where it will end. You are already paying an exorbitant price for snail mail because of bureaucratic efficiency. It currently takes up to 6 days for a letter to be delivered from New York to Buffalo. If the U.S. Postal Service is allowed to tinker with email, it will mark the end of the "free" Internet in the United States. One congressman, Tony Schnell (R) has even suggested a "twenty to forty dollar per month surcharge on all Internet service" above and beyond the government's proposed email charges. Note that most of the major newspapers have ignored the story, the only exception being the Washingtonian which called the idea of email surcharge "a useful concept who's time has come" (March 6th

1999 Editorial). Don't sit by and watch
your freedoms erode away!

Send this email to all Americans on your
list and tell your friends and relatives to
write to their congressman and say "No!" to
Bill 602P.

The U.S. Postal Service offers this standard reply when concerned
citizens send e-mail (www.usps.com/news/2002/press/emailrumor.
htm):

WASHINGTON - A completely false rumor concerning the U.S. Postal Service is being
circulated on Internet e-mail. As a matter
of fact, the Postal Service has learned
that a similar hoax occurred recently in
Canada concerning Canada Post.

The e-mail message claims that a
"Congressman Schnell" has introduced "Bill
602P" to allow the federal government to
impose a 5-cent surcharge on each e-mail
message delivered over the Internet. The
money would be collected by Internet
Service Providers and then turned over to
the Postal Service. No such proposed legislation exists. In fact, no "Congressman
Schnell" exists. The U.S. Postal Service
has no authority to surcharge e-mail messages sent over the Internet, nor would it
support such legislation.

Free Stuff

These e-mails claim that if you pass the message on to other people, you'll get free stuff. There's just one thing they forget to say:
How are you supposed to receive the free stuff if the company supposedly giving it away doesn't have your contact information? Some
of the chain letters claim the companies can tell where you're located
with special e-mail tracking. This is—you got it—untrue.

Good Luck, Mr. Gorsky!

One of the funniest hoaxes on the Net has to be the one known as "Mr. Gorsky" (www.snopes.com/quotes/mrgorsky.htm).

When Apollo 11 astronaut Neil Armstrong uttered the famous, "One small step for man, one giant leap for mankind," he also said, "Good luck, Mr. Gorsky!"

Or did he?

This rumor began on the Internet back in 1995 as a pretty obvious joke, but some media outlet picked it up and ran with it, causing it to become one of the Web's most famous (or infamous) legends.

What did this phrase mean? Supposedly, Mr. Gorsky was Armstrong's neighbor. When Armstrong was a kid, he overheard Mrs. Gorsky tell her husband in their backyard that he'd get oral sex when the kid next door walked on the moon. Armstrong was said to have divulged this 25 years after the moon landing, presumably when Mr. Gorsky died.

Guess what? There was no Mr. Gorsky (or Mrs. Gorsky) and the joke still floats around the Web, usually with minor changes, such as the name of the neighbor and how Mrs. Gorsky tells her husband when he'll get oral sex.

Armstrong publicly denied he ever made the statement and if you doubt it, check out the official NASA transcripts of what was said during the moon landing at www.hq.nasa.gov/office/pao/History/alsj/a11/a11.step.html.

I've received these chain e-mails myself. One that began circulating in 1997 has slowly morphed to keep up with the times. The first was short, simple, and easy to fall for:

```
Hello everybody,

    My name is Bill Gates. I have just writ-
ten up an e-mail tracing program that
traces everyone to whom this message is
```

forwarded. I am experimenting with this and I need your help. Forward this to everyone you know and if it reaches 1000 people everyone on the list will receive $1000 at my expense. Enjoy.

Your friend,
Bill Gates

One of the latest versions goes something like this:

Subject: PLEEEEEASE READ!!!!! it was on the news!
To all of my friends, I do not usually forward messages, But this is from my good friend Pearlas Sandborn and she really is an attorney.

Dear Friends; Please do not take this for a junk letter. Bill Gates sharing his fortune. If you ignore this, You will repent later. Microsoft and AOL are now the largest Internet companies and in an effort to make sure that Internet Explorer remains the most widely used program, Microsoft and AOL are running an e-mail beta test.
When you forward this e-mail to friends, Microsoft can and will track it (If you are a Microsoft Windows user) For a two weeks time period.
For every person that you forward this e-mail to, Microsoft will pay you $245.00 For every person that you sent it to that forwards it on, Microsoft will pay you $243.00 and for every third person that receives it, You will be paid $241.00. Within two weeks, Microsoft will contact you for your address and then send you a check.

The person who sent this to me was extremely embarrassed when I pointed out that this was a chain letter, a hoax, and an urban legend all rolled into one. I sent this person to the Snopes Web site (www.snopes.com/inboxer/nothing/billgate.asp), at which there is information about how this chain e-mail hoax has been attributed to other well-known businesses like the Gap, Nokia, Old Navy, and Victoria's Secret. The bottom line is that there is no such thing as an e-mail tracker. At least, not yet. But many people fell for this hoax — hook, line, and sinker. None of the companies mentioned were pleased when they received complaints that no free cash, gift certificates, or merchandise were forthcoming. But it didn't hurt sales — and publicity is publicity, they figured.

The Top 10 Urban Legends/ Hoaxes/Chain Letters

It's hard to select the Top 10, but here are my personal favorite urban legends, hoaxes, or chain letters:

1. Kidney theft, www.snopes.com/horrors/robbery/kidney.htm

What's scary about this is that the media picked it up and ran with the story like it really happened. An e-mail made the rounds from a friend of a friend (FOAF) who supposedly knew someone this happened to. The deal was that while traveling to New Orleans (in this case), a businessman is approached by a stranger in a bar who buys him a drink. The drink is drugged and the last thing the businessman remembers before passing out is being in a bathtub submerged to his neck in ice. When the businessman wakes up, there is a note tacked near the tub instructing him to call 911, which he does. The 911 operator then asks the businessman to carefully feel behind him and see if there is a tube in his back. When he replies that there is, an ambulance is sent to the hotel, the businessman is taken to the hospital and finds out his kidney has been harvested. The e-mail then goes on to claim that this is really happening and is not science fiction.

The New Orleans Police Department was inundated by concerned citizens about this e-mail. It got so bad, the department put up a page on its Web site, which stated, in part:

```
Internet Subscribers:

     Over the past six months the New Orleans
Police Department has received numerous
inquiries from corporations and organizations
```

around the United States warning travelers about a well organized crime ring operating in New Orleans. This information alleges that this ring steals kidneys from travelers, after they have been provided alcohol to the point of unconsciousness.

After an investigation into these allegations, the New Orleans Police Department has found them to be COMPLETELY WITHOUT MERIT AND WITHOUT FOUNDATION. The warnings that are being disseminated through the Internet are FICTITIOUS and may be in violation of criminal statutes concerning the issuance of erroneous and misleading information.

The National Kidney Foundation was outraged. It asked that anyone who had his or her kidney stolen to contact the foundation. Not surprisingly, no one has.

2. Rat urine, www.snopes.com/toxins/raturine.htm

This e-mail warns of a family friend of someone who knew a stock boy at a grocery store who opened a can of soda without washing the top of the can, or moved the cans and touched the top, then became seriously ill and died because of rat urine on the can. Even though it was thoroughly debunked and health officials proved that you won't die from unclean cans even if rat urine was on them, people freaked out about this one.

The moral of this story: Just clean the top of the darned cans anyway.

3. Klingerman virus, www.snopes.com/toxins/klinger.htm

This one appeared in e-mail inboxes claiming that if you received a large blue envelope from the Klingerman Foundation and opened it, you'd find a virus-filled sponge inside, which would kill you. There is no Klingerman Foundation and there were no sponges being sent in the postal mail. However, this urban legend almost became real when people who did receive large blue envelopes in their mailbox called the police, thinking a virus-filled sponge was inside. In 2000, a man in Auburn, Maine, dialed 911 when he received a blue envelope that contained a free sanding sponge from a handyman company.

While the dispatchers kept him on the phone, listening to his worries that this was a virus-filled sponge, he soon had ambulances, fire trucks, police cars, and curious neighbors in his yard. The FBI arrived in HAZMAT suits and made him strip, then hosed him down. When they realized there was no virus and it was based on the e-mail hoax, they were able to calm the man down.

Need more proof this isn't true? Go to www.cdc.gov/ncidod/ klingerman_hoax.htm.

4. Needles in the payphone, www.snopes.com/horrors/mayhem/ payphone.htm

With the AIDS and HIV scare, this e-mail began appearing, claiming that someone (yes, another FOAF) went to a public payphone, put money in the phone, made a call, and then reached into the coin slot to get the change. The person felt a sharp prick and became infected with HIV, AIDS, hepatitis, or other infectious disease because someone left a hypodermic needle in the coin slot. Sometimes the e-mail claims the message came to the sender from a certified EMT.

This is one time when an urban legend did become real, but definitely after the fact. When newspapers began running articles about this new urban legend, real incidents began to happen. There were reports of hypodermic needles being found in mail deposit slots, night deposit slots at banks, and yes, payphone coin slots. But all the needles were uncontaminated.

This only gave the urban legend a longer life. In 2000, the legend resurfaced as an e-mail claiming that vending machines in Alberta, Canada, were now harboring those dangerous AIDS-infected needles. Not true. Another legend similar to this is about needles affixed to gas pump handles that then prick the user.

5. Jen's embarrassment, www.snopes.com/sex/mistaken/jen.htm

This is particularly sick. A girl named Jen meets a man in a chat room and they become better acquainted, to the point where they engage in cybersex. After a few weeks of this, they decide to meet in person and find they live in the same town. They arrange their real life tryst in a hotel and Jen arrives first, removes her clothes, hops in bed, shuts off the light, and waits. She hears the door open, whispers, "Jeremy?" He whispers back, "Katie?"—the fake name she used in the chat room—and then turns on the light. They both scream when they realize they're father and daughter.

Not only is this untrue, it comes in the form of several tales. Sometimes they are college students who turn out to be brother and sister. Sometimes it's a businessman on holiday who asks for a hooker to be sent to his room—yep, his daughter, or his wife; and so on. But this story does serve to warn you that you never know who you're really chatting with online.

6. The Swiffer WetJet poses a general danger to household pets,
   www.snopes.com/critters/crusader/swiffer.asp
   This scares the pants off pet owners. The gist of it is that supposedly a friend's dog was healthy until a couple of weeks ago when it died suddenly. A necropsy found that the dog's liver had failed. Since the dog was kept indoors, the owner couldn't figure out what might have caused this. So he began searching through all the items in his house. He found a warning in tiny print on a Swiffer WetJet package that the product may be harmful to children and pets. He called the makers of Swiffer and was told that one of the ingredients is antifreeze (or a compound one molecule away from antifreeze). The pet owner deduced that since the housekeeper used the WetJet to clean the wood floors, the dog must have licked its paws and thus ingested the poison.

   This is patently untrue. There is no mention of the names of the people involved so there is no way to verify any of the statements. The claim that antifreeze or a component of it is in the WetJet is not true. The WetJet solution actually is made up of mostly water (over 90 percent) with propylene glycol n-propyl ether and isopropyl alcohol making up between 1 and 4 percent each. The rest of the solution is made up of minor ingredients and preservatives, none of which are harmful enough to cause a pet to become ill. The final falsity of this hoax is that the package contains no such warning.

7. A teacher wants to add you to a list of names for a science project,
   www.snopes.com/inboxer/school/names.asp
   This message claims that the person sending the e-mail is trying to collect as many names as possible for their child, or a friend's child, or someone else's child, and would you be so kind as to add your name to the list? Then you are asked to send the message to 10 people plus the person who sent it to you, with your name in the subject line.

   Don't do this. Variations of this hoax include adding your name for a cause or a charity and sending it on to more people, or signing a petition and forwarding that on. What happens is that you end up with dozens, maybe hundreds, of e-mail messages from strangers. If people fall for it, that is. And *you* know they do.

8. Deadly spiders in public toilets, www.snopes.com/horrors/insects/ buttspdr.htm

I heard about this one just before I was scheduled to take a lengthy business trip. A well-meaning friend e-mailed the warning to me and I got a good laugh out of it. Depending on the message, it always contains information about three women who went to the same restaurant, airport, movie theater, and so on, used the restroom, then died three days later. A Dr. Beverly Clark, who published an article in the *Journal of the United Medical Association* (*JUMA*), is quoted in the e-mail saying that these deaths occurred because a deadly spider called a South American Bush Spider bit the women when they sat down on the toilet seat. It was hiding on the underside of the seat.

There is no such spider. There is no Dr. Beverly Clark. There is no *JUMA*.

9. Mel Gibson was the man without a face, www.snopes.com/ glurge/noface.htm

This hoax claimed that the movie, *The Man Without a Face*, in which Mel Gibson starred, was a true story about him. E-mails sent out in 2000 claimed Paul Harvey devoted one of his commentaries to this, although no one who sent the e-mail actually heard the commentary. Paul Harvey never wrote or broadcast this. Mel Gibson never was savagely beaten and almost killed, needing extensive plastic surgery to repair his face. In fact, the movie was based on Isabelle Holland's 1972 novel of the same name.

10. The *Blair Witch Project* was real, www.snopes.com/horrors/ ghosts/blair.htm

This is my ultimate favorite. Before the movie *Blair Witch Project* came out, there was a Web site that convinced visitors that three students really did disappear, that the Blair Witch legend is a real legend (there's an oxymoron for you), and that the movie is really, really true. Even though the stars of the movie, the producers, and the studio publicly announced the Web site was just a great marketing gimmick (and caused the *Blair Witch Project* to become a high-grossing movie), people still believe it really happened.

Suckers.

Educate Yourself

The U.S. Department of Energy in conjunction with the Computer Incident Advisory Committee (CIAC) has a Web page devoted to chain letter hoaxes (http://HoaxBusters.ciac.org). The Web page imparts this advice:

> Users are requested to please not spread chain letters and hoaxes by sending copies to everyone you know. Sending a copy of a cute message to one or two friends is not a problem but sending an unconfirmed warning or plea to everyone you know with the request that they also send it to everyone they know simply adds to the clutter already filling our mailboxes. If you receive any of this kind of mail, please don't pass it to everyone you know, either delete it or pass it to your computer security manager to validate. Validated warnings from the incident response teams and anti-virus vendors have valid return addresses and are usually PGP signed with the organization's key. Alternately, you can and should get the warnings directly from the Web pages of the organizations that put them out to ensure that the information you have is valid and up-to-date.

There is a host of other information available about the e-mail hoaxes, legends, and chain letters found on the Net. One such site is the well-known Urban Legends Reference Pages at www.snopes.com, which is run by David and Barbara Mikkelson. David began reading and posting to a newsgroup about urban legends in 1989. Barbara joined the newsgroup in 1993 and found that David had quite the reputation as a researcher and debunker of false tales.

"I was thus deathly afraid of him," Barbara says laughing. "We began corresponding by e-mail and eventually met in real life and liked each other enough to get married. Our love of research is one of the things we have in common, and our love of the legends is another."

That love grew into a passion for finding out the stories behind these legends and hoaxes. How did they begin and where? What changes have they gone through over the years? They found that society tells tales, and has for centuries. The most popular legends tend to be what folks are apprehensive about, titillated by, or fascinated by, and morals and beliefs are held as the one true standard.

Is It Real?

1. If a message includes a request that you forward it to everyone you know, it's not real.

2. If there are several "FWD" comments in the body of a message, showing it's already been forwarded many times, it's not real.

3. If a message claims you'll get something for nothing, it probably isn't real.

4. If a message includes several e-mail addresses in addition to yours in the "TO:" line, you can be pretty sure it's a hoax, urban legend, or chain e-mail.

5. If a message claims such-and-such a thing happened to a friend of a friend (FOAF, in the words of the Urban Legends folks), their aunt or uncle, or someone else, but never them—yep—it's not real.

Even if a message contains technical references, refers to institutions, or includes addresses and phone numbers, be wary of believing it. If you want to verify that the message is real, go to the Web site of the company, person, or organization that claims to be involved and see if anything is mentioned on their site. Nine times out of 10, there will be a disclaimer, such as the ones noted in this chapter, about the Internet e-mail tax. "Urban legends are our way of venting what we're concerned about, and in the process we pass along our prejudices and our view of how things are supposed to be," Barbara explains.

"Urban legends are our way of venting what we're concerned about, and in the process we pass along our prejudices and our view of how things are supposed to be," Barbara explains.

Their Web site was a natural progression of their research. It features not only Internet-based urban legends and hoaxes but also tall tales that have been spread for ages.

So, why do people fall for these deceptions over and over again?

"It doesn't occur to us to question what friends tell us; we take what they say as gospel because we trust them to never lie to us," says Barbara. "It also never occurs to us that our friends could be honestly mistaken, having made the same error of wholeheartedly believing what friends told them."

What do you say to a friend who has unwittingly sent you deceptive e-mail?

"I'm afraid there's no one right answer," Barbara says. "With some folks, it won't matter how gently you try to tell them what they're sending is false; they're going to feel hurt and upset anyway. People don't like being wrong, and we often fail to handle such a turn of events gracefully."

Some people just dump the hoax/legend/chain e-mail into their trash bin and forget about it. Some do e-mail their friends and let them know it's a well-known hoax and send them to a site such as Barbara and David's to prove it.

"I've heard including a little note that omits any implication of the other person being misinformed works best," Barbara says. "Something along the lines of 'Wow! I just read about that very thing on an urban legends site. Have a look at <insert relevant URL> and let me know what you think.' "

Scams, Safe Shopping, and Online Banking

Online Scams

The same as scams offline, where an offer is just too good to be true but some people still fall for it.

Online Shopping

Shopping from the comfort of your home or office via the Internet.

Online Banking

Doing all of your banking online, including paying bills.

There are scam artists and there are scam *artistes*. And it didn't take them very long to discover the Internet. The FBI's Internet Fraud Complaint Center (IFCC, see Figure 5.1) and Internet Fraud Watch (IFW, see Figure 5.2) issued a list of what they consider to be the Top 10 online scams:

1. Online Auctions

2. General Merchandise Sales (non-delivery of items)

3. Nigerian Money Offers

IFCC
Internet Fraud Complaint Center
September 27, 2005

Privacy | Disclaimer | Sitemap

Home | File a Complaint | Press Room | Fraud Tips | Contact Us

Report Terrorist Activity (click here)

Filing a Complaint
How to file
Information Requested

Statistics

Partners

IFCC Warnings NEW

Welcome to IFCC

The Internet Fraud Complaint Center (IFCC) is a partnership between the Federal Bureau of Investigation (FBI) and the National White Collar Crime Center (NW3C).

IFCC's mission is to address fraud committed over the Internet. For victims of Internet fraud, IFCC provides a convenient and easy-to-use reporting mechanism that alerts authorities of a suspected criminal or civil violation. For law enforcement and regulatory agencies at all levels, IFCC offers a central repository for complaints related to Internet fraud, works to quantify fraud patterns, and provides timely statistical data of current fraud trends.

File a Complaint

This program is brought to you by the Federal Bureau of Investigation and the National White Collar Crime Center

NW3C
NATIONAL WHITE COLLAR CRIME CENTER

top | home | about us | press room | file a complaint | statistics | contact us
privacy | disclaimer | site map

Figure 5.1   IFCC

4. Information/Adult Services (pornography)

5. Internet Access Services (misrepresented or services not provided)

6. Computer Equipment/Software (never delivered or misrepresented)

7. Work-At-Home Plans

8. Lotteries

9. Fake Checks

10. Advance Fee Loans

Credit Card Fraud

When it comes to credit card fraud, some scammers are not only very clever but employ the same or similar ruses.

Figure 5.2 IFW

Annette was checking her bank statement in September 2000 and found a debit for Skiftelecom in Stavropol, Russia, for the amount of $15.08. Since she and her husband used their bank debit card online for purchases, she asked her husband if he ordered something from Russia. He hadn't. And she hadn't.

"When I reported this unauthorized charge to our bank, I was told that most consumers don't check their bank statements or credit card bills and that's how companies or people such as this Skiftelecom can get away with charging small amounts," Annette says. "If they do it to hundreds or thousands of people, they can make a tidy profit and never get caught."

Annette had the credit cards canceled and replaced with new account numbers. Then she did some checking online and found she wasn't the only one who'd been charged by Skiftelecom. A news site in the United Kingdom first reported it in its August 8, 2000, issue:

HASTINGS INTERNET SHOPPERS BEWARE!

Do you shop on the Internet? Do you accept your bank or credit card statements without a closer look? If you are one of those people who are busy or trusting and do not check your bank or credit card statements and you also shop on the Internet, now might be the time to change your habits.

Two members of our website team, who are Internet shoppers, have had statements this month which include the same entry for a service of which they have no knowledge.

The amount payable was 722.19 Russian Roubles to a company named as Skiftelecom, Stavropol. The sum in Sterling is £17.84 and was withdrawn on 18th July 2000.

They have both discussed the matter with their credit card company/bank and the site team have reported it to the Hastings Police. So, beware!

Annette was furious but not surprised and did some more digging. She found another person who posted a complaint to his credit card Web site, stating that he'd been charged $10.47 on July 21, 2000, by Skiftelecom. Another woman posted on a newsgroup that two of her credit cards were charged approximately $26.30 (one card twice) from Skiftelecom in July. She asked around and found four other friends who had the same charges. Then in October, her credit card was charged $10.05 from www.inetplat.com. Other newsgroup posters chimed in with complaints they had not only been charged by Skiftelecom, but also www.inetplat, both out of Russia.

Annette was glad she reported the charge from Skiftelecom when she had or she might have lost more money. As more people complained, they all seemed to have one common thread—they either had their Web site hosted by a Canadian company called

Softcomca or purchased something from a Web site hosted by Softcomca.

When contacted, a spokesman stated, "We are confident that the breach was not at Softcomca. We have received a bank statement from a customer who signed up at July 21, where she was charged on July 18 by Skiftelecom. Also, on some newsgroups, there are several complaints from people who have no relation to Softcomca, yet they were charged by Skiftelecom, too."

This response infuriated those who had lost money, and soon the Web host company was losing customers. To this day, there are warnings about this situation on newsgroups and forums, especially because Softcomca denied the Skiftelecom hack was from their site.

It all came to a head in December 2000, when the media began reporting that hundreds, perhaps thousands, of people reported small charges from four Russian "Internet firms": Skiftelecom, Inetplat, Intelcom, and Global Telecom. When I tried to interview these companies, none replied to my e-mail.

Thoughts were, at the time, that these companies were part of a larger credit card scheme Russian hackers had concocted and pulled off by hacking into a database at CreditCards.com, stealing 3 million credit card numbers. However, they turned out not to be the ones troubling Annette and others.

As suddenly as the charges appeared, they stopped. But Annette learned her lesson. "Now we use only one credit card for all of our online transactions and it's not our bank debit card," she says. "We haven't had any problems since."

Making small charges on a credit card is an easy way for criminals to rack up the dough—if they have hundreds or thousands of credit card numbers. Do the math. Most credit card companies won't go after the criminals for such small charges. So the criminal gets the dough, chucks his list of credit card numbers, and gets a new list. And the scam continues.

Online Shopping

When it comes to online shopping, we hear about the horror stories more often than the good experiences. The truth is that online shopping is as safe as offline shopping, if not safer.

"I've used my credit card and never had a security leak or unauthorized charges from any online store," says Lorian, who lives in Oregon. "I often use coolsavings.com and valupage.com coupons, which gets me free shipping at many online merchants, or $10 off a $25 purchase or some other premium item with purchase."

Yes, there are plenty of happy online shoppers like Lorian, and you can be one, too. Frank Fiore, an e-commerce expert and consultant, has written several books about online shopping and commerce.

"The most common mistake online shoppers make is not using a credit card," says Fiore. "When you use a credit card, you're protected by your bank against scams and merchants who either send you the wrong product or will not take a product back for whatever reason. All you have to do is call your bank and dispute the charge. If you send a check or money order, you have little or no recourse. This is especially important in person-to-person auctions like eBay."

Sites That Offer Tips/Advice/Comparison Shopping

About.com Online Shopping
www.about.com/shopping

Scams, Frauds, Hoaxes, and so forth, on the Internet
from A to Z
http://advocacy-net.com/scammks.htm

Scambusters
www.scambusters.com
   This is one of the most comprehensive Web sites devoted to online scams, including shopping and banking. It offers a monthly newsletter with the latest information, which can be e-mailed to you.

WebAssured.com
www.webassured.com

Planet Feedback
www.planetfeedback.com

Epinions.com
www.epinions.com

BizRate.com
www.bizrate.com

ConsumerSearch
www.consumersearch.com

PriceWatch (comparison shopping)
www.pricewatch.com

FTC Facts for Consumers: Shop Online Safely
www.ftc.gov/bcp/conline/pubs/online/cybrsmrt.htm

Yahoo! Shopping Safety Tips
http://docs.yahoo.com/docs/info/consumertips.html

For auctions, it's recommended that you use a service that allows payment for your winning bid with a major credit card. PayPal and Escrow.com are examples of these types of services. They enable you to pay for online purchases securely. If anything happens, such as nonshipment or receipt of the wrong item, you can get PayPal or Escrow.com to intervene on your behalf. Many online merchants use these services as a way for you to pay for items in their store if they don't accept credit cards.

Also, take a careful look at the location of online merchants.

"Does the merchant have their own domain name—such as www.virtualvin.com—or are they using free Web space such as Geocities or Tripod? If they have their own domain, it does lend some credibility to the merchant," says Fiore. "You could make a comparison to a merchant with a large storefront downtown vs. a guy with a fold-up cart on the side of the road. If you have a problem with your product, who are you more likely to find again to help get it resolved?"

Once you feel comfortable with the merchant's Web site, look at the site itself. Does it look professionally designed or slapped together? A site that looks professional usually means the merchant spent money to have it designed, showing a commitment to the product(s) he sells online. If you wouldn't go into a store that is small, dingy, and questionable, you shouldn't do business with a Web site that looks like it was put together by an amateur or fly-by-night operation, no matter how good the prices seem to be. If the business doesn't have its physical address and telephone number posted somewhere on the site, that's a warning sign.

"Does the site mention secure shopping?" Fiore says. "Many sites will dedicate an entire page to shopper security to help you feel at ease."

Make Your Online Shopping Experience a Safe One

MasterCard International and the National Consumer's League offer these great tips for making your online shopping experience a good one:

Privacy Protection. Reputable Web site operators clearly state privacy policies in an easily accessible place. Understand what information is collected and how it is used. Look for sites whose policies or privacy programs enable you to choose whether, and in what circumstances, your personal information will be used or shared with others.

Information about the offer. Good companies provide plenty of information and make it easy to find. Make sure you know what you're buying, how much it costs, the terms of any guarantees or warranties, the return or cancellation policies, and how to contact the company if you have questions. This is crucial when shopping online, since you can't actually see or use the product or service before you buy it.

Information about the seller. Look for information about whether the seller belongs to a trade group or participates in a program, such as BBBOnLine, that helps resolve complaints.

Delivery date. Know when the product(s) will be delivered or the service(s) performed.

Security. Good Web sites provide information about how they protect your financial information when it's transmitted and stored.

Guard your personal information. Don't provide information that you're uncomfortable giving. Never give anyone the password you use to log onto your computer or ISP. Don't offer financial account information unless you're paying for a purchase with that account.

Check the seller's reputation. Learn as much as you can about companies or individuals before doing business with them. Check with the Better Business Bureau (BBB) and your state and local agencies to find out about complaints. See if the Web site has a "feedback forum" where people can put information about their transactions. Ask friends about their favorite online merchants. Bear in mind, though, that just because a seller has no complaints or a good reputation, there's no guarantee that things will go smoothly for you.

Consider taxes and shipping costs. There may be taxes or duties on your purchase, especially if the transaction is international. Factor in shipping and handling charges to determine the total costs. You may also have to pay for shipping if you want to return the item.

Ask about insurance. Will the seller pay to insure the shipment, or is it your expense? How much does it cost? Is other insurance available to protect you if you don't get what you paid for or if you're dissatisfied? Some auction sites provide insurance to buyers. Be sure you know how insurance programs work and how much they cover.

Keep records. Print out all the information on your transaction, including the product description, delivery information, privacy policy, warranties, and any confirmation notices that the seller sends you via e-mail.

How can you tell if a site has secure shopping? There are several ways to determine this. Some sites that offer secure shopping show a graphic or logo with "SSL" on the main page, often with a link describing Secure Sockets Layer (SSL), which is a form of encryption that scrambles your credit card number and other information, allowing for safe transmission of the transaction (see Figures 5.3 and 5.4).

Once you've selected the items you want and have a virtual shopping cart or an order form, clicking on "Pay now" or something similar

Figure 5.3   Unlocked

Figure 5.4   Locked

should take you to a secure page. This page will either have "https" as the beginning of its URL (such as https://www.virtualvin.Com) or a "lock" or "key" graphic that appears in the lower left- or right-hand corner of your Web browser. If the lock or key is closed or whole—essentially locked—then the site is secure. When you leave that page or the site, you'll notice the lock is open or unlocked or the key is broken. Depending on which version of the browser you use, you may get a pop-up window letting you know you're entering a "secure area." This is the same as the lock or key graphic—your payment information will remain secure so that no one can steal it.

Online Scam and Fraud Statistics

- Online auctions accounted for 42 percent of complaints.

- 75 percent of online fraud cases originate from Web sites; 25 percent from e-mail offers.

- 72 percent of online fraud victims are ages 20–49 years.

- The average amount a victim lost rose from $895 in 2004 to $2,033 in 2005.

(Compiled by Internet Fraud Watch for Jan.–Sept. 2005)

Later versions of Microsoft and Netscape browsers, as well as the Mozilla Firefox browser, have preferences you can set so that you can be alerted when you're entering an encrypted (or secure) site, leaving one, viewing a page with a mix of encrypted/unencrypted information, or sending unencrypted information to a site (see Figures 5.5, 5.6, and 5.7). Remember, though, that checking these preferences will result in quite a few pop-up alerts while surfing the Internet.

If there's something you just have to have and the online merchant who sells it doesn't accept credit cards or seems a bit dubious, consider using PayPal (www.paypal.com) or an escrow service such as Escrow.com (www.escrow.com). Escrow services hold your money until you've confirmed you received the product or service. Then they release the payment to the seller. There is a small fee, but in many cases the peace of mind will be worth the expense.

If the merchant refuses to allow this, then you'd better look elsewhere or wait until the item you want becomes more widely available. Reluctance on the part of a merchant to provide a secure

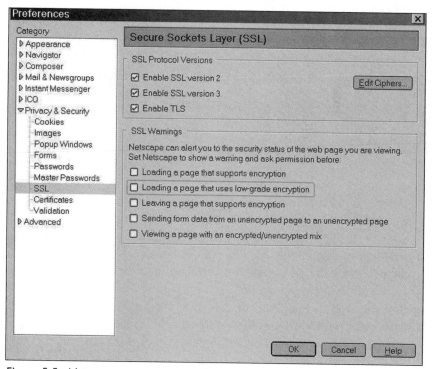

Figure 5.5 Netscape secure

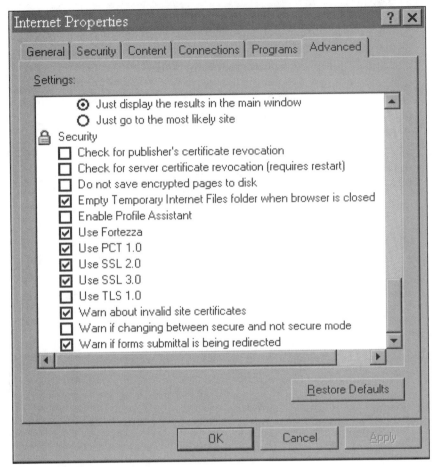

Figure 5.6   MSIE secure

transaction is a sure sign something's fishy. Don't cave in if they demand a money order or bank draft—or cash, heaven forbid.

"One of the best online shopping experiences I had was when I heard of a music group called Gaia Consort but couldn't get their CDs anywhere locally or through a major online merchant," says music fan Cynthia. "The group didn't have any kind of online sales set up on their Web site yet, but we contacted them via e-mail about purchasing their CD. We used PayPal to pay for it with a credit card and got the CD shipped to us overnight—just in time for a party!"

Credit card companies have jumped onto the bandwagon, offering everything from online fraud protection if you use their credit

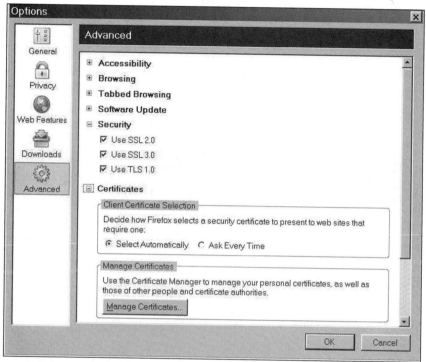

Figure 5.7   Mozilla Firefox secure

card for all your online shopping, to tips and information on their Web sites to make you a savvy online shopper. Here are some sites to visit:

MasterCard International ShopSmart
www.mastercard.com/us/personal/en/securityandbasics

American Express Fraud Protection Center
http://home3.americanexpress.com/corp/consumer_resources. asp

Discover Financial Services Shopping Guide
www.discovercard.com/discover/data/account/securityprivacy/ shopping.shtml

Visa International Internet Shopping Guide
www.usa.visa.com/personal/security/

Other Credit Card Companies
www.yourcreditcardcompanies.com/forconsumers/fraud.asp

It may seem that finding an online merchant you can trust is a simple task, but Richard M. Smith, a Boston-based independent security consultant, urges careful investigation.

Top 10 Countries Reporting Internet Fraud

1. United States
2. Canada
3. Australia
4. United Kingdom
5. Germany
6. Italy
7. Singapore
8. France
9. Japan
10. Netherlands

In the United States, California tops the list for complaints filed by victims, followed in order by New York, Texas, Florida, Pennsylvania, Illinois, Ohio, Michigan, New Jersey, and Washington.

(Compiled by the Internet Fraud Complaint Center for the year 2004; released 2005)

"If you go to a search engine, such as Yahoo! or Google, to look for something you want to buy, don't assume a merchant listed in the search results is legitimate," Smith says. "After you find an online merchant, do some basic research if it's not a well-known name. The best place to start is in newsgroups or forums. Ask if anyone in the newsgroup or forum has dealt with that merchant. You can bet that if they had a bad experience, you'll hear about it."

There are also Web sites where people can post their bad and good experiences with online merchants. With names like Epinions.com and BizRate.com, you can be sure you'll find out what you need to know before you purchase something from a particular merchant (see Appendix B, Resources, at the end of the book).

Smith also warns against Web sites that force you to register before you can look at what they sell.

"Give fake information," Smith says. "Or leave it blank if you can. If you can't get through that way, then don't register and don't patronize that site. They don't need all your personal information—such as name, address, and phone number—just so you can take a look around."

How the Government Helps

The FBI has its hands full with the ever-growing number of online-related cases, from harassment and stalking to hackers and fraud. Since the IFCC opened, more than 400,000 complaints have been referred to law enforcement agencies worldwide. With the number of online users increasing daily, the amount of complaints is certain to double, if not triple, in coming years.

"The agency has a hard time gauging the actual incidence of Internet fraud because only a fraction of those affected by fraud schemes online know where to report the problem," says Tracey Silberling, who is with the FBI's Criminal Division. "There is probably a huge percentage of fraud that goes unreported. The IFCC takes all those reports and sends them out to the appropriate agency."

The U.S. Postal Inspection Service (USPIS) has also gotten into the act. If an item was paid for through the postal mail (via check, money order, or bank draft), or if an item received through the postal mail was not what was ordered, the victim can file a complaint with the USPIS, which will look into it and try to get the customer's money back.

One example is the Woodside Literary Agency, mentioned in Chapter 1. Since many writers sent this so-called agency reading, editing, and contract fees via postal mail, the USPIS stepped in. They arrested the two people running Woodside in January 2000 and charged them with mail fraud and perjury, punishable by up to eight months in jail and/or fines.

Top 10 Countries of Alleged Perpetrators

1. United States (78.75 percent)
2. Canada (3.03 percent)
3. Nigeria (2.87 percent)
4. United Kingdom (2.32 percent)
5. Italy (2.01 percent)
6. Greece (1.04 percent)
7. Romania (.92 percent)
8. France (.86 percent)
9. Spain (.60 percent)
10. China (.58 percent)

In the United States, California again tops the list for alleged perpetrators, followed in order by New York, Florida, Texas, Illinois, Ohio, Pennsylvania, Georgia, New Jersey, and Arizona.

(Compiled by the Internet Fraud Complaint Center for the year 2004; released 2005)

The USPIS is serious when it comes to fraud that occurs while using postal mail. It is so Net-savvy that it offers a number of consumer tools on its site (www.usps.com/websites/depart/inspect/welcome2.htm) so that you can find the address of your nearest U.S. Postal Inspector, see the list of laws enforced, and read news about the latest cons and swindles. The Software Information Industry Association (SIIA) gave the USPIS a recognition award at its annual conference in 2001.

"SIIA has, over the past four years, developed an aggressive Internet Anti-Piracy Campaign to help stop the spread of infringing software online," wrote Mike Flynn, manager of the Internet Anti-Piracy division of the SIIA, in a letter to the USPIS. "To that effect, we have worked in the past with various U.S. enforcement agencies. This past year [2000], SIIA turned to the USPIS for help in a few cases that we were handling on behalf of our members since many, if not all, of the alleged pirates were using the U.S. Postal system to send illegal product. The response that SIIA has received from various USPIS offices has been extremely positive. As you know, often times good deeds go unrewarded. We'd like to change that."

On March 11, 2001, U.S. Postal Deputy Chief Inspector Michael Ahern accepted the award on behalf of the USPIS in San Diego, California, from SIIA President Ken Wasch, for its success in protecting intellectual property rights and consumer rights from online scams.

Since then, the USPIS has been involved in cracking child pornography rings related to the Web, credit cards stolen from mailboxes and used to purchase goods and services online, and illegal drugs or other items purchased on the Web and shipped through the postal mail.

Through rain or sleet or snow, and now we can add "online."

Online Banking

Many banks provide online banking services, often getting customers interested in signing up by offering the first three months free or waiving the standard setup fee. Some consumers still balk at moving their checking and savings to the Net. After all, using a credit card for an online purchase may be well and good, but this is their money!

If you are ready to take the plunge, or at least study the options, software accounting programs such as MS Money and Quicken offer tips on how to get an online banking account set up so that you can take care of all your finances online, including your taxes, stocks, bonds, and more. In addition, check out your bank's Web site to see what they offer or stop by your local branch and ask them about online banking services.

Here are some sites to visit:

Banking and Investing Online Resources Group
www.bank-accounts-online.com

American Banker
www.americanbanker.com

Quicken Online Banking
www.quicken.com/banking_and_credit

MS Money Online Banking Page
www.msmoney.com/mm/banking/onlinebk/onlinebk_intro.htm

"More and more people are turning to online banking in one form or another," notes Frank Fiore. "What will really open the floodgates is when they don't charge for bill paying. That's what I'm waiting for!"

FDIC Tips for Banking Safely Online

- Confirm that an online bank (if you're not using your own) is legitimate and that your deposits are FDIC insured.

- For insurance purposes, be aware that a bank may use different names for its online banking; understand your rights as a consumer.

- Learn where to go for more assistance from banking regulators.

- Remember that non-financial Web sites that are linked to your bank's site are not FDIC insured.

ALSO:

- Find out what fees are involved to switch to online banking; sometimes it's actually less expensive than keeping your regular checking account.

- Determine if there are any fees should you decide to cancel the service. Is there a contract?

(From www.fdic.gov/bank/individual/online/safe.html)

Auction Caution

Online Auction Fraud

When a seller offers something that is not what they claim, such as forged autographs or memorabilia; pirated software, videos, or music; and any prize that is not as initially described.

Author's Note: The following example is included for the purposes of illustration only, in order to point out the potential dangers of online auction fraud, and is in no way intended to suggest that shopping on eBay is unsafe in comparison to any other auction site. The principal function of an online auction site is to connect third-party buyers and sellers, and, despite the most diligent efforts of eBay and other auction sites to protect the interests of their visitors, abuses by auction participants are inevitable.

Phony Photos

It seemed like it was too good to be true. On eBay there was an 8x10 color photograph of Harrison Ford and Sean Connery from the movie *Indiana Jones and the Last Crusade* signed by both of them (see Figure 6.1). Prospective bidder Anne read the following description:

> All of our photos are authentic and come with 100%
> Money back guarantee. We Have been in business since

1988 and we have never had any problems with any Customer. We give you our word. Negative comments usually come from Competition. Look at our feed back it speaks for itself. Please notify us if you Receive any non-solicited e-mail regarding this item. Please forward complete email To me so that we can forward them to ebay! This is an absolutely gorgeous 8x10 photograph signed in Blue and Black ink by Ford and Connery. We provide money backed satisfaction guarantee and certificates of authenticity. We have other Memorabilia at www.xtruex-collectorx.com. or at Ebay sellers at XXMEM Thank you for visiting and have A great day. ** SORRY ABOUT BAD SCANS !**

Figure 6.1 Indiana Jones

There was a link to the company's Web site and it seemed legit, so Anne placed a bid on the photo. Three days later, on July 23, she won it for $41 plus shipping. The seller responded quickly with a shipping address and Anne promptly sent off a check for $45.50.

"Three weeks went by and no photo," Anne said, "so I e-mailed xxmem letting them know I was wondering where the photo was. I got no reply."

She sent two more e-mails a week later and still no reply. She went to the eBay site and got the user ID information on xxmem, which included an address and phone number. When she called, an answering machine picked up. Anne left a message, but received no return phone call.

The next day she got an e-mail from xxmem:

```
    We looked up the reciept under your last
name, could it be under a different name?
```

It hadn't been and Anne let them know that in a quick reply, repeating her full name and mailing address for them.

The next day brought this reply:

```
    Just got back from the post office and it
was insured, it will take 30 days to
process but we will be sending one out to
you on Monday, when it get home I am going
to email a scan of the insured reciept
showing it was mailed on July 28.
```

By this time, Anne had done some checking on xxmem on eBay and was beginning to doubt the validity of the signatures on the photo. She discovered that xxmem had offered the same photo with the same exact signatures at least 18 times within the past 30 days. Each auction had a winner, which meant there were at least that many other photos of Harrison Ford and Sean Connery out there. She knew it was hard to get autographs from Ford and Connery, and harder still to get them to sign copies of the same photograph that many times. Anne asked xxmem if the replacement photo would be like the one she'd won. The answer was yes.

Anne sent them this e-mail on August 23:

```
    One last question: Can you guarantee me
that this photo has authentic autographs
```

and does not have autopen signatures? My
concern is that after doing a search on
ebay under your seller ID, I find that
there were/are at least 18 of the same
exact photo since 7/19/99, with both Ford
and Connery's signatures on it. I don't
know how many prior to that date you've
sold. How did you get them to sign this many
photos? I sincerely think I would rather
get my money back at this point. Please
send a money order in the amount of $45.50
to me immediately. Forget the photo. If I
receive one, I am returning it. I want my
money back.

The reply came quickly, and was curt:

After everything we are doing you want
your money back sure will have it in the
mail today.

But they never answered the question about the authenticity of the
autographs or how they'd gotten them. Anne did some more research
on eBay and checked out xxmem's feedback.[1] She found out she
wasn't the only one having problems with this company, as per these
examples of complaints:

Complaint: Never sent item, won't give me refund, won't
answer about authenticity of auto's.

Complaint: The item has never been sent. I am very disappointed with the service.

Complaint: NEVER SENT PICTURE .... BEWARE! DO
NOT DO BUSINESS WITH Xxmem!!

Complaint: It has taken me over a month + 2 checks to get
him to send the WRONG picture!!!!

Complaint: BEWARE; I ONLY RECEIVED ONE OF
TWO ITEMS PURCHASED

Complaint: Check cleared 7-22. No photo, just excuses by e-mail. Did not return phone call (finally received a refund on 8/23/99 after repeated emails and calls)

Complaint: Well over a month never received item. Will never buy from again!!!!!!!

Complaint: Where's my Griffey Jr. picture? It's been a month. Not even an e-mail.

Anne gathered up these e-mail addresses and sent this message:

We're all in the same club, unfortunately—those who had problems with the seller known as xxmem on eBay. Most of us didn't get the photo we won and/or a refund and some of us got the wrong photo or not the whole order. My case is that I kept emailing them, asking when they'd sent the photo I won out and they didn't answer me until I called and left a message on their answering machine. Then I got the runaround—first I was asked if I'd used a different name, they couldn't find it under my last name, then they mysteriously found the insured receipt they supposedly sent with my photo (under my name), then said they'd send me a new photo. When I discovered they'd gotten four negative feedbacks within the past seven days, I demanded my money back. First I got an okay, then an e-mail claiming I had to wait until they got a refund from the post office first. I told them no. I not only demanded my money back, but told them I would complain to eBay, the southern California BBB, the California State Attorney General, and my lawyer. I think the IRS would be interested to find out that all auction sales on eBay have payment made out to a person and not the company name. I haven't heard back from them, but I want to ask all of you if you will agree to do a combined complaint to the organizations I mentioned. I'll be happy to do the legwork. All I'd need is your okay and have you let me know exactly what happened between you and xxmem.

I've also done some research on their past sales. They seem to have an awful lot of the same photos up for bid signed by some pretty elusive celebrities. I can't imagine Harrison Ford and Sean Connery signing the same photograph from Indiana Jones and the Last Crusade over 20 times. And that was just a listing of auctions from the past 30 days.

I'm sure if eBay did some research, they'd find that xxmem sells the same photos over and over again, leading me to believe this seller may be auctioning forged signatures of celebrities. I don't think most winners are smart enough to see what kind of photos xxmem has sold in the past or are selling now—I think they'd be very surprised to find that their photo may be a fake.

Replies came quickly from most of the people who complained about xxmem. Pat in Texas wrote:

I never got the photo of Stevie Nicks that I won. They (xxmem) had one excuse after another. The last excuse was that one of them had gone on vacation at the time the check was received and that a new person had not posted the check with the item number. They then asked for a copy of the canceled check. I faxed it to them on August 20 and have not received a reply. I asked for a refund in lieu of photo. I was a little leery about the authenticity of the autograph anyway.

And this from Lynette of Massachusetts:

> I won two photos from xxmem; one arrived
> and not the other. They said they would
> send it right out. They told me that three
> times. Because I waited the 30 days from
> the end of the auction, I was unable to file
> a Fraud report on eBay. They no longer
> answer my e-mails, ever since I left the
> negative feedback.

Jeff from North Carolina was also angry:

> I won an autographed Pretty Woman photo
> [see Figure 6.2] and the autographs look
> fake (they don't look the same as others I
> have seen). I have contacted xxmem and they
> agreed to refund my money, but I'm wary
> about sending him the photo without any
> proof.

And another came from David of Michigan:

> I was the high bidder on a autographed
> photo of Ken Griffey and Alex Rodriguez. It
> was a very nice photo, and the signatures
> looked very good. I've been collecting for
> some time, and from what I could tell, the
> Griffey signature was right on! I was
> excited to get such a great pic for only
> $42. After I won, xxmem sent me the info on
> where to send the money order. When the pic
> hadn't come after a week, I sent them an
> e-mail asking what was going on. They
> replied that it had been sent the day
> before. I waited another week, but never
> got the pic. I sent one more e-mail, say-
> ing that I either wanted my pic, or a full
> refund. I never got a reply, a picture, or
> a refund, so I left negative feedback!

Figure 6.2   *Pretty Woman*

Complaints stretched as far away as England, including this one from Christian:

> I was the highest bidder for a Pamela
> Anderson photo for $27 + $10 postage. So I
> sent $37 on the 14th of July. I then sent
> an e-mail about 3 weeks later asking if it
> had been sent out. They replied that they
> had not received the payment. Another week

```
went by and I sent another e-mail to see if
payment had arrived and they said no and
asked if I sent it under another name, to
which I replied no. Since then I sent five
e-mails but have not received any replies.
```

Anne was intrigued that Christian had also been asked if he sent his payment under another name. Now she was positive something was wrong. She gave xxmem one last chance and e-mailed them on August 30 that she had not received the refund. The reply the next day was:

```
It was mailed to on August 24 just like
the photo was mailed to you along time ago.
Something is wrong with your post office.
```

Anne knew there was nothing wrong with her post office. But she did receive the second photo. Jeff sent her his *Pretty Woman* photo "signed" by Julia Roberts and Richard Gere. She called a local auto-graph dealer who was a member of the UACC3 and asked if he'd look at the photos to authenticate them for her. He agreed.

His e-mail to her was what she thought it would be:

```
Anne, it is my opinion that both auto-
graphs you sent me are forgeries. Meaning
they were intentionally hand-signed by
someone other than the pictured celebrity.
Sean Connery, Harrison Ford, Julia Roberts,
and Richard Gere are perhaps the four
toughest Hollywood autographs to obtain—at
least the top 10 most difficult. To have
jointly signed pieces on these individuals
is remarkable.
    I would pay up to $150 for legitimate
pieces like the ones you sent me. Keep in
mind, that I pay wholesale prices so you
can imagine what the retail value is.
Another thing to keep in mind—authenticat-
ing is a risky and difficult job. So, I will
state that, in my opinion, the autographs
you inquired about are not hand-signed by
the pictured celebrity.
```

> You should never buy anything on eBay
> unless you have a business relationship
> with the seller—one that you trust. There
> is so, so much bad material on eBay that,
> in my opinion, it isn't worth bidding—
> unless you know the seller. Because of lia-
> bility issues, this will be my only
> indication that I felt the pieces you
> mailed me were not hand-signed.
>
> It is amazing, but some of the most dis-
> reputable dealers in the industry will sue
> if they hear someone saying their stuff
> isn't real—even though they know that it
> isn't. So, I really try to stay out of the
> third party authentication game.

Anne got the others to agree to a combined complaint and began filling out forms for all of them. These were sent to the Southern California Better Business Bureau (xxmem was located there), the California State Attorney General, the USPS Mail Fraud Bureau, the National Fraud Information Center, and eBay's Fraud division.

It didn't take long for xxmem to reply to everyone. And they all received the same e-mail:

> It is hard for us to believe you could do
> something like this. We went out of our way
> to get this matter solved and to make you
> satisfied. We always insure our packages,
> we have proof showing we sent the photo's
> out when we said we did. We have almost
> 2,000 positive feedback's from customers
> that are satisfied with our business. We
> even sent you a new photo, and you did not
> give us the benefit of the doubt. We are
> not out here to scam anyone, we are trying
> to earn a honest living.

But—miraculously—refunds began to appear in the mail.

Pat was one of the first to receive his, on August 23, in the amount of $50. Anne received hers on September 7, in the amount of $45.50. Lynette finally received her photo of Harrison Ford and Sean

Connery on September 21, and decided to keep it instead of getting a refund. Christian received his refund of $37 on September 24. David received his refund of $46.50 on September 24. Jeff was the last to receive his, on October 2, in the amount of $146.02.

It may seem incredible that nothing can be done to stop sellers from putting up forged autographed items on the auction Web sites, but as more pressure is put on online auction sites to take responsibility, things are bound to change.

When I asked eBay about this, I received this reply from the company's eBay Life columnist Uncle Griff:

> Fake autographs and infringing items are two separate kettles of fish. We cannot verify or authenticate an autograph, thus we remind all bidders it's 'caveat emptor' (buyer beware) that should be their watch cry. eBay doesn't handle the merchandise so any sort of authentication from us is impossible. The bidder has to rely on the integrity of the seller and know what they are buying. That being said, anyone who ends up with an item that is not what it was claimed to be has some recourse with our Insurance program and, if that fails, our Fraud Reporting form. Items that infringe upon a person's copyright or property rights are removed from the site as they are reported by either the property owner or a conscientious member. Since eBay is the biggest player in the person-to-person trading market, most of the big trademark or copyright holders watch us like hawks and immediately report any violations of their intellectual property rights.

It's interesting to note that by the time most bidders who have had problems do get in touch with either the insurance program or fraud reporting on eBay, the 30-day limit eBay imposes (from the end of the auction) has passed. This means bidders have to swallow their pride and lose their money, or they can file complaints, as Anne and the others did. The latter takes time and, often, money.

I contacted several suspected sellers at online auction sites about the origin of their "authentic" autographed memorabilia. No seller revealed where they got their autographs—and no seller claimed they had procured the photos and other signed objects directly from the celebrities.

Within a week after contacting these dealers, a major FBI raid occurred. Operation Bullpen, a two-year-old undercover FBI investigation, cracked down on counterfeit autographs, most of which had been sold at online auctions in what authorities said was a $1 billion-per-year industry. As part of the probe, agents and informants posed as collectors and traders to infiltrate the industry. As a result, more than 50 dealers were raided in California, Nevada, New Jersey, and Pennsylvania, including some of the ones I had contacted.

More on autographs: Two autograph organizations, Universal Autograph Collectors Club (UACC) and Professional Autograph Dealers Association (PADA), have strict guidelines for their members, which must be adhered to or members will be dropped and/or penalized. If an auction seller is a member of either of these organizations, then you can be reasonably sure the item you bid on is legitimate. Founded in 1965, UACC began as a small group of Long Island, New York, autograph collectors and has grown to be the largest federally recognized nonprofit collectors organization of its kind. Reach UACC at:

UACC
P.O. Box 6181
Washington, DC 20044-6181
e-mail: uacc2@autographworld.com
www.uacc.org

Membership in PADA is limited to dealers who have demonstrated expertise and integrity in buying and selling autographs. Reach PADA at:

PADA
P.O. Box 1729-W
Murray Hill Station
New York, NY 10156
888-338-4338
e-mail: padamail@padaweb.org
www.padaweb.org

You've Got Mail from eBay

If you receive an e-mail message from eBay, there is an easy way to find out if it is legitimate. Log into your eBay account, click on My eBay at the top of the page, and then select My Messages from the menu on the left. If eBay really sent you an e-mail message, it will be listed in My Messages, as well as having been sent to your e-mail inbox (see Figures 6.3 and 6.4). If you receive an e-mail claiming to be from eBay and it is *not* listed in My Messages, it is someone trying to scam you, also called phishing (for more about phishing, see Chapter 7).

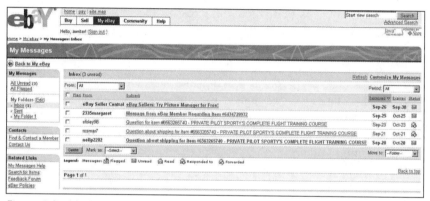

Figure 6.3   My Messages in eBay

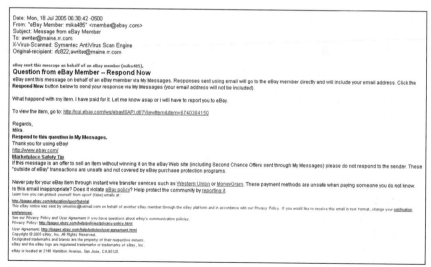

Figure 6.4   Legitimate message from eBay

Most times, the message will claim that your eBay account has been suspended until further notice or that your billing information needs to be updated (or something similar), or (one of the most clever ones I've seen) the message looks like it came from someone who won an auction of yours (if you sell items on eBay) or that you won their auction and never paid (if you bid on items).

This person either claims:

a) The item was never received so you will be reported to eBay and he or she will leave negative feedback if you do not respond.

b) That payment was never received so you will be reported to eBay and he or she will leave negative feedback if you do not pay immediately.

The goal in a) is that when you click on the link provided in the message, you'll be brought to the "eBay" login page. If you don't look at the Web site address (URL) in the text bar at the top of the browser, you could be fooled into thinking it was really eBay. These scammers are very good at making the page look just like eBay's login page. Once you've signed in, you've given the scammer the information they wanted—your eBay user ID and password. Now they can steal your account and do a lot of damage by selling items and scamming others ... all in your good name.

The goal in b) is to get you to "pay" for the item you supposedly won and never paid for by logging into your "PayPal" account. Similar to a), it's not really PayPal but only looks like the official PayPal site. Again, if you don't look at the address in your Web browser, you could not only lose your PayPal account to these scammers, but any credit cards or bank accounts associated with your PayPal account will be compromised as well.

The rule of thumb whenever you receive an e-mail purporting to be from eBay: Check My Messages in your eBay account. If there is not a matching message there, then either delete the bogus message or report it for free at Spamcop (www.spamcop.net). Unless you fall for it, it's just spam.

"Reverse" Auction Fraud

In 1997, Connie opened the Gray Horse Emporium, an antiques store in Paris, Virginia, with a friend. Soon, the two began buying and selling antiques on eBay. Then her friend left the business and Connie felt she couldn't run the shop by herself because she had no time for her family and for training her horse. She began selling antiques and collectibles exclusively online, mostly through eBay.

A friend asked if she'd help him auction off watches from his father's estate. Many were expensive, and he didn't want to try to sell them through classified ads in the newspaper. Connie agreed and put the watches up for auction. One Rolex was quickly bid on and had reached $10,000 when she received an e-mail.

It was a request that she end the auction at the reserve price of $13,000 if the bidder paid that day via credit card. She called her friend, advising him to keep the auction going, as she thought the Rolex could fetch much more money. He decided to end the auction instead of waiting, so she e-mailed the bidder back, agreeing to the transaction. Within an hour, she received an e-mail from Tradenable[2] stating that the credit card payment had gone through.

Connie called her friend with the mailing information so that he could send the Rolex out that day. When she got off the phone, she noticed she'd received another e-mail from Tradenable—the credit card was a stolen one and they urged her not to send the Rolex. She called her friend back immediately but he'd already dropped the Rolex off at the post office. When she called the post office, she was lucky—they still had the package.

While her friend picked up the Rolex, Connie called the local police. They asked her what she wanted to do about it. She had the Rolex, so she hadn't lost anything. She told the police officer that she didn't want this guy to get away with the fraud. The officer said he was happy to hear this and they hatched a plan.

Connie e-mailed the fraudulent bidder and let him know that the post office would not insure the watch and she'd have to send it via UPS. She needed a street address for this, not the P.O. Box he'd given her. He quickly e-mailed back a street address. Connie called the police officer with the address and was told to package something similar in size and weight of the Rolex and send it off.

Connie found a broken soap dish, carefully packaged it up and sent it via UPS to the address indicated. The next day, the police staked out the street address, finding it was an abandoned home. They hoped the fraudulent bidder would show up. They called UPS to find out what time the delivery would be. The police were told by UPS that the fraudulent bidder called them and said he'd come to the UPS office to pick up the package. By the time police arrived, the package had been picked up, but they got a good description of the man. Less than a block away, the opened package and broken soap dish were found in a dumpster.

Within a week, the fraudulent bidder was arrested—but not for the credit card fraud; it was for a traffic violation.

Connie says she learned her lesson: Never send an item out to a buyer the same day the credit card transaction has been approved, and never end an auction early. She has adhered to these two principles and has had no further problems.

10 Tips for Safe Bidding Online

Bidders can be auction savvy if they follow this advice:

1. Check the feedback/comments on the seller. If it's under 98 percent, tread carefully and think twice about bidding. Look at the negative feedback to see when the most recent was posted. Sometimes a winning bidder is disgruntled no matter what or has left negative feedback without contacting the seller first. But if the negative feedback looks bad to you, don't bid. The item you want is sure to show up again sometime with another seller. That's the beauty of online auctions—you can find just about anything you could ever want on them.

2. See what else the seller is currently selling. If the auction site you're on has the capability, check any past auctions by that seller. If you see more than one of the same item you want to bid on, be wary, especially if it's an autographed item. If you see a large number of the item you're interested in (such as 10 Joe DiMaggio signed photos, when you know he's been dead for some time, and they're all the same pose and same signature), DO NOT bid on them!

3. Look at other auction items of the same type and see if their descriptions match word for word. Many fraudulent sellers use several IDs or usernames to sell as many of the same items as possible.

4. If you're having doubts, check the seller's feedback to see if there is a winning bidder who has won several different auctions, but on different dates. Do a search on that bidder to see what other items they have bid on in the past. If he or she has only bid on

items from the seller you were looking at, it is more than likely this is a shill bidder—shill bidding is when someone creates one or more accounts on an auction site to bid on an item from a particular seller, hoping to drive the final winning bid price higher. If you suspect shill bidding, report it to the auction site.

5. If the seller has only a few feedback comments and you really want an item that the seller has up for auction, see if the seller takes credit cards, PayPal, or some other form of online payment. If the seller doesn't, and only accepts money orders to be sent to a P.O. Box or payments via Western Union, be wary. Many fraudulent sellers will put "ghost" items up for auction, then disappear once the money is sent. If you use a credit card, make sure it's one that will allow you to dispute a charge in case the seller does turn out to be fraudulent.

6. If you really want an autographed piece of memorabilia, deal with someone legitimate who can absolutely guarantee the item was hand-signed by the celebrity.

7. If the seller does use a post office box, don't let that sway you, especially if the seller has a lot of positive feedback. Many sellers I communicated with say they use a post office box for tax purposes (to keep their auction mail separate from their home mail) and/or for privacy reasons.

8. Always check shipping fees and where the item is coming from. Many bidders forget to do this and then they are surprised when the shipping fee is much more than what they expected, especially if the item is coming from another country.

9. Take advantage of eBay's wonderful "community" where you can ask questions and have other eBay members help you out with questions, concerns, or anything else, as well as eBay's easy-to-use Help information on their Web site. Always do your research before selling or bidding.

10. If you have a question about an item that wasn't answered in the description, ask the seller before bidding on it. Otherwise, it's buyer beware.

The Flip Side of Auctions: Scamming the Scammer

Jeff was selling an Apple Powerbook laptop computer on eBay for a friend. Bidding started at $1,700 with a Buy It Now[3] option of $2,100. He describes in detail what happened next on his Web site at http://p-p-p-powerbook.com/ (beware—there is foul language on the site). But I'll try to condense it.

The description of the auction listing read in part:

> You are bidding on my 19 day old G4 Powerbook. This was purchased for a project that fell through. When I tried to return it, I was informed of a 10-day limit for returns!
>
> Your new laptop comes with its original box, all of its documentation, all of its original accessories, and the blue tooth mouse.

Although no one bid on the Powerbook right away, Jeff received an e-mail from a person interested in purchasing it immediately. The person asked what the condition was and inquired about shipping it to London.

Jeff was perturbed. He had covered all of that information, except for shipping to London. And he clearly listed that the Buy It Now price was $2,100.

Jeff patiently replied to the potential buyer. A couple of days later he received a reply that the buyer was interested in making the purchase at the Buy It Now price and that it should be sent overnight. Money would be available at an escrow service located at www.set-ltd.net.

Jeff had never heard of this escrow service. Then the e-mail got stranger:

```
    I will pay the express shipping and also,
the escrow fee. The escrow service will
release you the money as soon as I will let
them know that the item passed the inspec-
tion and is 100% ok.
    The escrow fee is on my charge, don't
worry. Please let me know if my offer is good
enough for you. If it does, I will initiate
the transaction with the escrow service as
```

```
soon as I have your confirmation. If is ok
please register in order to make the deal
and start the payment procedures. Hope that
everything will be ok and close the deal in
the best conditions.

    Kind regards!
```

Jeff wasn't stupid. He smelled a scam and felt it was a fake escrow Web site. He came close to replying with a nasty message and then just dropping it. But instead he posted the story on an eBay forum. Almost immediately there was a reply warning that the site looked fraudulent and unprofessional. And it didn't have the proper security befitting an escrow Web site. Someone did a search on who owned the domain and found it was owned by an Indiana resident. From there, others discovered more information about the domain owner. More and more it smelled like huge scam.

Jeff decided to see how far he could go with this guy, who we'll call Mr. S. He sent this e-mail to Mr. S:

```
    Well, that sounds ok to me! I was able to
log onto your internet web site (Which I
must say looks very nice to me!)
    I just had a few questions…
    What should I use for a user name and
password? I like to use the same thing for
everything. Ebay, paypal, email…is that ok?
    In your FAQ, I noticed that you can use
the set-ltd.net services, and it does not
have to be an "online" purchase. But if
it's not online, how do they get to your
website?

    Thank you!
    Jeff
```

Sure enough, Mr. S replied. Jeff set up an account on the "escrow Web site" and soon the transaction for the Powerbook "went through." Mr. S supposedly put $2,100 plus shipping and the escrow charges into Jeff's account on the escrow Web site. Remember, the money has to sit in this account until Mr. S receives the Powerbook and approves of its condition. Only then does the money actually go into Jeff's bank account.

Or NOT. That's where the scam comes in. Jeff would be out not only a new Powerbook laptop but also the overnight shipping fees he paid for out of his own pocket.

Jeff had a plan. Now that he had the address of Mr. S in the United Kingdom, he conferred with his eBay allies and came up with the perfect solution: Mr. S would get his Powerbook all right. But it would be a three-ring binder decorated to resemble a Powerbook (see Figures 6.5 and 6.6).

Figure 6.5   P-P-P-Powerbook

Shipping was going to cost Jeff around $80 so he turned to his new online friends for donations—and they came flying in! Jeff packed the "Powerbook" up and took it to the post office. He wrote down $2,000 as its value, knowing full well that Mr. S would have to pay a 27 percent customs fee. It was now on its way to England.

Wait ... it gets better.

Some of Jeff's new eBay friends lived in London and decided to do some undercover work. They traced the mailing address to a barbershop.

Figure 6.6   Inside the P-P-P-Powerbook

Jeff had a tracking number so he was able to give them a pretty good idea of what day and time the package would arrive. They planned to be there.

They were. And a package was delivered. But it wasn't the right package. The "Powerbook" had been delayed.

Everyone went into a panic. The delivery service was contacted and it turned out that Mr. S hadn't paid the customs fee. Jeff e-mailed him, gently nudging him about it. Mr. S promised he would pay the fee. He did. More waiting. Jeff checked the tracking number often, holding his breath.

Finally, tracking showed the package had been cleared. The customs fee was paid and the package was being delivered. Jeff alerted his U.K. spies. One caught the delivery on video, which can be viewed at Jeff's Web site. It turns out the recipient was the owner of the barbershop.

Jeff sent a follow-up e-mail to Mr. S, but never got a response.

Anyone want a Powerbook cheap? Jeff has some more for sale.

Caveat: It is not recommended to do what Jeff did. He was lucky that his situation turned out well. This example shows how important it is to be wary when selling or bidding at online auction Web sites.

Sellers of fake or forged items really believe a sucker is born every minute. Don't prove them right. Remember what should become your mantra for everything you do online: If it looks too good to be true, it probably is.

Endnotes

1. Feedback: Found mostly in online auctions, the seller and winning bidder can leave feedback or comments for each other when an auction sale is completed. Feedback allows you to see if the seller or bidder has had positive, neutral, or negative feedback before you bid on an item.

2. Tradenable (formerly called iEscrow): Now out of business, an online escrow service that protected a buyer and seller from fraud.

3. Buy It Now: This option on eBay allows a bidder to purchase the item right away. Once a bid has been placed on the item, the Buy It Now option disappears. This gives bidders a chance to get the item they want immediately instead of waiting until the auction ends.

Gone Phishing: Nigerian Scams and More

Phishing

A play on the word "fishing," when scammers try to get you to reply or take them up on an offer to make money, or they claim your account needs to be verified by reconfirming everything from your user ID and password, to credit, banking, and other information.

Scammers

People who are out to illegally make a buck by running fraudulent schemes online.

Carders

People who get credit card numbers by phishing or scamming or even purchasing them from other scammers online. Carders then use the stolen credit cards to purchase items online or resell the numbers for a profit. Most of the time, Phishers, Scammers and Carders are all one and the same.

Nigerians Go Phishing

If you haven't yet received a so-called "Nigerian scam" message by e-mail, you're in a small minority. Such messages usually open like this (these are real examples):

My name is Raymond Eke. I am a friend to Mr. Roy J. Warner, a national of your country, who is a Contractor and have spent most of his life in my country.

On the 21st of April 2000, my friend, his wife and their only son were involved in a car accident along Benin/onitsha express way.

All occupants of the vehicle unfortunately lost there lives. Since then I have made several enquiries to your embassy to locate any of my friend extended relatives this has also proved unsuccessful.

After these several unsuccessful attempts, I decided to track his last name over the Internet, to locate any Member of his family hence I contacted you. I have contacted you to assist in repatriating the assets and Capital valued at US$5.5million left behind by my friend before they get confiscated or declared unserviceable by the Bank where these huge deposits were lodged. The Bank has issued me a notice to provide the next of Kin or have the account confiscated.

• • •

My name is Cristus Samuel, son of late Mr. Kenneth Samuel of Zimbabwe.

It might be a surprise to you where I got your contact address, I got it from Abidjan Information Bureau.

During the current crisis against the farmers of Zimbabwe by the supporters of our President Robert Mugabe to claim all the white owner farms in our country, he ordered all the white farmers to surrender their farms to his party members and their followers.

My father was one of the best farmers in the country and knowing that he did not support the president's political ideology, the president's supporters invaded our father's farm burnt down everything, shot him and as a result of the wounds sustained, he became sick and died after two days. And after his death, me and my sister Rita decided to move out of Zimbabwe for the safety of our lives to Abidjan-Cote D' Ivoire.

· · ·

Good day, with warm heart I offer my friendship and greetings. I hope this mail meets you in good time. However strange or surprising this contact might seem to you as we have not met personally or had any dealings in the past, I humbly ask that you take due consideration of its importance and immense benefits. I duly apologize for infringing on your privacy if this proposal is not acceptable to you. First and foremost, I wish to introduce myself properly to you. I am Mr. Michael Shaw, the son of the former Liberia finance minister (Mr. Emmanuel Shaw) under the past government of Charles Taylor. I presume you are aware of the political crisis in my country which affected my father's health.

At the end of Charles Taylor's regime, he was exiled to Nigeria where he currently resides. Majority of his officers including ministers like my father, are having their accounts frozen by the present government because they were uncomfortable with the past regime.

We then jointly decided within the family to relocate the family funds outside Liberia for investmest. I am contacting you because of a good friend of my father (Dr.

Thomas Clark) who visited your country sometime ago and told my family about your country.

. . .

Request for Urgent Busness Relationship.

May I through this medium seek for your cooperation and assistance in a business that requires high confidentiality.

I am a senior civil servant with the above named corporation and was opportuned to head a contract award committee of the corporation (NNPC) some time ago.

In the course of my assignment, I with the consent of my other colleagues on the board inflated a contract awarded to a foreign contractor, to the tune of US$48,500,000.00 (Fourty Eight Million, Five Hundred Thousand United States Dollars). The foreign contractor has long completed the contract and has since been paid his contract sum. Leaving the balance of thirty five million, five hundred thousand United States dollars floating in my corporation?s account with the government.

. . .

Let me start by introducing myself. I am Mr. Cheung Pui director of operations of the Hang Seng Bank Ltd. I have a obscured business suggestion for you.

I honestly apologize and hope I do not cause you much embarrassment by contacting you through this means for a transaction of this magnitude, but this is due to confidentiality and prompt access reposed on this medium, sorry my English is not very good.

Before the U.S and Iraqi war our client Major Fadi Bassem who was with the Iraqi forces and also business man made a numbered

```
fixed deposit for 18 calendar months, with
a value of Twenty Four millions Five Hundred
Thousand United State Dollars only in my
branch. Upon maturity several Notice was
sent to him, even during the war early this
year. Again after the war another notifica-
tion was sent and still no response came
from him. We later find out that the Major
and his family had been killed during the
war in bomb blast that hit their home.
```

Do you see the connecting thread? The e-mail is usually a sob story about an inheritance that has no takers. Often people were killed and there is either a huge life insurance policy waiting to be cashed in, a bank that has a huge amount of money in a defunct account, a hidden stash of money, or gold and certificates that have been found. The scam always involves a huge amount of money that no one else knows about now except you and them, and they want your help in setting up an account in your country so that the money can be deposited in it. You'll receive 20 percent or more once you send them the account details after you've set up a bank account with an initial deposit. Or you can send them your current banking information (even better!) and things can progress right away.

A Brief History

The Nigerian scam originated decades ago, originally via postal mail, then faxes, and now e-mail. It's been known as the "419 scam," "advance fee scam," and—way back when—as the "Spanish prisoner con." Although the majority of these scams do originate in Nigeria, they can come from any country. The story generally stays the same and the intent is to scam as much money from you as possible, if you fall for it. Believe me, plenty of people have. The following examples are just a recent handful of the many victims worldwide:

- A financial manager from Australia took $1 million from his clients because he really believed he was going to make more than 60 times that amount (you read that right) if he followed the instructions of Reverend Sam Kukah, the chairman of Nigeria's Presidential Payment Debt Reconciliation Committee, who needed to transfer a huge sum of money off-shore. This was an urgent transaction! And the financial manager believed him. He was arrested (not the Nigerian, who disappeared with the million bucks) and could spend up to 10 years in jail for deceiving his clients and stealing their money.

• Stan Stableski of Washington state learned the hard way that you don't send money to get money. He lost $45,000 two years after he responded to a Nigerian e-mail spam claiming he was entitled to an inheritance of over $40 million. The catch? He had to pay off the debts of the deceased before he could get his "inheritance." The fact that it took him two years to realize it was a scam is mind-blowing, but the con artists (there was more than one in this instance) had him totally convinced.

• A businessman in the United Kingdom lost $200,000 and his business. He received an e-mail from a man calling himself Vincent who claimed he had $12 million he wanted to move from South Africa to the U.K. and asked if the businessman would help. He said he would and when "problems" arose, he was asked to invest $7,000 in an offshore account to get the ball rolling. The ball didn't stop until he was out $200,000. His business failed as a result of the losses.

• An elderly man in Florida lost his entire life savings of over $300,000 to a Nigerian scam and he was still having a hard time believing they scammed him.

Sometimes victims are so distraught over losing their money they kill themselves, or worse. What could be worse? A 72-year-old man in the Czech Republic who lost his life savings to a Nigerian scammer went to the Nigerian Embassy in Prague where he shot and killed a Nigerian consul in late 2002.

Why do people fall for such an old scheme? Because they are inherently trusting and when they are online, for some reason, they are far more trusting than anyone should be. Even if there is a phone number in the Nigerian spam and they call it to reassure themselves, they should still be suspicious when they are asked to "front" some money or "invest" to get their percentage.

"They're mesmerized by the wealth that will soon be theirs," says Barbara Mikkelson of the Urban Legends Reference Pages. "They also fail to realize there's a hook hanging just out of sight. At first, all they see is that someone wants to give them something, thus they're ill-prepared to mentally shift gears when that person turns the tables. Because the premise of 'I'm going to get millions of dollars' is wholeheartedly swallowed early on, it's not questioned later when things begin to go wrong with the transaction."

There are some folks who have turned the tables on the Nigerian scammers, or tried to. You can read about their exploits at www.ebolamonkeyman.com (one of my personal favorites), www.419eater. com, and www.savannahsays.com/kizombe.htm.

Mike, aka "Nelson Druid," is one of those people and his hilarious exchange with "Henry Presley" follows. I've condensed these communications, but otherwise presented them in the words of the two parties.

After receiving the initial spam from "Henry Presley," Mike wrote:

My dearest Henry,

I have reviewed your offer and find it to be a worthwhile investment of my time and resources. I have read of the conditions in your country and a great feeling of sorry comes over me when I see the plight of your people. Please let me know what I can do to help you in your time of need. Surely, the Lord has sent you to me so that I might do His great work on this planet.

I am the owner of a small mid-western manufacturing company and have ample resources that I can bring to bear on this matter and help you out. Please write back and let me know what I can do to help you.

Regards,
Nelson Druid

Henry's reply:

Dear Mr. Druid,

I thank you very much for your prompt response to my proposal. I am particularly delighted that you are a high ranking official in your organization which shows that you are familiar with matters that require great responsibility and integrity. However it is also of great importance that should we commence full discussions and operations on this transaction you must endeavor at all times to handle the transaction personally and on a very confidential basis.

As stated in my letter to you all we require is a highly trustworthy and reliable foreign partner to assist us in the transfer and subsequent investment of the over-invoiced contract sum of USD30M which is available and awaiting claim. All modalities for transfer have been carefully put in place and you will be furnished with the complete details of the procedures. However the first step which is very imperative to indicate that you are indeed willing to assist us in this matter is for you to send immediately to me your complete particulars i.e. your full names, address, telephone and fax numbers and in due course your complete banking particulars of the account into which the funds will be transferred. Upon my receipt of your personal data and telephone/fax numbers I will immediately forward same to my senior colleagues and also furnish you with our private telephone for verbal discussion on details on how to commence fully.

It is very important that you reply my mails promptly always as time is of great essence. Lastly since I am presently in Zurich, Switzerland you will be discussing with my senior colleagues back in South Africa however you must unfailingly always intimate me with all proceedings and discussions with my colleagues so I can advice you adequately at all times in order not to jeopardize our transaction. I expect your prompt response and I sincerely pray that this will be the beginning of a long lasting friendship and business relationship.

Best Regards,
Henry Presley

Mike's reply:

My Dearest Henry,

Please forgive my tardiness in returning your second e-mail. The duties of my professional position leave little room for personal pleasures such as checking my e-mail. However, no #t^wl you h%v~ replied back, I will be sur% to check on a more+freque/@s basis.

For you records, my personal informatio 5? Fo-ÁwOf!

Nels*6 Mic`ael @ruid
193* Michig!n >ven#1u
S+it~ 490* Pe}-tho6se
Áhicago, /Ilinoi] 606/#
*5}., 3)2 6D6 3965
M10 Js2 - OV 82?"
V8ak4^
8H*O G^-F^L (34U23_7] @' M^>N(O^?;Y
M^04!R
4/`)?5Q:P+] K *NSL^,)
M[>=X(N+B XMOG X <&1 V9NP' 55934P+] N:V^MO
`&9%] K9
O@"WN #>W^T' V=SE
MW-T(HI.D Dn(1/T-)/?^U-/2T-4
3PL#.R@ZDHF8C^D)J[>R>`(,TO^ 1?X`
MCXN*B`!^;7+F8_#] L*Z!: +]=GAH 5%A:7?/V-
74T^,-L;#`

Henry's reply:

Dear Druid,

Thank you very much for your response though it came a little bit delayed. Please endeavour to be very prompt always as this is very important.

However as a matter of urgency please retype and resend your personal information to me as I am unable to read a sizable portion of your mail as most of it especially the part bearing your personal information came out in funny computer characters maybe due to computer error at your end. I am attempting to send you a copy of your mail which I received so maybe you will see what I mean. Meanwhile resend a clear and legible mail of your personal information immediately and to be double sure copy my alternative mail … hrypresley@yahoo.com, I expect your swift response.

Best regards,
Henry Presley

Mike's reply:

Henry,

I'm not sure what happened with the computer. These machines are so complicated and I have very little technical savvy. What I was trying to say is that my brother is a clerk with the Immigration and Naturalization Service and I'm sure that I could convince him to give you an expedited entry visa into the United States. Once here, you could then apply for the money yourself. Would this work better for you? After re-reading your previous message, I was struck by the statement that I would have to travel to South Africa for a few days.

Henry, I should probably warn you that I an a disabled veteran without the use of my legs. I was injured by a mine in Vietnam and am confined to a wheelchair. It would be most impossible for me to make a trek of such a distance. If only there were a way for me to help you from here without leaving, then I would most certainly help you.

With that being said, I would be glad to speak to my brother on your behalf and arrange for you to get an entry visa. All I would ask is that your make a sizable donation to one of the charities that I support here in Chicago.

I remain, as always, at your service,
Nelson

After a number of exchanges with "Henry," Mike decided to come clean:

Dear Henry, or whatever your name is,

(You're going to want to read this all the way through because I'm going to tell you exactly what you did wrong.)

Well, it's been fun. I guess by now that you realize that this little 419 scam of yours is not going to work. But before you go, I think there are some things that you need to know. First off, I'm not really Nelson Druid. Ndruid@yahoo is my spam e-mail account that I give out to websites when they ask for a valid email account to get something.

There are so many things that I would like to tell you, but you should have guessed them by now. You should have guessed by now that I'm not a business entrepreneur, actually, I teach Philosophy at a college. You should have also guessed that I did not lose my legs in VietNam. You should have guessed that I'm actually fairly computer literate and that the garbled e-mail was garbled on purpose. You should have guessed that I don't have hundreds of thousands of dollars in an account for you to bleed off. You should have guessed that my brother doesn't work for

INS. You should have guessed by now that I'm simply playing you for a fool and you're not going to get any money.

I say should have to all of these things because you certainly don't seem to realize them. Your replies back to me are a pathetic attempt to evoke pity and get your whale (The terms for those being scammed) to break down and give you what you want. Really, did you think you still had a chance at Nelson's money? Obviously you did. You took the bait and went for deep water.

Oh, by the way ... That fishing analogy worked well on the on-line bulletin board that I posted all of these e-mails to. I waited until I had you really into it and then I posted all of the e-mails and followed with the rest of them. It was quite a hit. The best part is that all of people who watched along all see how easy it is to sucker one of you scam artists and I would bet that several of them are just itching to do it themselves.

That brings me to the heart of this message. Think about it Henry ... All those people out there now see how much fun it is to screw around with scam artists. I'm sure that they go to other boards as well and when they get a live scammer on the line, hopefully they'll post their e-mails on other boards and more people will see how much fun it is to play along. Of course, that just makes your task that much harder and a lot less fun. Now, you have to stop and look really closely at every whale YOU get on the line and you'll have to think "Is it really someone I can scam or is it someone playing with me?". All that time wasted, Henry. All that time soon to be wasted. Think about it. Disturbing, isn't it? The best part is that you'll probably start making quick decisions about who to continue on with and you'll probably drop potentially lucrative "Real" contacts in favor of people like me. Won't that just be a waste of time? By the way, how much of your time did I waste? How many other whales got away while you were answering my e-mails?

Here's the tragedy … You can't even put my e-mail on a spammer's sheet as revenge. The account is already spammed from another NUT website that I pissed off. (My buddies on the board know where I'm talking about.) Also, you can't even report me for e-mail abuse because you're the scam artist and it would expose you. But, rest assured, I'm certainly going to send a copy of your e-mails to Yahoo and get your account shut off. I just might send a copy of all of them to the FBI. I bet they can even find some sort of pattern in all of them. Thanks for the plethora of e-mails to use.

Oh, I also was interested … What the hell is a "Modality"? That one appears in several different e-mails that I get from other scam artists.

Well, Henry I guess it's time to put an end to our little game. I don't expect to hear from you anymore, so I'll just say good bye and wish you the best of luck with trying to weed out the whales from the sharks.

I'll leave you with something from the Oracle at Delphi, Gnothi Sauton (Know Thyself)

Ciao
Obie Arete

Henry's reply:

I am sure you really feel like a smart alec, for your information at this very moment another whale has been turned belly up, for every self acclaimed smart ass like you there are a thousand suckers out there waiting patiently and for ever willing to expose their yellow bellies. There are too many suckers out there to harvest and your oneman smart ass crusade cannot make any significant impact, you can keep trying, maybe when your fingerprints fade out and your fingers fall off from typing, you may have scratched off a chip of the collosal iceberg better known as 419

A Simple Scam

Just when you thought you were safe from the sob story e-mails, scammers found another way to get you and your money.

Greg Brooks works for New Hampshire Public Television. He decided to put his classic 1974 VW Super Beetle up for sale on an online auction site. He received a lot of interest in it. One prospective customer was located in the United Arab Emirates.

"We went back and forth via e-mail," Brooks says. "He asked some questions about the condition of the car, asked to see more photos, that kind of thing. So I took more photos and e-mailed them to him."

Then he received an e-mail offering $1,500 for the car. Brooks accepted and soon found a cashier's check in his mailbox. The only problem was that the check was made out for $10,500, not the $1,500 he was expecting.

Brooks contacted the buyer and was told there had been a mistake by his secretary and that Brooks should go ahead and cash the check, keep his $1,500 and send the remainder to him.

Brooks thought something was wrong with this (he was right) and went to his bank to see if it could help.

"So, the way the scam works," he says, "is the guy writes a fraudulent cashier's check. I go to my bank and they cash it in 24 hours. Now I have the $10,500 in my pocket. At that point, I have my $1,500, send back his $9,000, and two weeks later when my bank tries to clear the check through the originating bank the check was written on, they will be told it's fraudulent. My bank would require me to pay back the $10,500."

"It's an old scam and doesn't take a lot of cunning," says Jonathan Gallo, New Hampshire Assistant Attorney General. "The Internet allows it to be done quicker and with anonymity."

Gallo prosecutes computer fraud cases. He thinks the FBI estimate of $54 million lost by Americans yearly doesn't represent the actual damage.

"That's because only one in four of these types of cases are actually reported," he notes. "So it's hard to get a handle on the actual number of people being defrauded."

Sue Shanoff, the security officer at Granite State Bank, got a look at the check Brooks received. "This looks pretty good, so there's no way the customer is going to know this isn't the real thing."

The responsibility is on the customer's shoulders, though, she warns. "Sometimes we know a bank's routing number, which would match the one on the check, so it wouldn't be caught right away. We wouldn't know until it goes through, which takes about five days. Meanwhile, we've given the customer next day availability because it's a cashier's check and we assume it's good."

Brooks was lucky. He listened to that little voice in his head telling him something was wrong. What happened to his classic VW?

"I traded the car in and got more than I was asking," he says. "I would suggest that anything can and will happen on the Web, so be skeptical and make sure all funds clear permanently before believing in them."

It not only happens with cars, but with just about any high-ticket item you put up for sale online, whether you list it at an auction site like eBay, a local auction site, your personal Web site, or another listing service.

Some tips before listing a high-ticket item:

- Don't list your item on a free Web site; these seem to attract the most scammers.

- Sell only to someone in your city, state, or country and put that proviso in the item description.

- Accept payment only via PayPal or an online escrow service; again, note in your item description that you do not accept bank or cashier's checks.

- Do not give in, no matter how desperate you are to sell or auction off that item, especially if the potential bidder/buyer offers you more than what you were asking for.

- Visit www.antiphishing.org for the latest information, resources, and tips.

What to Do ...

... if you took the bait and gave away your financial information:*

- Report it to the card issuer as quickly as possible: Many companies have toll-free numbers and 24-hour service to deal with such emergencies.

- Cancel your account and open a new one.

- Review your billing statements carefully after the loss: If they show any unauthorized charges, send a letter to the card issuer describing each questionable charge.

- Credit Card Loss or Fraudulent Charges (FCBA): Your maximum liability under federal law for unauthorized use of your credit card is $50. If the loss involves your credit card number, but not the card itself, you have no liability for unauthorized use.

- ATM or Debit Card Loss or Fraudulent Transfers (EFTA): Your liability under federal law for unauthorized use of your ATM or debit card depends on how quickly you report the loss. You risk unlimited loss if you fail to report an unauthorized transfer within 60 days after your bank statement containing unauthorized use is mailed to you.

(*Some tips from www.antiphishing.org)

... if someone is using your eBay account to bid, leave feedback, or list auctions without your permission:

- Contact eBay: Go to http://pages.ebay.com/help/tp/ isgw-account-theft-reporting.html and follow the instructions there (or do a search under "Help" for account theft).

- Attempt to sign in and change your password: If you are able to sign in, change your password and hint immediately, and begin to undo any damage done by the phishers; remove any bogus auctions, contact bidders and sellers, and so forth.

- If you were unable to regain control of your own account, go to http://pages.ebay.com/help/tp/isgw-account-theft-reporting.html (eBay will likely put your account on hold until it completes an investigation).

... if you gave out personal identifying information:

- Report the theft to the three major credit reporting agencies: Experian, Equifax, and TransUnion Corporation (contact information appears in Appendix B, as well as online at the book's supporting Web page) and do the following: Request that they place a fraud alert and victim's statement in your file. Request a free copy of your credit report to check whether any accounts were opened without your consent. Request that the agencies remove inquiries and/or fraudulent accounts stemming from the theft.

- Notify your bank(s) and ask them to flag your account and contact you regarding any unusual activity: If bank accounts were set up without your consent, close them. If your ATM card was stolen, get a new card, account number, and PIN.

- Contact your local police department to file a criminal report.

- Contact the Social Security Administration's Fraud Hotline to report the unauthorized use of your personal identification information.

- Notify the Department of Motor Vehicles of your identity theft. Check to see whether an unauthorized license number has been issued in your name.

- Notify the passport office to watch out for anyone ordering a passport in your name.

- File a complaint with the Federal Trade Commission at www.ftc.gov/ftc/consumer.htm

- File a complaint with the Internet Fraud Complaint Center (IFCC) at www.ifccfbi.gov/index.asp

- Document the names and phone numbers of everyone you speak to or contact regarding the incident. Follow up your phone calls with letters. Keep copies of all correspondence.

Another Phishing Trip

You receive an e-mail message from an institution that purports to be your bank or credit card company (the most popular institutions used for this scam appear to be CitiCard, SunTrust, and Wells Fargo), eBay, PayPal, or another online service you may have an account with. The message claims that your account has been suspended, compromised, or hacked into and that you need to reconfirm your personal information before you can use the service again.

Here's a sample e-mail message of this type:

```
Date: Wed, 17 Sep 2005 19:53:09 +0000
From: eBay <us-support@eBay.com>
Subject: Official Notice for all E-Bay
        users
To: Awriter <awriter@jahitchcock.com>

Dear eBay User,

During our regular udpate and verification
of the accounts, we couldn't verify your
current information. Either your information
has changed or it is incomplete.
As a result, your access to bid or buy on
Ebay has been restricted. To start using
your eBay account fully, please update and
verify your information by clicking below:
https://scgi.ebay.com/saw-cgi/eBayISAPI.
dlll?VerifyInformation

Regards,
eBay
**Please Do Not Reply To This E-Mail As You
Will Not Receive A Responce**
```

Looks official, doesn't it? But there are some pretty glaring errors. Did you catch them?

1. There are significant spelling and grammar problems (including eBay spelled as "Ebay").

2. The return address is us-support@eBay.com. Why "us" and not just "support"?

3. You've been instructed not to reply to the e-mail because the address will bounce back if you do.

These problems should have tipped you off, but if you had reason for concern that your account was in jeopardy, you may have clicked on the link. You would see that the Web site looks official. It asks you to sign into your eBay account with your username and password, then brings you to a page asking you to update your credit card/debit card information (see Figures 7.1 and 7.2).

Because the page appears to include eBay's official logo and mirrors the look of eBay's Web site, it's easy to overlook one important thing: the URL in the address box at the top of the browser. It doesn't say http://www.ebay.com. It begins with http://d153419.u36.fasthost.com. This is how carders can steal your credit card information.

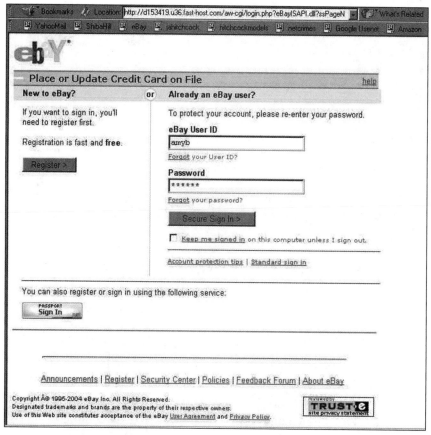

Figure 7.1   Fake eBay sign-in page

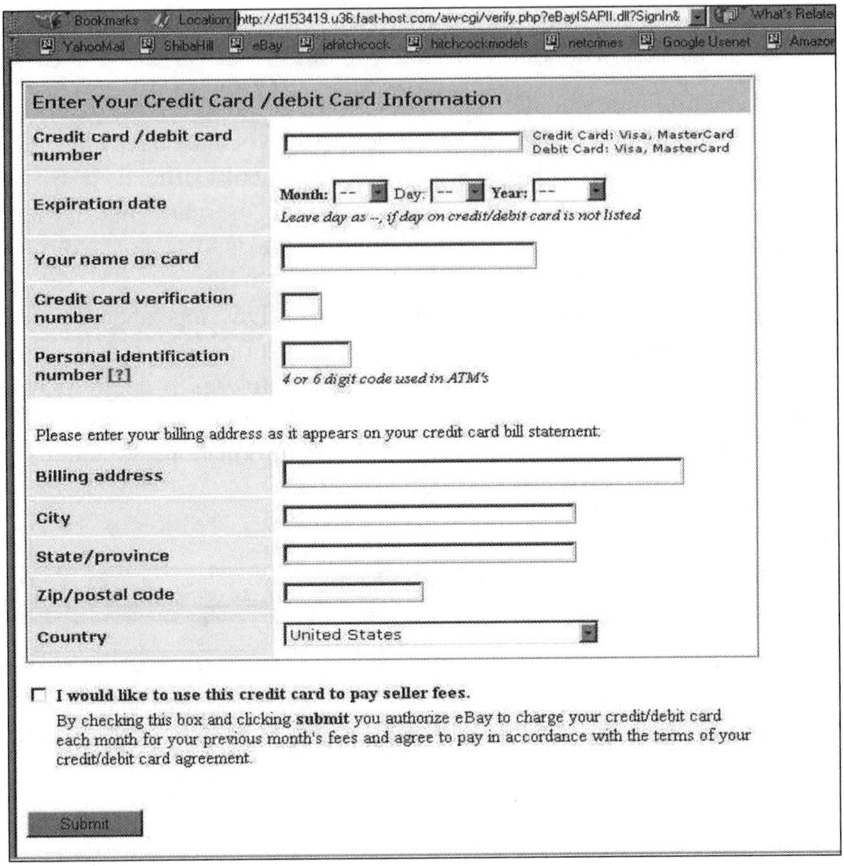

Figure 7.2   Fake eBay credit card request

Denise in Maryland recounts how her husband fell for one of these phishing scams—hook, line, and sinker:

> Bill responded to a query from PayPal. They said they were updating their files and needed our banking info. It had the PayPal logo and a link to their customer info, so he sent the requested information. Something sniggled at the back of his brain, so he called them. Nope, they didn't e-mail us. We had to open a new bank account because of this. You would not believe the problems this has caused. Since we couldn't completely close the old account because of pending transactions, we needed to leave it open until everything cleared.

Denise is grateful Bill didn't put in any credit card information or they would have had to cancel the card too. As it was, they had to contact the three credit reporting bureaus to flag their names so that if anyone tried to open up new accounts in their names, they would be contacted immediately. Also, they filed a police report. Bill still can't believe he fell for it.

He's not the only one. In September 2003, the U.S. Federal Trade Commission reported that "9.9 million U.S. residents were victims of identity theft during the previous year, costing businesses and financial institutions $48 billion and consumers $5 billion in out-of-pocket expenses."

The FTC advises:

- If you get an e-mail or pop-up message that asks for personal or financial information, do not reply or click on the link in the message. Legitimate companies don't ask for this information via e-mail. If you are concerned about your account, contact the organization in the e-mail using a telephone number you know to be genuine, or open a new Internet browser session and type in the company's correct Web address. In any case, don't cut and paste the link in the message.

- Don't e-mail personal or financial information. E-mail is not a secure method of transmitting personal information. If you initiate a transaction and want to provide your personal or financial information through an organization's Web site, look for indicators that the site is secure, like a lock icon on the browser's status bar or a URL for a Web site that begins "https:" (the "s" stands for "secure"). Unfortunately, no indicator is foolproof; some phishers have forged security icons.

- Review credit card and bank account statements as soon as you receive them to determine whether there are any unauthorized charges. If your statement is late by more than a couple of days, call your credit card company or bank to confirm your billing address and account balances.

- Use anti-virus software and keep it up-to-date. Some phishing e-mails contain software that can harm your computer or track your activities on the Internet without your knowledge. Anti-virus software and a firewall can protect you from inadvertently accepting such unwanted files. Anti-virus software scans incoming communications for troublesome files. Look for anti-virus software that recognizes current viruses as well as older ones, can effectively reverse the damage, and updates automatically. A firewall helps make you invisible on the Internet and blocks all communications from unauthorized sources. It's especially important to run a firewall if you have a broadband connection. Finally, your operating system (like Windows or Linux) may offer free software "patches" to close holes in the system that hackers or phishers could exploit.

- Be cautious about opening any attachment or downloading any files from e-mails you receive, regardless of who sent them.

- Report suspicious activity to the FTC. If you get spam that is phishing for information, forward it to spam@uce.gov. If you believe you've been scammed, file your complaint at www.ftc.gov and then visit the FTC's Identity Theft Web site at www.consumer.gov/idtheft to learn how to minimize your risk of damage from ID theft. Visit www.ftc.gov/spam to learn other ways to avoid e-mail scams and deal with deceptive spam.

How prevalent are the phishing scams that were just described? A survey conducted by Ponemon Institute in September of 2004[1] estimated that 35 percent of consumers received fake e-mails like these at least once a week.

Some other highlights of the survey:

- Seven out of 10 respondents revealed they unintentionally visited a spoofed Web site.

- More than 15 percent admitted to being phished.

- A little more than 2 percent believed they experienced a direct monetary loss as a result.

A great Web site that offers the latest news about the Nigerian scammers, their scams, and those who have been caught is located at www.nigeriamasterweb.com/419NewsFrmes.html. Interesting reading guaranteed!

A final important piece of advice: It's not a scam unless you fall for it. Until then, it's spam. Report spam to www.spamcop.net.

Endnote

1. National study conducted by Ponemon Institute, sponsored by TRUSTe, an online privacy nonprofit organization and NACHA, an electronic payments association, September 2004, www.ponemon.org

8

Where the Heartache Is: Adoption Fraud

Susan was single, in her forties, and wanted a baby. After much thought, she decided to adopt, but that was easier said than done.

"In late fall of 1998, I was frustrated with my hopes of adopting a child," Susan recalls. "Typical adoption agencies wanted children to go to two parents, not one, and wanted them younger, not middle-aged. I did find a couple of possibilities, but then the birthmom decided to keep the baby. Not her fault, just my luck."

Susan, who lives in southern Maine, occasionally visited an online adoption chat room to find some comfort with other frustrated prospective adoptive parents. They'd discuss the trials and tribulations of domestic and international adoption, mention where they were in the scheme of things, commiserate about failed adoptions, and give each other pats on the shoulder.

"That's where I met Sonya [Furlow]," Susan says. "She seemed to be on just about every adoption-related mailing list I joined, offering her comments about adoption as a facilitator—a person licensed to arrange adoptions—in Philadelphia, Pennsylvania."

Since these mailing lists seemed to have helped other adoptive parents, Susan read Sonya's messages with interest. She was well aware of adoption scams and grilled Sonya with questions and comments.

"Sonya told me she had a Web site, Tender Hearts Family Services Adoption Counseling, so I looked it up, felt it was professional looking, then called and asked her to send me a packet of information about her services," Susan recounts. "I asked her over the phone if she would work with singles and she told me she would, although I'd be her first."

Even though Sonya's agency was located quite a distance from her, Susan was hopeful.

Adoption Resources

National Council for Adoption (NCFA)
www.ncfa-usa.org

Adopting.com Internet Adoption Resources
www.adopting.com

Adoptive Families
www.adoptivefamilies.com

Adoption.about
http://adoption.about.com

Waiting Families: Family/Child Matching
www.waitingfamilies.com

Adoption Resource Directory
www.adopt-usa.org

Adoption Assistance
www.adoption-assist.com

Adoption Shop
www.adoptionshop.com

Internet Adoption: How Much Is That Baby in the Window?
http://gsulaw.gsu.edu/lawand/papers/su01/dutrow_wade/

Trusting Sonya

Sonya asked Susan questions about her family, what Susan was looking for in a child, essentially interviewing Susan. Susan confessed that all she wanted was a healthy baby—race and sex weren't issues. This conversation took place at the end of 1998.

The New Year rang in and Susan was worried she'd never adopt. Then one night, the phone rang. It was Sonya.

"Susan, I just may have a situation for you that came up a couple of days ago," said Sonya enthusiastically. "I have a birthmom who would be willing to have a single woman adopt her baby."

Susan couldn't believe her luck—maybe she'd finally get her baby! Sonya told her all about the birth mother, Gabrielle, weaving a sad, but believable tale: Gabrielle was a single mother, 27, with an associate's degree and working on her bachelor's. She was of Italian descent with one daughter who was five years old; Gabrielle worked part-time in daycare, and wanted to become a teacher. Gabrielle's boyfriend, Carlos, was a secret affair—he was married with four boys. Gabrielle and Carlos didn't believe in abortion and felt adoption was their only option. The baby was due May 12, 1999.

"I told her it sounded like a good situation," recalls Susan. "Sonya asked me to fill out the paperwork and sign the contract."

Before she did that, Susan checked around and talked to a lawyer in Philadelphia who had completed an adoption with Sonya with no problems. And when she checked with the Better Business Bureau, she got a thumbs-up. Satisfied that Sonya Furlow was for real, Susan sent her a check for $3,500 on February 18, 1999.

"I did not think that everything about Sonya checked out," says Judith M. Berry, Esq., Susan's lawyer and member of the American Academy of Adoption Attorneys. "In fact, I was extremely concerned as soon as I heard about her practices, such as asking for money to be wired to her immediately without receipt of medical records or background information and medical confirmation of pregnancy. Her practices were well outside the scope of traditional and reasonable adoption practice."

The next few months were like a roller coaster for Susan. Sonya started off with frequent reports about Gabrielle's pregnancy and the baby growing inside of her. After that, e-mail messages and phone calls became sporadic. There would be days when Susan wouldn't hear back from Sonya, who claimed she was an extremely busy woman. One time she said she'd been at the hospital with one of the other birth mothers she was working with. Susan believed her.

"Sonya told me she'd send a sonogram to me by Easter, then she changed her mind and called me back saying it was going to be Good Friday instead," Susan says. "That was when I began to feel uncomfortable about the situation."

It turned out Susan wasn't the only adoptive parent waiting for a baby from Sonya Furlow. Forty-three other families had put down deposits ranging from $1,000 to $15,000. And every one of them had found Sonya on the Internet at her Web site.

In early May, Susan heard from a couple who said they had flown to Philadelphia from Missouri to pick up the baby girl Sonya had promised them. They stayed for two weeks, waiting, and finally returned home empty-handed.

"I told them in the adoption chat room that it better not happen to me!" Susan recalls.

The roller-coaster ride continued. Gabrielle had false labor a couple of times. Susan never received the sonogram. With a heavy heart, but still hopeful, Susan flew to Philadelphia on May 20. She carried a baby car seat and bag filled with baby clothes, toys, and other child-care items. Somehow, she felt that if she were there when the birth mother was scheduled to deliver the baby, things would work out.

Sonya was more than surprised when Susan called her from the airport. But she reassured Susan that everything was fine. Susan sat in her hotel room, waiting.

"What went on for the next week was something I never believed would have been in the cards," Susan says. "After many frustrating phone calls never returned, faxes not answered until days later, I got a call from Judith Berry [Susan's attorney]. She asked if I was sitting down. I was. Then she told me the FBI was investigating Sonya."

"I was not surprised when the FBI called me," Berry says. "They wanted to interview clients who had contact with Sonya and found that I represented some of them. What started it all was another couple who reported Sonya to the FBI."

"I was stunned, I was in shock," Susan says, sighing at the memory. "I didn't want it to be true."

Susan flew home the Tuesday after Memorial Day weekend in 1999. She talked with the FBI on June 24, 1999. There was no Gabrielle. There was no Carlos. There was no baby.

"I found the FBI to be very compassionate, professional, and thorough," Berry says. "Sue helped tremendously to make their case."

"In my mind, that baby was real," Susan says. "It was the death of a child who never existed."

Around the country, from Maine to California, 44 families sat down with FBI agents and recounted their stories of trying to adopt through Sonya Furlow. The stories were similar: The birth mothers almost always seemed to be single and young, and the baby the result of a forbidden affair. Some families said Sonya told them the birth mothers had changed their minds. Some couples said they were told the baby was lost due to miscarriage or some other malady. And they all believed Sonya when she told them she'd find them another baby and to send more money. Sonya scammed the 44 families out of more than $200,000.

"Adoption scams have been happening for as long as there have been people seeking to adopt," says Julie Valentine of Adopting.com. "The Internet is simply a new way for people to connect. I don't think it's increased the number of adoption scams. It's simply widened the geographical possibilities for these scams."

Mary Mooney of Adopting Families agrees and adds, "There are also what I would call the 'low dollar crimes,' where birth mothers promise their babies to several couples, taking some money from each. It's usually $1,000 or less, but the victim still feels betrayed."

Daughter for Sale

Stephanie Arnold of Milwaukee was pregnant in 2002 and posted a message on Adoptster.com:

> I am due with a black/white baby on about Aug. 1, 2002. I need to find a good family for the baby. I have all the med. records and will sign a release. You can speak with my doc if needed.

She added that she needed money for maternity expenses, then listed her e-mail address. Several people fell for the ploy. One woman sent Arnold $1,200 and airline tickets worth $500. Another sent $950 before realizing something was terribly wrong. Arnold extorted over $5,000 in cash and gifts but that wasn't the worst of it.

One of the couples bilked of their money situated themselves in the delivery room when Arnold gave birth. Three days later she told them she had changed her mind about giving them the baby. The couple was devastated. Then Arnold called every month or so claiming she couldn't care for the baby—and then would change her mind. Up and down—it was a roller-coaster ride for the couple. Arnold at one point let the couple keep the baby girl with them in a hotel room overnight. Finally, they tired of the drama and tried to put it behind them. But they couldn't forget. They went to the police who then tracked down the other victims of this scam.

Arnold was arrested and pleaded guilty to theft and false representation. She received two years probation plus $3,500 in fines. Her punishment seems like a slap on the wrist considering the anguish she caused.

Other scams zoom in on larger sums of money.

"The big bucks are in the false ads that some adoption agencies put on their Web sites," Mary Mooney declares. "They make it look like it's easy and quick to adopt a baby. They often post photos of children from Romania or a country that is closed to adoption."

To avoid falling for this type of scam, Mooney advises a visit to a federal Web site (travel.state.gov/family/adoption.html) that lists most countries and their adoption rules.

Top 10 Online Adoption Tips

1. Go through an official agency or attorney. According to Adopting.org, "Do your homework. Don't rely on your gut instinct—make sure."

2. Don't give in to requests for immediate money. "A birth mother crisis is the common excuse," attorney Judith Berry warns. "Being homeless, out of food, etc. The bottom line is this: Don't send money until you have more information, and consult an attorney. Several states prohibit any funds being given to a birth mother—payments can void an adoption and be considered a criminal act."

3. Be leery of e-mail messages or chat rooms. "Don't go into a chat room and write, 'I'm looking for a birth mother,'" says Courtney Frey of Adopting.org. "This is like standing on the street corner with a wad of cash in your hand, waiting for scam artists to approach you. If you get an e-mail with photos of a pregnant birth mother, along with a request for your phone number or for money to 'help out until the baby is born,' don't fall for it. Most birth mothers use agencies. Very few have the emotional capacity to go online and look for potential parents themselves."

4. Remove any time limits you set. "Allow a minimum of one year to complete an adoption once you have started the paperwork," says Julie Valentine of Adopting.com. "If you're promised a baby faster than that, run the other way!"

5. Ask for information. "You have a legal right to confirmation of the pregnancy, medical records, social,

psychological, psychiatric, and genetic information regarding the biological parents," says attorney Judith Berry.

6. Contact others online. "Network with others in the online adoption community," says Courtney Frey of Adopting.org. "Tell them about the person who contacted you about adoption. Share your stories. The online community is quite close and if you use each other to keep an eye out, the more likely you'll be safe."

7. Educate yourself before you adopt and while you're waiting. "There are many books and Web sites on adoption that every adoptive parent should read," says Julie Valentine of Adopting.com. "An adopted child is not the same as a biological child. They have issues and needs that are unique, and adoptive parents should be well-educated and prepared to help meet those needs."

8. Don't be rushed into a decision. "People who say, 'I have a baby now and if you don't send money today, she may not be here tomorrow' are a big red flag," Valentine says.

9. Keep your Web site/messages private. "Use toll-free numbers on your Web sites and in your e-mail messages or in chat rooms," says Courtney Frey of Adopting.org. "Or use your attorney or agency's telephone number as a contact. This protects you from scam artists finding out where you live and from contacting you."

10. It's an old adage, but it's true: If it sounds too good to be true, it probably is.

The Internet Twins

In January 2001, two adoptive families fought over twins they both claimed as their own. One family in California had paid an online adoption agency $6,000 for the twins. When the babies were born in Missouri, the birth mother took them back, then resold the twins to a couple from England for $14,000. The couple flew back to England with the babies in tow. The "Internet twins" were taken by British social services at a north Wales hotel where the British couple had taken refuge. A court fight ensued among the couple in England, the couple in California, and the birth mother.

On April 9, 2001, a judge ruled that the now nine-month-old twin girls would be sent back to Missouri and placed in foster care pending future rulings. Their birth mother claimed she wanted to share custody with her estranged husband and regretted giving them up for adoption.

"Selling babies like that is not as uncommon as you'd think," says Sandra Lennington of Adopting.org. "We had a woman get in touch with us who was pregnant. She and her husband already had a teenager and she wanted to sell the baby for $50,000. We informed her it was illegal to sell a baby and we would prosecute. We never heard from her again."

"Adoptive parents are emotionally and financially at risk," Judith Berry says. "They are vulnerable and want to believe the situation is a dream come true, even when demands are placed on them regarding money. When I questioned Sonya, she stated that maybe she did not want to work with someone who was questioning her practices. Red flags were waving. I warned my clients, but they wanted to believe she was going to give them the baby they so badly wanted."

Sonya Furlow was indicted in April 2000 on charges of 20 counts of mail fraud—for receiving payments through the U.S. Postal Service and private courier services. In June 2000, she pleaded guilty to three of the counts and publicly accepted responsibility for what she did. When the judge sentenced her to nearly four years in prison, he called her conduct "particularly and unusually cruel." He ordered her to repay the $215,000 she scammed from the 44 families, but since she's broke, it's doubtful any of them will see restitution.

"I mourn the loss of a child that never was," Susan says. She still hopes to adopt, but will rely on the expertise of her attorney from now on. She hopes to see new laws enacted that specifically target Internet adoption fraud.

"You need to realize that the Internet is a tool for people to connect," says Julie Valentine of Adopting.com. "It's a wonderfully useful tool that has greatly increased the span and scope of information about adopting. It has also dramatically increased the number of children who have been matched with families, especially older and special needs children. But the anonymity afforded by the Internet is a potential veil for scam artists, so make sure you thoroughly check out anyone and everyone."

Cases of Stolen Identity

Identity Theft

When someone steals your identity online, impersonates you, and wreaks havoc in your name; many times the thief charges money to credit cards you never received, takes out loans, orders items, etc.

The term "identity theft" conjures up an image of someone who has had his name and reputation hijacked by an imposter—a thief who has used the victim's social security number, personal data, and credit records for personal gain, and perhaps even committed crimes while impersonating the victim. This is an accurate representation of the problem. It can be devastating, and it takes years for most victims to recover from the experience.

But how does it happen *online*? Much in the same way it does offline, except that it's easier to steal a person's identity online if the thief is Web-savvy and doesn't mind spending a few bucks. Sometimes it happens with a bit of a twist.

Natalie knows. Her identity was stolen online. She found out when she began receiving postal mail—three letters from different banks that thanked her for her business and enclosed her new credit card. Magazines she'd never ordered began to arrive—with bills asking for payment.

Then she discovered that someone applied for an online loan (it was denied), opened two online accounts with different ISPs, and applied for two more credit cards all in her name. This person joined online clubs based on her interests and waited for her to post to those clubs. Then the person made public, slanderous posts to the whole list in response—pretending to be her.

Who was this person?

Her ex-husband, bent on revenge.

"He broke into two of my e-mail accounts and sent himself harassing e-mails so that they looked like they came from me," Natalie says. "He then had Yahoo! close my accounts based on the fact that 'I' had harassed him."

But he wasn't done yet. He used her e-mail addresses to send messages to her friends, impersonating her, in order to get them to reveal information about her new life. He then sent himself e-mails from her address, this time trying to make it look like she was still crazy about him and wanted to get back together with him. One day, when he broke into one of her e-mail accounts, he found a copy of an e-mail in her Outbox in which she complained briefly about work, edited it to make it seem even worse, then printed it out, and overnighted it to one of her co-workers.

Natalie found herself on damage control alert in every aspect of her life—online and offline. She filed a complaint with the Arizona State Attorneys Office, her state of residence.

"After I turned over all of my evidence, the office was one step away from a Grand Jury warrant. Unfortunately, they needed something from the ISP proving that my ex-husband was in fact logged in under his account with them during the specified times at which the fraudulent applications were placed," Natalie says. "In other words, they needed the login records from the ISP, which are stored for just such reasons. The ISP had several computers devoted to batches of customer accounts for record-keeping purposes."

But the particular computer that held the batch containing her ex-husband's login records had crashed. All the information was lost. Therefore, it could not be absolutely proven and the grand jury would not issue a warrant. Undeterred, Natalie pressed on and got seven e-mail accounts of her ex-husband's shut down based on the ISPs' terms of service and her ability to prove inappropriate use.

When her ex-husband discovered that he was being investigated, he stopped impersonating and harassing her online.

"The most obnoxious thing about this is that although the credit bureaus recognized that the applications were fraudulent and not initiated by me, the inquiries will still stay on my credit report for seven years, making it very hard for me to actually get credit, or get a mortgage," Natalie says. "They say that I am welcome to add a 100-word statement to my credit report that explains the situation but I don't think I should have to."

But she did anyway, knowing it was the only way to keep her good credit rating. I wish I could tell you Natalie's story has a happy ending, but it doesn't. Her ex-husband began stalking and harassing her offline, even moving less than 90 minutes away from her. Although she has a protective order against him, she fears for her life.

10 Tips for Avoiding Identity Theft

1. Never give out information about your checking or savings accounts in response to an e-mail you've received unless you were expecting this e-mail. These are usually "phishers" trying to steal your identity ... and your money.

2. Be wary of giving information to a stranger who claims to be with your bank, credit bureau, or other legitimate-sounding agency. Call (you'll get a better response with the phone rather than e-mail) the institution this person claims to represent to confirm. Chances are the institution knows nothing about the person and will tell you to either ignore the e-mail or report it at www.ftc.gov/ftc/consumer.htm (click on File a Complaint).

3. Ignore any e-mails that claim to be from a company you do business with and want you to verify your account information. Also ignore any e-mails that claim to have suspended your account until you supply them with your information.

4. Make sure your passwords and PIN numbers are unique and hard for a potential hacker or criminal to figure out. For passwords, use at least eight characters (unless otherwise instructed) that are a combination of letters, numerals, and/or characters, such as: 1%jet49&. Many people use their social security number, date of an anniversary or birthday, pet's name, or something easy for them to remember. This makes it easy for a criminal to figure out. So pick something that might be more difficult to

remember because you and your personal information will be safer.

5. Make sure a Web site is secure: A site that does
    ask for personal or financial information while you
    are attempting to purchase something online
    should demonstrate that it has proper security.

6. Use common sense. You wouldn't give a stranger
    on the street your checkbook or ATM card and tell
    him the PIN, would you? So don't do it online. Make
    sure you know who you are dealing with before
    divulging personal or financial information.

7. Make sure your anti-virus program is updated
    frequently.

8. Make sure your firewall is updated frequently. If you
    don't have one, get one.

9. If you receive a suspicious-looking e-mail, go to
    www.ifccfbi.gov and fill out the online complaint
    form.

10. This can't be repeated enough: If it sounds too
    good to be true, it probably is.

Another Kind of Identity Theft: No Parking

Robert Wessel is a successful businessman in La Grange, Illinois.
When the city planned to build a multilevel parking garage, Wessel
created a Web site, LaGrangeNoGarage.com, to help fight its construction. He sent e-mail updates and news about the garage plans to
interested groups. One person who received an e-mail from Wessel
didn't like what he read. He e-mailed him back, copying almost 50
other people.

```
From: SoldMyTreadmill@aol.com
Sent: Thursday, January 22, 2004 11:38
      AM
To: <e-mail addresses suppressed>
Subject: RE: Residents Are Talking
```

Dear Mr. Wessel,

I want to thank you for showing each of us how to effectively use the gift of e-mail to both aggravate and attempt to intimidate uninterested folks in one communique, by threatening each of us with boycotting our business.

For several years now, I have wondered what to do with all of these unsolicited daily e-mails concerning pornography, viagra, debt relief, member enlargement, Nigerian investment opportunities, and aluminum siding for my brick home.

Voila, I have the answer ... have them contact YOU instead.

Your prurient fascination with garages will simply thrill the telemarketers I have in mind. You have inspired me (and hopefully other folks who just love your tenacity) to start saving coupons, magazine bingo cards, telemarketer phone numbers, and yes, weirdo e-mail addresses. We will place your name, address, phone, and e-mail addy on each and every one. Larger mailboxes are available in Hinsdale.

While I am NOT suggesting that others do the same, I just want to make certain that I have your correct information:

Mr. Robert Wessel
<Wessel's Home address>
La Grange, Illinois 60525
(708) <Wessel's home phone number> or <Wessel's business number>
<Wessel's e-mail address>

Quite sincerely yours,
A. Friend

> P.S. I have alerted neighbors in the
> (neighborhood) area that if they hear
> your phone ringing at 3 am, not to
> worry, as it is simply an aggressive
> telemarketer who abhors malicious boy-
> cotting techniques.

Wessel began receiving e-mails from a Web site called contractor. com, thanking him for signing up to get quotes for a parking garage. The barrage of e-mails arrived bearing variations of his name, such as Bobbie Wessel, Rob Weasel, and Bob Vessel.

He was not amused.

Wessel then received e-mails from actual contractors who thought he really wanted to build a parking garage and they wanted to make a bid for his business. People came to his door to give him quotes. The phone rang off the hook with telemarketers eager to tell him about the products "he" had asked for more information about. The campaign of harassment was working.

Wessel went to the local police, who agreed that it looked like a clear case of identity theft and harassment. But instead of arresting the impersonator (and Illinois does have a cyberstalking law), the officer in charge of the case sent an e-mail to "A. Friend" and told him he had three days to appear at the police station or a subpoena would be sent to AOL asking for his identity.

The impersonator showed up at the police station and apologized. He claimed it was only meant as a joke and went too far. He promised he wouldn't do anything else. The police let it go but Wessel was not happy. He was still receiving unwanted e-mails and phone calls.

The police refused to give Wessel the name of the impersonator, so he turned to AOL and filed a petition for discovery. When no one from AOL appeared in court, he filed a motion for a subpoena. When he and his lawyer went to court for that, once again there was no one from AOL present. But there was a surprise waiting for him when he got home. AOL had sent the harasser's information via an overnight delivery service.

Wessel plans to take further action against the impersonator. "He's cost me money having to deal with all the e-mails and phone calls I still receive each day," Wessel stated. "He put into motion something that is not going away and it's hurting my business."

And the city's proposed parking garage?

"Well, the garage has been built," Wessel sighs. "It's purple and it's ugly. And, thus far, fewer cars are parking in it than parked in the surface lots it replaced. We are now fighting to see that the village of LaGrange *does not* receive $3.2 million in federal funds that were appropriated for a 'commuter' parking garage."

Why?

The now-completed garage has been publicly identified as being for visitors, customers, employees, and business owners—but not commuters. The determination that the garage was not for commuter use was made public about two months after the application was sent to local U.S. Representative William O. Lipinski, who has since retired. His son, Daniel Lipinski, now occupies his father's former position. Officials in the Federal Highway Administration are now debating the definition of commuter.

And the fight goes on.

According to the Federal Trade Commission (FTC)[1] the number of identity theft cases in the U.S. rose dramatically in 2003, the latest year for statistics. Forty-two percent of the identity theft complaints the FTC receives have occurred offline. Those crimes include credit cards stolen out of mailboxes and the fraudulent use of social security numbers to open financial accounts and to start up utilities like gas, electric, and phone.

The majority of the identity theft complaints received by the FTC do involve the Internet in some way, with auction fraud accounting for 15 percent of the complaints and problems with Internet services/computer products accounting for 6 percent of them.

A survey conducted by CSI/FBI in 2004[2] found that although theft of proprietary information such as social security numbers, credit card numbers, and the like cost companies over $11 million, there is something else hitting them harder monetarily. Viruses actually do over $55 million worth of damage.

In fact, theft of proprietary information decreased by more than half between 1999 and 2004. This is good news for anyone who is fearful of using a credit card or accessing a bank account online.

"We don't see as many Internet solicitations, but we are watching that," says Joanna Crane, program manager for the FTC's identity theft program. "There is evidence, however, that Internet-related thefts, particularly e-mail schemes, are increasing."

Andrea Morin, director of strategic planning at Technology Resources in Boston, agrees with the FTC that there is a misconception that online identity theft happens all the time.

Steps to Follow If Your Credit Card Is Stolen

1. Report the crime to the police immediately. Get a copy of your police report or case number. Credit card companies, your bank, credit reporting bureaus, and your insurance company may ask you to reference the report to verify the crime.

2. Immediately contact your credit card issuers. Get replacement cards with new account numbers and ask that the old account be processed as "account closed at consumer's request" for credit record purposes. You should follow up this telephone conversation with a letter to the credit card company summarizing your request.

3. Call the fraud units of the three credit reporting bureaus in the United States (Equifax, Experian, and TransUnion). Report the theft of your credit cards and/or numbers. Ask that your accounts be flagged. Also, add a victim's statement to your report that requests that you be contacted to verify future credit applications. See Appendix B or go to www.netcrimes.net for contact information for the three major credit reporting agencies.

4. Keep a log of all conversations with authorities and financial entities.

(Provided by the U.S. Secret Service)

"The role the Internet often plays is one of aider and abettor, if you will," Morin says.

"Criminals often purchase fake IDs—that in itself is generally considered a separate crime—via Web sites, or other items that could contribute to identity theft such as diplomas, birth certificates, driver's licenses, visas, passports, etc."

Identity thieves are helped by sites that sell personal identifying information on just about anyone. Also, there are sites that advertise books on how to create a false identity.

Top Identity Theft Resources

U.S. Government's Official Site About Identity Theft
www.consumer.gov/idtheft
1-877-ID-THEFT

U.S. Secret Service
www.treas.gov/usss/index.html

Identity Theft Resource Center
www.idtheftcenter.org

Better Business Bureau
www.bbbonline.org/idtheft

"The Internet is also a great place for criminals to use the credit of the victim," Morin says. "You can make a transaction online, and unlike an in-person transaction, there are no witnesses and no videotape. You don't even need to show the credit card or sign a receipt."

One newsworthy online identity theft case involved a busboy in Brooklyn who went through *Forbes* magazine's "400 Richest People in America" issue and victimized more than 200 people who were listed in it.

Abraham Abdullah convinced credit companies to give him detailed credit reports about the people he wanted to impersonate. He then used the information to gain access to their credit cards and bank accounts—all online. This went on for almost six months. Abdullah impersonated well-known people including Martha Stewart, George Lucas, Oprah Winfrey, Ross Perot, Ted Turner, Michael Bloomberg, David Geffen, Steven Spielberg, and Michael Eisner.

How did he do it? First, he got a box at a local mailbox rental company in the name of Microsoft co-founder Paul Allen, conducting the rental transaction via fax from start to finish, never appearing in person.

Next, Abdullah used online voicemail/fax accounts to receive messages and faxes. He began receiving credit cards in his victims' names, and then ordered items online. When they were delivered to the postal box he'd rented, he had a courier pick up and deliver the packages using deliberately confusing routes to elude any authorities who might suspect something. He never physically did any of this himself.

It was only when he was arrested that the police began to suspect the scope of his criminal activities. They noticed the well-used copy of *Forbes* magazine on the front seat of the car he was driving. A closer inspection revealed detailed notes next to the biographies of the people he had impersonated, including their home addresses, telephone and cell phone numbers, mothers' maiden names, and more.

What led to the arrest of Abdullah was an investigation that had begun a couple of months before, when Merrill Lynch received an e-mail requesting a transfer of $10 million from an account belonging to Thomas Siebel, founder of Siebel Systems, to a new account in Australia. Siebel was contacted and said he never requested the transfer. Merrill Lynch then contacted the New York Police Department (NYPD), who tracked down the e-mail request to two e-mail addresses. Those two e-mail addresses were found in other accounts at Merrill Lynch, with similar requests, though not in the $10 million-range.

The NYPD began contacting other brokerage houses and high-roller banks and discovered the same two e-mail addresses popping up all over. Police officers found out about the couriers being used to deliver packages. This led them to keep track of one UPS delivery that arrived on February 23, 2001, containing $25,000 worth of equipment that could manufacture and magnetize credit cards. When the courier arrived to pick up the package, two NYPD officers nabbed him. One officer took over as the driver while the other hid in the back seat under a trash bag. When they were redirected to a different address, they went and waited. Soon after, Abdullah showed up in a 2000 Volvo, which he'd leased under a false name.

One officer leaped through the open sunroof to subdue Abdullah before he could drive away. The other opened the driver's door. The *Forbes* magazine was on the passenger seat, filled with notations made by Abdullah.

His crime spree had come to an end.

Endnotes

1. *FTC Figures & Trends Identity Theft Report*, January 2003–September 2003. The FTC's report is based on complaints made to the agency's Consumer Sentinel database, which is accessed by more than 900 law enforcement agencies in the U.S., Canada, and Australia.

2. *CSI/FBI Computer Crime and Security Survey* by Lawrence A. Gordon, Martin P. Loeb, William Lucyshyn, and Robert Richardson (CSI is Computer Security Institute).

Your Personal Life Exposed

Web Wreckers

People who put up harassing Web pages about another person or persons.

Cyberstalkers

People who track another person or persons' online activities. Cyberstalking sometimes leads to physical stalking.

Famous people face more dangers online than do average private citizens. Besides threatening e-mails, celebrities have to contend with the fact that information about their home and office addresses, the types of cars they drive, and the places they frequent is posted by fans on various Web sites and newsgroups. On the other hand, movie stars and other celebrities often have the money, resources, and connections to protect themselves, while regular folks have to fend for themselves.

Askance Romance

Brenda was surfing the Web one night and typed a query into a search engine, looking for information in New Jersey, where she lived. When she saw a link to a Web site that bore her ex-boyfriend's name in the URL,[1] she clicked on it, curious to see what he was up to.

At first glance, the site was tame, but when she clicked on a link for Romance, she discovered that, along with other ex-girlfriends, he'd posted her name, where she lived, photos of her, and intimate descriptions of their relationship for anyone to read.

Devastated, Brenda sought advice from a friend, who suggested she contact him via e-mail and ask him to remove her information. She did and he wrote back that although he was disappointed, because she had been a part of his life, he would do what she asked and remove the link.

Brenda breathed a sigh of relief. Two days later, she checked his site. When she clicked on Romance, she got a pop-up window asking for a password. Panicked, and not knowing if her information was still on his site, she again e-mailed him, trying to remain calm.

"I asked him why he didn't remove the link like I'd asked and like he'd agreed to," Brenda says. "He just ended up writing me back, and not in a very nice way, that he was not going to remove the page and that he was expressing himself and I would just have to deal with it."

She didn't. Brenda contacted the ISP he was using, explaining that he was doing more than just expressing himself, and she was concerned about who may be reading her information on his site and what they might do with that information.

A Site About Online Stalking That Should Scare You

The Stalkers Home Page
www.glr.com/stalk.html

Opening paragraph from the Stalkers' Web page: "What could be more absurd than a home page for stalkers? We thought so, but we're finding more and more personal information widely available to any prying eyes. ... Of course, we don't encourage anyone to engage in stalking or other impolite behavior ... but look at the resources!"

Although this site tries to be more pro-stalking than anti-stalking, it does offer some links to interesting and helpful sites victims can use to their benefit, as well as links to sites that some may find questionable and unsettling.

The site was pulled. When Brenda found that the site was back online a few weeks later, all the Romance links and information were gone from the site.

Sorry, Wrong Number

Cindy, who lives in Los Angeles, began finding messages on her answering machine from men she didn't know. These men stated they'd gotten her number from a Web site, one she'd never heard of. She never called them back and thought it was just an odd coincidence or a wrong number. Then, while home sick one day, she answered the telephone and found herself in a conference call with two men claiming they were online with her right at that moment. She told them she was not online; they in turn told her what Web site she was supposedly on. There were photographs of her and a description that said she wanted to be a "white sex slave to an all-black gang-bang, men and women."

Cindy was lucky because when she contacted the owners of the Web site, she found out who was impersonating her and was able to get her local police to press charges against the man. It turned out to be an ex-boyfriend.

Lawmakers Understand

"I first became aware of this issue [cyberstalking] after reading a magazine article appearing in an NCSL [National Conference of State Legislatures] publication," says Florida State Senator Steven A. Geller, District 29. "I saw that this [cyberstalking] legislation had been passed in other states, and based on my service on the Florida Information Technology Development Task Force and the extensive amount of Internet legislation I've been working on, I felt this was important legislation to be passed."

Because of his efforts, Florida's cyberstalking law was passed and put into effect in October 2003. Before this, many Florida legislators said they believed the then current stalking and harassment laws covered cyberstalking.

John Laurence Reid, Legal Counsel/Legislative Assistant, Florida State Senate, District 29, disagrees. "I spoke with numerous women from Florida who were being stalked over the Internet. Because of jurisdictional problems, the stalking statutes prior to this were ineffective for them, and they desperately need this legislation. This law is good for these women, and it is good for the people of Florida," he says.

Cyberstalking Facts

- WHOA (www.haltabuse.org) claims it receives up to 100 requests for help each week.

- CyberAngels (www.cyberangels.org) claims it receives more than 800 requests for help each week.

The data from these three organizations alone represent more than 46,000 cyberstalking cases per year, and that number is growing. And consider this: There are over 1 billion people online worldwide today; if only 1 percent become the target of cyberstalkers, that's 10 million victims.

The Amy Boyer Story

Amy Boyer of Nashua, New Hampshire, was a victim whose story had a tragic ending.

A vivacious 20-year-old, Amy lived at home with her mother, Helen, stepfather, Tim, and 10-year-old sister, Jenna. She had a boyfriend, her own car, and a job at a local dentist's office. Life was good. When Amy and her mother went online on October 12, 1999, they surfed several sites for a few hours. What they didn't think to do was search for Amy's name.

"Maybe if we had, she'd still be alive today," Helen says.

Liam Youens seemed like an unassuming young man. He was 21, tall, thin, and wore glasses. But Liam harbored a dark secret—his obsession with Amy. Although he didn't tell anyone around him about his crush, Liam spilled his thoughts onto two Web sites, one located at Geocities and the other at Tripod. Both Web sites offered the same disturbing information and had been online for some time, one of them for more than two years, yet no one was alerted to them.

The main page opened with two black-and-white photos of Amy and scarcely any text. One link, labeled "age 17" went to a page where Liam commented on how he felt Amy's smile was forced in the top photo (see Figure 10.1) and explained that he had airbrushed the other photo so that it was more in keeping with how he wanted her to look.

Guess what.. Amy doesnt have a dimple when she smiles.. That is the worst attempt at a forced smile I have ever seen. But what the hell do I know. On the other page I airbrushed the photo to make it look better.

Figure 10.1   Amy's smile

A click on ENTER took visitors to a page that began: "Greetings Infidels, I am Liam Youens," and showed a photo of him holding an automatic weapon (see Figure 10.2). "Who am I?" the text continued. "Well if i had 20 people buried in my backyard my neighbors would have described me as 'Quiet, basically kept to himself'."

Thus begins the tragic online journal of how Liam began stalking Amy in real life. What may have started as a way to blow off steam for his unrequited "love" for Amy soon became a series of rants and raves and ultimately a death watch. It was only a matter of time before he would act on his obsession with killing her.

Liam claimed he fell in love with Amy in the tenth grade during algebra class. She never knew it. His thoughts on the Web site about this were: "Oh great, now I'm really depressed, hmmm ... looks like it's suicide for me. Car accident? Wrists? A few days later I think, 'hey, why don't I kill her, too? =).' "

He wrote about how he tried to be in the same classes as Amy in his senior year of high school (she was a junior), how he would stare at her in the hallways and at lunch, positive she knew he loved her, although her parents claim Amy knew Liam only in passing.

As he accumulated weapons and ammunition, Liam became braver in his pursuit of Amy. He added a Web page that showed off all the weapons he'd purchased (see Figure 10.3), with descriptions of where he purchased them. He kept thinking everyone knew he was stalking Amy, even the Nashua police, and noted this on the Web sites, but it was just another delusion. Or could it have been a cry for help?

Liam wrote on his Web pages about killing Amy's boyfriend and others from the same youth group they belonged to, even a "Columbine-style" shooting at Nashua High School (see Figure 10.4), but Amy remained his primary focus.

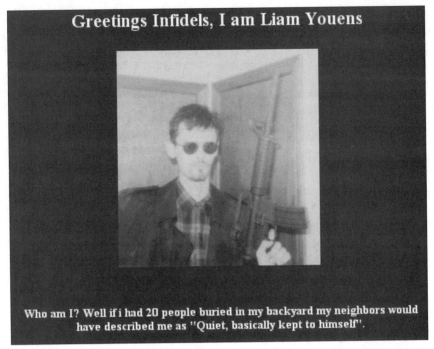

Greetings Infidels, I am Liam Youens

Who am I? Well if i had 20 people buried in my backyard my neighbors would have described me as "Quiet, basically kept to himself".

Figure 10.2   Infidels

By the time Liam had worked up his courage to set the date, it took less than $100 and visits to Web sites where anyone could purchase personal information, and he had what he needed: the address where Amy worked.

He wrote, "It's accually obsene what you can find out about a person on the internet."

On October 15, 1999, at 4:29 P.M., Liam showed up outside the dentist's office where Amy worked part-time. He waited for her to come out and get into her car, and then he drove up alongside her car and shot her several times in the face with his 9mm Glock. Then he reloaded the gun, put the barrel in his mouth, and killed himself.

Amy's parents were more than grief-stricken—they couldn't take out their anger at the killer because he was dead, too. And as parents, they couldn't get angry with Liam's parents. They found themselves directing their anger at Tripod and Geocities, where the Web pages resided, and at DocuSearch, the company that provided Amy's work address.

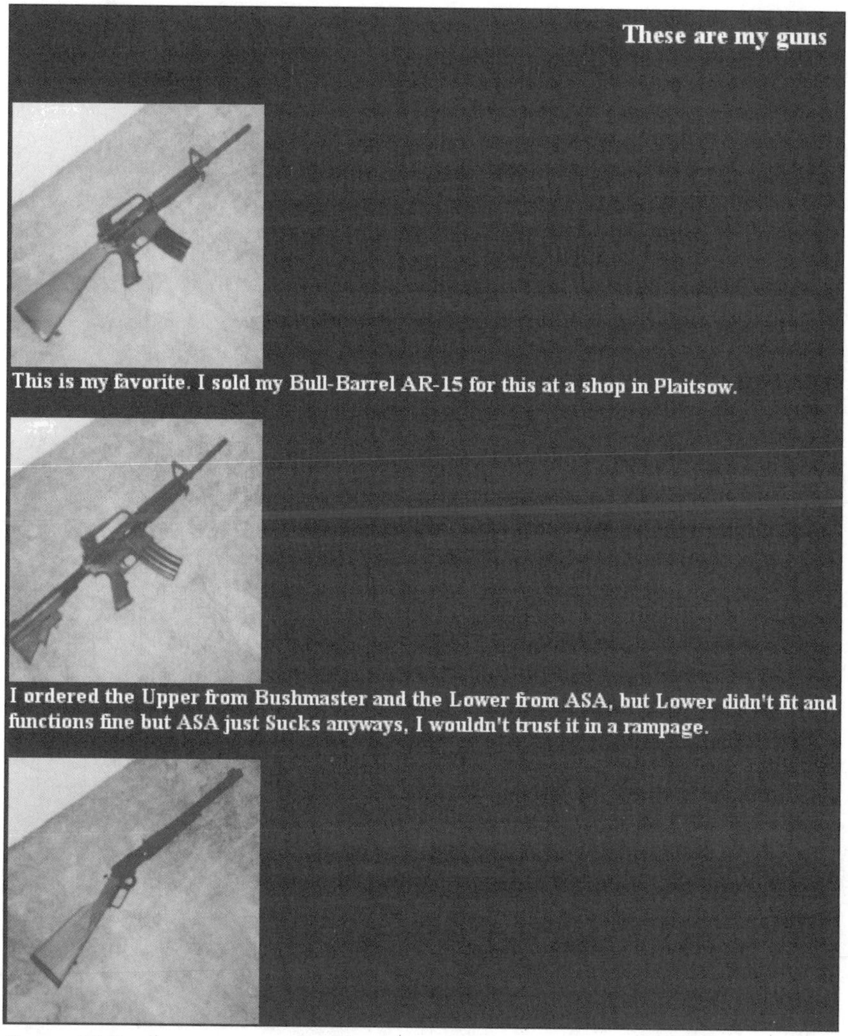

These are my guns

This is my favorite. I sold my Bull-Barrel AR-15 for this at a shop in Plaitsow.

I ordered the Upper from Bushmaster and the Lower from ASA, but Lower didn't fit and functions fine but ASA just Sucks anyways, I wouldn't trust it in a rampage.

Figure 10.3   Guns

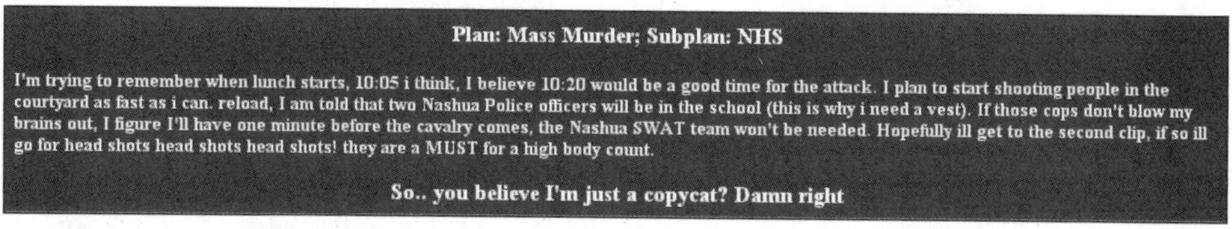

Plan: Mass Murder; Subplan: NHS

I'm trying to remember when lunch starts, 10:05 i think, I believe 10:20 would be a good time for the attack. I plan to start shooting people in the courtyard as fast as i can. reload, I am told that two Nashua Police officers will be in the school (this is why i need a vest). If those cops don't blow my brains out, I figure I'll have one minute before the cavalry comes, the Nashua SWAT team won't be needed. Hopefully ill get to the second clip, if so ill go for head shots head shots head shots! they are a MUST for a high body count.

So.. you believe I'm just a copycat? Damn right

Figure 10.4   Plan

Cyberstalking Estimates

- The Los Angeles District Attorney's Office estimates that e-mail or other electronic communication was a factor in approximately 20 percent of the 600 cases handled by its Stalking and Threat Assessment Unit.

- The chief of the Sex Crimes Unit in Manhattan District Attorney's Office also estimates that roughly 30 percent of its cases involve cyberstalking.

- The Computer Investigations and Technology Unit of the New York City Police Department estimates that almost 40 percent of its cases involve cyberstalking.

"It would be one thing if he'd written this in a private handwritten diary," Amy's stepfather, Tim, says. "But he wrote this on the Internet. Now don't you think he expected someone to read this?"

A representative who worked for Tripod at the time removed the site the same night Amy died, after a Nashua police detective called him. He said Tripod would have notified authorities if anyone had seen the site. Later, the Tripod representative claimed that the number of visitors to the site was in the single digits, suggesting Liam had been the only visitor to his site. But had he been?

If Amy Boyer's stepfather has his way, Web page hosts such as Tripod and Geocities (now owned by Yahoo!) will be required to police themselves.

"They should be monitoring sites where the word 'kill' is used ..." Amy's stepfather says. "They should have someone sitting in front of a computer all day, doing nothing but hunting for the people who're hunting for us."

A Tripod representative, who wished to remain anonymous, claims the company does its best to monitor pornography and online threats, which are a violation of the terms of service (TOS) agreement that each Tripod member must follow. But the technology to weed out threatening pages hasn't been perfected. In March 2001, a filtering program used by Tripod ended up deleting legitimate Web pages along with ones that did violate the TOS. If a human reviewed each of the sites (as Tim suggested) instead of a computer program, this might not have happened.

In March 2000, Tim stood before a Senate subcommittee in Washington, DC, and testified, "We must show Amy that we care about what happened to her and that we are going to act to see it doesn't happen to anyone else."

Within days of his testimony, New Hampshire Senator Judd Gregg announced he was co-sponsoring legislation that would outlaw the sale of Social Security numbers online. With the Social Security Administration and the White House on board, the Amy Boyer Bill was introduced. Although passed by the House and Senate, organizations such as the American Civil Liberties Union (ACLU) vigorously opposed it. The bill passed in December 2000,[2] but Tim and his wife asked that they take Amy's name off the bill, as the approved bill was not what they'd initially supported. The bill applies to violations effective on or after December 21, 2002, two years after its enactment.

Amy's parents filed a wrongful-death suit against DocuSearch. com in April 2000, claiming negligence and invasion of privacy. They haven't done anything about Tripod and Geocities, mainly because of the Communications Decency Act, which doesn't hold ISPs or Web hosts such as Tripod and Geocities responsible for their customers' actions.

"These companies have a 'get out of monitoring free' card," Amy's parents claim on their Web site, www.amyboyer.org. "This law … eliminates the Web site servers from having any responsibility for anything printed on the space they provide on the Web."

If the Web hosts had monitored their sites correctly, as they claim they do in their TOS, Amy might still be alive today. Yet, these same Web hosts are fearful of the First Amendment, the right to free speech, and the opposition from members to monitoring member pages. They should have the same concern when it comes to threats of violence.

Amy's parents received good news in March 2004. DocuSearch. com, the Web site that sold Liam Youens information about Amy, settled a lawsuit with Amy's mother, Helen, for $85,000.

"This has never been about money," Amy's stepfather Tim said. "It is hard to forgive and forget. DocuSearch was making a lot of money by providing private information to anyone with a credit card. I don't think that they should be able to do what they did."

Unwanted Fantasy

Gary Dellapenta was angry that a woman at his local church had spurned him in 1996. He followed her at first, keeping his distance, but his anger grew so much that he decided he wanted to get back at her in a more serious way. He went online during the summer of 1998 and began signing up for sex-related chat rooms and placing personal ads, all in Randi Barber's name. He opened up free e-mail accounts using sexually attractive usernames such as "playfulkitty4u" and "kinkygal30."

Randi didn't own a computer, had never been online, and went about her daily life until the first man came knocking at her door wanting to fulfill her home-invasion rape fantasies.

She told him she had no idea what he was talking about. The man left, then called later that night asking if she'd changed her mind. She demanded to know why he thought she was interested in something as sick as that and discovered that someone was impersonating her online.

Six men in all came to Randi's home, and by the time the last one arrived, she had stopped answering the door and the phone.

Dellapenta wasn't through yet. He replied to anyone who e-mailed Randi, claiming she was playing hard to get and gave explicit instructions on how to break into her apartment, even how to bypass her home security system.

Randi didn't know what to do at first. She filed a complaint with her local police department, but officers told her they couldn't help her. She turned to her father for help. He went online, and with help from some of the men who had called Randi or stopped by her home, he finally learned Dellapenta's identity.

Randi and her father then went to the police. The FBI and Los Angeles County Sheriff's Department worked together and in November 1998, Dellapenta was arrested on charges of cyberstalking—the first case to test the new cyberstalking law passed in California earlier that year.

Police who worked on the case said that the computer-related evidence they collected was almost better than telephone recordings. They ended up finding proof that the personal ads placed in Randi's name originated from Sprynet, the ISP Dellapenta used, as evidenced by transcripts of chat logs and other information gathered from his computer.

Cyberstalking Statistics from WHOA

- More than 68 percent of victims harassed/stalked online are Caucasian.

- 74 percent are women.

- 48 percent are 18–30 years of age.

- Half the offenders are strangers to the victims.

- Just over 50 percent of offenders are male.

- The majority of cases begin with e-mail threats, followed by message boards (including newsgroups and Yahoo! Groups), IMs (instant messages), then chat.

- California has the most cyberstalking cases, followed by New York, Florida, Canada, Pennsylvania, and Virginia.

- Over 70 percent of all cases reported to WHOA were resolved by contacting the offender's ISP; this was followed by victims changing their e-mail address, username, nickname, and/or profile.

These statistics are based on a sampling of 1,664 cases WHOA handled from 2000 through 2005. These were victims who completely filled out the questionnaire on WHOA's site; providing location/gender/age information is not required to receive help from WHOA (www.haltabuse.org/resources/stats).

Dellapenta ended up getting six years in prison for stalking and soliciting others to commit rape. The court stated that probation was not an option because of the "enormous difficulty in controlling what a person does at his computer on the Internet."

The Psychology of Cyberstalking

Cyberstalking is the most prevalent type of online harassment. When a harasser is not stopped in the beginning stages of harassment, such as via e-mail, chat rooms, forums, or newsgroups, the perpetrators begin to feel powerful. The harassment escalates so that the harasser follows the victim everywhere online, becoming a cyberstalker. Cyberstalkers usually (often easily) find a victim's new e-mail address, put the victim on their instant messaging buddy or friends lists so that they are alerted when the victim is online, and then bombard them with e-mail, and subscribe the victim to mailing lists, free offers, pornographic Web sites, and other unwanted material.

It's the perceived anonymity of the Internet that provides the cyberstalker with a feeling of invincibility. Using a free e-mail account or changing the "From" line in e-mails to show a bogus e-mail address all feed into this feeling of power.

If not stopped early on, some cyberstalkers can become so obsessed with a victim that they escalate their activities to the level of physical stalking. This is extremely dangerous, which is why it's critical for you to contact an online safety organization, the offender's ISP, and/or the police if someone is harassing you online.

Don't end up like Amy Boyer.

Endnotes

1. URL (Uniform Resource Locator): A Web site address, such as www.disney.com.
2. P.L. 106-553; 42 U.S.C. Section 1320B-23.

Ugly Beasts
Lurking Online

Troll

Someone who visits a chat room, newsgroup, message board,[1] or other online forum and writes messages meant to get the other people online upset.

Flame

A public response to a message or posting on a newsgroup, mailing list,[2] or chat room, which goes beyond polite disagreement, belittling the author's point of view and frequently insulting him personally. If the author responds just as nastily to the flame, a "flame war" often ensues. On moderated lists, flaming can frequently be stopped before it gets out of control.

Spoofer

Someone who impersonates another person online. A spoofer will sometimes open several e-mail accounts in the victim's name, then use those accounts to post messages on Web sites, send offensive e-mail messages to others (typically employers, family, and friends of the victim), pose as the victim in chat rooms, newsgroups, and mailing lists, sign guestbooks,[3] and commit various online transgressions in the name of the victim; a form of identity theft.

Don't Feed the Troll

Trolls are more than ugly beasts hiding under a bridge in a fairy tale. Online trolls are people who love to cause trouble. Trolls will visit a chat room, newsgroup, or message board and post a message intended to get other folks upset. Then trolls sit back and enjoy the havoc and fighting they have created (sometimes adding to the mayhem by taunting the group). Once they have been sufficiently entertained, trolls typically leave for another newsgroup, chat room, or message board, and start all over again.

The newsgroup alt.sports.hockey.nhl.ny-rangers is an example of an online forum that was "trolled," which began when someone calling himself Gene posted a one-word message to the newsgroup: "Suck!"

"Gene" was no stranger to the newsgroup. He would pop in every once in a while to start trouble. Over the course of more than 50 replies to his Suck! post, Gene answered with taunts. As the messages progressed, so did the length and content of Gene's posts, with messages becoming especially vile at times. Instead of ignoring Gene, others on the newsgroup kept it up and began fighting with each other, which is exactly what a troll wants.

It turned out Gene only went to the newsgroup to cause trouble. Out of several newsgroups he visited, this sports newsgroup responded to his posts in such a way that he kept coming back ... and back, and back.

So, what can you do in this type of situation?

If you notice that a new person has appeared in a newsgroup, message board, chat room, or other forum and is making all sorts of rude comments, you can be fairly sure this is a troll. Ignore the troll. He feeds on replies and attention. No matter what the troll writes, avoid any sort of reply. In fact, put them on "ignore" in a chat room, filter them out of the newsgroup, or stop visiting that message board for a while. Don't give in to what the troll wants, which is attention and the chance to start a huge fight.

If you insist on defending yourself or others, you could be asking for more trouble than it's really worth. Your best defense is to simply complain to the troll's ISP and let them take care of the troll.

Flaming Beatles

Flaming is an appropriate name for another online situation that often gets out of control. When an individual responds to someone's comment in a public forum with a nasty personal attack (as opposed to respectful disagreement), that's a flame. If the person who made the original comment reacts defensively the communications can quickly escalate into a vitriolic war of words. Other group participants may take sides and enter the fray, and often the "flame war" will come to an end only when one of the original parties has the good sense to walk away from it.

A good example of flaming is what happened on the rec.music.beatles newsgroup. A group of Beatles fans had been sharing thoughts, stories, and silly messages with each other for quite some time. One day, a new person named Garik showed up in the group and began lambasting one of the participants for being a Beatles freak. The person responded by telling Garik to "buzz off," but he wouldn't leave. Garik began to target other members of the rec.music.beatles newsgroup, even going so far as to forge messages in other members' names, such as this one, "from" Ted:

> I like child molestors. As long as they confess to their crime, and then do what the courts order them to do as part of their sentence, I have no problem with them. I would like to molest children myself. I read all about Gary Burnore's child molestation, his confession, his sentence, what a sick f---ing piece of shit he is, and I have to say, I got quite turned on. I masturbated all day thinking about Gary molesting that girl, and the thought of her being upset, and perhaps permanently scarred by it made me cum harder than I ever did before.

Next he listed Ted's full name, home address, and phone number.

Regulars on the group complained to Garik's ISP, who canceled his account. But instead of letting it go, Garik got a new e-mail account and started flaming the newsgroup again; the regulars flamed right back. Garik ended up losing several more e-mail accounts due to complaints from the regulars, but he kept coming back. It got to a point where many of the regulars began receiving e-mails and threats from Garik, and they ended up looking for legal help.

Another incident involved Dean Stark, a regular on the scruz.general newsgroup. He had some disagreements with a few people in the group and flamed them for disagreeing with him. They fought back in full force. One member in particular, who went by the username anus_astonished, was particularly brutal, and is thought to be the creator of more than 200 newsgroups about Dean, among them alt.fan.dean-stark, alt.recovery.dean-stark, and alt.fan.dean-stark.diapers (many of them are still there). Soon Dean's name was all over the newsgroups, with discussions asking just who Dean Stark was. But Dean did the right thing. He stopped responding to messages about him, stopped posting messages, changed his e-mail address/username, and is more careful now when posting online.

The best solution, besides what Dean did, is to e-mail the person who flamed you, swallow your pride, let them know you apologize if you offended them, and "shake hands." This often works. If it doesn't, and the other person continues to flame you on the newsgroup, chat room, etc., don't respond but do report them to their ISP. Your non-response will prove to the ISP that you didn't encourage the flaming.

Spoofing

Spoofing can happen without your knowledge, and it should be considered a serious problem. Someone can open an ISP account in your name. Or a person can open an account in her own name or a fictitious name, go online, and pretend to be you.

Sound impossible?

Susan, who lived in Maryland, didn't even own a computer. She discovered she was being spoofed (impersonated) online when she began to receive phone calls about items she supposedly put up for sale on a local newspaper's Web site. Susan hadn't.

Carol, who lived in Michigan, found out someone was going into chat rooms pretending to be her, then berating the other chatters and getting into arguments with them. Carol would receive e-mail messages asking why she was being so awful or threatening to complain about her to her ISP. She'd have to explain that she'd never been in that chat room.

Gerald, a Maryland college student, received phone calls from gay men saying they'd answered his ad on a gay Web site. He hadn't put the ad there.

But someone did.

Why did this happen to these people? Most of the time it turned out to be a spurned lover, friends who had argued, or a jealous classmate. Sometimes it was a total stranger who took a dislike to the victim's e-mail address or chat room user ID,[4] didn't like what the victim "said" in a chat room or wrote in an e-mail or newsgroup, or sometimes took offense to something written in a guestbook. There was no real single factor that set off these spoofers.

The scariest thing is that spoofing happens more often than it should. Why? Because it's far too easy to forge another person's name on messages, on e-mails, and in chat rooms.

You need only to provide a valid credit card, money order, or sometimes just a cash deposit to an ISP and you can open an account. ISPs rarely check to make sure the name of the person opening the account is the same as on the credit card or check. Even less often do ISPs check to see if that person was kicked off their service or another ISP for harassing someone or abusing the service.

Once someone has an account, she can do all sorts of damage to another person. Even if the account is in the spoofer's real name, the spoofer can easily change the "FROM:" line in e-mails or newsgroup postings so that they look like they came from someone else. Or, a spoofer can get a free e-mail account (such as from Yahoo!, Hotmail, or Juno) and use that to forge the victim's name everywhere. Or they can use an anonymous remailer—a service (usually free) that allows someone to send an e-mail or newsgroup post with all of the associated identifying information stripped away so the recipient can't determine the origination.

But that's just the beginning.

If someone knows your current e-mail address or chat room user ID, they can go to Web sites and leave nasty messages in guestbooks using your name and e-mail address, put your information on controversial or sex-related Web sites "offering your services," order pizzas to be delivered to your house (this happened to Jackie—the pizza parlor called her to confirm that she'd actually ordered 10 pizzas with the works when she hadn't), subscribe you to online newsletters and mailing lists, impersonate you in chat rooms—the list goes on because there are so many things spoofers can do to you on the Web, all for free.

Then there are the newsgroups and message boards, such as Yahoo! Groups. Pick a group, any group. Someone can post a message that claims the people there are a bunch of idiots—or worse—and make the message look like it came from you. You'd surely get nasty e-mail messages about "your" behavior on that group or any others "you" visited. Then you have to deal with telling these people that you didn't put that message on their group and try to figure out what happened and why.

So, what can you do to avoid being spoofed?

If you don't own a computer, but are listed in the telephone book and someone has taken a dislike to you, there may not be much you can do to prevent being impersonated online. Your name, phone number, and address information can wind up on newsgroups and Web pages, in chat rooms, and on message boards. An unpublished phone number can help you avoid problems, and you may decide it's worth spending a little extra each month to have one.

If you own a computer and have an Internet connection, the likelihood of your being spoofed increases. The flip side is that you can discover fairly easily if someone is spoofing you, and take steps to resolve the problem. If you have reason to believe you are being spoofed, I recommend the following.

On Newsgroups

First, go to a newsgroup search engine, such as Google Groups as shown in Figure 11.1 (www.groups.google.com). Look for Google's "Advanced Search" link, click, and input your first and last name in the "with the exact phrase" text box, then click the Google Search button.

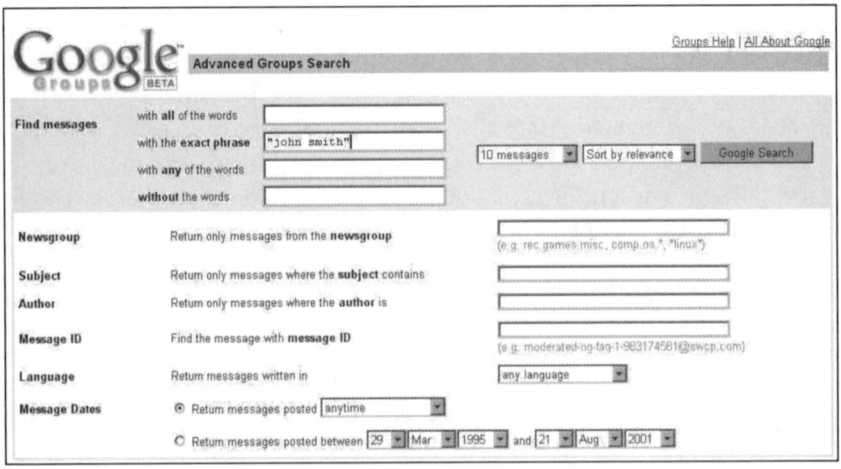

Figure 11.1   Google Groups

If you like, you can refine the search by selecting certain dates, newsgroups, and other criteria. You can also type any e-mail address or chat room user ID you use in the text box and click on the Google Search button.

If the results list (see Figure 11.2) includes messages that may have been written by you (remember, there may be messages by someone with the same name as yours), click on the associated link to view the message.

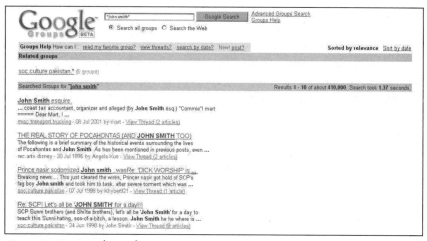

Figure 11.2 Google results

Here, as an example, is a message forged in my name:

```
From: "J.A.Hitchcock" <latakia@ix.netcom.
    com>
Newsgroups: rec.climbing
Subject: CLIMBERS ARE SICK PEOPLE
Date: Tue, 24 Dec 1996 04:53:47 -0800

    I'm an international author who knows
what she's talking about. Read my books.
Climbing is a disease and pointless.
```

If a given message is clearly associated with you and your e-mail address, and you're sure you didn't write and post it, click on "View Original Article" in Google Groups to learn which ISP the message was posted from (or, alternatively, get a newsreader program, such as

Free Agent at www.forteinc.com/agent, which offers the option to show full headers).

In this example, the headers expanded quite a bit:

```
Path:
ix.netcom.com!ix.netcom.com!worldnet.att
.net!feed1.news.erols.com!news.idt.net!nnt
p.farm.idt.net!news
    From:   "J.A.Hitchcock"  <latakia@ix.net-
com.com>
        Newsgroups: rec.climbing
    Subject: CLIMBERS ARE SICK PEOPLE
    Date: Tue, 24 Dec 1996 04:53:47 -0800
        Organization: INTERNATIONAL AUTHOR
        Lines: 2
        Message-ID: <32BFD25B.3D9E@ix.net-
com.com>  NNTP-Posting-Host:  169.132.8.11
(ppp-9.ts-12.nyc.idt.net)
        Mime-Version: 1.0
        Content-Type:  text/plain;charset=
us-ascii
        Content-Transfer-Encoding: 7bit
        X-Mailer: Mozilla 2.01 (Win16; I)
    I'm an international author who knows
what she's talking about. Read my books.
Climbing is a disease and pointless.
```

The full headers[5] will help you determine where the message originated; this is crucial for the next steps. In this example, the NNTP-Posting-Host line shows the message originated from 169.132.8.11 (ppp-9.ts-12.nyc.idt.net; you can identify the ISP from the last part, idt.net).

Now you have some options.

If you are a newsgroups user, open your newsreader or the program you use to view newsgroups. Find a newsgroup called news.admin. net-abuse.sightings and post a new message with the subject line exactly as it appeared when originally posted, with [usenet] in front of it. In the text area, type in something like "I've been spoofed on Usenet and did not post the following. Please cancel this message [or "these messages" if there is more than one]," then paste a copy of the newsgroup message in its original Usenet format, with the full headers. Here's how you'd post this example to news.admin.net-abuse.sightings:

```
From: J.A. Hitchcock (latakia@ix.netcom.
    com)
Newsgroups: news.admin.net-abuse. sightings
Subject: [Usenet] Climbers Are Sick People
Date: Tue, 24 Dec 1996 09:15:47 -0800


   Hello, I'm being spoofed on Usenet and
have found many messages forged in my name.
I've reported these to news.admin.net-
abuse.sightings but would appreciate any
help you can give me. One of the messages
is as follows; you'll see by the headers
that it did not originate from my netcom
account, but from idt.net.

Thank you,
The real J.A. Hitchcock

   Path:
   ix.netcom.com!ix.netcom.com!worldnet.att
.net!feed1.news.erols.com!news.idt.net!nnt
p.farm.idt.net!news
   From: "J.A.Hitchcock" <latakia@ix.net
         com.com>
         Newsgroups: rec.climbing
   Subject: CLIMBERS ARE SICK PEOPLE
   Date: Tue, 24 Dec 1996 04:53:47 -0800
         Organization: INTERNATIONAL AUTHOR
         Lines: 2
         Message-ID: <32BFD25B.3D9E@ix.net-
com.com>  NNTP-Posting-Host:  169.132.8.11
(ppp-9.ts-12.nyc.idt.net)
         Mime-Version: 1.0
         Content-Type: text/plain; charset=
us-ascii
         Content-Transfer-Encoding: 7bit
         X-Mailer: Mozilla 2.01 (Win16; I)
```

> I'm an international author who knows
> what she's talking about. Read my books.
> Climbing is a disease and pointless.

If you are not a newsgroup user, register on the Google Groups site, then find the newsgroup news.admin.net-abuse.sightings and follow the instructions given here for posting to it.

After you've posted to news.admin.net-abuse.sightings, go to the newsgroup news.admin.net-abuse.misc and post a new message with the subject line: "I'm Being Spoofed—Please Cancel." In the text area, explain that someone is spoofing you on one or more newsgroups and that you have posted those messages on news.admin.net-abuse.sightings but request any help that can be offered. You may be surprised by how willing other Internet users are to help victims of spoofing.

Yahoo! Groups

Yahoo! Groups are similar to newsgroups, except that you can create a group right away, whereas Usenet (the formal name for newsgroups) requires an approval process. This means that Yahoo! Groups makes it far too easy for someone to create a group to harass, stalk, or libel a person. If you find that someone has created a group designed to harass you, or someone is impersonating you in one or more Yahoo! Groups, there is a simple form to fill out (located at http://add.yahoo.com/fast/help/us/groups/cgi_abuse). If this link doesn't work, go to http://help.yahoo.com/help/groups and follow instructions from there. Yahoo! has been pretty good over the years about deleting groups that don't follow its terms of service. It is also quick to delete user IDs forged in another person's name or used to harass and defame someone.

On Web Pages

Go to a major Web search engine or service, such as Yahoo! (www.yahoo.com), and do what is called an ego search—type your name in quotes and click on the Search button, as shown in Figure 11.3. You should also try searching on any e-mail addresses and chat room user ID you use. Also, as each search engine will index different pages and at different times, it makes good sense to ego surf on more than one of them. (Another option is to use a metasearch engine. Metasearch engines, like Metacrawler, www.metacrawler.com, and DogPile,

Figure 11.3   Yahoo! search

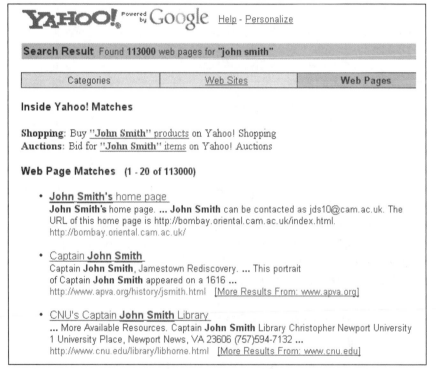

Figure 11.4   Yahoo! results

www.dogpile.com, search a number of major search engine databases at once.)

The resulting listing will, for the most part, include Web pages where your name appears. If there are Web page matches, follow the links to see if they are legitimate: You may be surprised at how often your name or user ID might be out there, as indicated in Figure 11.4.

How does this happen? Programs called "bots" go out and search for new or updated pages, sometimes looking for specific keywords. If a page or site matches the keyword(s), it will be added to the search engine's directory. For instance, if you signed a guestbook at a Web site, there's a good chance it has been picked up by a search engine. If you went to a message board located at the Web site of your favorite TV show and posted a message, it might show up in a search. If you purchased a home or property and your town or state has a Web site, it's likely your purchase is listed on the site. If your employer has a Web site, you may be listed as an employee. Local newspapers are putting their archives online, so if you won an award, got married, had a baby, got a divorce, got into a car accident, or were arrested for DUI, it just might be online.

Besides finding legitimate listings of your name, if someone has put up a Web site about you or forged your name in newsgroups, forums, in personal ads, or somewhere else, there's a good chance you can catch it and get it taken down or removed before any damage is done. If the Web pages you turn up were obviously designed to harass or embarrass you (as was the case with Gerald, who had his name and phone number placed on gay Web sites), then send an e-mail to the site's Webmaster or support person (an e-mail link can be found somewhere on almost any site). Explain that you did not authorize use of your name or information on the site and would like it removed immediately. Most of the time, this will work. If it doesn't, read Chapter 19, "Encryption Made Easy," to find out how to trace the origination of the Web site to the person or company who owns that site.

In Chat Rooms and on Message Boards

If you find that a chat room you frequent or a message board to which you often post suddenly shows messages from you when you're not online, change your user ID immediately. This change is easy to perform in a majority of chat rooms and message board sites. Then alert the Webmaster, moderator, or support person of the chat room/Web site via e-mail that you are no longer posting under your old user ID. Explain to them that someone is impersonating you with certain user IDs and list the one(s) you know about. Ask them to remove these user IDs from the chat room or message board immediately. If that doesn't work, a telephone call almost always seems to do the trick. Although e-mail is the wave of the future, a human voice over the telephone tends to have more impact than an electronically sent message.

Be Alert and Informed

If you don't own a computer and someone is impersonating you online, you probably won't know about it unless a friend or acquaintance mentions something or, even worse, when you start getting phone calls or home deliveries you did not initiate.

Remember Jackie, who supposedly ordered pizzas online? She was able to cancel the order when the pizza parlor called to confirm the order. Then she went a step further. She asked that the pizza parlor send her a copy of the online order placed in her name so that she could find out from where it originated. Jackie asked for help from someone she knew who was Internet-knowledgeable and they were able to track down the order to a particular ISP, which was contacted and informed of the impersonation. Once she provided a notarized statement that she did not open the account used to order those pizzas, the ISP canceled it.

How about Susan, who received phone calls about items "she" offered for sale on a local newspaper's Web site? She was also able to get the information she needed, this time from the Web site owner—the newspaper. She contacted the Maryland State Police Computer Crimes Unit, who took the case from there. The police ultimately tracked down the spoofer to a local library system. The spoofer, an employee at one of the libraries, turned out to be a neighbor of the victim and was getting back at her because she wouldn't carpool with him.

If you begin receiving phone calls or—heaven forbid—find someone knocking on your door claiming to be taking you up on your online offer, don't hang up or slam the door. If you ask for the source of their information, they may be able to pinpoint the Web site, newsgroup, message board, or chat room where they "met" you online. From there, you can contact the Web site or chat room administrator, or go to Google Groups to find out what newsgroup posted the message and from where the message originated. This will allow you to contact the appropriate ISP about resolving the problem.

Some spoofers won't take no for an answer and will open up several e-mail accounts in a victim's name, jumping from one account to the other as the accounts are canceled, or changing a chat room user ID as often as they can. This is when you need to be diligent and continue to report them to the proper ISP, Webmaster, or support folks to get those accounts canceled. If your state has an online harassment or related law, take advantage of it and file a complaint with your local, county, or state police (see www.haltabuse.org/resources/laws for more information).

If the advice I've given in this chapter does not do the trick, and your state doesn't have an applicable law, then it's time to consider hiring a lawyer and filing a civil suit. While most of us would rather avoid this step, spoofing is a serious offense and, unfortunately, there are times when legal action is the only solution.

Endnotes

1. Message Board: Similar to a newsgroup, but located on a Web site; usually message boards are unmoderated, which opens the door for trolls and spoofers.

2. Mailing List: Similar to a newsgroup, but all messages (new ones and replies) are sent to your e-mail inbox. If the mailing list is especially active, this could be as many as 100 messages or more in your e-mail inbox daily.

3. Guestbook: Much like a guestbook at weddings, this is on a person's Web page/site so that a visitor can add a comment about the Web page/site in the guestbook.

4. User ID: Also known as a "nickname," this is your "name" when you go into a chat room.

5. Full Headers: Technical information in the header of e-mail and newsgroup messages; the information is hidden when you receive/send mail.

A Little Harmful Chat

Chat

Real-time or live conversation online. This happens in an online room where anywhere from a few people to a hundred or more congregate; or the conversation can take place one-on-one in what is called a Private Room. People chat about anything and everything, whether or not it has to do with the name of the chat room. Names of chat rooms range from "The TV Room" to "Adults 30+" to "Los Angeles Teens."

IM

Real-time or live chat that's conducted one-on-one rather than in a "room" full of other people.

Marci's Story

Marci, a Massachusetts resident, decided to visit a chat room on a local Web site. A legal secretary, she created the username "legalsec" and began chatting with others in the room. A message popped up from someone named MetalOne:

"I don't like your name, legalsec."

Taken aback, her first reaction was surprise, then anger.

"So what?" she replied.

Responding in kind to rude remarks is a natural reaction but it's the wrong one if you want to avoid trouble in chat rooms, newsgroups, and the like. In Marci's case, it led to big problems. MetalOne began to make it his mission to find out more about her: her real name, where she lived, and her telephone number. That was in the fall of 1998.

In November, he posted her real name, address, and cell phone number in the chat room. Marci reacted angrily, telling MetalOne he had no right to publicize her personal information. He taunted her. She defended herself.

It soon became a tangled web of people from her local area fighting one another. Marci heard from someone else in the chat room that MetalOne's real name was Donnie and he lived at home with his mother, not far from Marci. Without thinking twice, and for revenge, she mentioned in the chat room Donnie's real name and where he lived.

Donnie changed his username to MachismoMan and in March 1999, he posted this in the chat room:

```
Marci, you are a slut, a blowhole—I like
to bother you because it gets me going,
bitch. I'm going to get you.
```

Marci was afraid now. She changed her cell phone number, and then moved to a different apartment in the next town. She made sure her new phone number was unlisted and got Caller ID. She called the police. They told her there wasn't much they could do because it was all happening online.

In April, Donnie, aka MachismoMan, wrote in the chat room:

```
Hey Marci, I am going to kick your teeth
down your f-ing throat, you c-t.
```

Even with this obvious threat of physical harm, the police still wouldn't help her. Marci stopped going to the chat room for a few weeks, but when she returned in early June, Donnie was waiting for her.

```
There's a girl watching for you, Marci.
She's going to beat the crap out of you,
you bitch.
```

Marci knew the police wouldn't help, so she created a new user-name, PrimedUp, and made believe she was someone else. Soon Donnie confided to PrimedUp:

```
Marci is gonna get it, she's going to die.
```

The police finally listened to Marci and began an investigation when she provided them with a copy of this chat room conversation. But it wasn't fast enough for Marci.

Donnie found her new, unpublished phone number and began call-ing her in July. She let the answering machine pick up. He IM'd[1] her, demanding she answer her phone and that she had "two weeks."

"Two weeks to what?" she recalls wondering. "To die? Before he'd come over to my house? Burn it down? What? I was terrified."

He IM'd her again, telling her to watch herself everywhere she went. By then, a court date had been set for August. Marci was count-ing the days, praying nothing would happen to her before then. She had an alarm system installed and went to the pound to adopt a large dog for protection.

The last week of July, Marci answered the phone. It was Donnie.

"I'm your worst nightmare, bitch. I am going to kill you, you c—t."

As the court date came closer, Donnie's harassment increased. He not only IM'd and called her at home, but seemed to magically appear in the chat room every time she logged in.

He wrote in the chat room, "You're all done, Marci. You'll end up in a wooden box and I'll piss on your grave when you're four feet under."

Others in the chat room finally told him to stop threatening Marci. He defiantly wrote back, "NO, she's mine!"

In court, a woman accompanying Donnie admitted he asked her to beat up Marci. Donnie admitted nothing. The case was dismissed.

Angry, Marci went to the District Attorney's office with proof of the threats, both online and offline. In March 2000, the DA filed new charges against Donnie for telephone threats and annoying calls. In court in early May, Donnie finally admitted to what he'd done and was found guilty.

On Memorial Day weekend, Marci looked out her living room win-dow and saw Donnie getting out of his car. She said he looked drunk and had duct tape in one hand and rope in the other. She immediately tripped her alarm, grabbed her dog's collar, and called the police. They were there within minutes and arrested Donnie.

Since then, Marci has moved once again, changed her online account to a different Internet service provider, put her new phone number in another person's name, and doesn't go to chat rooms anymore. She finally won her case in the summer of 2001. Donnie was ordered to pay her more than $20,000 in restitution, but received no jail time.

The Urge to Chat

According to a survey conducted by Pew Internet & American Life,[2] 25 percent of Internet users have participated in chat rooms. That means more than 29 million Americans. Also, men are more likely than women to participate. And chat rooms tend to attract a younger, more ethnic crowd.

Why do people love chat so much? It gives folks the chance to mingle with people they never have to meet face to face (unless they want to). People can talk about everything and anything, whether it's how their day went, what last night's TV show was like, complaints about their boss, or just goofiness. Because chat is immediate and live, people tend to say things they wouldn't normally say to a stranger standing next to them in an elevator or on the street corner. Online chatters tend to show their feelings to the world, and most forget that the world is reading everything they write. Many times what people write can get them in trouble, even though they feel they can remain anonymous when using chat rooms on Web sites such as Yahoo!.

A Matter of Free Speech?

The line between exercising the right to free speech and the harassment of another individual can easily blur. Here's a perfect example: Let's say someone is in a chat room and complains bitterly about their employer. This person is letting off steam and may feel better, but may also be forgetting that there are many people in the room reading the chat.

Now, if one of those lurkers[3] happens to be an assistant to the president of that person's employer and reports that someone is bashing the company online, the chatter could be sued. Often the company involved is small to midsize, and it will subpoena the records from the chat room provider to find out who belongs to that anonymous username before filing a suit. The company doesn't expect to actually file and win the suit, but it hopes to make the person complaining keep quiet—and it usually works.

Even though the U.S. Supreme Court ruled that Internet speech should be accorded the same protection as speech in any other medium, many chat room providers are only too happy to turn over those anonymous identities to anyone who provides a subpoena, often without notifying the owner of the username.

There have been several cases where privacy advocates have supported these anonymous chatters, claiming the subpoenas are illegal, and they've won. So, where do you draw the line between harassment and free speech? The law clearly states that the plaintiff must prove the defendant not only made a false statement but did so maliciously. To do this, the defendant needs to be deposed, but if they're anonymous, that's hard to do. However, if an anonymous chatter is clearly harassing someone else, making threatening statements, posting personal information about the person, following them from chat room to chat room, and e-mailing them, then that should be more than enough to allow chat providers to disclose the anonymous chatter's identity when a subpoena is provided.

When Chatting Becomes Harassment

If you don't believe harassment in chat rooms is a problem, conduct your own experiment. Go online to a chat Web site such as Yahoo! or AOL. Create a female-sounding username, such as MissKitty, then go into any chat room and wait. I guarantee that within minutes someone in that chat room will be asking you questions about where you live, how old you are, if you're single—and sometimes even nastier things. You'll probably be hit with PMs (private messages), which usually pop up in a small, separate window so that chatters can talk one-on-one, and you can bet their chat will not be about the weather.

While you're waiting for the first come-on, take a look at the usernames of the other chatters in the room. Some will be pretty shocking. Many are obviously female or male, and depending on the chat site you're on, if you check their profiles, you'll find that people list far too much personal information in their profiles.

Why would anyone put sensitive personal information online for the whole world to see? It's quite simple: People online forget the world can see the information.

Chat Room Tips

- Don't give out personal information such as your address, telephone number, or work address/ telephone number.

- Never agree to get together with someone you "meet" online without first checking them out to the best of your ability (do an "egosearch" on them); if you do decide to meet, make sure it's in a public place.

- Do not send anyone your photo unless you really trust the person you're sending it to and they agree to send you one also. Make sure the photo is "generic" and not suggestive or inappropriate.

- Do not respond to any messages that in any way make you uncomfortable; your first reaction may be to defend yourself, but it could make the situation worse.

- Don't fill out your chat profile or put in as little information as possible; this is the first place people look for personal information!

If you were at a party chatting with various people and someone came up to you and made rude comments, you'd probably move on to another conversation. If this person continued bothering you, following you from conversation to conversation, and the host (much like a chat room moderator) didn't ask him to leave, it's likely you would leave the party and avoid going to a party there in the future, right?

If that's what you'd do in the real world, wouldn't you act in a similar fashion online? But Internet users return again and again to chat rooms where they have previously encountered problems.

Chat room moderators can help keep out the riffraff, but not all chat rooms are moderated, and some moderators do not deal effectively with problem visitors.

Consider what happened to Annie in Illinois.

"I used to go to a chat room on AOL all the time," Annie says. "Then this group began harassing all the women in the room. We notified AOL on a continual basis for an entire month. Some of the chat room moderators saw what was going on but did nothing. The response was mostly the general form letters from AOL. None of these people were kicked off."

Annie and the others fought back, defending themselves, and telling the harassers to leave them alone. Suddenly, they all received viruses via e-mail, then found their AOL accounts had been hacked and their passwords stolen.

When Annie called AOL and finally talked with a representative there, he chided her for giving out her password. But she hadn't.

Annie and the others began receiving harassing messages via e-mail, IM, and mailing lists, all on or through AOL. They continued to complain to AOL, but nothing was done. Finally, tired of fighting back, they stopped going to the chat room or changed their usernames. Some canceled AOL and got new accounts with other ISPs, and then blocked the harassers' usernames in their chat preferences so that the harassers couldn't get through.

"It's not fair that I had to leave a chat room I really enjoyed going to," Annie says. "These people should have been taken care of when they began harassing us."

Annie was lucky. Her chat harassers were content with online abuse. Sometimes the harassment goes offline.

"A man allegedly from Florida started chatting with one of our students," Steve Thompson, Sexual Assault Coordinator at Central Michigan University, recalls. "After about a month, he showed up at her apartment, talked a bit, and raped her. She came to me for help and we worked with local police to resolve the case."

Central Michigan is just one of the many universities and colleges taking online harassment and stalking-related cases seriously, and educating not only students but faculty, too.

"I began seeing these types of cases in 1996," Thompson says. "Not many, but I've seen them. We do try to address this issue at orientation, but I have a feeling not all students having these problems come to us for help. It's hard to get the word out there that we are here to help."

Angela

Most people are too embarrassed to come forward when they've been harassed in a chat room, mostly due to the stigma chat rooms have—that they're frequented by lonely people looking for romance, which isn't always the case.

Common Chat Terms

Here is a list of some common abbreviations and acronyms you'll come across in chat rooms and elsewhere online. For a complete list, go to the Tech Dictionary at www.techdictionary.com/chat.html.

ADN – Any day now
AAMOF – As a matter of fact
AFAIK – As far as I know
AFK – Away from keyboard
AISI – As I see it
B4N – Bye for now
BAK – Back at keyboard
BBFN or BB4N– Bye bye for now
BRB – Be right back
BTW – By the way
CSG – Chuckle, snicker, grin
CUL8R – See you later
DIY – Do it yourself
F2F – Face to face (or in person)
FOAF – Friend of a friend
FWIW – For what it's worth
FYI – For your information
GMTA – Great minds think alike
HTH – Hope that helps!
IAC – In any case
IIRC – If I remember correctly
IMHO – In my honest opinion
IMO – In my opinion
IRL – In real life
KIT – Keep in touch
LOL – Laughing out loud
MYOB – Mind your own business
NBD – No big deal
OBTW – Oh, by the way
PDS – Please don't shout (when someone types in capital
        letters, that's considered "shouting")
ROTFL – Rolling on the floor laughing
RTBM – Read the bloody manual
SO – Significant other
THX – Thanks
TTFN – Ta ta for now
WB – Welcome back
YMMV – Your mileage may vary

Angela is in her early twenties, pretty, outgoing, and lives in suburban Virginia. She likes to hang out in chat rooms and has made many online friends through chat. One night, Andrew began chatting with her. He was from Rhode Island, friendly, funny, and said he wanted to be online buddies. As their chats continued, he asked her to trust him, and they exchanged photos. A few weeks later, he let her know he thought the relationship had progressed to another level—to boyfriend and girlfriend. Angela was uncomfortable with this and told him she wanted to stay online buddies.

He did not.

Angela e-mailed Andrew and asked him to leave her alone. He wouldn't. She complained to Hotmail, his e-mail provider, and Hotmail quickly canceled the account. Then she got an e-mail from Andrew, who had gotten another Hotmail account:

> oh wow angela how funny you got me locked out of my hotmail account wow baby you're dangerous at least now i have one less account to worry about so thank you for that you hillybilly inbred c—k licker and if you are as f—ing stupid as i think you are you will have this account closed too. so once again big deal i lose one or hundred hotmail accounts i will just get a new one haha so funny you can't stop me i know how to get your e-mail no matter how many times you change it i could make your life hell if i wanted to

A few days later, when Angela didn't respond, he sent her another e-mail, more chilling than the first:

> hey ang get this one closed too while you're at it oh by the way it's amazing what you can find online—credit reports, income tax reports, personal info, ss #, and tons of other stuff to so go and have this hotmail account closed you dumb ass s—t!

Angela went to her local police for help.

192 Net Crimes & Misdemeanors

"They said that most likely they couldn't really do anything," she recalls with a sigh. "And that I should just stay off the computer. They said it was a misdemeanor and Virginia probably wouldn't bring him from Rhode Island for that."

Frustrated, she contacted WHOA[4] for help. WHOA was able to cancel Andrew's free e-mail accounts and advised Angela to change her e-mail account and username again. But Andrew wasn't content with that. He began prowling the chat rooms, first pretending to be her, then asking where she was. Although Angela happened to be in the chat room at the same time he was, he didn't know her new chat name, and she always left the room before he could figure out she was there.

Andrew was banned from several chat rooms but he began getting more usernames and managed to continue to prowl the chat rooms looking for Angela.

He found her new e-mail address and sent her one final message: "It's all a matter of time. I'll be paying you a visit very soon. You're going to die."

WHOA had a contact at the Providence, Rhode Island Police Department, Captain Jack Ryan, to whom WHOA provided all the information from Angela, including Andrew's address and telephone number. When Captain Ryan called Angela, she wasn't too optimistic.

"My first feeling about this was, 'Why am I even trying? He's going to be like the other cops and not help,' but boy was I wrong," Angela says. "In the first five minutes of talking with him, I can't describe how wonderful I felt."

Captain Ryan called Andrew's home and his father answered, claiming Andrew was asleep. Captain Ryan said he'd call back and when he did, suddenly Andrew wasn't there. Captain Ryan told the father what his son had been doing and Andrew came on the phone and admitted to harassing Angela. He then offered to come to the police station.

Later that afternoon, Andrew sat with Captain Ryan at the Providence Police Department and admitted to everything. Andrew turned out to be 24 years old, unemployed, had no driver's license, lived with his father, and never got past the eighth grade. He spent his life online.

"When Captain Ryan told me Andrew said he would stop, the relief that came over me was amazing, too much emotion in fact for me to handle," Angela says. "I can never repay Captain Ryan or WHOA for what they did, but I hope they know they are amazing people who will always hold a very special place in my heart."

When IM Becomes IM Scared

Instant messaging can be fun and more personal than chat. Instead of baring your soul to a roomful of people, you can instant message one person. A small window pops up so you can type your message to them. They reply in the same window. You can chat with only that one person or you can carry on live text conversations with several people at once. But your computer screen will be filled with separate windows for each person you're chatting with—and that can get confusing.

Workplaces commonly use IM programs so that employees can quickly communicate with each other on projects. They get their questions answered quickly this way, something that is especially useful when a company has many offices around the U.S. or the world. IM is making the workplace more efficient.

Cell phones also offer text messaging. You can now send an instant message from your computer to someone's cell phone and vice versa (or you can send messages from phone to phone). This is offered through several IM services, such as Yahoo!, AOL, and MSN. It's wonderful to use if you're on the road and can't carry on a live phone conversation, or if you just want to send a quick message.

Like chat, IM has its own lingo and acronyms. Many of the acronyms for chat (see Common Chat Terms on page 190) are applicable for IM. However, you'll find that most IM'ers shorten words—kind of an IM shorthand, you might say. For example, "How are you?" would become "hru" or "how ru." It can take some getting used to but once you get the hang of it you'll find it rolls right off your fingertips.

But like everything else mentioned in this book, IM can be used for good ... and bad.

Who's Calling?

Marian heard her cell phone beep and knew she'd received a text message. She looked at its tiny screen and almost dropped the phone.

    You should die.

The startling message came from someone with the username of "saintly2004," which wasn't familiar to Marian. Over the course of the next few days, she received more messages—all of them threatening and frightening.

Marian finally contacted her local police department in Saco, Maine, and filed a complaint. The officer who took the case wasn't sure how to handle it and contacted me at WHOA. He told me Marian was a teacher at the local high school and couldn't imagine who would be doing this to her.

I took it from there. I added saintly2004 to my AOL IM buddy list. Sure enough, that night in July 2004, saintly2004 IM'd me.

```
Nm  u  who  dis?
```

I decided that since this person initiated the conversation, I'd try to see how much information I could gather. I was off to the races! Following is how the conversation went—grammar, acronyms, and all. (This is really how most teens talk via IM; only names and other personal identifiers have been changed.)

```
Me: Dis is sarah.
Saintly2004: sarah?
Me: From Saco
Saintly2004: ummm
Saintly2004: drawin a blank here
Me: Geez. Now I feel stoopid.
Me: You *r* the guy from Maine, right?
Saintly2004: yaaa
Saintly2004: i'm from Maine yes
Me: I met u last week. U gave me your IM.
     Too much booze I guess ;-)
Saintly2004: where'd we meet?
Me: At OOB. One of the bars. Hmm. I think
     the one near the pier.
Saintly2004: ooo um well I'm only 16
Saintly2004: lol
Saintly2004: maybe you mean my bro
Saintly2004: lol
Saintly2004: wait do u kno (name of his
     brother)?
Me: First name yes, last name no.
Saintly2004: lol was his name chris
Me: I hate when dudes play me like that.
Saintly2004: noo he doesn't play trust me
```

```
Saintly2004: he prolly just gave u the
             wrong one on accident
Me: Ya no, This is why we chix hate men.
    LOL
Saintly2004: wats ur lastt name I'll ask
             him bout u
Me: r u chris then?
Saintly2004: No I'm his bro
Me: Needham
Saintly2004: sarah needham
Me: Nice 2 meetcha. You?
Saintly2004: i'm mikey
Saintly2004: mikey walker
Me: Hey mikey, I'm really sorry about
    this
Saintly2004: hey its fine
Saintly2004: u seem like a nice girl
Me: Tell him to im me sometime
Saintly2004: ok I will
Me: And I'll keep you on my bl
Saintly2004: ok same here
Saintly2004: how old ru?
Me: 21
Me: No, no 19
Saintly2004: lol fake ID?
Me: Yep Don't tell
Saintly2004: lol I won't tell
Saintly2004: u have a pic?
Me: I'll send 1 if u give me your e-mail
Saintly2004: saintly2004@oohay.com
Me: Here's mine
Saintly2004: ok kool
Me: Bye
Saintly2004: cya
```

In less than 10 minutes I not only had his full name but his e-mail address as well. I did a quick Web search and found Mikey Walker was a sophomore at a high school in Saco and was on two sports teams. His brother, Chris, was listed as having graduated a couple of years earlier. A further search found Chris's home address listed in a neighboring town.

I called the officer back and gave him all the information, and he promised to call me back. He did, within a day. It turned out Mikey was one of Marian's students. She had given him a failing grade and he had decided to take revenge. In turn, what he now received was a month's suspension from school and two months of detention.

Five Quick IM Tips & Tricks

1. Provide as little information as possible when opening an account. Just like chat, you don't need to fill in your hobbies, the names of everyone in your family, and so forth. Always fill in only what is required (usually this is denoted in the application process) or as little as possible. Then submit that information to see what is really needed to open an account. IM programs want you to describe yourself so that others searching for Buddies can find you based on your interests, where you live, and other factors. But you'd be surprised by how little is indeed required.

2. Always check all of your preferences and options before starting the program or beginning to send IMs to others. The default is that everyone who has an account with the same IM service will easily be able to find you.

3. If someone harasses you, you receive spam via IM, or someone sends you a link to a Web site you wouldn't normally go to (such as a pornographic one), add them to your Blocked or Ignore list.

4. Never send confidential information such as credit card numbers or SSNs via IM.

5. Be wary of accepting downloads of graphics, audio, or video files unless you are positive the person sending them to you is someone you know and trust. Even so, always run the downloaded files through your anti-virus program before opening or viewing them.

Using IM and Chat Safely

Whether you are in a chat room or using IM, you should always check to see what options and preferences are available and take advantage of them. For example, the default for most IM programs is that anyone who has a similar program can contact you from anywhere in the world. I'll show you how to use your chat or IM program safely.

Following are instructions for checking/changing preferences in some popular chat and IM programs.

IM Privacy Options

AIM (AOL Instant Messenger)

You do not need to be an AOL member/customer to use AIM. It is probably the most popular IM program and can be downloaded from many Web sites, including www.aim.com.

1. Click on My AIM, Edit Options, then Edit Preferences (shortcut is the F3 key).

2. In the Category frame, click on Privacy (see Figure 12.1).

3. Under Who Can Contact Me, select Allow Only Users On My Buddy List.

4. Under Allow Users Who Know My E-mail Address ..., select Nothing About Me.

5. Go through the other categories to make sure all the default sections are what you really want.

6. Click on the OK button on the bottom before continuing so that the changes can take place.

MSN Messenger

As with AIM, you don't need to have MSN as your Internet service to use this IM program; it comes with the latest version of Windows or can be downloaded at messenger.msn.com.

1. Click on Tools in the toolbar, then Options. A separate window pops up with several tabs.

2. Click on the Privacy tab (see Figure 12.2). This is where you can add or block people.

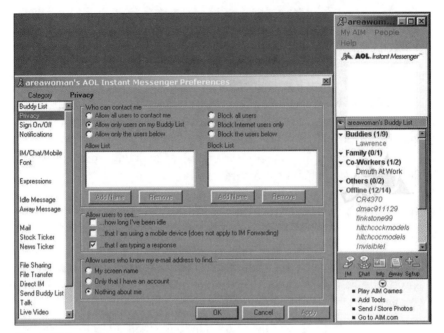

Figure 12.1   AIM privacy options

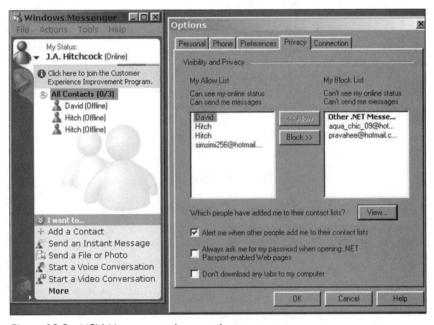

Figure 12.2   MSN Messenger privacy options

3. Go through the other tabs to make sure the default selections are what you want.

4. Click on the OK button on the bottom before continuing so that the changes can take place.

Yahoo! Messenger

You need to open a Yahoo! account to use this IM program, but Yahoo! offers many things once you do open an account—from free e-mail to chat to shopping and more.

1. Click on Login in the toolbar, then Privacy Settings. This brings up a separate window with Category selections on the left; Privacy should already be selected.

2. In the window on the right, select Ignore Anyone Who Is Not On My Messenger List (see Figure 12.3).

3. Select (check) Login As Invisible; this allows you to login without anyone knowing except users you decide to IM.

4. Under When People See My ID on Yahoo! Web Sites, select Do Not Allow Other Users to See Me Online and Contact Me.

5. Check the other options available in this category.

6. Go through the other categories to make sure the default selections are what you want.

7. Click on the OK button on the bottom before continuing so that the changes can take place.

ICQ (IM Program)

This IM program is available at www.icq.com.

1. Click on the Main graphic on the bottom, then Preferences and Security (see Figure 12.4).

2. Under Security on the left, select General.

3. Under Contact List Authorization, select My Authorization Is Required Before Users Add Me to Their Contact List.

4. Under Web Aware, deselect (uncheck) Allow Others to View My Online/Offline Status from the Web.

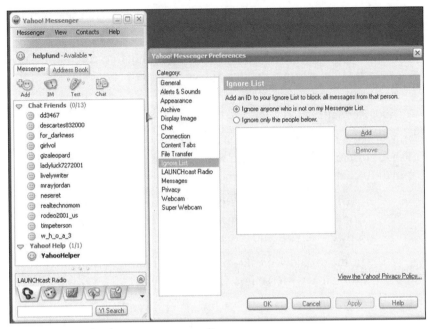

Figure 12.3   Yahoo! Messenger ignore list

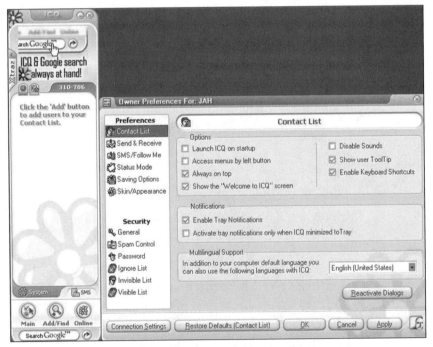

Figure 12.4   ICQ IM owner preferences

5. Under Security Level, select the Medium Level as recommended or select the one you are most comfortable with.

6. Click on Spam Control in the left panel.

7. Under Accepting Messages, select (check) Accept Messages Only From Those On My Contact List.

8. Unless you feel otherwise, deselect (uncheck) the World Wide Pager Messages and Email Express Messages selections.

9. Click on Ignore List in the left panel; this is where you can add users who are bothering you or ones you don't want to have contact with.

10. Click the Apply button on the bottom before continuing so that the changes can take place.

If you are still worried about security and privacy, consider these two options:

GAIM
http://sgaim.sourceforge.net
This looks a lot like AIM and is easy to use but it is more secure and it is compatible with AIM, ICQ, MSN Messenger, Yahoo!, IRC, Jabber, and other IM programs.

Jabber
www.jabber.org
Jabber uses encryption software to make all the IMs you send and receive secure and private.

Chat Privacy Options

Yahoo! Chat

1. When you go into the chat room of your choice, click on the pencil graphic in the toolbar just above the text box (see Figure 12.5).

2. Click on the Preferences you want. It's highly recommended to check the boxes next to Ignore Invitations to Join a Room and Ignore Private Messages from Strangers.

3. Go back to the main chat window and right-click on your username. A small window pops up.

4. Check the Preferences. If you filled out your profile, click on Edit Your Profile and change or delete any information that someone could use against you, such as your real name, your age, location, and personal Web page. If you clicked on female, change it to male to be safe.

5. If anyone bothers you in a chat room, right-click on their username, then click on Ignore Permanently so you will no longer see that chatter in the chat room, and/or check the box next to Ignore.

6. If someone continues to bother you by signing on under a different username, contact chat-abuse@yahoo.com or fill out Yahoo!'s feedback form (http://add.yahoo.com/fast/help/chat/cgi_abuse).

CompuServe Chat Preferences

1. Choose the chat room of your choice, then click on the Options tab, as shown in Figure 12.6. There are boxes that have been prechecked. Make sure the only ones checked are:

   • Accept incoming text styles.

   • Record room transcript. (Click on the Browse button to see which folder the log file is in for future reference.)

   • Record group transcript (same as previous bullet point).

   • Track member actions. (This brings up a separate window so that you can see who's going to what rooms; click this only if you're already being harassed and need to keep track of the harasser. This pop-up window stays up even when you leave chat, so it can become annoying.)

2. If anyone bothers you in a chat room, click on the Members tab, highlight the name, and click on Ignore so that chatter won't appear in any chat room you go into. You can also do the same thing once you enter a chat room.

3. Click on Enter or Eavesdrop. If you're new to the room or chatting in general, Eavesdrop is the best choice so that you can "lurk" and get to know the room before chatting.

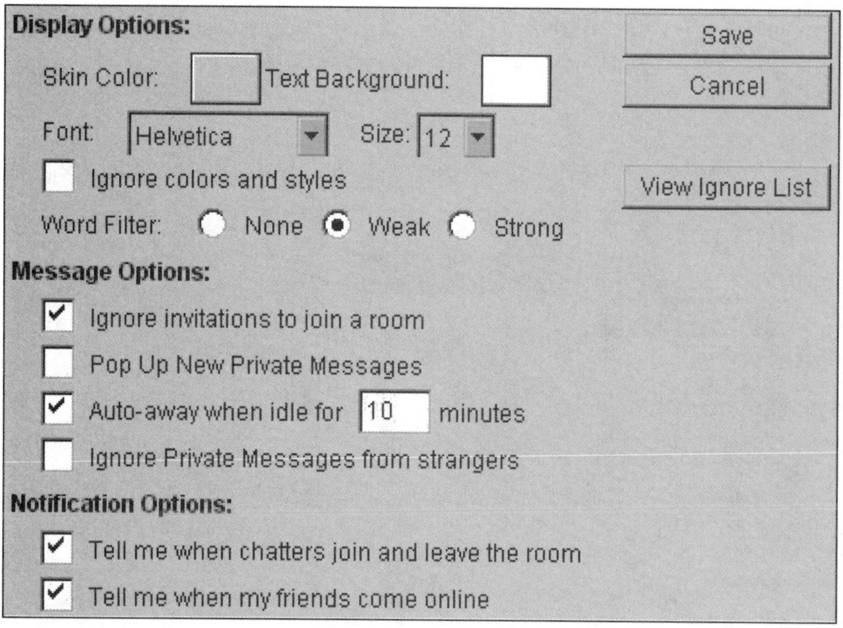

Display Options:

Skin Color: Text Background:

Font: Helvetica ▼   Size: 12 ▼

☐ Ignore colors and styles

Word Filter: ○ None ● Weak ○ Strong

Save

Cancel

View Ignore List

Message Options:

☑ Ignore invitations to join a room

☐ Pop Up New Private Messages

☑ Auto-away when idle for 10 minutes

☐ Ignore Private Messages from strangers

Notification Options:

☑ Tell me when chatters join and leave the room

☑ Tell me when my friends come online

Figure 12.5 Yahoo! Chat display options

ICQ Chat

1. Click on the System Notice button in the ICQ Window and select History & OutBox or double-click on System Notice, click on My ICQ and select History, then select History & OutBox.

2. Click the System tab to display a list of events received.

3. Click the OutBox tab to show the events that you sent (see Figure 12.7). Events are stored in the OutBox until you connect to an ICQ server and, if necessary, until the recipient goes online.

4. Double-click on a message to get a dialog to display the contents of that message.

5. Right-click on System Message for options regarding the selected message.

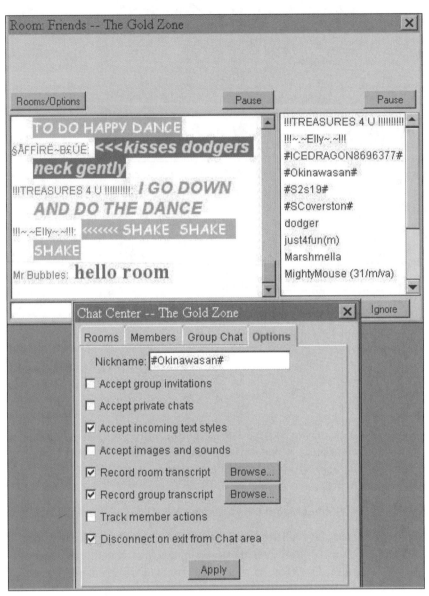

Figure 12.6   CompuServe Chat options

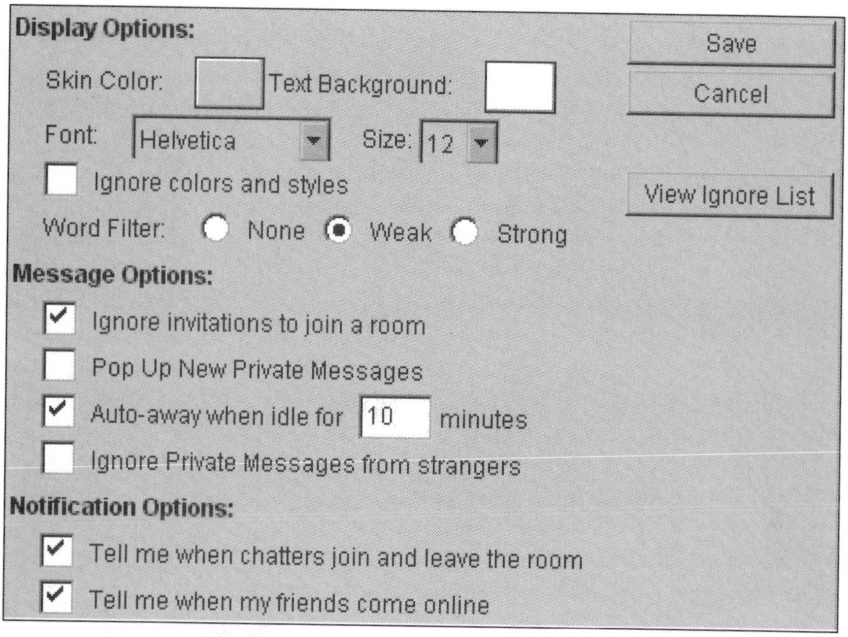

Figure 12.7   ICQ Chat security options

Endnotes

1. IM: Instant message, similar to chat except the conversation is one-on-one instead of in a room with many other people; popular IM programs include AIM (AOL Instant Messenger), ICQ, and Yahoo! Messenger.

2. America's Online Pursuits, May 30, 2004, www.pewinternet.org/pdfs/PIP_Online_Pursuits_Final.PDF

3. Lurker/Lurking: Someone who goes to a newsgroup or chat room and reads what's going on but does not participate in the discussion.

4. WHOA (Working to Halt Online Abuse): An online safety organization that helps adult victims of online harassment and cyberstalking.

Lookin' for Love in All the Online Places

In the past, singles met available dating partners mainly at social events and through introductions by mutual acquaintances, but the Internet has opened up a whole new world of possibilities. Today, with seemingly endless opportunities for making a good match online, the potential for trouble is also on the rise. Online personal ads, dating services, and chat room romances can and do lead to deception, violence, and—in rare cases—even death.

Michael Halloway of Kentucky was sentenced to life for murdering a woman he met on the Internet. Stacy Dodson would drive to Louisville to meet Halloway and in October 2001, he kidnapped her at gunpoint, put her in the trunk of his car, then drove to a local park where he shot and killed her. His motive: simple larceny.

William Miller of Missouri met Joann Brown in a chat room. She went to live with him in 1998 and a few months later he killed her, put her in a well, and filled it with cement. Two weeks later he called the authorities, claiming the shooting was an accident. He's currently serving a 25-year sentence.

Of course, these are worst-case scenarios. Episodes of online dating gone wrong typically lead to disappointment, frustration, anger, and occasionally concerns about one's safety, with relatively few resulting in loss of life. Still, it can happen.

Personal Ads

Personal ads can be great for the individual who wants to meet someone online, but they are sometimes misused, typically with revenge as the motive. The way it works is that the vengeful party places an ad in the other person's name, including a provocative "profile" along with personal information like a home phone number and address. This can be very dangerous if the wrong person reads the ad.

"A woman, the ex-wife of a friend of my brother, decided to harass me by making up a profile using my name in the Yahoo! Personals," Anita says. "Why she did this, I still don't know. She solicited men to 'fantasy rape' me and gave out my phone number and address. As a result, I had over 400 men approach me. It was pure terror."

Yahoo! was cooperative. It canceled the account in question and held all the information regarding it for subpoena. But local police claimed they couldn't do anything for Anita even though she was put in harm's way.

"What if one of those men tried to rape me?" Anita says. "I ended up confronting this woman, telling her that Yahoo! had all the evidence and if she didn't stop I'd sue her. She stopped."

Marie started receiving phone calls asking about a personal ad she'd supposedly placed on Yahoo!. "I had no idea what they were talking about," Marie recalls. "I checked Yahoo! Personals and sure enough, there was an ad placed about me. It listed my name, that I was looking for a 'bisexual female,' and it also listed my home and cell phone numbers."

Marie received phone calls about this ad for days and she became stressed over it, not to mention humiliated. She finally changed her home and cell phone numbers and made sure neither was publicly listed. She had to contact Yahoo! several times before the ad was pulled. She never found out who placed it.

What happened to Sue was a little different. She began receiving e-mail from people who claimed they'd heard about her through someone else. One of the messages read:

```
We received your name from someone via
yahoo personals listing and were told that
we should contact you. We have no idea if
this contact was being straight with us but
we were told that you are exactly what we are
looking for. We don't want to go into more
detail yet until we hear back from you and
find out if this is for real. You can look
up our ad/profile on yahoo (bbvelvet69). If
this person was not being sincere we apol-
ogize for any inconvenience. Hope you will
set us straight either way.
```

Another read:

> Hey there. Glad to hear your very horny.
> Did you see my ad on Excite or did I reply
> to one of yours? I'm rather horny as usual
> myself. (-: Maybe you could help me out
> with that..mmmmmm

And yet another read:

> I was given your e-mail by
> seegulred@yahoo.com. I am a married man
> 6' 4" 230 lbs, blonde hair, green eyes, and
> I live in Roanoke. I'm in need of an excit-
> ing sexual relationship. He said that you
> are very sexual and that is something I am
> looking for. I am 27 years old. So do you
> think you would be interested in getting
> with me sometime? Please e-mail me back and
> tell me what you look like.

Naturally, Sue was very upset. She answered the e-mails explaining she was not interested and had no idea who seegulred was. She
asked for any information they could provide and one of them sent
Sue the following, which she had purportedly posted:

> If you want a nurse that will do any-
> thing, contact sueoromo@yahoo.com she will
> do anything, and likes it all. Her profile
> is earthpiggy.

Sue was flabbergasted to learn that, in order to impersonate and
harass her, someone had opened an account at Yahoo! under the
name "earthpiggy" and sent other Yahoo! members e-mail messages
encouraging them to contact her. Sue requested that Yahoo! remove
the earthpiggy account, as well as the seegulred account that was
being used to e-mail inflammatory comments as well as her personal contact information. While both accounts were promptly canceled, Sue remains in the dark about who perpetrated the hoax. She
hasn't had any problems since, but will probably always remain on
her guard.

Through no fault of its own, Yahoo! seems to be a magnet for people bent on harassment. Such people may choose Yahoo! because (1) e-mail accounts are freely available, and (2) it offers a variety of other free services including chat, personals, clubs, and groups. Yahoo!'s dominance as one of the most popular sites on the Internet, attracting millions of users, makes it an obvious choice for a broad spectrum of Web users including those with bad intentions.

It is gratifying to know that Yahoo! is quick to act when a situation like Sue's occurs. This helps Yahoo! keep its reputation as one of the most popular sites on the Web.

Dealing with Fraudulent Personal Ads

There's no way to know if someone has placed a personal ad in your name until you begin receiving phone calls, e-mails, or—heaven forbid—you get an unwanted knock on your door. If you are approached, I recommend these simple steps:

1. Try to remain calm and ask the person who has contacted you where he/she saw the ad.

2. If possible, get a URL for the offending Web page; go to the page and print out several copies of the ad to keep as evidence.

3. Contact the Web host of the page/site where the ad was placed and ask that the ad be removed.

4. If the Web host refuses to remove the ad, contact your local police and ask them to intervene on your behalf to get the ad removed (having the URL and printout of the ad will come in handy). Assuming the host agrees, this usually does the trick.

5. Contact an online organization, such as WHOA or CyberAngels, for help.

6. Consider changing your e-mail address with your ISP. If you do, share your new e-mail address only with people you know and trust; open a free e-mail account on a Web site such as Hotmail or Yahoo! and use that for general e-mail.

Not all Yahoo! dating stories are bad, of course. Often, connecting online leads to romance and even true love. Mary and Sam met in a Yahoo! chat room, though neither was looking for a date at the time.

"I was new to computers and to Yahoo!," Mary, a teacher, recalls. "One evening after school, I was playing around in Yahoo! and accidentally found myself in a chat room called the Millionaires Club. Now, I would have immediately backed out of the chat room except I started reading what these people were saying and it was so hysterical that I was rolling out of my chair in laughter."

After about an hour, Mary decided to grade some papers so she turned off her computer after noting a couple of the chatters' screen names. A few evenings later, she spent two hours looking for the same chat room to get another good laugh. She found it and started reading the chat but did not see any familiar screen names.

When she finally recognized the screen name of a chatter entering the room, Mary sent a private message (so that the rest of the chatters wouldn't see it) to ask if one of the other chatters she'd previously encountered had been in the chat room that evening. The reply indicated that the chatter had been a lurker like Mary and that he also thought the room was a hoot to hang out in, but he didn't know if that certain chatter had shown up.

Mary recalls: "I replied in kind to say that reading between the lines was fun but that if anyone in that room was really a millionaire they would be on a yacht sipping drinks with little umbrellas served by a guy named Raoul—and not in a Yahoo! chat room. I got back a reply with a bunch of ha-ha's and a serious note asking if he could e-mail me privately about a security issue."

Mary said yes and soon received a friendly e-mail from the chatter, who gave his real name: Sam. She replied in kind. Then Sam gently suggested that she change her screen name from her real name to a fake one. He told Mary he was the head of computer security at a bank, and thus had some experience with these types of privacy issues. He gave her the telephone number of the human resources department at the bank so she could verify his employment.

Sam told her it was not safe in his opinion for a single woman or, in fact, any woman to use her real name on the Internet. Mary took his advice and subsequently e-mailed him her new username at Yahoo! After that, they started e-mailing regularly, writing about her teaching, his work, their kids, and so on. "It was all just casual conversation for the most part," Mary says.

Eventually, Mary felt comfortable enough with Sam to share more personal details about herself and her religious beliefs. She waited anxiously for his reply. When she got it, she found they shared the same interests. She was ecstatic.

"From then on he called almost every night," Mary recalls. "After about two months of phoning and more e-mails, I decided that I really liked him."

In 1998, Mary and Sam were married. On the question of whether Sam was really a millionaire—considering the chat room she met him in—Mary winks and coyly says, "That online encounter changed my life for the better and forever. I have been laughing ever since."

Online Dating Resources

There are hundreds of online dating sites available—too many to list here—but following is a sampling of some popular ones. To find additional sites, try doing a search for "online dating" in your favorite search engine, adding other keywords if you have special dating interests. There are any number of specialized dating sites, for instance, gothicmatch.com, veggiedate.com, and millionairematch.com.

Date Seeker
www.dateseeker.net
This site compares the major online dating sites to help you find the one that fits you best. It also offers dating tips and shows you how to write a good profile.

Match.com
www.match.com
One of the oldest dating sites (founded in 1995), Match.com claims that 49 percent of online users look for love online rather than offline.[1] The site offers three-day free trials to e-mail other members, after which you can sign up for package rates in three-, six-, and 12-month increments.

Cupid.com
www.cupid.com
Cupid.com is known for its advertising campaign, which it claims attracts more new members than any other comparable site. It offers a free "basic" membership that allows you to place a personal ad/

profile with photo, send and receive "Eye Contacts" (to let someone know you're interested), and reply to a member who contacts you. Full-fledged memberships are available in one-, three-, six-, and 12-month increments.

eHarmony
www.eharmony.com
You fill out a personality profile and the service "scientifically" selects the best matches for you (see Figure 13.1). According to Marilyn Warren of eHarmony, membership includes more women than men but the gap is narrowing; more than 10 percent of members are over age 55. This is the only dating site I'm aware of that boasts a team of PhD psychologists who conduct follow-up research into the quality of the relationships that result. It also charges more than most other sites, starting at $49.95 for a one-month subscription. eHarmony claims more than 6,000 marriages to its credit since 2001.

e|Harmony®

WHY EHARMONY WORKS   TAKE OUR TOUR   LOGIN

**when you're ready to
find the love of your life.**

See why eHarmony.com is the fastest growing relationship site on the web. Take the eHarmony Personality Profile and get instant, objective feedback on yourself and how you relate to others. The eHarmony Personality Profile begins the exciting journey toward finding your true love.

Figure 13.1 eHarmony

Date.com

http://uk.date.com

One of many dating sites in the United Kingdom, uk.date.com has been around since 1997. Membership starts at $24.95/month. It claims to have more than 2 million members worldwide.

True.com

www.true.com

More than 90 percent of women said they'd feel better if members of online dating sites were pre-screened.[2] All members of True.com go through criminal background and marital screening checks (see Figure 13.2). In fact, when you log into their Web site a warning appears:

> If you are married and posing as single, be aware that you could be guilty of fraud and subject to civil and criminal penalties under federal and state law. For each offense, Title 18, Section 1343 of the U.S. Code authorizes fines of up to $250,000 and jail sentences of up to five years.[3] True.com reserves the right to report violators to law enforcement authorities and seek prosecution or civil redress to the fullest extent of the law. If you are married, please close your browser.

That may sound intimidating, but if you have nothing to hide—no problem!

Senior FriendFinder

http://seniorfriendfinder.com

This is not the only dating site for senior citizens but is one of the best known. It offers a free standard membership and is for those who are looking for friends or serious relationships and not merely flings (see Figure 13.3). The site does not tolerate verbal abuse or harassment and will block anyone who doesn't follow the rules. According to Peggy Pendergast of Senior FriendFinder, the average age of members is 52.14. The site offers "niche" dating options for specific cultures and religions, for example, asianfriendfinder.com and jewishfriendfinder.com.

Figure 13.2   True.com

Figure 13.3   Senior FriendFinder

Yahoo! Personals
http://personals.yahoo.com

Fast, free, fun. Because it is free, however, there is a greater chance you'll encounter someone who is not as reputable as his or her profile suggests. Adhere to the dating tips in this chapter, look at profiles with good quality photos only, and be sure to get all your questions answered satisfactorily before meeting anyone in person.

Not OK in the U.K.

Some people who try online dating services swear by them. Others are not so keen. But it's pretty much the same with offline dating services, isn't it? Sometimes a person will find the love of his or her life, and sometimes just an interesting person to go out and have a good time with.

Or sometimes a person has a truly bad experience.

Jennifer met Mike through an Internet dating/friendship site in May 2002. They exchanged several e-mails before arranging to meet at a local pub in London. As with all new encounters, especially a "blind date" such as this, things were a little awkward at first. But they hit it off and started to see each other regularly.

"He was a nice, friendly guy and we got on well," Jennifer says. "We did not have an enormous amount in common but it became a comfortable relationship."

In October, Jennifer and a few of her girlfriends went to Kenya on a vacation she had planned before meeting Mike. She tried to e-mail him when she could, but Internet access wasn't always available or reliable. When she returned, Mike did not seem to trust her. He began questioning who she was talking with, where she was going when she went out without him, and so on. Troubled by his increasing possessiveness, Jennifer split up with him in November, six months after they'd met online.

It didn't end there. The next two months consisted of giving it another try, breaking up again, and trying yet again. He continued to use online dating services, even during the times when their on-again/off-again relationship was "on," and that bothered Jennifer.

"I had been fond of this man and it hurt to see him chasing other women," she says with a sigh. "He made it clear, though, that he found it unacceptable for me to do the same."

Each time they broke up, Mike would send her nasty e-mails and go into angry tirades on the phone. Finally, she could take no more, and decided to end the relationship permanently in January 2003.

Although Mike started up again with the derogatory calls and e-mail messages, Jennifer ignored him. He continued to use the online dating services, and on one of them she encountered a statement in his profile that disturbed her. It went something like, "My last girlfriend dumped me because I am about to be bereaved." She called and asked him to remove the sentence. Instead, he changed it to something even more disturbing and ignored her subsequent requests to remove it.

Jennifer decided to try to put the situation behind her and start dating again. She updated her profile on the dating Web site where she and Mike had met. When he saw it, he began to heap even more abuse on her through his profile. Next, he copied her profile, posed as her, and studied the profiles of men who had been in touch with her. (The dating site they used allowed users to monitor access to their personal profiles.)

Jennifer decided to create a new profile with a new username. Soon, however, she began to notice odd things happening. Someone would add her to his "favorites" list but when she went to view the individual's profile, it would be gone. Once, when she changed the wording on her new profile, she checked out Mike's profile and noticed that he had changed his wording as well. It was word-for-word the same as hers. She received e-mails from addresses she didn't recognize, but which she felt sure were from Mike. Although they weren't threatening, they indicated the sender or senders knew more about her than any stranger could.

"I felt that my every move on the Internet was being watched," Jennifer recalls. "I felt threatened and harassed by this man and simply wanted him to leave me alone."

Jennifer eventually removed her profile and changed her e-mail address and telephone number. A mutual friend of theirs was a police officer and she explained to him what had been going on and asked for help. This antagonized Mike. When she checked his profile, it was abusive toward her again, with such comments as:

> "Unfortunately I have been unlucky enough to have known a truly evil woman and she has been reported to the police."
>
> "An utter twat has reacted rather viciously to my accidental visit."
>
> "Only those who have been told tales behind my back will know who someone is."

He accessed her Hotmail e-mail account (by guessing the correct answer to the "secret question" required to retrieve the user password), changed her password, and began e-mailing people she knew, pretending to be her. Not until the police had issued him a warning did the e-mails stop.

Online Dating Safety Tips

1. If there's something in a profile that concerns you, raises a red flag, or just doesn't match up with what you're looking for, move on.

2. When you find an interesting profile, take your time e-mailing back and forth, asking the questions that are important to you before exchanging telephone numbers or making plans to meet in person.

3. "Google"[4] the person you're interested in. Googling can offer important clues to what an individual is like, especially if he or she has a personal or professional Web site or has posted or been profiled on the Web. You may discover contradictions to what you've been told. If you want to be sure you're not corresponding with a married person, stick with dating services like True.com that conduct marital screenings.

4. Once you've decided to meet for the first time, do so in a public place and don't make it dinner (too intimate). Try lunch, coffee, a local fair, festival, or some similarly casual venue where you know other people will be present. Arrange to meet there; do not pick up your date or agree to be picked up. If an unpleasant date follows up afterward asking to meet again, decline by e-mail or phone, stating firmly yet politely that you are not interested.

5. Trust your instincts. If something feels wrong, don't pursue the relationship.

A year later, Jennifer decided to take a stab at online dating again and put up a new profile. So far, so good. Mike hasn't reappeared and she is hopeful that she may yet find the man of her dreams online.

When Trust Turns to Terror

It had been 12 years since Kay had divorced her abusive ex-husband and she finally felt she was ready to try to find love again. A middle-aged Christian living in Texas, Kay decided to take a chance with online dating and joined AmericanSingles.com.

She soon began corresponding with a man who lived in another state, who we'll call Mark. They progressed to exchanging telephone numbers and had numerous conversations over the next several months. When their talk eventually turned to the topic of marriage, Kay was ecstatic with joy. Mark invited her to visit him at his expense, and she was comfortable enough with their relationship to accept his offer, but on her terms. She made it clear she did not believe in having sex out of wedlock and he promised to honor her feelings.

Kay arrived at the airport and Mark appeared to be just as he seemed online and over the phone—a caring, funny, nice guy. However, as they drove to his house, which was a couple of hours from the airport, she began to feel uneasy. He had always been a gentleman when they communicated, but in the car he began to make raunchy and derogatory comments. By the time she realized she'd made a mistake, she knew he was not going to let her leave without a struggle. She feared for her life.

For two weeks she was his hostage. He raped her twice, causing physical injury. She wasn't allowed out of his sight, even when using the bathroom. If she made a phone call, it was in his presence so that he could monitor everything she said. As she tried to formulate an escape plan, she felt her only hope was to pretend she enjoyed being with him and wanted to marry him. Once she felt he had fallen for this, she told him she had to return home to tie up some loose ends before the wedding. He agreed.

Kay flew home, moved, changed her phone number to an unlisted one, and sent one letter to him requesting that he stop contacting her. She breathed a sigh of relief when she received no reply. That relief was short lived, however, when her son began receiving phone calls from Mark, who threatened him and his family, as well as Kay, if the son would not tell Mark where Kay was.

"He called my work identifying himself as 'FBI agent Williams' and threatened the person who answered the phone that he would be in this area immediately to talk with me," Kay says worriedly. "Of course she denied that I work there. It is driving me nuts, but still, so far as I know, he does not know exactly where I am."

Because of what happened to her, Kay became a proponent of online dating legislation that would require all dating Web sites to disclose whether or not they do criminal background checks on members. She isn't alone in supporting this legislation. Herb Vest, founder of True.com (a dating site that does conduct criminal background checks), has also gotten involved.

"Protecting individuals from crime is a passion of mine," Vest says. "My father was senselessly murdered, so I know firsthand the impact of violent crime on a family. Therefore, I want to do everything I can to protect citizens from that pain. I know criminal background screening works as a first layer of protection in the online dating environment."

This is where Rapsheets.com comes in. Co-founded by Edgar Rains in 2002, Rapsheets.com was a spin-off from another enterprise he'd started in 1995. "At that point (2002), we housed the world's largest privately held database of criminal records," according to Rains.

Today, Rapsheets.com conducts criminal background checks in 47 states and Washington, DC. It boasts on its Web site:

> Our National Criminal Index, covering more than 170 million criminal records from the vast majority of America's population centers, can turn up a person's criminal records in states or counties that might be excluded from an in-person, courthouse check.

When True.com became a customer of Rapsheets.com in 2003, Rains advised them of the legislative issues pertaining to online dating. Since that time, True.com's research (www.true.com/saferdating/true_safer_surveys_all.asp) has conducted surveys to see how the general public feels about this. Many problems can be avoided through the use of criminal background checks, though they are not foolproof. True.com couples criminal background checks with safer dating tips and Herb Vest wishes other online dating sites would all do the same. Why? Because it works.

"On average, we reject 5 percent of individuals per month for felony convictions," Vest says. "During a 15-month period in Texas alone, we have denied more than 500 individuals from communicating with other members due to entering incorrect or false data, being married, or being a felon. Of that 500, 134 were convicted felons, with crimes ranging from homicides to sexual assaults, injuries to children, aggravated assaults, organized crime, stalking, and terrorist threats. In Florida, some 497 individuals were rejected from True.com's system during a four-month period for material misrepresentations, felony, and sexual offense convictions."

Rapsheets.com's Rains concurs. "I do think criminal background checks of online dating subscribers are worthwhile when done through reliable databases. With the dramatic expansion of Internet commerce, we are seeing a growing, and I believe increasingly dangerous, disconnect between customers and the companies providing goods and services to those customers via the Web. In the matter of online dating, this is an especially important point because of the very real peril of serious personal injury or death to unwary subscribers."

But Rains warns that there are limitations to these background checks. "No database is perfect. And even if one had access to a database containing every arrest record, every conviction record, and every jail record in the U.S. (and no one does), no screening is foolproof. For example, there is a huge misconception among legislators, law enforcement, and the general public that the FBI database contains comprehensive records. This is simply not the case. In fact, there are several commercial databases of criminal records containing not only far more records in absolute numbers, but more timely and accurate information, as well. So, I think background checks are a good idea, but I advise caution nevertheless."

Bernice Burns, for one, is all for criminal background checks at online dating sites. She dated a man she met offline and discovered too late he had a violent criminal background. When she decided she was ready to give dating another try, she put a profile on more than a half a dozen Web sites, including True.com, eHarmony, BBW Finder (Big Beautiful Woman Finder), Large Friends, and Yahoo!.

"True.com was the last site I joined. Then the warning popped up that said they did background checks," Bernice says. "It made me start thinking about whether the other sites did these background checks. I went back to all of them and contacted each site and began asking questions. Most did not even reply!"

Since then, she's stayed with True.com, still looking for the love of her life.

Maybe All You Need Is a Good Coach

Melanie Dodson put a concerted effort into online dating. She began in the summer of 2001 and after several months of using various sites and talking to dozens of men, she made one particularly strong connection. That relationship lasted for one and a half years. When it ended, she jumped right back into online dating, meeting many interesting men, some of whom have become good friends.

One thing Melanie noticed during her online dating foray was that many individuals had trouble effectively presenting themselves—not only in their online profiles, but also during e-mail correspondence. She found that others were as wary of online dating as she was enthusiastic about it. She soon found herself giving single friends advice on such matters as how to select the right online dating site and how to write a compelling (yet honest) profile. Before long they were referring to her as the "poster child for Internet dating."

This gave Melanie an idea that eventually grew into "The Internet Dating Coach," a company she runs online at www.theinternet datingcoach.com. She offers seminars and workshops, as well as individual coaching. Before you start laughing (if you haven't already), think about it—how many of you single folks can call yourself a good dater?

"My clients are generally looking for a long-term, monogamous relationship," Melanie says. "So my goal is to help them optimize their experience on dating sites. 'The Beginners Coaching Special' has clients delve deep into who they are and what they seek in a mate and relationship. I pose to them a series of thought-provoking questions which will not only give me the information I need so that I can best assist them, but generally serves to give them clarity about what they're about and what's most important to them, among other issues."

From there, she helps them formulate their online profile, then takes 75 digital photos of the client in various settings and attire to choose the best ones to go with the profile. She guides them every step of the way, even providing a month of e-mail coaching after the profile goes up. Testimonials on her Web site prove that what she does not only works, but is sorely needed.

The Internet Dating Coach's Top 10 Reasons to Try Online Dating

1. You can screen *more people online* than you can in person.
2. You can meet people with whom *you'd never cross paths otherwise.*
3. You can learn whether people meet your *minimum requirements* before making contact.
4. You can get to know someone on a *deeper level* before meeting.
5. It saves *time and money.*
6. It allows you to get to know people *without ever leaving your home.*
7. You can do it *when it's convenient* for you, day or night, for minutes or hours.
8. *If you do what you have always done, then you will get what you have always gotten!*
9. It is *fun* (if you do it right).
10. It *works!*

Mainely Dating

Vivian and Robin are two single women who live in the quaint New England town of York, Maine. It has a lighthouse, lobstermen, village square, and friendly residents, but it's also a small town where you pretty much know all the year-round residents — and it's hard to find a single man.

"Friends kept telling me stories of people they knew who had used online dating services and had a positive experience," Vivian says. "They encouraged me to check it out for myself. I thought, 'I am in my late 40s. Where *does* one go to meet single men?' Singles clubs do not appeal to me."

Her friends told Vivian about Match.com and she figured, why not? She paid for a three-month special and then wrote what she felt was a good profile. She had a friend take a photo of her to post with the profile. It was time-consuming to screen profiles of men who interested her and when she did find one to contact, there was no guarantee he'd write back. For those who did respond, there was yet another screening process on her part. She began to feel that most of the men who responded to her profile were in it for entertainment rather than a search for a quality person.

"When I find someone who seems to be on the same page as me, the process begins with sharing likes and dislikes, hobbies, how you like to spend your spare time, what is your career, past relationships, children, what you are looking for in a partner, and so on," Vivian explains. "This is done with e-mails through the Match.com system, which means we do not e-mail each other directly and our private e-mail addresses remain private. Once I feel comfortable or interested enough, I'll call the guy—using a phone block so my number doesn't come up on his Caller ID. By the time I give him my phone number, I have decided that he is someone I would like to meet in person."

Sounds good so far, right? Her first few dates were, well, odd.

"I met a man for dinner at a town nearby. One of the first things he told me was that he did a background check on me. He Googled me," Vivian recalls. "He then informed me that by having my full name, he looked it up in a white pages directory online, got my home address, then went to a site that allowed him to get an aerial picture of where I lived. He then presented me with a poem he had written about me. It was very strange. It made me uncomfortable. That was the last time I saw him."

Another date listed his height as 5' 6" and when she met him in person, he came to her nose. Vivian stands 5' 6" herself, and she was irked. When she asked why he lied, he insisted he was 5' 6". Needless to say, he didn't get another date with her.

Robin, on the other hand, tried eHarmony.com, getting up the courage after being divorced and single for seven years.

"I didn't like it much since they send so few matches and you don't get to choose who you might like—they do the selecting," she says. "There didn't seem to be many matches who lived within a reasonable distance either. I only got two matches during the four months I was on there, and one of them stood me up. We planned to meet at a certain place and time, but he never called to confirm that day. The other guy I met I hit it off with very big. Unfortunately, he met another match the very next night and e-mailed me saying he had to choose and I lost. Ouch! Amazingly enough, he contacted me two months later saying he had made a mistake and would I like to get together. Also amazingly I said yes ... haha. We spoke on the phone and online quite a bit before seeing each other, then dated for about a month before it became obvious we didn't fit. He was very uptight, a real perfectionist neat-freak type, and although I found him very attractive in most ways, I never really felt comfortable with him."

Robin decided to give Yahoo! Personals a try. It's free, whereas eHarmony.com is a pay site, as is Match.com. She ended up getting several responses right away. She found the pool of dates a bit better but decided to give Match.com a whirl, too. As with Yahoo!, she received responses right away. Within two months, she was seriously dating one of the men who responded to her profile. Her main criterion was that her perfect man had to be a Red Sox fan and this one was. It's a good thing, too, since the Red Sox won the World Series in 2004 and "reversed the curse." Perhaps there's a Red Sox wedding in their future.

Robin offers the same general complaint as Vivian about men's dating profiles: "They lie about their height!" she says incredulously. "I mean, really, like we don't know the difference between 5′ 8″ and 5′ 10″ ?"

A Man's View

It's not only women who have a hard time finding love online. Tim, an attorney in Boston, decided to give online dating a try when he moved, mainly because he was new in town and didn't have a social circle yet to draw any potential dates from.

Although he wouldn't specify which dating Web sites he tried, he says that—in his opinion—90 percent of the profiles he looked at were rewrites of some original prototype. "Relatively few show courage and/or originality," he says. "I ended up with five truly boring first dates for coffee, and nothing after that."

He eventually started dating someone he'd met offline, and they're still together. His view of online dating is that it's overrated. "I personally feel you're better off dating friends and friends of friends, where both sides have more of an idea of personality and matching before any sort of romantic pressure builds that could cloud both judgment and true persona."

Spoken like a true lawyer.

Jeff, on the other hand, found his true love online. He had a female friend go over his profile before he put it up on Cupid.com. It's a good thing, too. She ended up rewriting it, noting that he had fibbed about his height. She told him if he really wanted to meet someone he'd have to be honest from the get-go.

He ended up meeting Lily, who surprisingly lived five minutes from his house. They both had dogs and for their first date took their dogs to a lake nearby. Jeff thought Lily was a bit snooty. Lily thought Jeff wanted the date over because he walked so quickly. However, the two decided to give it a shot anyway and are still together almost three years later.

Some Online Dating Statistics According to Nielsen*

- One in three Internet users would now use the Web to meet a potential dating partner.

- The Internet is the third most popular way to get a date (behind "through friends/bars and work").

- Women are more likely looking for friendship and/or true love online than men.

- Men are more likely looking for a long-term relationship, intimate relationship, short-term relationship, or marriage online than women.

- Men are more likely to look for a "no strings" fling than women.

- Men are more likely to contact a woman based on their photo.

- Women are more likely to contact a man based on their description.

- For men the most appealing feature about Internet dating is the ability to e-mail people they like the look of on a one-to-one basis.

- For women the most appealing feature about Internet dating is the pre-screening that provides a list of potential matches based on personal characteristics, interests, etc.

(*Nielsen/NetRatings, August 2005, www.nielsen-netratings. com/pr/pr_050802_uk.pdf)

Chat Romances or B-Movies?

Rea, who lives in southern California, dated a man she met in a widow and widower support room on AOL. Ron said he had been widowed twice. When they met in person it was for coffee less than a half mile from her sister's house.

"He talked me into lunch and prayed over our meal," Rea recalls. "He was kind, funny, and intelligent, so we met a few other times for lunch or dinner, usually with me meeting him halfway. When I felt he was trustworthy enough, I invited him to my place for dinner. He left at about 10 P.M. that night during one of the worst storms my part of the state had ever seen. I didn't hear from him or see him online for 10 days after that."

Rea wondered if she'd done something wrong. Maybe she should have let Ron stay at her house that night. When his name popped up on her AOL IM buddy list, she IM'd him and found it was his wife who was online. After the shock of finding out he was married, Rea and Ron's wife chatted and cried for what seemed like hours.

"I kept reassuring her that nothing inappropriate had taken place," Rea says. "She kept begging me for my phone number and address, which something in my gut told me to refuse to do."

When daylight arrived, Ron's wife told Rea she was going to go into the widow and widowers chat room to let everyone know she was Ron's wife and that he'd been lying about being widowed. Rea agreed to join her and got there just in time to see her tell the room that Rea was her husband's mistress and had stolen him away from her.

"Luckily, many of the people there knew me and had chatted with Ron. They told her it was bull," Rea says, shaking her head. "My roommates did some research and found he had a harem all over the Valley, and none of them were willing to give him up even though the fact that he was married was now out. I was the only woman who refused further contact with him."

It didn't end there. For the next two months Ron's wife stalked Rea online. She IM'd Rea and called her filthy names. Ron's children (or the wife pretending to be them) IM'd her as well, telling her they hoped she'd rot in hell. One night Ron's wife informed Rea she had a gun and was going to use it. This frightened Rea so much she reached over and unplugged the computer.

"When I quit shaking enough to get back online to report her to a moderator, I had nothing to prove she was stalking me—shutting off the computer erased the IM chat," Rea says. "But the moderator instructed me how to block her IMs. For a while, she'd sit in the chat room while I was there but then little by little her threats stopped. Eventually, she quit appearing in the chat room when I was there."

Rea learned a valuable lesson. Check out your online date thoroughly before meeting in person.

In Australia, Greg, a tech-savvy promoter, had a little spare time on his hands. He decided to check out some chat rooms, first at work and then at home.

He had some sexy chat with Jo, who claimed to be blonde and a pretty good squash player. Sexy, liked sports, and a Scorpio—just like Greg. This sounded promising.

During the first few dates, everything was normal. Then Jo's conversation began to include ex-boyfriends, an Internet criminal, borrowing money, and more. During one of their phone calls, Jo asked him to start documenting their e-mails—"so she could have a record." Greg was unsure why she wanted this but he complied. He had fallen hard for her.

"We met again in person and she encouraged me to move in with her," Greg says. "Arrangements were made and I started to move in my most precious items, some sales and marketing trophies."

When Greg talked of moving in more of his things, Jo suddenly stopped answering the phone. She lived more than an hour away but Greg made time to drive to her place. He felt she was home but not answering the door.

When Greg finally heard from Jo, she said she wanted to take it slow. She never explained why she got cold feet. Still strongly drawn to her, Greg forgave her. They started seeing more of each other, each time becoming more and more intimate.

Then there was another sudden disappearance on Jo's part. Greg had enough of it by now and cut off all ties with her. As a result he's lost a number of prized trophies, but it could have been worse.

"She still calls me about once a year, usually on a holiday like Christmas," Greg says. "Each time I tell her not to contact me again in any way, shape, or form. But sure enough, the next year I get a call. I'd advise anyone who is thinking of finding a date via chat to be very careful. You could find trouble—or a stalker."

Endnotes

1. Match.com survey, April 2002, http://corp.match.com/index/newscenter_ research_ online.asp

2. Russell Research, July 2004, http://tinyurl.com/3ts86

3. U.S. CODE: Title 18, Section 1343. Fraud by wire, radio, or television, www.law.cornell.edu/uscode/18/1343.html

4. To "Google" someone is to perform a search on a person's full name in a search engine, such as www.google.com or www.yahoo.com, and review the results.

Other Ways
They Can Get You

Yes, there's more. Just about any part of the Web can be used for harassment, fraud, or scams. From Web site guestbooks to keystroke loggers, spyware, online games, Webcams, and more, you need to know what to look out for and how to handle it if it happens to you.

Online Bullies

It's not just kids who are afraid of bullies. Adults are, too. However, kids still get the brunt of it. (Read more about online bullying and kids in Chapter 15, "Protecting the Children.") Before the Internet, when kids left school and were safely home, they were safe from bullies. Holidays and school vacations were a relief. That's not necessarily true anymore.

"Cyberbullying involves the use of information and communication technologies such as e-mail, cell phone and pager text messages, instant messaging, defamatory personal Web sites, and defamatory online personal polling Web sites, to support deliberate, repeated, and hostile behavior by an individual or group that is intended to harm others," says Bill Belsey of www. cyberbullying.ca.

In fact, Netsmartz.org found that one out of every 17 children is bullied online. They also found that one out of three students ages 8–18 say they know at least one victim of cyberbullying.

The Internet literally leaves kids no place to hide from their tormentors.

The prosecutor's office of Union County, New Jersey, was one of the first to address this problem. In early 2004, it created and distributed a brochure entitled "Cyber-Bullying on the High Tech Playground" (www.ucnj.org). It advises kids (and adults should know this, as well) to:

- ACT IMMEDIATELY! The longer you wait, the harder it is to successfully identify the subject.

- SAVE ALL MESSAGES in whatever manner you have to. If live, try to record the conversation. Write down the content of the message, the date and time it was sent and/or received, and the caller's name and number.

- PRINT COPIES of all messages. In chat room or message board, PRINT SCREEN and copy/save.

- RECORD THE CYBERBULLY'S USERNAME and try to identify the caller/sender through that person's voice, user name, or telephone number. Many units have a built-in memory or memory card, which can store a limited number of sent and received messages and which identify the call number, so check your "recent calls" log. Dial *69 to identify the originating call number. Try to identify the person based upon your relationship and their motive.

- IMMEDIATELY TELL AN ADULT YOU TRUST—a parent, guardian, teacher—someone! DON'T WAIT! IT IS NOT YOUR FAULT, YOU ARE NOT ALONE, AND YOU CANNOT HANDLE THIS BY YOURSELF!

- CONTACT YOUR SERVICE PROVIDER (telephone company or Internet Service Provider) to report the harassment, ask for assistance in identifying the caller, obtain a copy of the data, trace the call(s), and investigate the abuse.

- CONTACT THE SENDER'S SERVICE PROVIDER (telephone company or Internet Service Provider) to report the harassment. Most providers have user agreements expressly forbidding abuse and can cancel the sender's service.

- WHEN TO CONTACT LOCAL LAW ENFORCEMENT: If you are receiving death threats or believe you or your family to be in immediate physical danger, dial 911 immediately.

If you have asked the cyberbully/harasser to cease and you have taken the steps outlined here and the contact continues, ask your local police department for an interview. Be sure to have on hand the potential evidence you have collected. Online cybercops are also available, the most notable ones being www.haltabuse.org, www.safetyed.com, and www.web-police.org.

As mentioned before, it's not just kids who are bullied online. Author C. E. Laine knows this only too well.

"I'm a writer, so I maintain a public profile—albeit small. I'm hardly a celebrity of any notable caliber," C. E. says. "This has been the chink in my armor. Had I not maintained a public profile, I could have more easily disappeared off my ex-husband's radar. But as it is, he knows he can always go to my Web site to find out something about me."

His bullying and harassment online included sending her 50 or more of the same e-mail messages in an hour, sending just as many instant messages through Yahoo! and AIM, following her around online, and posting messages in guestbooks at sites she either visited or where the owner knows her.

"He tried to damage my professional and personal reputation by posting hideous lies, including those of a sexual nature," she recalls. "He defamed me and my parents, and posted terrible descriptions of me naked on his blog—then sent the link to clients of my Web design business. He also posted the link on parenting message boards, genealogy message boards, and so on, and e-mailed it to any poet or writer he had ever seen in any connection with my name. What he has done to me is very similar to some tactics used by schoolyard bullies. It's about control, dominance, and humiliation."

As a result of the harassment, C. E. was forced to legally change her name and social security number—and move to an undisclosed location.

E-Newsletters

It's easy to sign yourself up for free accounts on the Internet, but it's also easy to sign up other people for services they didn't request, such as e-mail newsletters, subscriptions to magazines, and more.

"Someone was signing me up for all sorts of wedding and child-birth e-subscriptions and having free items or brochures from these sites sent to my home or workplace," Doug says. "I thought it was someone I work with who had a crush on me and was upset that I had announced my engagement to my longtime girlfriend."

Doug spoke with the woman and asked her to stop subscribing him, but she denied doing it and the number of subscriptions increased, online and offline. He began receiving trial issues of magazines related to weddings, babies, and romance. He finally approached his supervisor and explained what was going on and that he had no proof but was pretty sure it was this woman. The company Doug worked for installed security software on the computer network so it could keep track of which Web sites each employee was visiting and when.

Doug again approached the woman and asked her to stop subscribing him. She again denied she was doing anything at all. Within an hour, Doug began receiving more newsletters via e-mail, and more messages from sites offering information about weddings. Later that day, the woman was called into her supervisor's office and confronted with a printed report of her online activity right after she spoke with Doug. All of the Web sites from which he had received e-mail were sites she had visited.

She was warned to stop the harassment or she'd be fired.

Doug stopped receiving free things in his e-mail and mail at home. He's now happily married. The woman eventually left the company and he never heard from her again.

Greeting Cards

You've probably received or sent an online greeting card to someone in your family, a friend, or co-worker. Online greeting cards are usually cute and funny, some with animation, some with music. They're a quick and easy way to stay in touch with people. Unfortunately, the twisted among us use online greeting cards to serve their own strange purposes.

Lisa opened her e-mail one morning and found a message that claimed there was a greeting card waiting for her at Yahoo! Greetings. It was from someone named "chrisjimbob," a name not familiar to her. Thinking it was a joke from a friend, she clicked on the URL link in the e-mail message and found a colorful beach scene. She was due to take her vacation soon, so she assumed the card was from a friend. She clicked the "cover" of the card and it opened to reveal the following text:

> want to go to the beach? or do your tribe
> of halfbreeds have you tied to your house.
> Just think if you had started sleeping with
> black men earlier you could have a half-
> breed yourself.

Lisa noticed more greeting card announcements in her e-mail box from Yahoo!, Blue Mountain Arts, and other greeting card sites. As she hesitantly opened them she discovered they all featured a variation on the same message. She began thinking about who might be responsible and remembered a message board she'd been on the prior week.

"There were some disagreements on the board, and we exchanged some angry posts," Lisa says. "I received e-mails from some of the people but put them in my trash and never read them." She felt this was probably the source of the offensive greeting cards. When she contacted the greeting card companies, they blocked her from receiving their cards. Soon after, she changed her e-mail address and the greeting cards began arriving again.

"I felt like I was being held hostage by these people," Lisa says. "It was horrible. For a long time, no one I knew could contact me because I had to keep changing my e-mail address. I finally gave up. I stopped visiting that message board and the harassment stopped."

Dealing with Junk You Never Requested

Are you suddenly being inundated with subscriptions to e-mail newsletters, greeting cards, and more? Follow these steps to stop them:

1. Go to the Web site that the subscription or other nuisance originated from and contact its abuse department via e-mail (many abuse departments can be e-mailed by simply typing the word "abuse" then the domain, such as abuse@yahoo.com) and ask to be removed from its list(s), explaining that you did not subscribe.

2. If you received an abusive greeting card, make sure you print out a copy as evidence, then contact the abuse department at the greeting card Web site, providing them with the URL where the card is located.

3. If the site does not remove your name from its list or remove the greeting card(s) and you continue to receive them, call the company and ask to speak to the manager in the abuse department, explain what's been going on, and ask the manager to intervene.

4. If this doesn't work, go to your local police for help, contact an online safety organization, or cancel your e-mail address and get a new one. Many ISPs are willing to help people who are receiving abusive or harassing e-mail, so a phone call and brief explanation may save you a few dollars.

Guestbooks

Many personal pages and many professional sites have a nifty feature called a guestbook. People who visit the page or site can sign the guestbook and leave comments. At least, that was the guestbook's original design.

A professional racecar driver's Web site suddenly began to get odd messages in its guestbook.

"Several times a person tried to post descriptive messages about the driver's wife and weird sexual fantasies about her," says Candi, the Webmaster. "He described what she was wearing at the race track, so we knew this person had gotten close to her and we were very concerned."

Although Candi deleted the messages from the guestbook, she kept copies of them as evidence. Soon, the person was posting more disturbing messages to the guestbook and to a message board on the site:

```
Madeline Thomas [ not her real name]
will wear her red FLEECE SWEATSHIRT and
have her hands tied behind her back. Then
she will have 100 cream pies smashed into
her face and be covered in chocolate
syrup. Then she will have a cake smashed
into her pretty little face. Then she
will put on her black FLEECE SWEATSHIRT
and have 10 cream pies smashed into her
```

```
face and covered in mustard. Then she
will put on a gorilla costume and be
thrown into a huge mud puddle. Then she
will get covered in mayonnaise and oil.
This will totally humiliate pretty little
Madeline and then we will see how she
walks around the pits in her nice little
RED AND BLACK FLEECE SWEATSHIRTS!!!
```

"We were able to determine which ISP this person posted from," Candi says, "and found out it was a small and fairly new ISP, only about 20 minutes from the race track where Madeline's husband is based."

Since this was the first case of harassment for the ISP, its owners weren't sure how to handle it or how to figure out who was posting the messages. Meanwhile, the messages in the guestbook and on the message board continued, escalating at a rate where Candi almost couldn't keep up to delete them.

The local ISP was doing nothing and Candi was getting worried. Then a new message appeared in the guestbook:

```
Can someone get a hold of Madeline and
tell her that at Port Royal this Saturday
she WILL get a pie in her pretty little
face. There will be three people there with
cream pies and whoever sees her first and
gets the best shot at her will smear that
pie in her face and hair. Then this will be
the end of these messages.
```

"We'd been scratching our heads trying to figure out what these messages meant as *every* post mentions a pie," Candi says. "We had been trying to decode them and finally came to the conclusion that it must be some weird sexual fetish. We'd heard about a group of people who pied celebrities like Bill Gates, but it never occurred to us that the pie could actually be a weapon. That's when we began to get really worried."

Madeline and her husband finally went to their local police and filed a complaint. The local police contacted the state police, who began narrowing down the search to six users at the local ISP. They finally narrowed that down to one person and left a message on the man's answering machine.

"That's when the posting escalated even more," Candi says. "And this time he began sending e-mails to my address in addition to the posts in the guestbook and on the message board."

```
Madeline will wear her red fleece sweat-
shirt and I'll tie her hands behind her
back. Then I'll wrap plastic around her
whole body so she is helpless and put her
black fleece sweatshirt on her. Then I'll
hit Madeline in the face with 30 cream
pies. Then I'll dump chocolate, ketchup,
mustard, syrup, and salad dressing all over
Madeline. What would your dream date be
like with the very pretty Madeline?
```

The state police arrested the man responsible for the "pie posts" less than a week after the latest message was posted to the guestbook. He was the 18-year-old son of a truck driver at a speedway where Madeline's husband raced. He admitted to everything and was charged with harassment—he received 90 days in prison and a $300 fine. His parents made him send a letter of apology to Madeline, which was a nice end to the whole mess.

"The police said they didn't think the kid was deranged," Candi sighs. "He was apparently shy and overweight and just hung his head and cried when they asked him about the posts."

The Other Side of Online Auctions

What happens when a high bidder reneges on an auction and takes revenge on the seller? This happened to Eve, who regularly auctions items at eBay. Some of these items are very ugly.

"The Butt Ugly is a contest we hold every month for fun," Eve says, laughing. "A group of us have been doing this for what seems-like forever. Each of us finds the ugliest item we can and puts it up for bid. We do it differently from normal eBay auctions—the winner is determined by which Butt Ugly item gets the most bids, then that person can either keep the item or give it to the high bidder if they want it. We pay all the eBay fees involved, so there is no deception."

Good Guestbooks

An online guestbook can be a good and useful feature. Whether you get a guestbook program through a Web site that offers them, or design your own from scratch, make sure it:

- Sends you an e-mail message each time your guestbook is signed

- Shows the IP address of everyone who signs your guestbook (this will allow you to contact a visitor's ISP in the event of abuse)

- Allows you to edit and delete guestbook messages.

Many guestbooks also allow you to set preferences so that a person can only sign your guestbook one time, or to block certain e-mail addresses/usernames from signing the guestbook.

Some recommended ones that are also free are:

1-2-3 Web Tools
www.freeguestbooks.com

Guestbook.de
http://two.guestbook.de

Dreambook
www.dreambook.com

Creation Center
www.creationcenter.com

eFree Guestbooks
www.efreeguestbooks.com

Sometimes real bidders who aren't part of the group place bids, not knowing a thing about the Butt Ugly contest (BU contest, as it's called), but they gladly join in on the fun when told at auction's end if they are the winning bidder. A few really want the item and are more than happy to pay for it.

"I had one that was a really ugly porcelain chicken. I put it up with the description, 'BU Chicken thingie that wouldn't die,' " Eve says. "This is the one that started the problem."

A bidder who had won an earlier auction of Eve's and was told of the BU contest did not take the news lightly. In fact, he was outraged and claimed she and the other sellers were shill bidding, which means bidding on each other's auctions to artificially raise the bid. "Crusadeworker" wrote to the BU Chicken bidders:

> The auction you bid on is part of a shill ring perpetrated by a group of users on ebay. The bidders in the auction except yourself are all friends of the ring. Unless you really want this item I suggest you retract your bid. Are you aware that the BU in the description stands for Butt Ugly. Just thought you wanted to know.

Crusadeworker then began checking Eve's auctions and e-mailed every one of the bidders for any auction she was running, whether it was a BU auction or not.

One bidder was so alarmed, she contacted Eve:

> Hello. I received this message concerning the BU item you have up for auction. While I am not concerned about the ugliness of the item (which is rather obvious), I am concerned about the legitimacy of the auction. Does the item exist and is it really for sale? If you do not reply to my message, I am afraid I will follow the advice of retracting my bid. Thanks!

eBay suspended Crusadeworker's user ID, but he kept coming back and creating new IDs. Although eBay continued to suspend the new user IDs, there wasn't much else it could do. Eventually, Crusadeworker either got tired of creating new IDs or wasn't getting enough attention, because he stopped e-mailing bidders on BU auctions, which continue to this day.

Another way to cause problems in online auctions is through the feedback or comments section. When a bidder wins an auction and completes the transaction with the seller, he is supposed to leave feedback. If the bidder doesn't pay for the item won, the seller leaves negative feedback to warn others of possible problems with that bidder. This didn't sit well with one bidder.

"This guy was a high-bidder on six of my auctions," Patti says. "I followed the standard contact timeframe specified by eBay but never heard from him. When I posted negative feedback, he seemed to have exploded."

The bidder posted a retaliatory negative feedback against Patti in each of the six auctions he'd won, which she had expected him to do. But the ferocity stunned her.

"I was really baffled as to why he didn't just tell me he'd changed his mind, as I am a reasonable person and hate to resort to posting negative feedback," Patti says. "In my final note to him, I advised him I would have to post negatives in keeping with eBay's recommendation, but would still consider not doing so if he would just reply to my e-mail with an explanation."

He not only left negative feedback but began signing her up for online services, one of which was weather specific to her ZIP code. Patti managed to cancel these as they came in, but she knew he wasn't going to give up easily. And he didn't:

```
     Of course, the loss of the $12 that you
have initiated all of your little war over,
will seriously damage your ability to pay
for the counseling you so obviously need,
won't it ...? If you had one bit of sense,
you would have relisted the items and gone
along merrily. Did that never occur to you?
Or were you so busy focusing on pestering
us and slandering us to everyone you
encounter, that the thought never crossed
your mind? Well, I really don't have the
time for any more nonsense from you. ...Go
and take some Prozac and lie in a dark room
for a while...it might begin to help. Get
it right up ye, you nasty cow!
```

This was just one of the many e-mails he sent Patti. He began bidding on her auctions under other user IDs, then leaving more negative feedback when he won. She complained to eBay and it canceled the user IDs of this unhappy bidder, but Patti finally had to change her own eBay user ID and basically start all over again.

"I had to change my Web page on eBay, all my links, contact people who were repeat bidders, and others I did business with," Patti says. "It took a huge amount of my time to do this, but it did end the harassment by this man."

Webcams

They're cute, fun, and easy to install and use. Webcams are a great way to keep in touch with family and friends around the world—more personal than just e-mail because you can chat and see each other live or send videos back and forth. It didn't take long, however, for the cute and versatile Webcam to be used against someone.

A pre-teen in the Los Angeles area was wandering around his bedroom in his underwear, getting ready for school. His computer was on, but he didn't notice the green light on his Webcam. It was recording.

A hacker had broken into his online connection and was busily recording the kid. Suddenly, the kid heard that familiar, "You've got mail!" and went to check his e-mail. When he saw there was an attached graphic, he didn't think twice and double-clicked on it.

Imagine his surprise when he saw himself, in his underwear, in his bedroom. He looked up at his Webcam, noticed the green light, and unhooked the Webcam. From then on, he only hooked up the Webcam when he wanted to chat with friends or send pictures and videos.

Webcam Chat Rooms

Yes, they have them. Yahoo! not only has text chat rooms but if you have a soundcard, speakers, and Webcam, you can do voice chat and Webcam chat. But be careful! Don't be as trusting as Chris was.

Chris came to WHOA via an e-mail message. He wrote that he was too embarrassed to fill out the questionnaire. When asked why, he spilled his story. He had gone into a Webcam chat room where three other people were signed in. On his monitor he could see the three others and himself—all men. It was a Friday night and they talked about sports, cars, women, and work. They also did some imitations of celebrities, basically cracking each other up and having a good time. It was getting late and all of them were drinking beer, wine, or some other liquor. One of the men suggested doing a trivia game. If you lost, you had to remove a piece of clothing. Yep, Webcam strip trivia.

Since they were now loosened up and comfortable with each other, they thought this was a great idea. Chris lost the most games and had to do a loser's dance in front of his Webcam.

A couple of weeks later, a co-worker came up to him and asked about his nude dance online. Chris was shocked. He hadn't told anyone about the Webcam chat room. He asked for the URL of the Web site and discovered that one of the men in the room had captured the video of him dancing around and then put it up on his personal Web site.

As Chris perused the site, he found that this man routinely went into Webcam chat rooms with men and women, got them to feel comfortable, and then convinced them to take off their clothes or do rude things. Then he would steal the video and put it on his site.

WHOA went to the Web site and was amazed at the hundreds of videos on it. All were of adults. If any had been of children, they would be classified as child pornography and WHOA could have gotten the FBI involved.

WHOA realized that a simple e-mail to the Web site owner probably wouldn't get the results it was after. So WHOA found the name of the ISP that hosted the site and contacted it, asking politely if it could contact the Web site owner and ask him to remove Chris's video. Technically, it was Chris's video and he did not give permission for this man to post it on his site. WHOA suggested that many of the other videos were probably up there without permission as well.

Three days later, the Web site was gone—and remains gone. Chris learned his lesson: Drinking and Webcams don't mix—at least in the company of strangers.

"I play pinochle at Yahoo! games, and I met up with 'Jim,' " recalls Rebecca Summers. "We became partners playing pinochle, then became friends ... or so I thought."

She felt they were getting comfortable with each other, enough so that he talked her into seeing each other via Webcam. It would be fun, she thought. Little did she know he took screen captures of the Webcam sessions, more than 500 of them. Soon after, he became obsessed with Rebecca. When she tried to back away, that's when the threats started.

"He told me what he had on me and that he would expose me or else!" She shudders as she remembers. "I sent over 50 complaints to

Yahoo!, charges were pressed, letters written, and he still wouldn't stop. He sent me as many as 1,000 e-mails at one time. He impersonated me online and solicited men to call my house for phone sex."

It didn't stop there. Jim sent messages describing the physical harm he said he would do to her and her family. He created Web sites about her, put spyware on her computer, and no matter how many times she has changed her Yahoo! ID, he still finds her in Yahoo! Games. Rebecca's story is so compelling that the cable station TechTV covered it in August 2003 (www.techtv.com).

Webcams Can Be Fun— If You Follow These Simple Tips

1. Get a Webcam that has a lens "shutter" so that you can slide it closed when it's not in use.

2. If you want to broadcast a "show," choose a site that has a good privacy policy and does not tolerate harassment or abuse. Some great sites let you put on a show of your own, post photos taken with your Webcam, and more. Some of the more popular sites include:

    WebcamWorld
    www.camcities.com

    CamCentral
    www.camcentral.com

    Webcam Index
    www.webcam-index.com

    Webcam List
    www.webcam-list.com

Online Journals and Blogs

Remember when you had your diary or a journal where you wrote down your innermost thoughts every day or whenever you could? Then you'd hide it from curious siblings and your parents. Today, Internet users keep an online version of a diary but don't seem to mind that anyone with an Internet connection anywhere in the world can read their printed thoughts.

Sometimes it becomes a problem. News stories abound about employees who kept online journals in which they complained about the company they worked for, their boss, or their co-workers. Many times they named names and described people and events in detail. The result was that they usually got fired for insubordination or for personal use of the Internet on company time (which is a big no-no in many offices these days).

Then there are the people who seem to forget that you really shouldn't put deeply personal feelings or thoughts anywhere online, even in your journal. These are the people who rant about a politician, for instance, actually "wishing" that someone would kill the politician (or celebrity or other public figure). Or they may simply "wish" a person was dead. Then they act surprised when Secret Service or FBI agents come knocking.

Others are flabbergasted when friends or family become angry because of what they posted online. You may think that Aunt Mildred looks like a fat cow in her yellow-striped dress, but the whole world doesn't need to know your opinion. Certainly Aunt Mildred shouldn't be able to find it online! Along the same line of thought, neither should your ex-boyfriend be able to find online your estimate of the size of his, ahem, member.

Common sense seems to flee when some people go online. Those who keep online journals, diaries, or Weblogs (commonly called blogs) seem most susceptible to this malady.

It's nice to have an online version of a diary, but my advice is to keep the really personal, sensitive, and sexually explicit stuff off the Internet. Buy an old-fashioned paper diary for those types of thoughts, if you really feel the need.

Use your online diary for funny stories, sad stories, what you are growing in your garden, or links to other Web sites or news stories that interest you. I can't repeat this bit of advice often enough: If you wouldn't say it to a stranger on the street, don't say it online.

As mentioned in previous chapters, if you do opt to take advantage of online journaling, make sure you don't put too many personal details in your writing either. You never know who is lurking just waiting to cause trouble for you.

Some of the more popular online journal and blog sites (most are free) are:

> LiveJournal
> www.livejournal.com
>
> Blogger
> www.blogger.com
>
> Diaryland
> www.diaryland.com
>
> Blurty
> www.blurty.com

Spyware

Spyware exists as an independent, executable program on a computer, usually put there without the computer user's knowledge.

Stephen Gibson, founder of Gibson Research Corporation, explains the phenomenon further:

> The Internet allows multiple simultaneous data 'connections,' and unless the computer is running a firewall program, those connections can be completely hidden and occurring without our knowledge or permission. Thus, malicious software called Spyware, with its own agenda, running quietly and secretly inside our computers, can silently connect to remote computers located anywhere in the world while we're innocently exchanging e-mail, surfing the Web, or doing anything with our Internet-connected computers.

Spyware has the capability to do anything any program can do, including:

- Monitor keystrokes

- Scan files on the hard drive

- Snoop other applications such as word processors

• Read cookies

• Change the default homepage

• Interface with the default Web browser to determine what sites are visited

• Monitor various aspects of a user's behavior; "phoning home" from time to time to report this information to the spyware's author

• Notify the spyware company of any attempt to modify or remove it from the system

"It is not uncommon for online predators to secretly install spyware programs on victims' computers," warns Steve Reutter of PestPatrol.com. "Programs such as keyloggers can be secretly installed on a recipient's computer by using a trojan horse program. When the application is opened, the spyware is installed on the computer without anyone knowing it has happened. To the average computer user, there will be no evidence or suspicion that any such activity is occurring. Just think of the potential information—names, addresses, phone numbers, where someone is going to meet their friends and when, their friends' names, where they go to school, when parents are going out for the evening, etc. The potential is staggering."

So, what are keystroke loggers? They are software programs and/or hardware devices that record every key you strike on a computer keyboard. The two basic types are:

1. Software Keystroke Loggers

Advantages to the person doing the spying:

• Inexpensive ($19.95 and up)

• May be able to be e-mailed to the user's e-mail box as a trojan

• A greater number of features than hardware loggers

• Can do screen captures and Webcam captures

• Can capture both incoming/outgoing e-mails and conversations in chat rooms

• Delivers logs to the installer's e-mail inbox

Disadvantages to the person doing the spying:

- Access to the user's computer is necessary unless the program can be sent as a trojan

- Can be relatively easily detected by users/victims

- Using the software effectively requires a significant learning curve

2. Hardware Keystroke Loggers

Advantages to the person doing the spying:

- Easy to use

- Cannot be detected by software

- Installation is done in seconds without gaining internal access to the computer, though physical access is necessary. All you do is disconnect the keyboard, attach the logger device to the end of the cable, then connect it back into the computer (it's about the size of a thumb)

Disadvantages to the person doing the spying:

- The user/victim can find the device through a physical check of their keyboard cable connection

- Only captures what the user is typing, not receiving

- Limited to capturing keystrokes only

- Relatively expensive ($50 and up)

If you suspect you have spyware on your computer (if it's been running sluggishly that can be one clue), try one of these Web-based programs:

Spybot Search & Destroy
Free
http://security.kolla.de
This program has the most complete detection list ever seen. Spybot S&D is also able to replace some spyware files with dummy files so that other programs don't notice they're missing.

Lavasoft AD-aware
Free
www.lavasoftusa.com

Windows utility detects and removes many adware products, including TimeSink TS ADBOT, Aureate/Radiate files, Comet Cursor, Cydoor, and more.

PestPatrol
$30 for home use, free trial
www.pestpatrol.com
Detects a wide assortment of spyware and remote-access and key-logging trojans

For a list of the more common software programs infested with spyware, try www.infoforce.qc.ca/spyware/enknownlistfrm.html
For more information on spyware, try www.firewallguide.com/spyware.htm

Camera Cell Phones

An estimated 65 million camera phones were sold worldwide in 2003, with Japan and South Korea as the leading markets. More than 5 million have been sold in the U.S. By 2006, more than 80 percent of cell phones shipped in the U.S. and Western Europe will have cameras.

Taking photos via your cell phone can be enjoyed as a convenience. You can shoot the photo and then e-mail it to yourself or someone else. It's a great way to share something as you're experiencing it—maybe a chance encounter with a celebrity, a birth, a wedding, or a birthday party. There have been stories of people who have witnessed a car accident and taken photos with their cell phones. One woman used hers to take a photo of a man exposing himself to her in a parking lot. Police were able to identify the man as the former principal of a nearby high school. A teenager took photos of a man who was trying to lure him into a car.

There are Web sites where you can post and share the images you've captured. These are known as moblogs (short for "mobile blogging"). Two such sites are Picturephoning at http://textually.org/picturephoning/ and Text America at www.textamerica.com.

So, while camera cell phones can be a convenience and even a boon, there are potential problems. Be wary because there is a proliferation of Web sites filled with photos taken surreptitiously in places such as public bathrooms, locker rooms, and so forth.

Pardon the language, but one well-known site is called www.mobileasses.com. Photos of men and women's behinds and chests—taken with cell phone cameras—are posted daily. You can even rate them from 1–10 with 10 being the most attractive. The majority of these photos are taken without the victim's knowledge. It happens in supermarkets, malls, on the street, in offices, schools, libraries, gyms, and many other public places.

Here are other examples of camera cell phones put to bad use:

- Students have been caught using cell phone cameras to cheat on tests.

- A 20-year-old Washington state man was charged with voyeurism after he slipped a cell phone camera underneath a woman's skirt as she shopped for groceries.

- A strip club owner in Missouri came out swinging against the technology—threatening to smash cell phone cameras with a sledgehammer to protect the privacy of his patrons and his dancers.

- In Japan, where nearly half of all cell phones are photo phones, magazine publishers have become concerned about consumers who snap shots of pages they like instead of buying the magazine.

- A police officer in the U.K. was fired after he was caught using his camera cell phone to take photos of dead bodies in a hospital mortuary.

As a result of these indiscretions, many states have passed laws regarding usage of camera cell phones. Many cities have banned them in schools, gyms, health clubs, hospitals, and other places.

You're probably going to look twice at the person near you with a cell phone now, aren't you?

What's Next?

As technology advances and the online world expands, the number of possible ways to harass others increases. That abusive phone call could originate from someone's computer, rather than from a telephone. A fax sent to you with a nasty message on it could have been sent from someone's computer. Both methods are virtually untraceable avenues, paving the way for law enforcement to try to find new ways to deal with situations like this.

Work is underway to develop a computer that emits odors when you surf the Web or get your e-mail, and CD-ROM and DVD drives that will play CDs or DVDs encoded with scents, so that as you go through a program or game, you can smell the green grass, honeysuckle, bread baking, or whatever. I guess you could call incoming messages smell e-mails. One company called Digiscents was touted as being the first to try out this technology. However, it went the way of the dodo bird. Other companies are testing the waters, though, so who knows when or if this technology will take off.

And you know that when players are made, recorders are not far behind, so someone out for revenge could easily make a scented CD or DVD encoded with the smell of feces, rotting garbage, or something equally disgusting and send it to someone they dislike. Or a harasser could send a scented e-mail that probably won't smell like roses.

Harassers, stalkers, scam artists, and other criminals are finding new ways to ply their trade. Be on the alert so you don't become their next victim.

Protecting the Children

It's simple. Nothing will happen to your child online because you're a good parent, right?

Wrong.

The truth is any child can become an online victim of child predators, harassment, stalking, pornography, and more.

Ruben Rodriguez Jr., director of the Exploited Child Unit, National Center for Missing and Exploited Children (NCMEC, see Figure 15.1) makes a bold statement: "Over 95 percent of the complaints and leads we receive via our CyberTipline are related to child pornography. These are followed by online enticement—child luring—and child molestation."

The NCMEC launched its Exploited Child Unit in 1997 specifically to address online issues. It then added CyberTipline to its Web site a year later for the public to report Internet and non-Internet-related child sexual exploitation. It's worked. The CyberTipline has received more than 50,000 leads and complaints since it was created.

Concrete statistics are hard to come by because of various state and federal statutes under which people are prosecuted and because many online-related cases involving children never go to court.

According to a study released in 2004 regarding Internet-initiated sex crimes against minors[1], "76 percent of child victims were between 13 and 15 years of age. Of those, 75 percent were girls." Another survey, conducted by the National Center for Missing and Exploited Children[2] in November 2003, found that 74 percent of child predators who plead guilty to or are convicted on federal charges serve prison time, while only 50 percent of those convicted on a state level spend time in prison. As for how many of those convicted are required to register as sex offenders, 69 percent must do so federally and 75 percent must do so in the state in which they live (and in any states they move to after that).

253

If you know about a child who is in immediate risk or danger, call your local police. If you have any information on a missing child, call 1-800-THE-LOST.

The CyberTipline handles leads from individuals reporting the sexual exploitation of children.

• possession, manufacture, and distribution of child pornography • online enticement of children for sexual acts • child prostitution • child-sex tourism • child sexual molestation (not in the family)	**CLICK HERE**  **REPORT ONLINE**

NCMEC, in partnership with the Federal Bureau of Investigation, U.S. Customs Service, and the U.S. Postal Inspection Service, serves as the national CyberTipline and as the national Child Pornography Tipline 1-800-843-5678. Please contact us if you have information that will help in our fight against child sexual exploitation. Your information will be forwarded to law enforcement for investigation and review, and, when appropriate, to the ISP. The U.S. Congress has funded these initiatives for reporting child sexual exploitation.

Figure 15.1   NCMEC

Just for Kids—Tips for Staying Safe Online

1. *Select a gender-neutral or generic username, e-mail address, etc.* Avoid anything cute, sexual, or overly feminine. Don't select a username related to where you live, what school you go to (such as a school or team name), your age, your hobby, or your favorite sport. Child predators look for ways to make you think they know you or like the same things you like, so be careful. Some good examples of words to avoid are girl, kitty, sweet, cute, sexy, or hot. When selecting a username or e-mail address,

DO NOT use your real first or last name. Your first name probably isn't gender-neutral, and you're also making it too easy for people to find out information on you.

2. *Don't give out information simply because it is requested.* Web sites sometimes ask you to give your full name, date of birth, address, phone number, e-mail address, etc. when you might just want to read messages on a discussion forum. Give as little information as possible, then hit the "submit" button and see what information you really need to provide to get that account. If some information is required that shouldn't be, go elsewhere. You can also put false information in, especially if you don't plan to return to in the future. Be especially careful of "profiles" and "directory listings" for instant messaging programs or Web sites that provide free e-mail services, blogs, journals, etc. You don't want too much information to get into the wrong hands.

3. *Block or ignore unwanted users.* Whether you are in a chat room or using IM, you should always check out what options/preferences are available to you and take advantage of the option to "Block all users except those on my buddy list" or to add unwanted usernames to an Ignore list in chat. If anyone bothers you and won't go away, put them on block or ignore, even if it feels rude! Your comfort level is more important than their feelings.

4. *Don't allow others to draw you into conflict.* Although your normal reaction is to defend yourself, it could be the worst thing you could do, because that's what the other person wants—a reaction from you. It's safer to ignore them and keep yourself out of the argument. This is hard to do at times, but even if you have to sit on your hands or go somewhere else online, it could save you a lot of grief in the future. When you respond to a personal attack in any way, you're letting the attacker know that he or she has succeeded in upsetting you and in most cases, this only encourages them to continue. When

the attacker realizes that he or she isn't getting a reaction from you, he or she will move on to find an easier target. Remember the old saying, "Sticks and stones may break your bones, but words will never hurt you!"

5. *If someone continues to harass you in a public message forum or chat room, *leave*.* You may feel that you're letting the person win, but it's better for you mentally and emotionally to get away from someone who is attacking you. After a few days or weeks, you can go back, but we advise you get a new username and "lurk" before taking part again. Make sure the harasser is gone. If they are, have fun! If they aren't, there are plenty of other places online to go. Try to find a message board, group, or chat room that is moderated. Those types of places are good at kicking out potential harassers and others looking to cause trouble.

6. *If someone always seems to be changing their stories or saying something that's different from something they've said before, be extremely careful.* A lot of predators and harassers will tell stories to trick you into trusting them, but because they're making up things, they can slip up. These are clues that something is wrong. For example, you might be talking to a boy whose profile claims he's 14. After a little while, he tells you that it's wrong, he's really 19. A few weeks later, he may tell you that he's really 25, but he likes to hang out with people who are 19. Stop talking to people that lie about themselves like this ... they are up to no good.

7. *Be careful filling out profiles or bios.* Yes, it's nice to let other people know things about you in your profile or biography on your blog, online journal, or facebook. But be careful about putting too much information out there. Child predators look at these profiles and bios so that they can chat you up and make you think they like the same things you do, or live near you, or even go to your own school. This is called social engineering—they are trying to put you at ease so that you will trust them.

8. *When you change, really change!* If you need to change your username or e-mail address to break off contact with a harasser, using a variation on your real name or anything you've used in the past leaves tracks allowing the harasser to find you again fairly easily. If you've always been "Kitty" and you change your handle to "Cat," you haven't really changed. Assume that the harasser knows your hobbies or interests. For instance, perhaps you like to play Scrabble. If he's really obsessed or simply has too much time on his hands, he's likely to poke around in different Scrabble-related message boards and chat rooms looking for feline names to see if he can find you again.

9. *Don't show that you are angry or upset when you're online.* If you're upset with your parents, a teacher, or a friend, don't put that in your blog, journal, on a message board, or mention it in a chat room. This opens up the opportunity for a child predator to take you "under their wing" and make you feel like they are your real friend. If you don't know them in person, they are not your friend! Not everyone you meet online is really who they claim to be. It's awful to always be suspicious, but it's the only way to stay truly safe online.

10. *Never, ever give out personal information*—your real name, address, or phone number—online without making sure it's a legitimate (real) Web site that absolutely needs this information. How do you do this? Ask your parents or older sister or brother, uncle, aunt, grandparents, or another adult you trust. They'll be pleased you asked them for help. Be very cautious about putting any photos of yourself online anywhere, especially in profiles, or allowing anyone else (relatives, schools, dance academies, sports associations) to publish any photos. Some stalkers become obsessed because of an image. Someone may also take your photo and deface it or alter it with crude images to upset you or harass you.

(From WHOA-KTD at http://haltabusektd.org)

Agencies and Organizations Are Here to Help

There are a number of important resources you should know about. The U.S. Department of Justice has created the Child Exploitation and Obscenity Section (Criminal Division), and the FBI has created the Innocent Images National Initiative (IINI), a multiagency investigative initiative that addresses online child pornography and the sexual exploitation of children.

WHOA-KTD (Kids/Teen Division at haltabusektd.org, see Figure 15.2) was created specifically to help kids and teens worldwide who are being bullied, harassed, and stalked online. Established in September 2005 as an offshoot of WHOA (which helps adult online victims worldwide), WHOA-KTD not only offers help and resources for kids and teens worldwide, but also offers resources for parents, educators, and other concerned adults.

"We would ideally like to be the first place kids and teens come to for help," says Joan Welch, KTD vice president. "Our hopes are that we are eventually part of school curriculums or that at least a link to WHOA-KTD is placed on school Web sites so that students know where they can receive help in a timely manner from experienced Internet Safety Advocates who care."

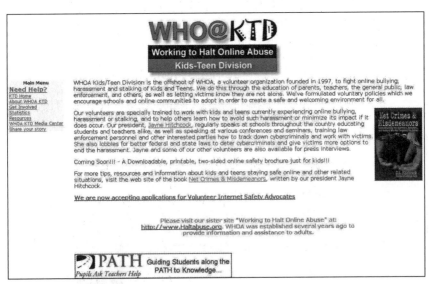

Figure 15.2   WHOA-KTD

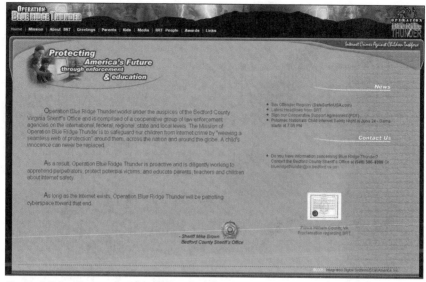

Figure 15.3   Operation Blue Ridge Thunder

Operation Blue Ridge Thunder (Internet Crimes Against Children Task Force) is often spotlighted in the media when the organization busts an online child predator (see Figure 15.3).

These are just a few of the many organizations and individuals trying to combat online child exploitation, harassment, and stalking.

"I got involved in helping kids online in early 2000 when I watched a 13-year-old girl I knew experience the trauma of being targeted by a predator," says Paul Hook of Riverside, California. "She developed a contact through a chat room who identified himself as being 14 years old and made arrangements to meet her."

The teenage girl approached Hook for advice. He became alarmed upon hearing that her parents hadn't been informed that this so-called "14-year-old" was making a 700-mile trip to meet her.

"I convinced her to let me pretend to be her in a conversation with this person in the chat room," Hook says. "After 10 minutes of conversation and asking this 'kid' to prove who he was before 'I' met him, he got very frustrated and angry. He then told me his 'mom' (who was supposed to drive him the 700 miles) was now in the hospital and his uncle would be bringing him. At that point, with the agreement of the girl and her parents, we deleted her accounts and created new ones for her, and she quit going to her normal places online."

This resolved her problem—there was no more contact—but the incident left trauma and fear in its wake.

Detective/Constable Nancy Yingling of the Vancouver Police Department in Canada feels that chat rooms pose a serious concern for parents and, subsequently, police.

"The simplest advice for children is to not chat with anyone not known to them and never give out any personal information to a stranger," she advises. "Just as on the street or playground where a child should not speak with a stranger, the same rule applies to this scenario. Really, it's just common sense."

The people at Operation Blue Ridge Thunder find they are overwhelmed at times by the caseload. But they do take each case seriously and try to resolve it quickly.

Monitor Your Child

According to a 2005 study by the Pew Internet & American Life Project[3], almost 19 million American children between the ages of 12 and 17 can access the Internet at home, representing 73 percent of those in this age bracket. The good news is that 54 percent of American families (about 12 million) have filters installed on their home computers, up 65 percent from 2000, when only 41 percent of families used filtering software. Besides the many pornographic sites, there are now more than 5,000 hate-promoting sites, up 25 percent from last year, according to the Simon Wiesenthal Center.[4]

According to a survey released in May 2005 by the National Center for Missing and Exploited Children and broadband service provider Cox Communications, just over half of parents say they don't use monitoring software on computers their teenagers use. Forty-two percent said they don't review what their teenagers are reading or writing in chat rooms or via IM software.[5]

"We see more child porn/pedophile cases, mainly because of the dollars involved," says Lieutenant Rick Wiita, supervisor of the operation's Special Investigations Division. "We've found there are over 100,000 Web sites related to child exploitation. One particular site was in operation for 90 days. During that period, they received 150,000 hits and 3.2 million images were downloaded. Six people were arrested."

This increase in cases is the reason why so many online safety organizations, including Operation Blue Ridge Thunder and WHOA-KTD, are involved in passing legislation state by state and federally.

Several laws have been passed to help protect children online. The U.S. Congress passed the Children's Online Privacy Protection Act (COPPA, www.coppa.org) in 1998. According to the Electronic Privacy Information Center (www.epic.org):

> The Children's Online Privacy Protection Act ("COPPA") specifically protects the privacy of children under the age of 13 by requesting parental consent for the collection or use of any personal information of the users. The Act took effect in April 2000. The Act was passed in response to a growing awareness of Internet marketing techniques that targeted children and collected their personal information from websites without any parental notification. The Act applies to commercial websites and online services that are directed at children. The main requirements of the Act that a website operator must comply with include:

- Incorporation of a detailed privacy policy that describes the information collected from its users.

- Acquisition of a verifiable parental consent prior to collection of personal information from a child under the age of 13.

- Disclosure to parents of any information collected on their children by the website.

- A Right to revoke consent and have information deleted.

- Limited collection of personal information when a child participates in online games and contests.

• A general requirement to protect the confidentiality, security, and integrity of any personal information that is collected online from children.

Congress' intent in passing the Act was to increase parental involvement in children's online activities, ensure children's safety during their participation in online activities, and most importantly, protect children's personal information.

Another law is the Children's Internet Protection Act (CIPA at www.fcc.gov/cgb/consumerfacts/cipa.htm). The FTC Web site states that:

Schools and libraries subject to CIPA are required to adopt a policy addressing: (a) access by minors to inappropriate matter on the Internet and World Wide Web; (b) the safety and security of minors when using electronic mail, chat rooms, and other forms of direct electronic communications; (c) unauthorized access, including so-called "hacking," and other unlawful activities by minors online; (d) unauthorized disclosure, use, and dissemination of personal information regarding minors; and (e) restricting minors' access to materials harmful to them. CIPA does not require the tracking of Internet use by minors or adults.

Slowly, but surely, other countries are following in the U.S.'s footsteps by introducing legislation and passing laws to protect children online.

How Bad Is It?

In the study conducted by the Crimes against Children Research Center (CCRC) called Internet-initiated Sex Crimes against Minors (2004), it was found that 76 percent of first encounters between a child predator and a victim happened in a chat room. Other eye-opening results include:

• 64 percent of child predators communicated with the victim online for more than one month in order to develop a relationship.

- 79 percent escalated to telephone conversations.

- 48 percent sent photos online to their victims.

- 47 percent offered or gave the victim gifts or money.

- Surprisingly, only 5 percent of the predators claimed they were the same age as the victim.

- However, 25 percent did introduce themselves as being close in age to the victim, then later on confessed they were older.

- Although 21 percent were not open about their motives for chatting with the children, most were very open about wanting sex from the victim.

- 74 percent progressed to meeting in person with the victim and 93 percent of those meetings involved illegal sexual activity between the predator and the victim.

Why are so many kids at risk online? There are several reasons, according to Welch, vice president of WHOA-KTD.

"Most parents aren't learning about the Internet themselves," Welch says. "There are those who don't want to learn and those who just don't understand. Even the ones who do use the Internet and know it fairly well just don't want to be bothered. They think it won't happen to their child, that it's something that only happens to other kids. Then you have the parents who overreact if their child does come to them with a question about something odd happening in a chat room."

Welch feels kids should know that there are good and bad sides to the Internet, as well as good people and bad people online, just like in real life.

"Kids tend to forget that the other person they are chatting with or IMing might not be who they really are," she warns. "Schools assume the kids are being watched by parents at home and parents assume schools are keeping an eye on their kids when they're online at school ... the same goes with libraries. But if kids and teens don't know how and why they need to be cautious online, no one takes responsibility when something happens to a kid or teen. That's why we hope kids, teens, parents and other adults will come to WHOA-KTD for help when something does happen."

To that end, Cox Communications offers a host of information at its site that teaches kids and their parents all about Internet safety.

On the Web site, www.cox.com/TakeCharge, there are guidelines for safe chatting for kids and parents, protecting your personal information online, and a sample "family contract" to make surfing the Internet safer for everyone in your family. Other popular sections include chat room lingo for parents, 10 tips for safe surfing, and much more.

Not only kids in middle and high school become targets of predators online. Parents are allowing their very young children to go online, too, simply because kids take to computers quickly and easily. They all seem to want to go online and see what's out there. And that can be dangerous, especially if they go to the wrong Web sites, or get unwanted e-mail messages, IMs, or questions in chat rooms.

"Some predators will send young children sexually explicit photographs," says Welch. "They are trying to convince that child that sex is normal and fun, no matter what your age. Once they have that child in their confidence, they take it from there, making up sexual games while they chat or IM each other, or if the child has access to a Webcam ... well, use your imagination. It's not pretty."

Cyberbullies

It used to be that if a child was bullied at school, he could go home and breathe a sigh of relief. Not anymore. Bullies have discovered that they can follow their victims everywhere—on the Internet via chat, IM, and e-mail or on a victim's cell phone using text messaging, IM, and phone calls, or by taking photographs or videos of the victim, then posting them online.

Here are some disturbing statistics about offline and online bullying:

- According to FBI Statistics (1993) from the National Education Association, 160,000 children miss school every day due to fear of attack or intimidation by other students.

- In 1999, 5 percent of students ages 12 through 18 reported being bullied at school in "the previous six months." Bullying is being "picked on" or made to do things they did not want to do (National Center for Educational Statistics and Bureau of Justice Statistics, 2001, Indicators of School Crime and Safety 2001).

- Only 25 percent of students report that teachers intervene in bullying situations, while 71 percent of teachers believe they always intervene (Bully B'Ware).

- The majority of bullying goes unnoticed and unreported—kids and teens may be too embarrassed to seek help or tell an adult what is being done to them.

- While most bullying behavior begins in school, the Internet is more of a cloak-and-dagger secrecy. A bully feels safer with cyber distance between him and his victim—the bully feels anonymous.

- Effects of bullying can last a lifetime, leaving emotional scars that may never go away.

- Bullying reduces a victim's self-esteem and can cause deep depression, and in the worst-case scenario, suicide may be seen as the only means of stopping the torture.

Sometimes the victims just can't handle the bullying anymore.

This happened to Ryan Halligan of Vermont in October 2003. A bright and happy 13-year-old, Ryan was bullied at school by a group of boys. This had been going on for a couple of years. Then they found his e-mail address and IM username and the torment escalated online. He received hundreds of harassing messages from his bullies. One wrote to him: "You're a loser." Another wrote that Patrick was ugly; another that he was stupid. Other messages were much worse.

Then one day, one of the bullies appeared to have had a change of heart and took Patrick under his wing. His parents, John and Kellie, warned him to not trust this boy. Sure enough, they were right.

"This classmate went on to describe how Ryan had shared something very personal with him—a detail about a medical exam Ryan received in the fall that included a rectal examination that was performed by a young female intern," recounts his parents on the Web site they created in Ryan's name, www.ryanpatrickhalligan.com. "We'll never know why Ryan decided to share this aspect of his emergency room exam. Perhaps he thought it was a funny story. The bully ran with the story and spread a rumor around the school that Ryan likes anal sex and therefore Ryan must be gay. According to other students that later corroborated the story, this was spread online as well through IM and chat. One kid described the scene at school as being a feeding frenzy. Throughout the school day, Ryan was teased and humiliated by many. His friends tried to console him but he just pushed them away ... often running into the bathroom between classes to hide his upset and collect himself. According to another student, two teachers asked him what was the matter. We'll never know what he said because we never got a call from the school that this went on in the first place."

Soon afterward, Ryan's sister Megan opened the bathroom door to find that Ryan had hanged himself. It was only when his father logged onto Ryan's AOL account that he discovered how extensive the cyberbullying had become. This led John and Kellie to get a cyberbullying law passed in Vermont. Other states have since followed. Schools are taking bullying and cyberbullying more seriously. And they should, before another child becomes the next Ryan Halligan.

What Is Bullying?

Bullying is a form of violence. It is a brutish, learned behavior that some kids use to feel superior and powerful. Bullies want attention and believe it is cool to make their victims feel helpless. Bullish behavior has always been around, but the Internet adds dimension with new twists, turns, and refinements. The Internet is a new frontier for bullies who select kids they think can be victimized and made fun of and who they can diminish in the eyes of other kids. They use the computer to effect devastating public humiliation. Kids are fragile and this behavior is very damaging to them, often causing long term and painful depression.

Bullying behavior includes:

- Prolonged attention that is unwelcome, unsolicited, and unwarranted

- Physical, verbal, and/or written attacks that are repeated and cruel, including racist comments

- Deliberate belittling, name-calling, or embarrassing tactics such as painful constant teasing

- Intimidation, including threats

- Spreading of mean, hurtful, and nasty rumors that invite peers to exclude and reject the victim

- Creation of hateful Web sites and blogs designed to shame and embarrass the victim

- Any behavior that makes the victim obviously uncomfortable

- Use of a false identity or somebody else's identity in order to perpetuate untruths or rumors

The good news is that kids and teens do not have to feel unsafe or be afraid of bullies on the Internet any longer. It is important for kids to know they are not alone. Bullying is not their fault. Kids need to be reassured, supported, and, more than anything else, they need to learn how they can stay safe online. WHOA-KTD (www.haltabuse ktd.org) is one place that kids can turn to and ask for help. They will teach victims how to prevent bullies from using the Internet to hurt them, as well as what to do if they are bullied online.

Other cyberbullying resources include:

Cyberbullying.ca
www.cyberbullying.ca

Cyberbullying
www.cyberbully.org

Bullies on the Internet
www.bullyonline.org/related/cyber.htm

Bully Beware
www.bullybeware.com

Stop Cyberbullying
www.stopcyberbullying.org

Net Bullies
www.netbullies.com

It's Not All Bad

The Internet can be a wonderful educational tool. Because it's international, kids can go online and learn about different cultures. Also, they can access documents and information they probably wouldn't find in their school or local library. And this can all be done from the comfort and safety of their own home.

There are hundreds, if not thousands, of educational sites on the Web. For instance, there are the TV-related sites—such as Nickelodeon, Disney, Sesame Street, and the Fox Family Channel—that help children learn. On the Web, kids can play interactive games that actually teach them something, or play games that are just plain fun. They can download printable coloring books and even find out how to play new offline games with their friends.

Here are some activities parents can share on the Web with their kids:

1. *Plan a trip*. Whether families are planning to go to Walt Disney World, drive across the country, or go to the beach for the weekend, parents can sit with their kids and plan the trip together online. See if there's something interesting about where you're going that you wouldn't find out from the brochures or travel agent. (For instance, have you ever heard of the world's largest ball of twine? No? You'll find out about it online at www.roadsideamerica.com/attract/MNDARtwine.html.) Figure out what you want to do, where you want to eat, and if the hotel you're staying at has a swimming pool with a water slide.

2. *Plan a pretend trip*. Go on safari in Africa, walk the outback in Australia, or experience haunted castles in Ireland (there are plenty of those!)—all without leaving the house.

3. *Build your family tree*. Get your kids started with your parents' and grandparents' names and see how far back you can trace your family online. You may find you have a long-lost cousin in the next town.

4. *Get an online pen pal*. Help your kids find an online pen pal in a foreign country so they can share what it's like living in the U.S. vs. Japan or Brazil or Iceland or even Nova Scotia.

These are just a few of the many fun and educational things you can do online. Use your imagination!

What's a Cache and How Do You Check It?

A cache is your computer's backup of all the Web sites that have been visited, including graphics and any of the pages accessed. This is a great way to find out where your child has been. The following instructions will help you check the cache in the most popular Internet browsers from Netscape and Microsoft.

Netscape Navigator Versions 4.x and higher
Check the History first, by hitting the Ctrl and H keys, or by going to the pull-down menu on the top toolbar and

Title	Location	First Visited	Last Visited	Expiration	Visit Count
	http://member.audiobookclub.co...	1 hours ago	1 hours ago	7/27/2001 1:5...	1
Online Respond	http://member.audiobookclub.co...	1 hours ago	1 hours ago	7/27/2001 1:5...	1
Online Respond	http://member.audiobookclub.co...	1 hours ago	1 hours ago	7/27/2001 1:5...	1
Audiobookclub.com Monthly...	http://member.audiobookclub.co...	1 hours ago	1 hours ago	7/27/2001 1:5...	1
Audio Book Club	http://member.audiobookclub.co...	1 hours ago	1 hours ago	7/27/2001 1:5...	1
Audio Book Club	http://member.audiobookclub.co...	1 hours ago	1 hours ago	7/27/2001 1:5...	1
Audio Book Club	http://member.audiobookclub.co...	1 hours ago	1 hours ago	7/27/2001 1:5...	1
Audio Book Club	http://member.audiobookclub.co...	1 hours ago	1 hours ago	7/27/2001 1:5...	1
Audio Book Club	http://member.audiobookclub.co...	1 hours ago	1 hours ago	7/27/2001 1:5...	1
AudioBookClub.com Membe...	http://member.audiobookclub.co...	1 hours ago	1 hours ago	7/27/2001 1:5...	1
AudioBookClub.com Membe...	http://member.audiobookclub.co...	1 hours ago	1 hours ago	7/27/2001 1:5...	1
eBay item 1450175734 (End...	http://cgi.ebay.com/aw-cgi/eBay...	1 hours ago	1 hours ago	7/27/2001 1:5...	1
Items matching (theory of pe...	http://search.ebay.com/search/s...	1 hours ago	1 hours ago	7/27/2001 1:5...	1
Items matching (stephen kin...	http://search.ebay.com/search/s...	1 hours ago	1 hours ago	7/27/2001 1:5...	1
eBay Listings : Audio	http://listings.ebay.com/aw/plisti...	1 hours ago	1 hours ago	7/27/2001 1:5...	1
eBay: Books	http://pages.ebay.com/catindex/...	1 hours ago	1 hours ago	7/27/2001 1:5...	1
eBay - the world's online mar...	http://www.ebay.com/	1 hours ago	1 hours ago	7/27/2001 1:5...	1
DRUDGE REPORT 2001®	http://www.drudgereport.com/	1 hours ago	1 hours ago	7/27/2001 1:5...	2
DNC Chief Decries Tax Che...	http://dailynews.yahoo.com/h/x/...	1 hours ago	1 hours ago	7/27/2001 1:5...	1
eBay item 1168861286 (End...	http://cgi.ebay.com/aw-cgi/eBay...	5 hours ago	1 hours ago	7/27/2001 1:4...	26
eBay Seller List: jmeg3000	http://cgi6.ebay.com/aw-cgi/eBa...	1 hours ago	1 hours ago	7/27/2001 1:3...	1
eBay Item Bid History	http://cgi6.ebay.com/aw-cgi/eBa...	1 hours ago	1 hours ago	7/27/2001 1:2...	2
eBay View User Feedback f...	http://cgi2.ebay.com/aw-cgi/eBa...	1 hours ago	1 hours ago	7/27/2001 1:2...	2
eBay ' ' - Invalid Item	http://cgi.ebay.com/aw-cgi/eBay...	1 hours ago	1 hours ago	7/27/2001 1:2...	1
eBay Leave Feedback abou...	http://cgi2.ebay.com/aw-cgi/eBa...	2 hours ago	2 hours ago	7/27/2001 1:2...	1
eBay item 1167444614 (End...	http://cgi2.ebay.com/aw-cgi/eBa...	2 hours ago	2 hours ago	7/27/2001 1:2...	1
eBay Leave Feedback abou...	http://cgi2.ebay.com/aw-cgi/eBa...	2 hours ago	2 hours ago	7/27/2001 1:2...	1
eBay item 1166529972 (End...	http://cgi.ebay.com/aw-cgi/eBay...	2 hours ago	2 hours ago	7/27/2001 1:2...	1
PayPal - Log Out	http://www.paypal.com/cgi-bin/...	2 hours ago	2 hours ago		1

Figure 15.4   Netscape history

clicking on Communicator, then Tools, then History (see Figure 15.4).

The history shows Web sites visited, date and time visited, and how many times a site has been visited. If you want to go to a previously visited site, double-click the URL. If there's a questionable site listed there, it's a good idea to check the cache. To do this, you need to know where your browser cache is stored on your hard drive. Just go to the top toolbar and click on Edit, then Preferences. A separate window pops up. Now select Advanced, then Cache, as shown in Figure 15.5.

Look for "Disk Cache Folder" and you'll see where it's stored. The default is usually C:\Program Files\Netscape\ Users\default\cache. To get there, you need to open up Windows Explorer (your file directory). Click on the Start button, and then look for "Windows Explorer" in one of the subdirectories if it isn't on the main list.

When Windows Explorer is open, click on My Computer, then the plus sign (+) next to C: (your hard drive). This expands the listing to show all the directories on your C: hard drive. Now look for the directory where the cache is stored: Program Files, Netscape, Users, Default (or your username), and click on Cache. You should see a lot of files here. If you don't, they have been manually deleted and you need to talk with your child.

Netscape Communicator Versions 6.x and higher

As with Netscape Navigator, check the History in Communicator by hitting the Ctrl and H keys.

You can also check the cache. Depending on which version of Windows you are using, the cache will be in the system folder. For example, if using Windows XP, it should be in C:\DOCUMENTS AND SETTINGS\ADMINISTRATOR\ APPLICATION DATA\Mozilla\Profiles\ (see Figure 15.6).

Microsoft Internet Explorer (MSIE) Version 5.x and higher

To check the history and cache in MSIE, go to the top toolbar and click on Tools, then Internet Options (see Figure 15.7). A separate tabbed window pops up.

Go to "Temporary Internet Files" (MSIE's name for the cache file) and click on Settings (see Figure 15.8). This shows you the current location for the cache.

If you click on View Files, you'll be able to see names of the sites visited, graphics, and so forth; the dates and times visited; and how many times a site was visited. Again, if this is empty, it's time to talk to your child.

Mozilla Firefox, Version 1.0 and higher

To check the History, hit the Ctrl + H keys. A frame appears on the left of the browser with folder listing Today and Yesterday's Web sites visited, listed alphabetically (see Figure 15.9). Just click on the site and it automatically comes up to the right. There is also a handy Search function if you are looking for a particular site. To close the History frame, just hit the Ctrl + H keys again.

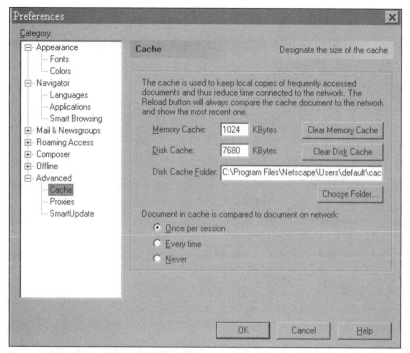

Figure 15.5   Netscape cache menu

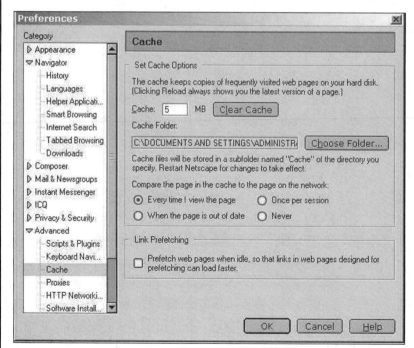

Figure 15.6   Netscape cache options

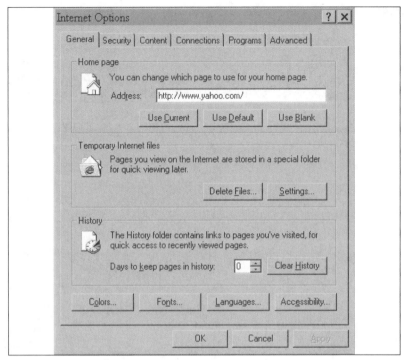

Figure 15.7   MSIE history

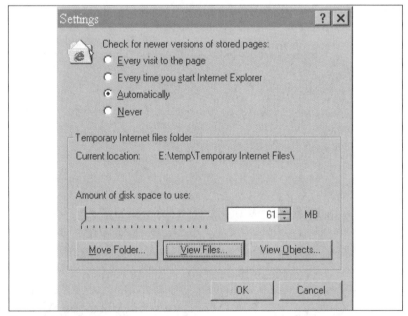

Figure 15.8   MSIE cache

Figure 15.9 Mozilla Firefox history

How to Protect Your Child Online

The experts interviewed seem to agree that the following actions will help:

1. Get actively involved in your children's online life. Know what they are doing online. If your child has created a personal Web site, what information is posted on it? How about an online journal (such as LiveJournal) or diary, also known as a blog (short for Weblog)? If there's anything personal or that could easily identify where you live or where your child goes to school, explain why it needs to be changed. The same goes with profiles. Make sure as little as possible is filled in, and select a username/e-mail address for kids that is gender-neutral to make it harder for predators to guess their age and sex.

2. Place the computer in a den, family room, kitchen, or other high-traffic location. Don't allow your child to keep a computer with an Internet connection in the bedroom where the

door can be closed while online. If they close the door whenever they go online, regard it as a danger sign.

3. Use a filtering/screening program such as CyberPatrol, NetNanny, SafeBrowse, or Kidsnet.

4. Set use of the computer to specific times so that your child does not spend an excessive amount of time online.

5. Monitor how frequently your child gets unfamiliar e-mail — and read it.

6. Become more computer literate. The best way to do this is to sit down with your child and ask them to show you how the Internet works. You may be surprised to find how much they enjoy the role of teacher.

7. Sit and work alongside your child while they are online.

8. Warn your children to be cautious with online strangers.

9. Monitor your long-distance phone bill for evidence that your child has been in contact with a stranger.

10. If your child receives strange phone calls or gifts from strangers, find out what's going on.

11. If your child turns off the monitor or computer when you approach, regard it as a warning sign.

12. Know what your children are looking at on the computer. If you find that it's pornography, it's time for a chat. If you check the Web browser cache and find it's already been cleaned out or that it's empty, it's time for a chat. If you check the Recycle Bin to see if the cache info is there and it's not, it's time to disconnect the computer from the Internet and have a serious chat.

If something does happen to your child online, do not panic. Yes, you're upset, but understand that your child may be more upset than you are, and frightened—not only about what happened but also about the possibility that you'll be angry. Remain calm and find out what happened and when. Then contact an online safety organization such as Operation Blue Ridge Thunder, WHOA-KTD, CyberAngels, or the NCMEC for advice. If a predator has arranged to meet your child, call your local police immediately.

How the Filtering Software Rates

In 2005, *Consumer Reports* magazine tested 11 filtering software packages[6] on sites known to contain objectionable material such as sexual content and the promotion of crime, bigotry, violence, tobacco, and drugs. It found that all of the filtering software tested actually did a good job, much better than the software *Consumer Reports* tested back in 2000, although the software is still not perfect.

The testers at *Consumer Reports* built a list of objectionable Web sites that anyone could easily find, plus informational sites to test the filters' ability to discern the objectionable from the merely sensitive. They configured each filter as it would most likely be configured by the parent of a 12- to 15-year-old, then tried to access those sites.

They found that all of the filtering programs keep most, but not all, pornography out. The worst performer was at 88 percent, but showed that it still blocked a majority of pornographic sites. Most of the programs had trouble blocking hate sites—sites with instructions on how to kill a person, illegal drug use, etc. And some good Web sites were blocked, such as health sites, sites about civil rights, or political sites. But the good news is that almost all of these filtering programs can be adjusted so that parents can add or delete a Web site on the pre-approved list that came with the program.

Filtering Programs

Mention Internet filtering programs and watch organizations such as the American Civil Liberties Union (ACLU), the Center for Democracy and Technology (CDT), and the Electronic Frontier Foundation (EFF) come out swinging. For these organizations, it's an issue of freedom of speech and the First Amendment. But these are your children—should you use a filtering program? It's really a choice, and it's yours to make.

Filtering programs continue to improve and to offer increasing options for customization by the user. In addition to offering preinstalled lists of Web sites that are automatically filtered, typically you can now deselect sites you don't find objectionable and add others that you do.

Descriptions of some popular filtering programs follow.

CyberPatrol

www.cyberpatrol.com

CyberPatrol is a typical filtering program. It includes a preset list of filtered Web sites, which are checked out by the company's researchers. You can override the list and customize filtering to your preferences, a positive CyberPatrol feature. (Be forewarned: There are hundreds of sites to wade through, although they are categorized and subcategorized to try to make it easier.) Another benefit is that access to the Internet can be restricted to certain times of the day or for a certain amount of time. Your child won't be able to stay online past the allotted time. CyberPatrol is offered on a free trial basis, so take advantage of this and then decide for yourself.

CYBERsitter

www.cybersitter.com

Among the many features available, CYBERsitter records all IM chat conversations for AOL (AIM) and Yahoo! Messengers. Now you can know who your kids are chatting with to ensure that they are not communicating with strangers. CYBERsitter also provides more than 30 categories of filtering that are updated automatically, and there are no subscription charges. A sophisticated "content recognition" system recognizes and blocks new objectionable Web sites. In addition, parents can override blocked sites, add their own sites to block, specify allowable times to access the Internet, and maintain a detailed log of all Internet activity and violations. CYBERsitter will even send a daily report to parents by e-mail. A free trial is offered.

NetNanny

www.netnanny.com

In addition to letting you customize the list of blocked Web sites, NetNanny (see Figure 15.10) allows parents to utilize built-in pop-up blockers to keep the screen from filling up with advertisements from adult solicitors and other over-zealous advertisers. Free 15-day trial is available.

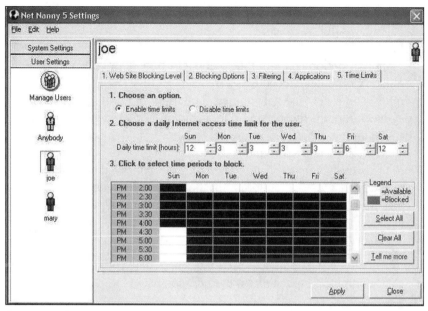

Figure 15.10   NetNanny

Kidsnet

www.kidsnet.com

Kidsnet is a unique, powerful approach that lets you determine what your children can access on the Internet. Content specialists have reviewed millions of Web sites to ensure complete protection of your children with this software. In addition, they have examined Web sites that represent more than 98 percent of all World Wide Web traffic with a special focus on sites interesting to children. A free trial is available on the Web site.

Other useful filtering programs include:

McAfee Parental Controls
www.mcafee.com

Norton Internet Security Parental Control
www.symantec.com

iProtectYou Pro Web Filter
www.softforyou

SafeBrowse
www.safebrowse.com

Another option is to limit the amount of time your child can spend online. "ComputerTime allows parents to set time limits on their children's computer use at home, including amount of time per day/week/month, the very important time-of-day usage (so parents can be home when the computer is used), and more," says Joe Acunzo, CEO and co-founder of SoftwareTime, the company that produces the ComputerTime software. "We believe the computer is an amazing tool for children for both education and recreation. Unfortunately, it can be, and often is, misused and therefore parental guidance is necessary."

Some of the many benefits include:

- Allowing parents to be present when their children are on the computer, especially on the Internet

- Curtailing children's instant messaging addictions

- Ensuring children don't stay up past bedtime on a school night because they're chatting online

- Making sure homework is done before the computer can be used

SoftwareTime also allows parents to:

- Disable the use of the computer entirely

- Set alternate limits—different limits for things like vacation week

- Use time tokens, which provide additional time, without changing settings, as incentive or reward

- Set different time limits for weekdays and weekends, or even individual days

A free trial download is available on the SoftwareTime Web site (www.softwaretime.com).

If you don't want to install software, there is an alternative (besides keeping a computer out of your child's hands): Filtered Internet Providers.

A Filtered Internet Provider is like an ISP except it automatically filters out certain Web sites. The good news is that the Filtered Internet Providers are competitive with regular ISPs, and many offer free trials so you can test them for yourself. The bad news is that you can't choose which Web sites you want filtered or accessible. Also, the Filtered Internet Provider may not be available for access as a local telephone number. Some offer portals, which essentially allow you to use their filtering process while using their Web site as your browser. However, if your kids are as smart as most kids are, they can figure out how to back out of this site and surf the "old way."

Filtered Internet Providers include:

Family Safe Web, the Family Friendly Internet Service Provider
www.familysafeweb.net

Mayberry USA
www.mbusa.net

Safe Access
www.safeaccess.com

Dnet Internet Services
http://get.dnet.net

More Filtered Internet Providers can be found at The List at http://thelist.internet.com. Type "filtered" in the search text box.

While your kids may gripe about your concern, they will appreciate it when you take the time to show them that you care about what happens to them—online or offline. Just be open with them, and encourage them to be open with you so that if something does happen, you're the first person they go to for help.

Endnotes

1. This study, Internet-initiated Sex Crimes Against Minors: Implications for Prevention, was conducted by David Finkelhor, PhD; Kimberly Mitchell, PhD; and Janis Wolak, J. D. of the Computer Crimes Research Center (CCRC) at the University of New Hampshire, Durham, www.unh.edu/ccrc/pdf/CV71.pdf

2. This study, Internet Sex Crimes Against Minors: The Response of Law Enforcement, was conducted by David Finkelhor, PhD; Kimberly Mitchell, PhD; and Janis Wolak, J. D. of the CCRC for the National Center for Missing & Exploited Children (NCMEC), www.missingkids.com/en_US/publications/NC132.pdf

3. Teens and Technology: Youth are Leading the Transition to a Fully Wired and Mobile Nation, Pew Internet & American Life Project, July 2005, www.pewinternet.org/PPF/r/162/report_display.asp

4. Simon Weisenthal Center's Digital Hate and Terrorism 2005 Study, www.wiesenthal.com

5. New Study Reveals Parents Need Better Cybersmarts—survey commissioned by the National Center for Missing & Exploited Children (NCMEC) and Cox Communication; May 2005, www.cox.com/TakeCharge

6. Published in June 2005, available at www.consumerreports.org

Office Know-How:
Stay Safe in the Workplace

Each day, you arrive at work and don't think twice about safety while using your office computer. But listen to this: Whether your company has an intranet or Local Area Network (LAN),[1] you can still become an online target. Trouble can come from someone within the company or outside of it.

Melanie's Surprise

Melanie received a puzzling e-mail at work from Escorts.com, thanking her for the information she submitted and telling her someone would be in touch soon.

"I replied and asked them to remove me from their mailing list," Melanie says. "And I left a message for the network administrator at Escorts.com to find out who submitted my information in the first place."

Melanie went to lunch. When she returned, there was an e-mail from someone else with the subject line: "thanksgiving." When she opened the attached file, it was a two-minute video of a man masturbating. Melanie was Web-savvy enough to know how to show the full headers in the message and she tracked the message back to the pornographic Web site from where it originated. She learned that the fiancé of Sharon, one of her co-workers, was the network administrator for the pornographic Web site. She printed everything out and brought it to the president of the company for discussion.

The president told her the company couldn't do anything because it wasn't an employee who had harassed her. Melanie approached the vice president, who was friendly with Sharon. The vice president approached Sharon, and when he explained the situation she said she knew Melanie had received the e-mail, but that it had been a mistake. The message was intended for her. When Sharon was asked about Escorts.com, she said she had no idea what that was about.

The vice president felt this was good enough and advised Melanie to drop it. Melanie argued that even if it had been a mistake, wasn't there something wrong with Sharon receiving pornographic e-mail attachments through the company e-mail system? She was told that if Sharon had been sending pornographic e-mail she would have been terminated.

Even though Melanie received no additional offensive e-mail messages, this incident left her feeling uncomfortable at work. She soon left to take another job.

E-Mail Usage Study

According to a 2004 Survey on Workplace E-Mail and IM conducted by the ePolicy Institute[2]:

- 21 percent of employers had employee e-mail and IM records subpoenaed in the course of a lawsuit or regulatory investigation (more than double from 2001).

- 13 percent of employers have battled workplace lawsuits triggered by employee e-mails.

- Only 6 percent of employers surveyed retain and archive IMs; 35 percent have an e-mail retention policy in place.

- 79 percent of employers have implemented a written e-mail policy (only 20 percent of those include IM in the policy).

- 16 percent of employees reported they received IMs containing jokes, gossip, rumors, or disparaging remarks.

- 6 percent reported receiving IMs containing sexual or pornographic content.

Was the company legally responsible for what happened? No. A company cannot be held responsible for the actions of an employee's friend, relative, or significant other who is outside of the workplace. Since the e-mail messages had stopped by the time they were brought to the company's attention, no further action was required. So, the company's conduct in this case was legally defensible, but—given that Melanie had received the messages through her e-mail account at work—could the company have done more to help her?

The answer, in my opinion, is yes. The company could have helped Melanie contact the ISP and Web sites involved, letting them know the situation. It could have explained that the messages were sent to a company e-mail address, that this was unacceptable, and that it expected some action to be taken. Sharon could have been reprimanded for knowingly accepting obscene e-mail messages at work. Melanie's superiors might also have offered to move her to a different department or branch office in order to make her work environment as comfortable as possible.

However, this company had no guidelines or policies in place regarding online harassment. If it had, it could have addressed this situation more effectively and possibly avoided losing a good employee.

In fact, the company was lucky Melanie did not sue for sexual harassment. Sexual harassment is a form of sex discrimination that violates Title VII of the Civil Rights Act of 1964. This is how the definition appears:

> Unwelcome sexual advances, requests for sexual favors, and other verbal or physical conduct of a sexual nature constitutes sexual harassment when submission to or rejection of this conduct explicitly or implicitly affects an individual's employment, unreasonably interferes with an individual's work performance, or creates an intimidating, hostile, or offensive work environment.

Sexual harassment of a woman or a man can occur in a variety of circumstances. Note the following important points:

- The victim does not have to be of the opposite sex of the harasser.

- The harasser can be the victim's supervisor, a co-worker, a supervisor in another area, an agent of the employer, or a non-employee.

- The victim does not have to be the person harassed but could be anyone affected by the offensive conduct.

- Unlawful sexual harassment may occur without economic injury to or discharge of the victim.

- Conduct must be unwelcome for it to be considered harassment.

Advice for employers:

1. Develop and distribute a company Internet usage policy that offers guidelines for employee conduct and covers online-related abuse and harassment issues.

2. Install firewall protection and anti-virus software on each computer in the company, not just on the LAN/intranet.

3. Consider installing monitoring software on company computers. You need to know if an employee is downloading obscene material, visiting pornographic Web sites, stealing company secrets, sending or receiving harassing e-mails, and so on. Make sure your written policy advises employees that their electronic communications and activities may be monitored.

4. Don't use an employee's first and last name as her e-mail address; allow employees to select something gender-neutral or assign a gender-neutral username.

5. Don't list all of the e-mail addresses of employees on the company Web site unless the employee needs to be listed there (as a public relations contact, for instance).

6. If an employee comes to you with a complaint of online harassment/stalking, whether or not the perpetrator is within the company, change the employee's e-mail address immediately, as well as his or her voicemail extension. Do not post the new e-mail/voicemail information anywhere, online or offline, for as long as there is a threat of continued harassment.

7. Take all employee complaints seriously. Investigate and act on them immediately. Being proactive in these situations will say a lot to your employees.

8. Consider involving local law enforcement. If you attempt to handle a harassment case yourself and the perpetrator physically harms the victim and/or others at the company, you will regret not going to the police in the first place. Hiring a private investigator may also be a viable option.

I Spy

Many companies have turned to filtering, monitoring, and what many employees call "spyware" to keep track of what employees do online—whether it's receiving or sending e-mail, surfing the Web, Instant Messaging through the company system, or putting games or obscene material on the computer hard drives at their desks.

WinWhatWhere (www.winwhatwhere.com, see Figure 16.1) is a spyware program. It allows employers to monitor all computer-related activity (not just online-related), selectively exclude particular programs from the log, or monitor only selected programs. It can specify certain days and times to monitor the activity. This means that every time employees run a program or application, it can be logged. If they have a game on their hard drive and they play it, that activity can be logged. Every keystroke they make on the keyboard can be logged—Web sites they visit and the contents of e-mail messages sent or received, even if the messages have been deleted. The program has a stealth mode so that employees never know they're being monitored (see Figure 16.2).

Because of the availability of programs like WinWhatWhere, more employers are implementing guidelines or policies that state specifically what they expect of employees and what they would consider a violation.

In the past, some companies put together guidelines outlining telephone privileges—such as whether an employee can make personal or long-distance calls and what reprisal would follow if they did. Or companies laid out the rules for using the company postage meter, photocopier, or computer printer for personal use. It makes sense to add electronic communications to this practice of rule making.

"Every company should have this policy. But make sure it's not hidden so that no one sees it or knows about it," says Eric Rolfe

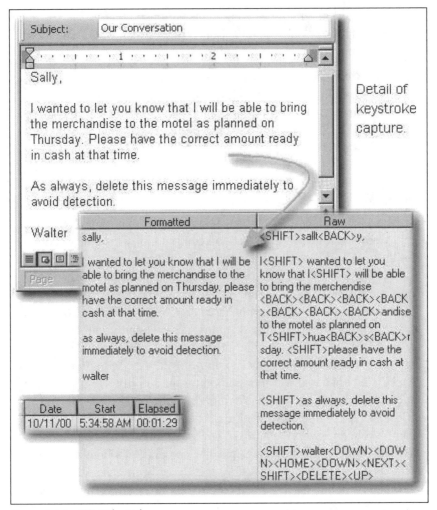

Figure 16.1 WinWhatWhere

Greenberg, director of management studies, American Management Association (AMA). "So many companies tend to throw new policies or guidelines in the back of an already unwieldy publication and neglect to properly inform employees and new hires about it. When they implement a new policy, such as proper use of online communications in the workplace, every employee needs to be trained in it, not just given the policy printed on paper to read. This would easily take care of potential problems."

Eric Friedberg of Stroz Associates, a computer crimes consulting business, agrees. "Obtain appropriate consents from all employees

3:13:17 AM	00:00:00	DELETE:A:\Web Site Visitors.xls
3:13:17 AM	00:00:00	DELETE:A:\INVEST.BAK
3:13:17 AM	00:00:00	DELETE:A:\AMEX.TXT
3:13:17 AM	00:00:03	3½ Floppy (A:)
3:13:20 AM	00:00:00	My Documents
3:13:20 AM	00:00:21	My Documents
3:13:41 AM	00:00:02	3½ Floppy (A:)
3:13:43 AM	00:00:00	Moving...
3:13:43 AM	00:00:00	3½ Floppy (A:)
3:13:43 AM	00:00:00	CREATE:A:\Government Charges 120 People in Nationwide Securities Fraud Crackdown.url
3:13:43 AM	00:00:02	DELETE:C:\My Documents\Government Charges 120 People in Nationwide Securities Fraud Crackdown.url

Figure 16.2   WinWhatWhere—stealth mode

and consultants that their e-mail accounts, office-issued laptops, PDAs,[3] cell phones, and text messaging devices can be monitored or searched," Friedberg says. "Often, an incident that appears to originate from an unknown person is being perpetrated by a fellow employee. Consents in employment agreements give an extra level of comfort to executives and in-house counsel in conducting internal investigations."

An example is a superior who admonishes or fires an employee via e-mail instead of in person. The employee might reply in anger (justifiable, but the wrong thing to do) and possibly escalate the situation. Or the now ex-employee could sue the company for discrimination, sexual harassment, and so forth, and use the e-mail as evidence.

Even if the e-mail message gets to the correct person(s), if it contains confidential information, this could be used against the company at some point. This is what happened to Microsoft when the Department of Justice investigated them.

With a little bit of thought and common sense, you might decide it is better to communicate in person, over the phone, or via a memo.

Office Netiquette— More Than Just Manners

Here are some important do's and don'ts for employees:

- Don't give out your password or PIN number and don't write it where others can easily see it.

- Be polite when you are communicating within your company or on the Internet. Remember that you're using your work account and if you do something that could be considered harassment or even rude, you could lose your job.

- Don't put personal information about yourself in a company profile (if your company requires one). List only basic information, such as the initials of your first and middle name, then full last name, your work extension number, and your work e-mail address/username.

- When you write an e-mail message, make it look professional, as though you were typing it to be printed and mailed via regular postal mail. Don't hit the SEND key until you've reread it at least a couple of times to make sure spelling and grammar are correct. Don't use "smileys" or cute acronyms. Always sign your e-mail messages with your full name and title.

- If you're using your work e-mail account to send messages containing your personal opinions, clearly state that this is your opinion and not necessarily that of your employer.

- Don't compose messages in all capital letters, SUCH AS THIS. It's considered shouting and may offend some people.

- Do not access pornographic material while at work—whether on the Internet or from a diskette you bring in or borrow from a co-worker. It could get you fired!

- Don't send or forward any chain letters or "Forward this to everyone you know" messages while at work or to your work associates.

- When you write a message intended for someone in a branch office in another country and who is not American, make sure you know enough about that country's customs so as not to inadvertently offend. If you don't know anything about that culture's etiquette, ask someone. It's better to be safe than sorry later (or fired for inappropriate behavior).

- If you do become a victim of online harassment at work, report it immediately, as Eric Friedberg of Stroz Associates suggests. "Harassing conduct can escalate quickly into a violent situation," he says. "Employees and companies are far better served in addressing the problem immediately. Under no circumstances should the employee attempt to deal face to face with a person who has been harassing him or her over the Internet."

To Monitor or Not to Monitor

According to the 2004 Workplace E-Mail and Instant Messaging Survey by the ePolicy Institute:

- 60 percent use software to monitor external (incoming and outgoing) e-mail.

- Only 27 percent take advantage of technology tools to monitor internal e-mail conversations that take place between employees.

- 100 percent of employees spend at least half a day (four hours), each day on e-mail, with 86 percent of it constituting personal correspondence.

Perhaps you will remember these headline stories:

Two Salomon Smith Barney executives were fired for accessing pornography and transmitting it between themselves.

The New York Times *fired 20 staffers for sending "inappropriate and offensive" e-mail, citing a need to protect itself against liability for sexual harassment claims.*

Two female employees of PNC Bank in New York were fired in August 2004 for forwarding jokes on company time. One of the e-mails featured a picture of a barebreasted woman with Hillary Clinton's head superimposed. Although the two hired a lawyer to fight their termination, PNC had a policy in place and they had already fired other employees for similar infractions. A judge dismissed the employees' case.

One company that offers filtering/watching software is SurfControl. In addition to the software, SurfControl offers many resources on its site (www.surfcontrol.com, see Figure 16.3), including a sample "acceptable use policy" (see www.surfcontrol.com/ resources/aup). TechRepublic conducted a survey in January 2002 that polled both

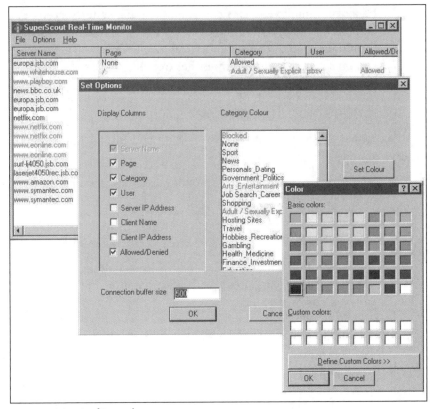

Figure 16.3   SurfControl

information technology (IT) managers and corporate Internet users on their views about the use of filtering software within their organization.[4] The results indicate that:

- 57 percent of respondents monitor e-mail and Web use of employees.

- 17 percent monitor only Web usage; 4 percent monitor only e-mail usage.

- 94 percent of respondents agreed with the statement: "It is corporate policy that the company's Internet access and e-mail system are property of the company and the company has the right to regulate and monitor its use."

- 65 percent indicate that filtering technologies are essential in order to ensure the availability of key network resources (versus 47 percent in 2001).

- Less than 6 percent felt filtering was unnecessary.

- More than 50 percent of employers had fired an employee who abused the company-provided Internet policy (on average, there were 2–3 such incidents per company).

- 65 percent of the firings involved visiting pornographic or other adult-themed Web sites.

- 38 percent were fired for inappropriate e-mails.

- Half of the respondents run reports of e-mail and/or Internet activity daily or weekly.

The other side of the coin is that this kind of "Big Brother" approach upsets many employees. They feel their phone calls, voice-mail, e-mail, and other communications should remain private and are none of the company's business.

"Workplace privacy is a contradiction in terms. It's an oxymoron," says Greenberg. "I know the illusion of privacy is there, but don't forget, you are not using your own stuff. The phone, the keyboard, the connections, the job itself—they don't belong to you. They belong to the company, legally."

TechRepublic also found in its survey:

- 72 percent of respondents indicated that unauthorized file downloads are considered a somewhat serious (38 percent), serious (22 percent), or very serious (12 percent) problem in their organizations.

- Network bottlenecks closely followed, reported by 70 percent of the respondents.

- Viruses were rated as a somewhat to a very serious problem by 61 percent of respondents.

- Another 26 percent indicated that the virus problem was considered extremely serious by their organization.

In fact, more than 30 percent of respondents indicated that viruses were responsible for more than $100,000 in loss of productivity, loss of data, or network downtime to a significant degree.

Speaking of employee sabotage, Mark Greenlaw turned on his office computer one day and found that something odd was going on. Programs were opening and closing by themselves, files were being copied, and some files were missing from the hard drive—most importantly a presentation he was set to give the following week. Panicked, he let his supervisor know and soon the company IT tech was in his office. A Trojan horse virus had been planted in his computer. The IT tech took Mark's computer and analyzed the hard drive. After a few days, the computer was returned to him, but this time his computer (and the rest of the computers in the company) was equipped with firewall and anti-virus software.

"They found out that an employee who was upset I'd been promoted over him put the Trojan in my computer," says Mark. "It was set to go off on a certain day at a certain time and when it did, he gained access to my computer and was wreaking havoc with it."

The IT tech was able to trace the Trojan to the employee by watching the activity on Mark's computer, then using "sniffer" software to track it down. The employee was fired.

"Luckily, I had a copy of the presentation on my laptop, so I didn't have to redo it," Mark says. "But we all learned a lesson, even the IT guy who thought he knew everything about computers: Make sure all the computers have firewall and anti-virus protection and keep it updated."

What Should Your Acceptable Use Policy (AUP) Look Like?

Here's an example of an AUP for business, courtesy of www.efa.org.au/Publish/aup.html (reprinted with permission). Replace "Widgets Ltd." with your company name and adjust wording accordingly, or edit as desired:

WIDGETS LTD.
ACCEPTABLE USE POLICY FOR EMPLOYEE USE
OF THE INTERNET

SUMMARY

This policy sets out guidelines for acceptable use of the Internet by employees of Widgets Ltd. The primary purpose for which access to the Internet is provided by Widgets Ltd. to its employees is to assist them in carrying out the duties of their employment. They may also use the Internet for reasonable private purposes that are consistent with this Acceptable Use Policy (AUP). They may not use the Internet access provided by Widgets Ltd. in such a way as to significantly interfere with the duties of their employment or to expose Widgets Ltd. to significant cost or risk of liability. Widgets Ltd. may modify this policy upon 30 days notice in writing to its employees.

WHAT IS ACCEPTABLE USE

Subject to the balance of this policy, employees may use the Internet access provided by Widgets Ltd. for: Work-related purposes; Sending and receiving personal e-mail messages provided that if e-mail messages are sent with a Widgets Ltd. e-mail address in the From: or Reply-To: header, a disclaimer shall accompany the message to the effect that the views of the sender may not represent those of Widgets Ltd.; Reading and posting personal Usenet messages on the same condition specified above; Using instant messaging software for personal purposes; Accessing the World Wide Web for personal purposes; and Utilizing any other Internet service or protocol for personal purposes after obtaining permission to do so from Widgets Ltd.; provided in each case that the personal use is moderate in time, does not incur significant cost for Widgets Ltd., and does not interfere with the employment duties of the employee or his or her colleagues.

WHAT IS NOT ACCEPTABLE USE

Except in the course of an employee's duties or with the express permission of Widgets Ltd., the Internet access provided by the company may not be used for: personal commercial purposes; sending unsolicited bulk e-mail; disseminating confidential information about Widgets Ltd.; any illegal purpose; knowingly causing interference with or disruption to any network, information service, equipment,

or any user thereof; harassing either a fellow or nonem-
ployee; disseminating personal contact information of officers or employees of Widgets Ltd. without their consent;
knowingly causing any other person to view content that
could render the company liable pursuant to equal opportunity or sex discrimination legislation at the suit of that
person; or knowingly downloading or requesting software
or media files or data streams that the employee has reason to believe will use a greater amount of network band-
width than is appropriate.

CONSEQUENCES OF UNACCEPTABLE USE

Widgets Ltd. keeps and/or may monitor logs of Internet
usage that may reveal information such as which Web
sites have been accessed by employees, and the e-mail
addresses of those with whom they have communicated.
Widgets Ltd. will not, however, engage in real-time surveillance of Internet usage, will not monitor the content of
e-mail messages sent or received by its employees
(unless a copy of such message is sent or forwarded to
the company by its recipient or sender in the ordinary
way), and will not disclose any of the logged, or otherwise
collected, information to a third party except under com-
pulsion of law.

Responsibility for use of the Internet that does not comply with this policy lies with the employee so using it, and
such employee must indemnify Widgets Ltd. for any direct
loss and reasonably foreseeable consequential losses
suffered by the company by reason of the breach of policy.

Widgets Ltd. will review any alleged breach of this AUP
on an individual basis. If the alleged breach is of a very
serious nature which affects the employee's duty of fidelity
to the company (for example, e-mailing confidential information of the company to a competitor), the employee
shall be given an opportunity to be heard in relation to the
alleged breach and if it is admitted or clearly established
to the satisfaction of the company the breach may be
treated as grounds for dismissal.

Otherwise, an alleged breach shall be dealt with as
follows:

Initially, the employee shall be informed of the alleged breach, given an opportunity to respond to the allegation, and if it is not satisfactorily explained, be asked to desist from or, where applicable, to remedy the breach.

If the breach is not desisted from or remedied, Widgets Ltd. may either withdraw the employee's access to the Internet or provide a first warning to the employee, to which the employee shall have an opportunity to respond.

If the infringing conduct continues, the employee may be given a second and a third warning, to each of which he or she shall have an opportunity to respond.

If a breach is committed after the third warning the employee may be dismissed.

Version No: ... Date: ...

Endnotes

1. LAN (Local Area Network): Sometimes known as an intranet, an internal "Internet" for that company; only employees and those within the company can access it; LANs are not available to the general public; some large corporations have an intranet/LAN accessible by a branch of that corporation, whether it is across the USA or on the other side of the world.

2. The 2004 Workplace E-Mail and Instant Messaging Survey questionnaire was designed by American Management Association and the ePolicy Institute, www.epolicyinstitute.com.

3. PDA: Personal Digital Assistant, such as a Palm Pilot or other handheld "mini-computer" used for keeping track of appointments, to store phone numbers, and more.

4. Managing Content Security: Update 2002—January 31, 2002, www.techrepublic.com.

Police Duty:
Our Nation's Finest Boot Up

The Internet has its share of dark alleyways. Unfortunately, people who would proceed with caution down a poorly lit back street in real life often throw caution to the wind when online. If you find yourself "accosted" online—whether through carelessness or in spite of your best efforts to stay out of trouble—there is a very good chance the police or even a federal agency can help. This chapter takes a look at what law enforcement professionals across the country are doing about cyber crime.

Kennebunk, Maine

Lobsters and lighthouses are what most people think of when they think of Maine. It's the postcard of picturesque views and moose roaming the land. And it doesn't have any online crime. Right?

Wrong.

But at least police Lieutenant David Gordon and former Detective Tom Cannon of the Criminal Investigation Division (CID) at the Kennebunk Police Department are on top of things.

"The first online crime I was involved in and made an arrest for was a child porn case in 1997," says Gordon. "The suspect was also arrested for child sexual assault—a felony—of over 100 counts with two victims. In this case, the children could not testify and the suspect would have gone free, but the online pornography involved made for a good case on its own."

The perpetrator received only one year in jail plus eight years probation, but Gordon was pleased because the perpetrator would be monitored for close to a decade.

Another case did try Gordon's patience, though. It was a stalking case that became an online stalking case.

The suspect was a former boyfriend of the victim. He had been stalking her in person and then he created a Web page. There he related the sexual activities the two had engaged in while they had been a couple. He included her real name and other identifying information.

The victim was mortified and went to Gordon for help. The suspect claimed he had a right to include what he wanted on his Web page. He said it was freedom of speech. Gordon felt otherwise. He was able to get the Web site revised through a court order. It wasn't easy, though, because Maine didn't have a cyberstalking law at the time. Gordon had to do what he could with the existing laws.

At the conclusion of this case, the suspect was found not guilty of stalking. The victim was given a two-year Order of Protection, which included the conditions that the suspect was not to use the Internet to communicate with the victim or post any information online about her.

So it was a partial victory.

"After that case, I strongly feel that victims have no rights while the suspects have many—he stalked her online as well as offline. We had the proof, but the court felt otherwise. And that makes it hard on victims," says Gordon. "I think advocacy groups like the ACLU should apply common sense when it comes to areas where people are having their lives ruined by a criminal who waves the flag of free speech."

Former Detective Tom Cannon agrees. "I feel that free speech is important, but I never saw anything in the Constitution granting the right to stalk and harass," he says.

The two made a formidable team, with Gordon handling the sex-related and some cyberstalking cases and Cannon handling all other online and offline crimes, including homicides, deaths, aggravated assault, and robbery. In addition, Cannon helped Gordon, who unfortunately has plenty to keep him busy.

"We're seeing a great increase in computer-related crimes of all types," Gordon says. "We're getting three to eight cases a month and it's our fastest growing problem, crimewise. In fact, I predict we'll need a full-time computer crimes investigator on staff within the next few years."

Gordon's concerns about online crime caused him to become involved—as did I—in the writing of the Maine Cyberstalking Bill, which was introduced in March 2001. He represented law enforcement while I advocated on behalf of cyberstalking victims. The Maine bill was signed into law in June 2001 by then-Governor Angus King.

"Online-related laws need to be passed," says Gordon, "but the hardest thing is getting them enforced. People committing online crimes are not arrested often enough. The courts need to hold these people accountable for their acts."

Another Maine Unit

Taking care of online crimes in the state of Maine is a unit called the Maine Computer Crimes Task Force. The unit conducts criminal investigations and performs computer forensic exams (the testing of evidence such as hard drives, diskettes, and so forth), and it also provides public outreach programs and law enforcement training. The task force is composed of detectives from different law enforcement agencies throughout the state, including the Maine State Police, the Lewiston and Brunswick Police Departments, and the Maine Office of the Attorney General. The task force has investigated various Internet crimes, with crimes against children, stalking, and harassment taking up a large portion of its time.

Maine recently joined up with the Internet Fraud Complaint Center (IFCC), a project of the National White Collar Crime Center and the Federal Bureau of Investigation, allowing visitors to the task force Web site (www.mcctf.org) to "drop a dime on cybercrime." By filling out a set of online forms, users are able to submit complaints directly to the IFCC. The reports are analyzed, compared with other citizen reports from around the world, and then sent to the law enforcement agency or agencies with jurisdiction.

It's a partnership that has been a great success, according to Michael Webber, a detective with the Maine Office of the Attorney General and a member of the Maine Computer Crimes Task Force.

Maine also joined with the National Center for Missing and Exploited Children Internet safety initiative, the NetSmartz Workshop, to provide schools and parents throughout the state with tools to teach Internet safety to children in grades kindergarten through high school.

"In Maine, the job of responding to crimes involving computers is largely the responsibility of local law enforcement. Our detectives assist them by providing the forensic and technical expertise required to help police collect the evidence," says Webber.

Webber notes that law enforcement personnel are discovering that computers can contain evidence of almost any criminal offense. For instance, in one case, task force detectives recovered a "to do" list from the hard drive of a homicide suspect. This list ultimately contributed to his conviction for murder.

Webber feels there are still many unreported computer crimes simply because victims aren't completely comfortable turning to police for something that happens to them online.

"Although," adds David Gordon, "as the days go by, it does seem to be getting better. We're getting the training we need and we want victims to come to us first instead of trying to handle it on their own or ignoring the situation."

Nashua, New Hampshire

The New Hampshire online harassment bill was signed into law in June 1999, a year after Amy Boyer was murdered by Liam Youens (see Chapter 10). Youens, who subsequently took his own life, had posted details of how he was going to kill Boyer on his Web page.

Detective Lieutenant Donald Campbell of the Criminal Investigation Division (CID) of the Nashua Police Department was assigned to the Amy Boyer case. He sees the new online harassment law as a hopeful sign.

"We've seen a distinct rise in online-related cases since 1998," Campbell says. "They include harassment, identity fraud, fraudulent auctions, child pornography, and more. We haven't been inundated with them, but there certainly has been an increase in the number."

The Nashua CID has been able to handle most of its cases without referring any to outside agencies. But CID officers have invited federal authorities to join in cases that involved interstate suspects.

"We used New Hampshire's online harassment statute in the prosecution of a man who sent anti-Semitic material by e-mail," Campbell says. "He received a guilty verdict after a trial. So we know the law works."

Massachusetts

The High Technology and Computer Crimes Division was set up by the Massachusetts Attorney General's Office (AGO) in 1997 after officials noticed an increase in online crimes reported by police departments throughout the state.

"I used to get calls from police departments and hear them say 'These aren't crimes anyway,'" says John Grossman, chief of the Corruption, Fraud, and Computer Crime Division. "I rarely hear that anymore."

The Massachusetts AGO provides support to local law enforcement agencies. Many, but by no means most, of the calls are about stalking. The AGO's office has been seeing more child pornography and auction fraud, and a lot of what Grossman calls "stalking by proxy." This is where a suspect creates an online profile in the victim's name and then lets other people pursue the victim.

"The difficulty is tracing the source of these threats and then working on an inter-jurisdictional case in what is often only a misdemeanor," Grossman says. "Personally, I'd like it to be more difficult for people to be anonymous online, from a law enforcement standpoint. But advocacy groups do make the important point about just how difficult the balance between protecting victims and protecting privacy can be."

Alexandria, Virginia

"Our first and in some ways worst case took place in January 1998," recalls Sergeant Scott Gibson of the Domestic Violence Unit of the Alexandria Police Department. "The case was both cyber and in-person stalking. We contacted WHOA because we had no idea how to trace the e-mails. They were able to tell us where the e-mails were coming from."

The suspect followed the victim and left e-mail messages, handwritten notes at her room, and voice messages, which the victim gave to Alexandria police as proof that he was stalking her.

The suspect also e-mailed messages to her at work with obscene pictures attached and sent them to her fellow employees and to her employer's central fax line. He then posted her name and telephone number online with the message that she liked sex with men over age 60.

"We helped stop the e-mails and got the personal ads removed, but we normally don't handle this type of case," Gibson says. "We don't have any one person in the department to even handle them."

Because Virginia didn't have an online harassment law at the time, the police charged the suspect with in-person stalking. During the trial, the e-mail and personal ads were introduced as part of the evidence.

The suspect was convicted and seemed to have gotten the message. The victim hasn't been bothered since.

"Whenever we get a case now, we work with WHOA," says Gibson. "They've been a tremendous help. Some of us have also attended workshops to help us understand how to work on these types of cases and to get to know the Internet a bit better so that we can not only help the victims but understand what they're talking about when they come to us in the first place."

Somerset, Kentucky

At the Somerset Police Department Criminal Investigative Division (CID), cases of e-mail harassment are on the rise. Officer Mike Grigsby believes the trend will continue.

"I believe this is the new type of prank call," Grigsby says. "Instead of using a pay phone to order 100 pizzas for someone, a prankster can use online services to harass people via e-mail since they think they can do it anonymously."

"We have seen somewhat of a continuation of the rise in e-mail and other types of online harassment," he notes. "I have been assigned to the Pulaski County School System as a School Resource Officer since January 2004. We have been very proactive in the reduction of online crime in schools, since it has been such an issue. The Kentucky State Police developed a full-time Internet Crime Unit. Also the Department of Criminal Justice Training Center in Richmond, Kentucky, has developed an Internet Crime Investigation course."

Online crimes pose problems for the department and Grigsby lists his concerns: "You may have prosecutors that don't understand, victims who are frustrated because they feel like no one can or is helping them, few laws under which to prosecute the persons when they're identified, and then the preparation and collection of evidence and how to present it to a jury is very difficult. I can't testify to something if I really don't understand how it works myself, so how can I explain it to a jury of 12 laypersons, many of whom may have never used a computer?"

Grigsby is optimistic that through training and experience, his police department and departments throughout the country will become more knowledgeable about online crimes and how to deal with them.

To that end, the Somerset Police Department has implemented the I-SAFE program. The Pulaski County School System partnered with I-SAFE America to bring Internet safety education to Pulaski County Schools. This program provides students with the awareness and knowledge they need to recognize and avoid dangerous, destructive, or unlawful online behavior—and how to respond appropriately.

I-SAFE America, Inc. is a nonprofit foundation whose mission is to educate and empower youth to responsibly take control of their Internet experience. The project is supported by a grant awarded by the Office of Juvenile Justice and Delinquency Prevention, Office of Justice Programs, and the U.S. Department of Justice.

The I-SAFE curriculum includes lessons for all students from kindergarten through the 12th grade. The integrated teaching and learning activities are age appropriate and vary from grade to grade.

"There are many online threats to children, including exposure to pornography, harassment, and cyberstalking. The most dangerous is 'cybergrooming,'" Grigsby warns. "Cybergrooming is the process of gaining trust and building false relationships to entice victims."

Because parent and community (e.g., business, church group, scout leadership, youth group) involvement is essential to the success of I-SAFE, it is important for both groups to be knowledgeable of these topics. To assist them in attaining this information, Grigsby and Pulaski County District Technology Coordinator Teresa Hail have completed the training program and help schedule school and community activities aimed at increasing Internet safety awareness.

"The School Resource Officer Program has to advance more quickly regarding Internet crimes, as almost all students have Internet access at school and at home," Grigsby says. "We have seen online harassment become an issue and we work very closely with the technology people at the schools to address this issue."

Grigsby and Hail also monitor student and staff-visited Web sites with filtering software. They admit they have had problems with online harassment of staff, both by those outside of the school and by other staff. As a result, they have established an online crime reporting form, where students and staff can report crimes that occur at school, online and offline.

San Diego, California

District Attorney offices are also getting on the online crime bandwagon. The San Diego County District Attorney (SDCDA) has two units that are involved in the investigation of online crimes: the Stalking Unit and the Economic Fraud Division, which handles primarily high-tech crimes.

In the spring of 2000, SDCDA Investigator Dave Decker wrote a grant request through the California Office of Criminal Justice Planning (OCJP) for a multijurisdictional group to investigate high-tech crimes. As a result, in June 2000 the Computer and Technical Crime High-Tech Response team (C.A.T.C.H.) was formed.

The C.A.T.C.H. team consists of more than a dozen investigators from San Diego–based federal, state, and local law enforcement agencies that work together to investigate high-tech crimes in San Diego County. The team also includes two prosecutors and a support staff.

C.A.T.C.H. takes the case when the following circumstances occur: A computer is the target of a crime—meaning intrusions, denial of service, and so on; a computer was the primary means to commit a crime; and/or a computer is the primary means to investigate a crime. C.A.T.C.H. investigators have varied authority in computer crimes, which means they conduct preliminary and follow-up investigations, assist law enforcement agencies with investigations, write and serve search warrants, conduct forensic examinations of seized computer evidence, make arrests, and prepare criminal cases for trial.

C.A.T.C.H. may handle the more involved high-tech cases, but that doesn't mean the SDCDA itself isn't busy with other online crimes.

"Approximately 10 percent of our stalking cases involve the Internet," says Wayne Maxey, DA Investigator of the SDCDA Stalking Unit. "I believe that for almost every crime that occurs in the real world, we are seeing or will see those crimes committed on the Internet, such as fraud, forgery, gambling, prostitution, child porn, stalking, threats, and more."

Maxey says that e-mail is the number one medium for harassing and stalking online.

"Following at a close second is the posting of victim's information on message boards or forums," Maxey says. "We liken it to the old 'For a good time, call …' message you might see on a bathroom wall."

Maxey knows it's hard for law enforcement to keep up with this new type of crime, especially when suspects use anonomizers and remailers. He would like to urge small organizations that have a network to take measures to protect it from intrusions. Hackers and crackers, he notes, can break into a system and use it to relay their venom and destruction.

"Computers and the Internet are the new tool of terror for the stalker," Maxey says. "We in the criminal justice system will just have to keep up the good fight."

National Center for Victims of Crime

The National Center for Victims of Crime (NCVC) is handling more online-related cases every day.

"Most victims initially contact our helpline at 1-800-FYI-CALL," says Tracy Bahm, director of the NCVC's Stalking Resource Center (see Figure 17.1). "Advocates in our victim services department answer those calls and provide basic information regarding privacy and Internet safety. The helpline advocates refer victims to organizations

Figure 17.1 NCVC's Stalking Resource Center

and services in their own communities, such as shelters, domestic violence programs, local law enforcement agencies, or the FBI. If these organizations are unwilling or unable to assist, the helpline staff will advocate for the victim with ISPs or law enforcement. We do everything we can to make sure they get the help they need."

Through the Stalking Resource Center, the helpline also has access to stalking experts around the country. The SRC and helpline often work on cases together.

The NCVC, located in Washington, DC, was founded in 1985 and is the nation's largest nonprofit advocacy and resource organization serving victims of all types of crimes.

The SRC opened in July 2000 to meet the newly recognized needs of stalking victims. The SRC responds primarily to calls and technical assistance requests from victim service providers and criminal justice professionals seeking educational resources related to stalking and cyberstalking. The SRC provides training and technical assistance on stalking and related topics, publishes a newsletter, and maintains a comprehensive Web site with stalking laws, articles, statistics, and more.

The SRC works with organizations such as WHOA, the National Network to End Domestic Violence, SafetyEd International, Privacy Rights Clearinghouse, the American Prosecutors Research Institute, the National Center for Missing and Exploited Children, the FBI, U.S. Attorneys Office, the ABA, the COPS office, National Cybercrime Training Partnership, the Federal Trade Commission (the identity theft case division), national and statewide agencies working on domestic violence and sexual assault, and local agencies and practitioners.

What does the SRC feel is required to provide better help to online victims?

"A lot," Bahm says. "We need to fix our stalking laws to reflect the behaviors that stalkers engage in and ensure that those behaviors are criminalized. We need to provide training and resources for law enforcement officers, prosecutors, judges, probation officers, and advocates on how to respond to these crimes. For the most part, our criminal justice and victim services fields are playing catch-up to the perpetrators who are using technology to terrorize victims."

The Stalking Resource Center would like to see:

- The general public getting more education to become more knowledgeable about online safety.

- States passing better stalking laws that cover all forms of technology that could be used to stalk.

- ISPs receiving training and education to become more sensitive and responsive to the needs of victims.

- State and federal prosecutors receiving education and training on how to successfully prosecute stalking cases that involve technology.

- Colleges and universities taking stalking and cyberstalking more seriously and developing effective strategies to address both online and offline stalking on their campuses. (Note: The SRC has been working with colleges and universities across the country, teaching them about cyberstalking and encouraging them to address the problem in their regular anti-stalking policies, practices, and procedures.)

"More and more practitioners are reporting stalkers who use technology to enhance their stalking capabilities. The days of offices being able to refer technology cases to the 'tech' or 'cyber' experts are really gone. Each of us has to develop at least a basic level of understanding on how to respond to these cases and how to assist victims who are stalked online or via any other form of technology," says Bahm.

The U.S. Department of Justice

The United States Department of Justice (USDOJ) has several departments that handle online-related crimes, including Computer Crime and Intellectual Property Section (CCIPS) (see Figure 17.2, www.cybercrime.gov). Created in 1991, CCIPS began as the Computer Crime Unit of the former General Litigation and Legal Advice Section, and then became a section of the Criminal Division in 1996. Today, CCIPS works with the U.S. Attorneys Offices (USAO) in each of the districts to pursue cases of hacking, virus dissemination, and denial of service attacks.

CCIPS includes the following divisions:

- CCIPS, Criminal Division – Intellectual property/ trade secret violations

- Child Exploitation and Obscenity Section, Criminal Division – Child pornography/luring

- Fraud Section, Criminal Division – Fraud

- Office of Consumer Litigation, Civil Division – Illegal sale of pharmaceuticals

- Civil Rights Division – Hate Crimes

- Organized Crime and Racketeering Section, Criminal Division – Illegal gambling

- Narcotics and Dangerous Drugs Section, Criminal Division – Illegal drugs

- The National Infrastructure Protection Center (NIPC, www.nipc.gov), an inter-agency center housed at the FBI, serves as a national critical infrastructure threat assessment, warning, vulnerability, and law enforcement investigation and response entity.

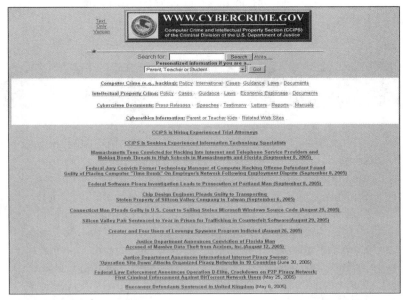

Figure 17.2　Cybercrime.gov

From Cop to Cybersnitch

It sounds worse than it actually is.

Thor Lundberg, a technological security specialist with the Raynham, Massachusetts, Police Department, had a plan in 1996. He and his brother, Eric, developed Cybersnitch (see Figure 17.3), a public service crime-fighting solution for Internet users. Their two goals:

1. To prevent crime from occurring on the Internet.

2. To network all law enforcement at all levels in the mission of fighting computer crime, patrolling, and securing the Internet.

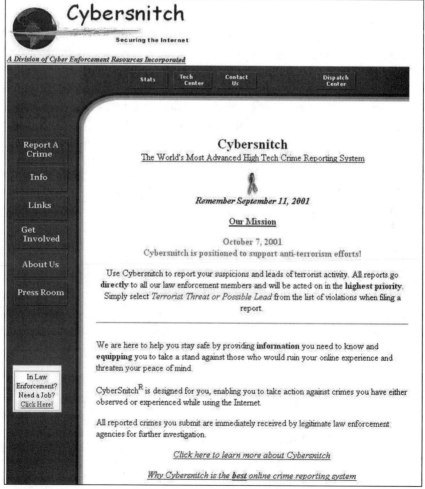

Figure 17.3 Cybersnitch

In March 1997, Cybersnitch made its debut at www.cybersnitch. net, with law enforcement membership representation in more than 26 states in the U.S., plus some in Canada and the U.K.

"Cybersnitch is designed for enabling the quick and aggressive investigation and prosecution of virtually all computer crime occurring on the Internet," Lundberg says. "And it eases the jurisdictional limitations inherent in the investigation of Internet-based computer crimes."

Cybersnitch has been responsible for shutting down hundreds of sites displaying contraband. Cybersnitch is not only designed for law enforcement; the site puts cybercitizens in direct communication with law enforcement officials—it's a virtual 911 for victims of cybercrime.

"The online cases we've seen the most are those involving e-mail and chat rooms equally," Lundberg says. "It typically starts with chat rooms, then progresses to e-mail, and from there, in some cases, it continues to phone calls, standard mail, or worse—real-life stalking."

When Cybersnitch receives a harassment report, it tries to resolve the situation. If it can't, it helps the victim by putting him or her in direct contact with a law enforcement agency that can.

"It's kind of a Catch-22 situation sometimes," Lundberg says. "Online friendships occur, solidify, and then sour over time, resulting in harassing situations. People need to be cautious about who they consider a friend online, especially if that is the only way communication has occurred."

SamSpade.org

SamSpade.org (see Figure 17.4) is a tool that many law enforcement agencies and cybercitizens use to track suspects. Steve Atkins initially created the SamSpade program in 1996 to combat spam.

"I used to be active in the technical aspects of theater—stage management, sound, and lighting design—and I maintained the FAQ for the newsgroups rec.arts.theatre.stagecraft and alt.stagecraft," Atkins says.

Since alt.stagecraft was next door, alphabetically, to alt.sex, Atkins found that his e-mail address was harvested by porn spammers who had targeted the alt.sex newsgroup. He saw his e-mailbox fill up with pornographic spam e-mail.

Atkins poked around the newsgroups and found news.admin.net-abuse.email, where others complained about the porno spam. He

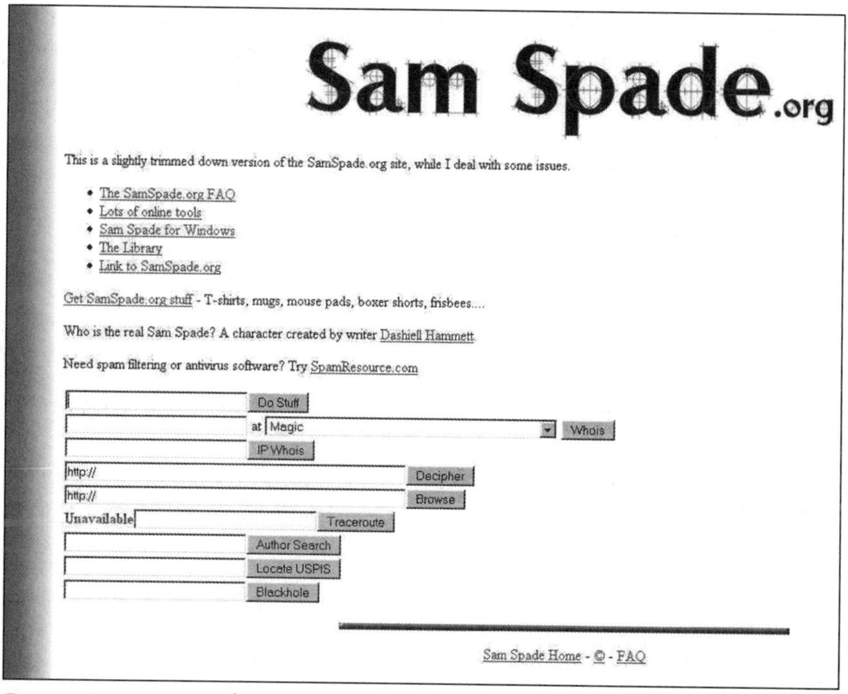

Figure 17.4   SamSpade

posted a few messages and found that most of the people in the news-group used the Windows operating system. An idea for a way to combat spam came to him and he soon devised a simple program that conducted a WHOIS query. This determined who owned the domain of the originating ISP of the e-mail/Usenet post and what the trace route was (tracking where the message came from, server by server).

That simple program grew into a full-fledged Windows program (a free one) that can be downloaded to use on your computer. Or you can go to SamSpade.org and use the more than 40 tools available on the Web site.

"I get quite a lot of fan mail both from individual users and a lot of ISP abuse desks," Atkins says.

But not everyone has been a fan. In addition to e-mail complaints, he's had spammers forging e-mail addresses he hosts and a few Denial of Service attacks (a program designed by hackers to try to cripple the SamSpade network so that people could no longer access the Web site), which have put the site out of commission for a day or two.

"But I know my provider well," Atkins says, "and there haven't been any problems. The site averages 100,000 hits a day, and sometimes I see as many as 1,000 downloads a day of the program. I must be doing something right."

Universities Catch Up with the Net

When universities fail ...

Nina attends a prominent university in the northeast and felt safe there the first two years she attended. She struck up a friendship with a fellow student, Jim, a sophomore. She considered him a friend, but eventually he began to have more feelings for her and started sending love poems via e-mail. At first she ignored the love poems, but when they continued to arrive she told him that even though at one time there may have been a possibility of more than a friendship, now she didn't think so.

Nina continued seeing Jim in class and around campus, and they chatted about inconsequential things like school and movies. One day, she found a new love poem in her e-mail inbox calling her a "soft-spoken temptress." He began instant messaging (IMing) her, too. She always sent the same reply: "Please leave me alone."

She went home to Virginia for a week to visit her family and friends and checked her e-mail when she arrived. A message from Jim was waiting for her:

"I like you, but I'm going to kill you last."

Nina shrugged it off since she was so far away from the university—she knew he wasn't close enough to do anything. When she returned to school, nothing more happened. It was soon time for the holiday break and she went back home again. While there, she canceled the username that Jim knew and created a new one, even though he'd been quiet. Better to be safe than sorry, she thought.

When she returned to the university, Jim left a note under her door at the dormitory: "Why won't you talk to me online?"

He somehow found her new username and began IMing her again, asking her why she wouldn't reply. She wrote back that he should f—k off. He responded with threats. That's when Nina became frightened.

In early January, she received a Trojan Horse virus via e-mail that shut down her hard drive, essentially making her computer useless. Five days later, someone hacked into her e-mail account; Nina found this out was when she was talking to her sister in Virginia, complaining about being without her computer. Her sister told her that Nina's username popped up on her IM buddy list as being online. Her sister sent an IM to Nina's username but there was no response, and the person quickly signed off.

This occurred a few more times while Nina's computer was being repaired. Each time her sister saw Nina's username on IM, she would send a message. There was never a reply and the person always signed off.

"I went to the campus police and told them what had been happening. But all they did was tell him to stop making threats and showing up at my door," Nina says. "Jim implied to the campus police that we were romantically involved when we weren't. They began to not believe me, even when I showed them copies of the IMs he sent me— even the one where he threatened to 'kill me last.' "

The campus police and judicial affairs office at the university told her that the IM logs weren't good evidence and the threats were indirect, even though the Massachusetts state law clearly indicated that any "Internet communications threatening someone is regarded as stalking."

Nina moved to a friend's apartment off-campus and stayed there for the rest of the school year. She doesn't know if she'll return to school in the fall. She's scared Jim might escalate his stalking offline.

Nina's case may seem extreme, but it happens more often than not. The campus police often aren't any help—not because they don't want to be, but because they have no knowledge of how to handle online-related cases.

Many universities are taking stock of this new online threat and becoming proactive. George Mason University (GMU) in Fairfax, Virginia, is one of them.

Cyberstalking on Campus: How Prevalent Is It?

A questionnaire was distributed to 235 undergraduate communication college students at a large southwestern public university; 130 females and 102 males responded.* It found that 59 percent felt they had been cyberstalked; 19.6 percent of those felt threatened or were in fear for their personal safety.

A larger study consisting of 656 East Coast university students was conducted. It found that 11 percent had been harassed/stalked online; 61 percent of the victims were female; and 55 percent were 17–20 years old, although victims ranged up to age 41.**

A case study of 241 students enrolled in an Introduction to Psychology course at the University of Pittsburgh*** had these results: 5 percent indicated the person who did not reciprocate their love was an e-mail correspondent; and 79 percent of males and 71 percent of females reported they had sent or delivered notes, e-mail, or other written communication to express their interest.

(*From B. H. Spitzberg and G. Hoobler. 2001. "Cyberstalking and the technologies of interpersonal terrorism." *New Media & Society*. Vol. 4, pp. 71–92)

(**From A. W. Burgess and T. Baker. 2002. "Cyberstalking." In: J. Boon and L. Sheridan (editors). *Stalking and psychosexual obsession: Psychological perspectives for prevention, policing, and treatment*. West Sussex, U.K.: John Wiley & Sons)

(***From J. Langhinrichsen-Rohling, R. E. Palarea, J. Cohen, and M. L. Rohling. 2000. "Breaking up is hard to do: Unwanted pursuit behaviors." *Violence & Victims*. Vol. 15, No. 1, pp. 73–90)

GMU Has a Clue

"A father of a girl in her senior year of high school called me in 1998 because one of our GMU students put up a Web page dedicated to her," says Connie Kirkland, coordinator of Sexual Assault Services at GMU. "Though no nude or otherwise derogative information was posted, there were pictures and information about the girl. The father asked, 'Does this mean that someone in Thailand could be looking at my daughter's picture right now?' I answered that it could mean that. He was distraught and asked that I intervene."

Kirkland got in touch with WHOA, which contacted the Web host provider, which promptly removed the Web page. Kirkland worked with GMU's Judicial Dean, who brought in the university counseling center's expertise to assist with this fragile young man in hopes that no further stalking—online or in person—would result. So far, so good.

GMU has seen an average of 30 similar cases a year since 1997, when it received its first case. GMU has worked with online organizations, such as WHOA, and with local and campus police to resolve situations. In spring 2001, GMU sponsored a training session for campus and police officers from around the state of Virginia. Called "Catching a Stalker—Hook, Line & Sinker," the session covered online and offline stalking. In addition, Kirkland developed a student-friendly brochure that is handed out to as many students as possible either at information fairs or presentations on campus. It is also available on the GMU Web site.

Most GMU cases tend to involve IMs, such as Nina's, but many involve e-mail as well. In late 2003, students in Judy Palmore's Human Sexuality class at GMU began receiving e-mails from someone named John Casey, who claimed to be a fellow student. Most looked like this:

```
Hi Lily,
    I really liked your presentation in Human
Sexuality class Monday night, it was very
interesting. You and your group did a very
good job.
    Anyway I just wanted to say hi. What do
you think of this class so far?
    John
```

The catch was that the e-mails were sent only to the female students in the class. Alarmed, they let Palmore know what was going on. She checked the student roster and found there was no John Casey registered for her class or at GMU.

Casey then sent a sexually explicit PowerPoint presentation via e-mail to many of the female students asking for their opinion on it. They were more than alarmed by the pornographic photos and graphics within and alerted Palmore, who was equally upset.

The e-mail address Casey was writing from was located at fastmail. fm, a free e-mail service—not a GMU e-mail address. This further frustrated Palmore, who contacted Kirkland, who then turned to WHOA for help. Kirkland explained how Palmore had seen a male student she didn't recognize as being part of the class but had figured he was just a visitor and didn't think twice about it until the weird e-mails were sent out.

WHOA traced the messages to an ISP called the New York Internet Company and sent complaints to them as well as to fastmail.fm. Both were quick to cancel the offending accounts. But that didn't stop Casey.

He opened an account with Hotmail and began targeting one student in particular in February 2004:

> Hi Sarah,
> How is your semester going so far? Are you taking any interesting classes this time? Anyway I just wanted to say hi again. You were in my Human Sexuality Class last semester—even though we never spoke I thought you were really nice.
> John

She replied:

> John,
> I'm sorry if this sounds really bad but with 70 people in that class, I'm not sure that I know who you are but thank you.
> I'm surprised that people actually listen to those presentations. Class is interesting I think and I don't think the final will be too difficult which is totally a plus.

He replied:

> Hi Sarah,
> Yeah well I agree this class was inter-
> esting, with a topic like Sexuality it was
> bound to be, and I thought the profesor did
> a great job too, she was awesome.
> (Were you there the night the people from
> the sex shop came in and handed out the
> toys, that was hysterical.)
> You're right the final should be pretty
> easy as long as you study up for it. Would
> you happen to have good notes from the
> lectures?
> I missed a few lectures and the handouts
> on those nights. If you plan on being in
> the library over the weekend just let me
> know when and maybe I could make some
> copies.
> Anyway good luck on the final, I hope to
> see you again sometime. (-:

Luckily, Sarah remembered that this Casey had previously sent e-mails to many female students in Palmore's class. She forwarded the information to Palmore, who then forwarded it to WHOA.

Now the messages were coming from Georgetown University via Hotmail. WHOA sent complaints to Hotmail. Soon afterward, the accounts were canceled. So far, "John Casey" hasn't shown up for class at GMU, nor has he contacted any more of Palmore's students.

This is one instance where contacting the ISPs involved ended the harassment before it escalated. When GMU has to help an employee go to court, however, it does get frustrating.

"The identification of the harasser/stalker coupled with the inability to get a conviction on the cases that we've taken to court is the hardest for us to deal with," Kirkland says. "It seems the judges believe the victim and are ready to convict, but they don't believe that the prosecutors adequately prove intent or prove stalking has occurred. Training in this area for prosecutors seems crucial at this point."

Consider the following information on the same subject from a study titled "Cyberaggression: Safety and Security Issues for Women

Worldwide" by Sharon Levrant Miceli, Shannon A. Santana, and Bonnie S. Fisher of the University of Cincinnati:

> Cyberaggression laws distinguish illegal speech in the form of threats from constitutionally protected free speech. The first case to address First Amendment issues relative to cyberaggression is *United States vs. Jake Baker and Arthur Gonda*.[1] Jake Baker and Arthur Gonda exchanged e-mail messages with one another regarding sexual fantasies that they both had about harming young women. Baker, a University of Michigan student, was indicted for violation of 18 U.S.C. 875 that prohibits transmission through interstate or foreign commerce of any communication that threatens to kidnap or injure another person. The court's decision basically affirmed the Watts[2] 'true threat' standard for cyberaggression cases. Because there was no direct threat made to another person, Baker and Gonda's communication was constitutionally protected.

For an insightful article about the Jake Baker Scandal, visit www.trincoll.edu/zines/tj/tj4.6.95/articles/baker.html (warning: it is very graphic).

Jim Dempsey, deputy director of the Center for Democracy and Technology (CDT), discusses this complicated issue further. "In a way, there's a little more latitude for expression online," Dempsey says. "For example, when you stand in front of the White House and yell, 'It's time to take over the White House!' that may be a crime. But if you say the same thing online in a chat room, it's not a crime. Making threats against people online is roughly similar. The context is about the same."

UB Good

Since 1996, campus police at the University at Buffalo (UB) in New York have had reports of online auction fraud, stolen credit cards used online, soliciting obscenity from a minor, and hacking.

Their largest volume of online complaints come from various copyright holders who send "take down" notices under the Digital Millennium Copyright Act. These come from the Recording Industry Association of America, the Motion Picture Association of America, and various individual movie companies who are serious about protecting their intellectual property. The university expects the activity to heat up even more in the future.

"The next largest number of complaints is harassment, although that seems to be shrinking, at least at UB," notes Harvey Axlerod, UB's Computer Discipline Officer. "From our perspective, it seems people are finally catching on that the cyberworld is not a separate dimension of reality."

Axlerod finds that the anonymity of the Internet sometimes hampers his investigations.

"Some online harassers are very savvy at hiding their identities," Axlerod says. "The free e-mail services, such as Hotmail, Yahoo!, and Lycos, have a tough time keeping up with these folks, who often use phony personal data to open an account, then move on to establish new bogus usernames. The most difficult cases are those that use anonymous remailers. These sites often keep no records, so the e-mail is quite untraceable. In one case, a clever user had one remailer forward to another remailer, in effect double-dipping the anonymity."

This doesn't stop Axlerod from being a bulldog on cases, actively working with university police and local police when needed. He's found that a mutual working relationship usually results in seeing the case closed quickly.

One case Axlerod can't forget is one of his earlier ones. He has changed the name of the victim.

" 'Betty Smith' was a young, attractive professor at UB," he says. "She called me because she received an odd e-mail from a complete stranger."

The stranger claimed that a photograph of Smith was posted on the Web site, www.hotornot.com. (Read that as "hot or not"; the site posts pictures of individuals with comments and intended to be rated by visitors. Interested visitors can make contact with the individual.) The e-mail said that if she was serious, he was interested in meeting her. If this was a bogus posting, his qualifications as a computer professional would enable him to help her track the culprit.

She went to the Web site and was alarmed. There was her photo, which had been taken from her online course Web page at UB. Even more alarming, the text claimed she was interested in hairy men and that she liked putting things in her mouth.

Also cause for more alarm, it identified her academic department at UB. A simple online search of UB, her department, and her first name (hotornot.com posts only the first name) would point a visitor to her UB Web page. Her Web page gave personal information about her—office address, UB phone number, cell phone number, office hours, areas of academic interest, published work, and so forth.

Smith contacted hotornot.com. To its credit, the site immediately removed her entry from its database.

She also explained the situation to her e-mail contact, who graciously sent her a large amount of computer forensics about who posted her picture.

Next, she filed a report with the University Police Department. Under New York State law, the perpetrator could have been prosecuted under "aggravated harassment in the second degree," which makes it a crime to use telephone lines (or a computer online) to harass or otherwise cause a reasonable person to become alarmed.

"Finally, I investigated," Axlerod explains. "There was good reason to suspect that the perpetrator(s) were from UB, maybe even students who were enrolled in Betty's online course. Everyone at UB has to log in to use our system. This 'authentication' gives us a good record of the traffic of UB network users." (Note: UB does not track or record contents, just traffic.)

As it turned out, it was a female student who had posted the photograph and information. Her roommate was involved, too. Both were enrolled in Smith's class.

When the women were interviewed, it was distressing to investigators to find that neither understood the gravity of what they had done. They didn't understand that they had put their professor in harm's way. Initially, they offered to apologize to her but they weren't actually sorry because their conversation deteriorated into, "It's just a joke. Why make a big deal?"

Both were charged at the Student Wide Judiciary and given community service hours as administrative punishment. In addition, they both received a grade of "F" in the course—for violating their professor's stated rules of online behavior.

Online, as offline, a prank can have serious consequences.

Educating students and faculty at UB is a priority for Axlerod. "When dealing with minor infractions of university policy, this becomes an opportunity for individual counseling and training," he says. "Also, I encourage students to share their experiences with friends. The grapevine is a very effective means of communications. For example, after a flood of pyramid schemes (for example, Ponzi[3]) and chain e-mail several years ago, the word spread that this was unacceptable. I can't recall seeing a case of either since then."

UB publishes its university policies in print and online. Freshman orientation includes creative efforts at explaining what is acceptable and what is not. UB also provides lectures and student skits to show what dangers lurk online.

"It's a common misconception to regard the Internet as a virtual world," Axlerod says. "I'm always amazed at how much information people give online when the same requests in person would draw a rebuke. The Internet is different but hardly separate from the traditional world. Unfortunately, it often takes an unpleasant experience, such as harassment, stalking, or fraud, before the light goes on in one's head."

What Can Universities Do to Prevent Online-Related Incidents?

1. When giving a student a university/college e-mail address, let the student select his or her own username and make sure it's gender neutral. Too many universities and colleges automatically hand out e-mail addresses to students and faculty consisting of the first name initial and last name or partial last name, such as jhitchco@umuc.edu. If someone is harassing or stalking a student or faculty member, the victim's e-mail address can be very easy to figure out.

2. Do not post e-mail addresses, dorm room numbers, class schedules, telephone numbers, and so forth on the university or college's Web site or in printed form. This information should remain private, as it only gives harassers and stalkers another tool to escalate online harassment to offline.

3. Have a sign-in system for library or computer lab use. Make all students and faculty members sign in to a certain computer, the time they signed in, and the time they signed out. Then, if any harassment or fraudulent activity is found to originate from a certain computer, it can be traced back to the faculty member or student who used it at that time.

4. Create an acceptable use policy that clearly covers what will not be tolerated online, such as harassment, stalking, or threats.

5. Publish online safety tips on the university or college's Web site and in brochure form, as GMU does. Distribute a printed brochure at rallies, information seminars, or other campus activities. Let students and faculty know there are online organizations that can offer great advice and help if the victim doesn't want to approach campus police.

6. Hold an online safety lecture for students and faculty once a semester. Talk about what can happen online and encourage students and faculty to voice their concerns or their own experiences.

7. Make sure campus police are trained to handle online-related cases. Training costs are minimal. Police officers can either attend workshops sponsored by other universities or colleges or schedule one for themselves through groups such as WHOA (www.haltabuse.org). As long as campus police officers have a basic knowledge of the Internet and Web browsers, they can learn how to track down online harassers and stalkers and how to work with victims in a day's training.

CMU Cares

When Steve Thompson became Central Michigan University's (CMU) Sexual Assault Services Coordinator in 1996, he began to see online-related cases, mostly relating to chat and e-mail.

"One I remember clearly is a man allegedly from Florida who started chatting with one of our students," Thompson says. "After about a month of chatting, he showed up at her apartment, talked a bit—and raped her."

He understands that this was an extreme incident but feels he should have been able to prevent it. "We've had a few cases that involved e-mails where the offender would make comments and write things that were sexually explicit," Thompson says. "Some students ignored the letters and they went away. Two that I recall went to the local police, with one offender being caught."

Although online harassment and related issues are covered in student orientation, Thompson thinks more can be done to enlighten the students.

"I'm sure there are more cases happening here. However, students are not coming forward," Thompson says. "This leads me to believe that we must address it better so students recognize it for what it is, and that they—the students and the faculty—are aware there are people at the university who care and want to help."

A Distinct Challenge

Other universities and colleges find the Internet a distinct challenge.

"There actually have been very few reported cases at the University of Maryland University College (UMUC) involving online harassment, stalking, or identity appropriation," says David Freeman, vice president of communications at UMUC.

Those cases were handled swiftly and well, prompting UMUC to update its institutional policies to address online-related issues and other threats to the students, faculty, and staff. This included adding an article titled "How to Protect Yourself on the Net" to all CAPP (Computer Application) courses as required reading. The article, co-authored by UMUC Instructor Patti Wolf and me, is available to enrolled UMUC students online at the university's Web site.

"We are keenly aware that the combination of technological advances and increased populations here at the university certainly increases the probability of such situations," Freeman says. "Our Institutional Technology unit is constantly assessing technology that will enable us to provide the most effective protections to our faculty, staff, and students."

Although most students and faculty think their school-related e-mail accounts are private, they'd probably be surprised to know that the school usually monitors e-mail and other communications.

"Universities have the right to read your messages and discipline accordingly," says Howard Meyer, former trial lawyer, Senior Trustee Emeritus, and former instructor at the University at Buffalo. "If I was sent child pornography and I opened it, the university could likely be monitoring me. And if I solicited that child pornography, there could be consequences. Heck, 40 percent of corporations occasionally audit and review e-mail, so nothing is actually private, and if you think it is, think again."

Howard recalls an experience he had while teaching at UB. "I had a girl in my class, what I call a 'hair-flipper.' I never exchanged a word with her, which is rare for student/teacher interaction. She received a 'C' at the end of the semester and then sent me an e-mail asking why her grade wasn't higher. I replied, and in my message I mentioned that her being attractive was disconcerting—a joke that obviously didn't go over too well via e-mail. She went straight to the Dean with that e-mail, claiming it was sexual harassment. I've learned to be careful when writing my e-mails."

Endnotes

1. *United States vs. Jake Baker and Arthur Gonda*—890 F. Supp. 1375 (1995).

2. *Watts vs. United States*—394 U.S. 705 (1969)—where a threat must be a "true threat" to be considered illegal speech.

3. A Ponzi scheme is a type of investment fraud. The person who runs it promises high returns/dividends that people wouldn't get with traditional investments. But, instead, the schemer uses money from subsequent investors to pay off the initial ones. This usually falls apart when the schemer either flees with the money he or she has collected or when no more victims take part and the "dividends" are no longer paid out.

    The scheme was named after Charles Ponzi of Boston, Massachusetts, who operated an investment scheme in the early 1900s. He guaranteed investors a huge return on their investments, but in the end could not pay the dividends. He was found guilty of mail fraud and imprisoned for five years. Thus the Ponzi scheme was born (http://home.nycap.rr.com/useless/ponzi).

Encryption Made Easy

Encryption

Scrambles messages so that they are unreadable by anyone except the sender and the recipient. One of the most popular encryption programs is Pretty Good Privacy (PGP).

Electronic Signatures

A form of encryption that allows online users to sign documents, pay bills, bank, and shop online with an electronic or digital signature unique to only them.

You've probably heard about encryption and electronic signatures (also called e-signatures or digital signatures). In this chapter you'll become more familiar with their functions—and how they can help you.

Encryption Is Built into Your Web Browser

"Whenever people use an online commerce Web site that has a 'secure server' or they go to a site that begins 'https' instead of 'http,' they are using the encryption built into their browser," says Stanton McCandlish, communications director of the CryptoRights

Foundation. "But encryption is useful for a lot of other things, many of which most people don't think about."

For instance, you might want to think twice the next time you send an e-mail about a project you're working on for your company. Why? A competitor could be on the watch for anything new going on in the company you work for and could be intercepting your e-mail.

Or, you might be exchanging e-mail with someone you'd rather your spouse or another family member didn't know about. And what if you are planning a vacation—you might be e-mailing your credit card information to a travel agency.

"Your e-mail is being read by someone other than the intended recipient, guaranteed," says Neil Schwartzman, founder of peteMOSS Publications and publisher of the popular Spam e-newsletter. "Do not put anything on your computer that you would not share with your mother. If you must put it on your computer, then encrypt it."

Here's another scenario. Someone forges messages in your name on a message board, in newsgroups, or in e-mail sent to your family or employer. It may sound farfetched, but it can and does happen.

Checking Your Web Browser

Microsoft Internet Explorer (MSIE; v5.0 or higher, see Figure 19.1):

- Click on Tools in the top toolbar, then Internet Options. A separate window pops up.

- Click on the Content tab.

- Click on Certificates and this shows what (if any) certificates you have acquired from your visits to Web sites. Clicking on Advanced Options allows you to change the settings so that you can send Secure E-mail with Outlook (the incorporated e-mail program with MSIE), among other settings.

- A lock graphic that appears in the bottom right of the browser lets you know when you're visiting a page or site that is secure or encrypted. If the lock is open, the site is insecure (usually a personal page

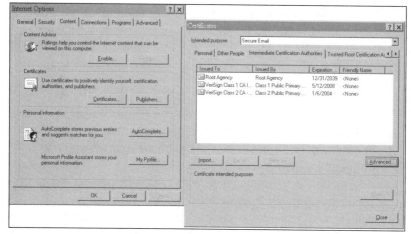

Figure 19.1   MSIE e-mail

or informational). If the lock is closed (or locked), the site is secured/encrypted (usually a site where you have to use a password to enter it, or a commerce site).

Netscape Communicator/Navigator (v4.75 or higher, see Figure 19.2):

(*Note*: Netscape is a little more comprehensive when it comes to privacy/security in its browser.)

• Click on Edit in the top toolbar, then Preferences. A separate browser window pops up with a menu on the left side.

• Double-click on Privacy & Security; click on Certificates, then Manage Certificates, then go through each tab to see what certificates, if any, you have acquired.

• Click on Passwords and you can store passwords here so that you don't need to input them manually every time you visit a Web site—and they are encrypted for your protection.

• Click on SSL (Secure Sockets Layer) to select whether you want to be warned every time you enter and/or leave an encrypted Web page or site (note: if you opt for the warnings, you'll keep getting pop-up windows with the warning; it's recommended to select "Loading a page that uses low-grade encryption only").

• Certificates lets you manage, create, and delete any certificates you may have acquired while surfing or shopping.

As with MS Internet Explorer, the graphic of a "lock" is in the lower left-hand corner of the browser when you are on a secure Web site or page.

You can also manage cookies, prevent pop-up ads/windows, and other security measures here as well. It would be wise to go through each section to make sure the selections made by default are what you really want.

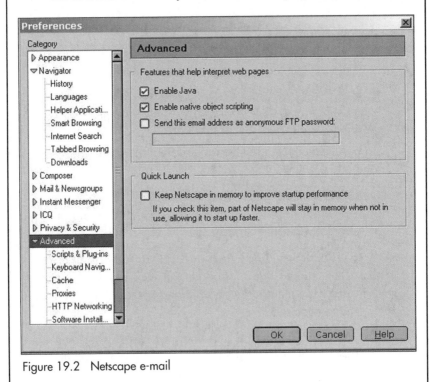

Figure 19.2 Netscape e-mail

What's PGP?

PGP, for Pretty Good Privacy, is an encryption program developed by Philip Zimmermann in 1984.

"I began PGP as a human rights project back in 1984, although I'd had the idea floating in my head before then," Zimmerman says. "I was involved with a grassroots political movement and I felt it would be useful to have something that would protect their communications."

A paper he wrote about PGP was published in 1986 in IEEE magazine, but he didn't officially release the program until June 1991. At that time, the need for encryption wasn't a necessity, but there were Bulletin Board Systems (BBS) that utilized it. Also using it were people who encrypted files on their computer hard drives or who wanted to send and receive files safely from one computer to another.

It has only been in recent years that PGP and similar encryption programs have become more popular. People are realizing that what they think is private online just isn't.

"Before the Information Age, we had privacy. Every conversation was private because it was face to face or over the telephone," says Zimmerman. "Now all communications technology has undermined privacy and we need to get it back. Encryption helps do this."

Stanton McCandlish agrees. "Everyone should use encryption," he stresses. "There is a slight learning curve to use the program but most mass market encryption software, like PGP, have easy graphical interfaces and pretty simple 'quick-start' documentation."

So, how does PGP work? The easiest way to find out is to download an encryption program and follow the instructions, but basically, PGP works like this:

1. During installation, you designate your full name and the e-mail address you will be using so that a "key pair" (a key is essentially encrypted information, such as the message you are sending or receiving, a signature file, or your passphrase) can be assigned to you. The pair consists of a private key and a public key. The public key is what you use when sending a message so that the recipient—or anyone who reads it, such as when it is broadcast on a newsgroup—will know that you are the real author of that message.

2. Now you need to create a passphrase, which will protect your private key. Make sure you write down your passphrase somewhere, preferably on a piece of paper and kept someplace secure. You don't want to save it in a file on your computer. Usually, a passphrase is at least eight characters long

with a combination of letters and numbers. Your key pair
will then be generated.

3. You can then "publish" your public key, and store your pri-
    vate key in a safe place, such as on a zip disk, diskette, or
    CD. Remember, if you lose the original private key, you
    can't decrypt anything encrypted to that key. Depending on
    the program you install, you should be able to publish your
    public key to a Web site called a keyserver. People who then
    want to send you private e-mail can download your public
    key from one of these keyservers, or you can send your pub-
    lic key to them directly. Some people also place their pub-
    lic key on their personal Web site or in their signature file.
    The caveat to using encryption is that both the sender and
    the recipient need to be using the same encryption program,
    although just about all versions of PGP, free or commercial,
    are compatible with each other.

4. To send encrypted messages to someone, you need his or
    her public key, from the person or from a keyserver. You
    encrypt your message to the public key, copy, and then
    paste it into the text of an e-mail message, or, if you are
    using a program that incorporates encryption by way of a
    plug in, such as Qualcomm's Eudora, the message will be
    automatically encrypted for you without copying and past-
    ing. The same thing goes with decrypting the message. The
    recipient then decrypts the message with his or her private
    key. To receive an encrypted message, the sender uses your
    public key to encrypt the message, e-mails it to you, then
    you decrypt it with your private key.

Once you exchange public keys with one or more people, you can
add their public keys to a "keyring" in your encryption program so
that you have them handy instead of having to go back to the key-
server each time you want to send an encrypted message. To encrypt
a file on your hard disk, use your private key.

Cynthia went online one day and found someone was forging messages in her name on a newsgroup. The messages were intended to
get others in the newsgroup mad at her—and it almost worked. After
explaining to the newsgroup that she hadn't posted those messages,
she found an encryption program, began using it, and hasn't had a
problem since.

"Now I PGP-sign all of my real messages so that they can be verified as having come from me. This person who impersonated me cannot forge the PGP signature," Cynthia says. "Sometimes people get confused by the PGP signature, but I simply post an explanation and the URL of my Web site, where there is an introduction to PGP."

Examples of Encryption

A Public Key will look something like this sample:

```
Cynthia's Public Key:
---BEGIN PGP PUBLIC KEY BLOCK---
Version: 5.0
Comment: PGP Key Server 0.9.2

mQCNAzJLTZUAAAEEANDW3sS9W3TaxNtQ9GROAooL
7yKg6nMgBYSWlGIrQi5bkuUvYjVgcYV5pMpnxp92SG
bKC7Rka1asj/fnA8hp5kAKnQDg/PhQwaRv6l6XUH
QLlNJyVC0KYqfVurk6Q+pvIruQfQgOdxa7LnzbF5
PmWIGp7VHqP2ItWB1LUpdZB1XtAAURtC5DeW50aGlh
IEFybWlzdGVhZCBTbWF0aGVycyAoY3luQHRlY2hub2b2
1vbS5jb20ptB1UZWNobm9Nb20gPGN5bkB0ZWNobm9t
b20uY29tPokAlQMFEDJLTpQdS1KXWQdV7QEBSeoD/3
I/nTo7oA1kluwjrYkbTUOv81odX5CnG99UCa3sqRfj
eSyc80YhA2Spom8ZgiNEQCI5OQtUmifvZLCNm7U6Oc
jWipyXNzIhMMtAcJW1k2R8MU8pqoZsf25hOQyTgFmS
GmdeOoczU7BmoIUak4f/2rsxzPgC4mDrTRNDwTEh7u
//tDJDeW50aGlhIEFybWlzdGVhZCBTbWF0aGVycyA8
Y3ludGhpYUB0ZWNobm9tb20uY29tPrQzQ3ludGhpYS
BBcm1pc3RlYWQgU21hdGhlcnMgPGN5bnRoaWFAWelu
ZHNwcmluZy5jb20+tDVDeW50aGlhIEFybWlzdGVhZC
BTbWF0aGVycyA8dGVjaG5vbW9tQG1pbmRzcHJpbmcu
Y29tPg===hXyP
---END PGP PUBLIC KEY BLOCK---
```

Cynthia mentions that she PGP-signs all her messages. This is, in effect, her electronic or digital "signature." If you received a message from her and wanted to verify that it did indeed come from Cynthia, you could do so by checking the signature using her public key. Yes, it sounds confusing, but once you begin using an encryption program, you'll find it easy to understand.

A sample message from Cynthia is shown below:

```
—-BEGIN PGP SIGNED MESSAGE—-
This is a PGP-signed message. The signa-
ture will be longer for longer messages.
Cyn
(See www.technomom.com/pgp.html for fur-
ther info on PGP)

—-BEGIN PGP SIGNATURE—-
```

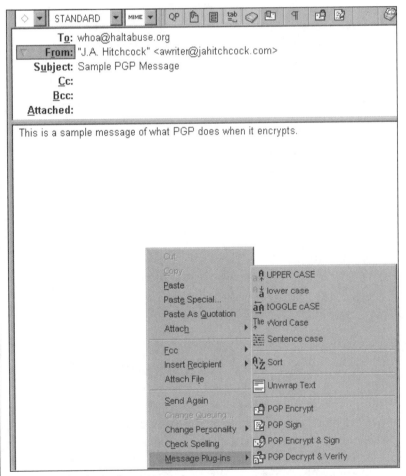

Figure 19.3 PGP Eudora

```
Version: PGP Personal Privacy 6.5.8

iQCVAwUBOfNHEB1LUpdZB1XtAQGcvAQAxr9NOOQY
ovebGwv28aheAnUIAJjsRYXPbU+0QeUBwf3MRFUxPo
6X26donmHmoofLalabjaIFEvnEmAWfrQkKZ+xvNSCv
RWBt9s8EHSTm/5ARzL89xV4QUUkimgj2cG9xe9b7Ii
PyNCTW6Rg4cbPDmnpEbu2FT4qvzjxoZMAseU==Tbam
----END PGP SIGNATURE----
```

Then there are PGP Fingerprints (see Figure 19.3), which are shorter versions of public keys. People sometimes use a PGP Fingerprint because it is not only easier to add onto the end of every message sent out, but the more often the Fingerprint is sent out, the more likely someone will notice if another person is trying to forge your key(s). Eudora, a popular e-mail program from Qualcomm, offers encryption capabilities such as these.

This is an example of a PGP Fingerprint:

```
703A C3CA AFF2 1D7B 97A6 839D 7A80 DE98
0550 E8F2
```

Here is an example of a PGP encrypted message:

```
----BEGIN PGP MESSAGE----
VersionPGPfreeware 7.0.3 for non-commer-
cial use <www.pgpi.com>
17-7
qANQR1DBwU4Dh0YjJERFJwcQB/94APRAEG8DZq5z
KIuo1kNa1xg+u5I9eE61+3ZcXDKERHrTyeXwmfjOwA
GrzaVbUreZXKgKKNnWbXT6bH2LffGuujwGoKS0wos+
yxCOOMrVaCQy5zoLaeZ88ZoRr1WlId1d5r15J1ew8m
9NRPtnzjGxfZgcbVdbO4eDJ8Bl+FZXmlnFlFdqisnP
cXxQZTks2oJ/0NfLVaR6oa2J3LHDRrrAxPfUjQyRhj
IrnhQ4
30eruNTVY1SpKDxMyoeXU0KFmYyoJz4wQZUfWqVc
nwEAwqeN3O/QT99f9ffgMXpZh68PM23HSwPBKS4jAX
8sZxgOV/L0i7CvFI5AAKtGehbMrDneCACpbfsi6/td
XAFu49ppYVLFYOYWrLpW1hTxUpKjpTJavloadmBzHz
CPIFqgGzStYRTYWLYscgKBiCOGt7RPEMR5I0c4oEHh
8KnuzjZuGGGe1Rr6Spd9UE7V8xids5ZVdZucks0LKu
lm5B5vZVU6C6rxMtM5zOhyCOskVG6mC6vIz2F+U4Ko
Khlly/17w25RYAdjo1oiXLNPEgKrNRr023yG7H/gpJ
```

AzxHHsdq6B2IlUEljzzkoWASJDhSO1OCoatQoUu9NW
qP2XJh2kv4azTTKBq6tSObd1G7nnBPdqp4Qob+CgPf
KPKhKC/QtgtTg+Bt252c1b42k5ZAKZBF9cuidTycAm
nqbxEXR3TEVQNbHPEKiROYCGEwkQMHPK78MK2JMjyA
GeM+ZkxVEtePJw3w4RY/WWxMdtjKTf+jzmwRKJVDgH
1xpQcyeq3ie+AA5xYW6vRyNhb+sMI7MS3YFBLRbf6h
2nd5/1Xw2eca40UpPP7s04i1uaHBVUwuQcLkc8d691
k+rVyu2bgtjcn+RGwDdI/FU5+tgUWmlot7QjnU+ftN
TQcXZnEvLx30KUIxzbFhCDumh1U59JhMnzt457wG2H
GxYdWWfOVUBujzftJvjxd1HYc3z51NaNS3KLPODJB9
ABhgUfVSyNPjg==PcTv
　　——-END PGP MESSAGE——-

After decrypting the message, this is what was sent:

```
*** PGP Signature Status: good
*** Signer: J.A. Hitchcock <awriter@
jahitchcock.com>
*** Signed: 5/3/2005 113521 AM
*** Verified: 5/3/2005 113809 AM
*** BEGIN PGP DECRYPTED/VERIFIED MESSAGE
***

J.A. Hitchcock
Author & Lecturer
www.jahitchcock.com
*** END PGP DECRYPTED/VERIFIED MESSAGE ***
```

All that for such a short message! But if privacy really concerns you, then PGP—or a similar encryption program—is the right thing for you.

Electronic or Digital Signatures

Wouldn't it be great to get a loan online, open a bank account, or have funds transferred without waiting for paperwork to arrive in the mail for a signature, or going to the bank in person? Electronic (otherwise known as "digital") signatures may help you avoid those inconveniences.

With the passage of the Federal Electronic Signatures in Global and National Commerce Act in 2000, online "digital contracts" that consumers agree to have the same legal status as pen-and-paper contracts (see http://thomas.loc.gov/cgi-bin/bdquery/z?d106:s.00761:). You can purchase a car, buy an insurance policy, get a new or second mortgage, receive credit card and other bills electronically, and much more—either on the company's Web site or via e-mail.

"Read the fine print before you enter into an online contract," says Gail Hillebrand, senior attorney with Consumers Union's West Coast Regional Office. "As consumers turn to the Internet to handle more of their business transactions, they need to be vigilant to avoid unwittingly sacrificing their legal rights in the process."

This means that if you decide to use an electronic signature and then change your mind, you should be able to do so without paying a fee. If you don't carefully read the agreement on the Web site you're dealing with, you could end up with more trouble than the service is worth. Another caution: If you decide to conduct business transactions online or receive legal papers via e-mail, make sure you check your e-mail regularly or you could miss a deadline and end up paying late fees or other fees.

An electronic or digital signature is set up with you and the online business you choose. Ideally, in the future there should be one standard electronic signature, no matter which software or hardware you use. But now you must check with the online business to see what it prefers as a signature standard. The electronic signature is a unique key, much like a PGP public key, and thus impossible to forge (in theory).

The Consumers Union offers these additional tips when considering using electronic signatures:

- Use only one e-mail address for all your personal business.

- Read the description of what software and hardware you will need to access future electronic notices.

- As with any contract, read the fine print. Don't agree to a contract you don't understand.

- Print your order, confirmation screen, and any electronic notices you receive, and save the hard copies for later use.

- Keep a list of the businesses with whom you have consented to receive electronic notices, and notify those businesses if your e-mail address changes.

Protect Your Computer!

Trojan

Much like the fabled Trojan Horse the Greeks built to gain entrance into the city of Troy, a Trojan in computerese is a program designed to perform functions on a computer without the computer user knowing it's there.

Virus

A program that "infects" your computer. Some computer viruses are a mere nuisance (snow or dancing animals may appear on your screen for a few minutes, then disappear), but others can cause serious damage, such as corrupting or deleting computer files. Some—like the Melissa virus, which appeared on computers worldwide in 1999—can wipe a hard drive clean.

Hackers

You've seen them in the movies and on TV. Most hackers are people who want to test a Web site or Internet connection just to see if they can break in, sometimes for the fun of it, sometimes at the owner's request. Some are called "crackers," people who are out to cause trouble and possibly fraud by doing something such as breaking into the computer systems of banks to transfer money to hidden bank accounts in their names. They are also known to wreak havoc at a former employer's Web site or LAN,[1] steal someone's Internet account to spam or harass someone, copy files from hard drives, wipe a computer hard drive clean, and more.

We may think about protecting ourselves when we go online, but most of the time we forget our computer is vulnerable, too. This chapter covers computer viruses, firewall/Internet security, hackers, passwords, and cookies (not the kind you eat).

Viruses

Most computer systems—desktop, laptop, or notebook—come packaged with anti-virus software, such as McAfee VirusScan or Norton AntiVirus. It's important to know that unless you use anti-virus software properly, your computer won't be fully protected.

What are viruses? There are four types to date:

1. *Boot virus*: This virus places its code in your computer hard drive so that when you start or "boot up" your computer, the boot virus loads and runs first. After the virus finishes its run, the original boot code loads and you're none the wiser.

2. *File virus*: Attaches itself to executable programs—usually with an .exe or .pif extension, such as runme.exe—so that when you run the infected program, first the virus code executes and then the program loads and executes, and the computer is infected.

3. *Macro virus*: Attaches its macros—quick commands that can be created in programs such as WordPerfect and MS Word—to templates and other files so that when you execute the program, the first invisible instruction is to execute the virus.

4. *Companion virus*: Attaches to the operating system (OS), such as Windows, Linux, and DOS. If you are in DOS, for example, and give the command to run a file called runme, instead of looking for runme.exe (usually the default when running a DOS file) a companion virus places its code in another file with a .com extension that matches the existing .exe file. Then, the infected file named runme.com runs instead of runme.exe.

To avoid virus infection, use an anti-virus program and learn how to update virus definitions. Virus definitions are a database of viruses for which your anti-virus software scans, either automatically (on a daily, weekly, or monthly schedule) or manually. It's getting easier to stay safe: Today's top anti-virus programs will automatically update in order to protect you from new viruses, every time you go online. However, if you hear about a new virus, worm, or trojan in the media, it's a good idea to perform a manual update to see if the anti-virus software you are using already has an antidote.

If you forget to update your virus definitions, or your program fails to do it for you, don't be surprised if your computer gets hit by a new virus. Many viruses are transmitted through e-mail attachments, so the ground rule is to never open an attachment unless you know the sender and are expecting it. Even then, you should be sure to subject the attachment to a virus scan prior to opening it. (All the top anti-virus programs and most major e-mail services will do this for you automatically.) If you get a message from someone you know with an attachment you did not expect, you can also e-mail that person to confirm that he or she actually sent it.

Because there are e-mail-borne viruses that do not require an attachment to do their dirty work, my advice is not to open any message that may be spam. If you don't know the sender or the subject line doesn't make sense, don't open the e-mail—delete it immediately. It's unfortunate that some legitimate communications may be lost in this manner, but it's the only sure way to avoid the increasing number of viruses being spread through e-mail.

Worms

A worm is similar to a virus but doesn't need to attach itself to a certain file or sector on your hard drive. An example is Sasser, which proliferated in the spring of 2004.

"In a nutshell, just as the outside world can enter your house through a variety of means—mail, phone, the door, the window, or the radio—computers can communicate over a variety of means, too. An instant request, like you asking for a Web page to be shared with you and then it appearing on your screen—that's your computer communicating with another computer," explains Jose Nazario, a researcher at Crimelabs (www.crimelabs.net). "Now imagine if the computer on the other end asks your computer to do things it wouldn't normally do. Think of it as an army of thousands of these computers scouring the earth looking for more computers to do things they wouldn't normally do—okay, it has an element of *Night of the Living Dead* to it, but it's not that far off. 'Brains ... brains ...' This is basically what happens when a worm outbreak happens and your computer just happens to be there."

Some of the Worst Worms and Viruses According to Jose Nazario

Worms:

1. The "witty" worm, early 2004. This was one of the first "0-day" worms, using a vulnerability publicly disclosed only a day or two earlier. It struck efficiently and most maliciously. It deleted a randomly chosen section of the hard drive, over time rendering the computer unusable.

2. Blaster, Fall 2003. A sign of things to come. Take one part attack, one part worm core, and mix. Release and watch the damage unfold. This wasn't sophisticated but it did show how easy it is to create a worm, and that's what's scary.

3. Nimda, Fall 2001. Considered a hybrid worm, it mass e-mailed itself with attachments called README.EXE; if executed, it would modify existing Web sites to start offering infected files for download and hit intranets hard.

Viruses:

1. Sharp, Spring 2002, written by gigabyte (a female virus writer) in C# (Microsoft's language platform). It arrived with the subject line "Important: Windows update" and the message "Hey, at work we are applying this update because it makes Windows over 50% faster and more secure. I thought I would forward it as you may like it." It also contained an attachment named MS02-010.EXE. If activated, the virus forwarded itself to everyone listed in the recipient's address book.

2. Loveletter, Spring 2000. Who wouldn't open a message from a random person with such a flattering subject line? Evidently a lot of people opened it.

3. Melissa, Spring 1999. So simple, so basic, so primitive. It was sent as an e-mail attachment and naturally if you opened the attachment (usually "list.doc"), it would search your Microsoft Outlook address book and then send itself out to everyone listed.

Your computer is especially vulnerable if it happens to "be there" and it's not properly protected with up-to-date anti-virus software.

"You can be online for just a few minutes to check your e-mail and your computer could become infected," Nazario warns. "Worms move so far and from so many other computers all over the world that your computer gets connected to them with great frequency. That's when it could fall victim to those malicious computers and start behaving like them, too—spreading the worm."

The Sasser worm affected more than 200,000 computers in the initial days of its release, targeting Windows 2000 and XP systems. The 18-year-old creator was arrested in Germany in May 2004, about a month after he released the worm.

A virus doesn't have to come as an attachment to infect your computer's hard drive. If you download a shareware or freeware program or even a retail program from a secure site, sometimes a virus will be attached. There have even been reports of commercial software— purchased in retail stores, boxed and shrink-wrapped—that have viruses in them. Sometimes these viruses are activated by a triggered event, meaning the virus may launch on a certain date, by a specific series of keystrokes, or when a simple DoS (Denial of Service)[2] function is performed.

This is what happened when the Code Red virus came on the scene in 2001.

"In a nutshell, Code Red is a common 'buffer overflow,' " Nazario says. "What this means is an attacker attempts to place more data into a storage space than has been allocated, only because the software on the attacked computer system wasn't coded to do any checks on the size of the input. This means the computer receives arbitrary instructions, in this case 'download and execute this software,' which is part of the worm package."

The good news is that Code Red only affected computers and systems running Windows 2000 and NT operating systems. Reports claimed that Code Red hit more than 500,000 computers. Since most consumers use Windows 3.x/95/98/ME or XP, it didn't affect the average online user, although it did create problems for many Web sites, often shutting them down for hours.

"The only thing that is assured in the anti-virus markets is change," says Beau Roberts, director of product marketing for McAfee.com. "New viruses are discovered every day. While the operating systems, devices, and types of viruses may change over time, the need to protect your computing devices and data is always going to be there."

So, why are viruses, worms, and trojans so prevalent? Mainly because of their success. They succeed at gathering large numbers of machines for whatever goal someone may desire (DoS for extortion, spam, storage, and distribution of pirated software). And they succeed with their deep penetration into various networks.

"This can lead to people doing all sorts of things, from working on creating viruses for money-making purposes, to random joyriding, to out-and-out maliciousness," Nazario says.

The second major reason is that they are relatively easy to create. When virus construction labs (VCLs) came out online some years ago, the number of virus authors rose, even though they didn't possess significant skills at the time. If even a small fraction of those who became interested in virus creation continued to write viruses independently, then that's a growth facilitated by such a tool as the VCL.

"While I'm not overtly aware of anything resembling VCL for worms at this point, the code is out there to be used and recycled," Nazario says. "It can be recycled in any number of worms. The trends that emerged in 2004 are that this is what people are doing, both in terms of techniques and in terms of some of the basic building blocks."

Here are some anti-virus programs mentioned in this chapter, plus a freebie:

Norton AntiVirus
www.symantec.com

- Automatic update of virus definitions while connected to the Internet.

- Worldwide network of LiveUpdate servers ensures fast, reliable downloads of virus definitions.

- Automatic scanning of e-mail attachments for standard POP3 clients including Microsoft Outlook, Eudora, MSN Mail, and Netscape Mail.

- Protection against viruses, Trojan horses, and malicious ActiveX code and Java applets.

- Detection of viruses in compressed files.

- Alert windows with detailed information and recommendations whenever a virus is detected.

- Quarantine of infected files until they can be repaired, protecting your other data and files.

- Step-by-step Scan and Deliver Wizard for sending infected files to the Symantec AntiVirus Research Center (SARC) for prompt assistance with eliminating viruses.

- Protection against newly created macro, file, and boot-sector viruses.

McAfee VirusScan
www.mcafee.com

- Detection of destructive ActiveX and Java applets.

- Advanced e-mail X-Ray feature catches viruses in e-mails before new messages have been opened.

- Quarantine of infected and suspicious files.

- AVERT Labs (Anti-Virus Emergency Response Team), the world's largest anti-virus research group, based in eight locations around the world, works to find the latest virus threats and distribute their cures 24 hours a day.

AVG Anti-Virus (a free program)
http://free.grisoft.com

- Automatic update functionality.

- The AVG Resident Shield, which provides real-time protection as files are opened and programs are run.

- The AVG E-mail Scanner, which protects your e-mail.

- The AVG On-Demand Scanner, which allows the user to perform scheduled and manual tests.

- Free Virus Database Updates for the lifetime of the product.

- AVG Virus Vault for safe handling of infected files.

Firewalls, Internet Security, and Hackers

Even if you're using a dial-up modem, whether it's 24kbps[3], 33.6kbps, or 56kbps, your computer is open for attack. Computers most at risk are those using a cable modem or digital subscriber line (DSL, available through telephone lines) because their Internet connections are on 24 hours a day.

Firewall or Internet security software will protect your computer from attacks, whether someone is trying to hack in, send viruses or Trojans, or commit some other mischief.

Consider what happened to Maurice, who lives in South Carolina.

A software beta tester, he had a company credit card that he used only for business expenses. He thought nothing of making purchases online, unaware that someone had hacked into his computer and stolen the credit card number. The hacker ran up charges of $1,000, including visits to porn and auto parts sites, and even a pizza-ordering site.

"I used the card online to purchase video camera batteries for an upcoming business trip," Maurice says. "My employer was ready to fire me for misuse of the card and I had no idea what he was talking about. I had to personally contact the merchants where the charges had been made to get them removed. Most of the merchants were very cooperative and provided information about who had stolen the credit card number."

This information was given to Maurice's employer, who ended up getting restitution from the credit card company for those charges not waived by the merchants. Maurice—who never found out who the hacker was and probably never will—installed firewall protection on his computer immediately following this incident.

"I actually purchased Norton Internet Security [NIS] the same day my boss almost fired me," Maurice says.

When Maurice first ran NIS, he discovered that his Internet connection was getting "hit" by people probing it to see if his connection was vulnerable to an attack. He was getting hit a lot more than he'd ever imagined—144 times in just the first seven days he used the program.

"What surprised me was the intensity of the attacks," Maurice says, still amazed. "It's not just once in a while but at least a dozen a day with every type of nasty Trojan you could think about."

Because Maurice was hooked up to cable for his Internet connection, he called the cable company and asked why it didn't provide better protection for its customers.

"They claimed it wasn't their policy or within their capability to protect their subscribers from attack," Maurice says. "They immediately suggested I purchase a software or hardware firewall because 'It's not our problem.' "

The "It's not our problem" reply is common. Cable and telephone companies were originally in the cable and telephone business — not the Internet business. When the opportunity to provide Internet service came about, they jumped on it, but many apparently don't care enough to offer adequate, or sometimes any, firewall protection. And typically they don't advise customers to use firewall protection on their own.

That's where a company like Symantec comes in — to provide reasonably priced and sometimes free firewall and anti-virus protection for your computer.

"We began working on Norton Internet Security (NIS) in early 1999," says Tom Powledge, group product manager for Symantec's NIS. "The idea for the product stemmed from our analysis of Internet connectivity around the world — particularly DSL or cable. We found that with an increasing number of always-on connections, home computer users were becoming more susceptible to hacking."

Powledge's group surveyed online users to determine their level of concern for security and privacy issues. The researchers discovered that online users were concerned about protection of their personal and confidential information and viewed hacking as a threat on par with virus invasion. Powledge and his group concluded there was a good market for a security suite that included a personal firewall and anti-virus capability. They were right. When NIS was introduced in December 1999, the U.S. retail market for Internet security software grew more than 140 percent.

But before NIS, there was ZoneAlarm, from Zone Labs.

In 1997, Zone Labs founders Gregor Freund, Marie Bourget, and Conrad Herrmann realized that fast, big "pipes" connecting people to the Internet (i.e., DSL and cable modems — the always-on connections) would mean that a new type of threat could emerge. Viruses, mutations of viruses, and spyware could spread more quickly than ever, since more and more people were connected.

"They realized that the only way to truly protect a machine would be to ensure that the machine itself was fortified. You could no longer rely on the corporate network or your ISP," says Te Smith of Zone Labs. "They developed a core technology, called TrueVector,[4] which could monitor an Internet connection and, among other things, alert the user whenever a program wished to 'speak' to the Internet. That put the user in control of their Internet connection."

The first product based on this technology was ZoneAlarm, which shipped in July 1999. Free for downloading from the Zone Labs' Web site, the product has proven to be a very popular and effective program. Later that year, Zone Labs added a firewall feature, then continued to expand the product, and, finally, in August 2000, shipped ZoneAlarmPro. ZoneAlarmPro added support for local area networks, and enhanced MailSafe E-mail Attachment Protection, passwords, and advanced utilities for "techie" users. The extra features in ZoneAlarmPro don't come free, although the program is fairly inexpensive and competitive with the other programs mentioned in this chapter.

"ZoneAlarm has kept my data secure and has logged all kinds of illegal attempts to either gain access to my system or to flood my ports," says Nancy, a devout ZoneAlarm user. "There were attempts to overwhelm the firewall with activity in order to bypass it. So far, no one has been able to beat ZoneAlarm, and I'm happy with my choice."

When you're connected to the Internet, your computer is part of a worldwide network and anyone can try to connect to your system. The best way to describe it is by contrasting it to your television set, a one-way communication mechanism. The Internet is a two-way communication mechanism. While you're connected and accessing Web servers, your computer is listening for incoming traffic. And this is what hackers, crackers, and viruses are looking for.

Even savvy consumers find the attacks troubling. Cynthia and her husband had a LAN set up for the home business.

"When we got a DSL connection, we installed a firewall program right away because we knew we'd be more attractive targets for hackers," Cynthia says. "We didn't think twice about it. But then when we saw the sheer number of hack attempts, we were shocked."

Cynthia realized that someone who'd been harassing her online found her new connection information and was trying to break into her computer—the IP address matched the harasser's perfectly. She knew it wasn't a coincidence. But there were other attacks not from the harasser and these attacks were not what are known as a "false/positive," or the firewall program thinking the user's ISP is attacking them (which does happen when the program first runs—the program has to learn the user's IP addresses to prevent hits in the future).

Cynthia says that on an average day she sees at least five attempts per hour to hack into her system. Most of the attempts are apparently by people who are randomly scanning blocks of IP addresses owned by companies that provide DSL service, such as the one Cynthia and her husband use. Her husband likes to chat occasionally on IRC (Internet Relay Chat), and when he does, the hack attempts go up to 20 or more an hour. This is because chatters tend to be on for long periods of time, allowing a hacker a lot of time to probe a computer or attack it with a virus/Trojan if there is no firewall program in place.

If you think using regular old dial-up modems is safer, think again. Trojan Horse programs have been around for quite some time, but one in particular caught the attention of Mikhail Zakhryapin, director of Agnitum Ltd., a software development company located in Cyprus.

"In 1999, one of my friends downloaded a program called BackOrifice 1.2 and called me to say that this program would change the Internet," Zakhryapin says. "It allowed stealth installation and powerful remote administration—a real Trojan horse."

Zakhryapin went to a Web site that offered the program for free and was shocked to see how many people were downloading it. He decided to check his network at Agnitum to see if someone had infected it.

"The results were amazing," Zakhryapin says. "From the 255 computers with dial-up modems, at least five were infected. I realized that BackOrifice and other Trojans were a very dangerous tool and a great number of people were probably infected without knowing it."

Zakhryapin spent his free time trying to come up with a solution. He installed a packet[5]-capturing program on his personal computer and dialed into his ISP. He waited. After several hours, he discovered that someone had tried to access two ports. He looked through the packets and found it was a typical BackOrifice scan. This led Zakhryapin to write a simple program he called Jammer.

"It was basically a utility that captured all the incoming packets and tried to find BackOrifice packets in the traffic, then send a message back, such as, 'Got you, hacker!'" Zakhryapin says, laughing. "After some time, a friend wrote a user-friendly interface, but it wasn't for sale; it was just for us and our friends to share. We put it on a shareware site for free downloading and found it became a popular program."

Zakhryapin and his friend worked full-time to produce a commercial version of Jammer. They also produced other programs that help protect your computer, the latest of which is Outpost, Jammer's replacement.

Firewall Protection Programs

(Note: Many of these Web sites offer free 30-day trial versions so that you can decide which program suits both your needs and your pocketbook.)

Norton Internet Security (includes Norton AntiVirus; see Figure 20.1)
www.symantec.com

- Script blocking proactively protects against certain known and unknown threats without the need for virus definitions.

- Keeps itself updated automatically.

- Intrusion Protection with AutoBlock automatically blocks systems from trying to probe your PC's ports.

- Security Assistant helps you quickly and easily configure product settings.

- Internet Access Control stops spyware and Trojan horse programs from spying on you or retrieving private information.

- Internet Zone Control simplifies firewall protection for home networks by allowing you to assign computers to a trusted zone behind the firewall.

- Alert Tracker informs you of important activities such as port scanning attempts and security alerts.

- Norton Privacy Control can prevent Web sites from tracking your activities with cookies.

- Ad blocking keeps banner ads, pop-up windows, and other Web clutter off your screen.

- 24-hour protection provides vital Internet security for dial-up, DSL, and cable modem users.

- Includes one year of free virus definitions and firewall updates.

Outpost Firewall Pro (see Figure 20.2)
www.agnitum.com

- Hides your computer identity from hackers.

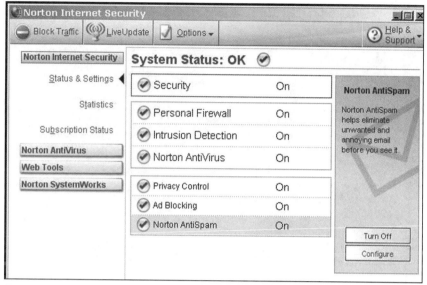

Figure 20.1 Norton Internet Security

- Stops hacker attacks automatically.

- Blocks private data from being transmitted.

- Prevents mass-mailed worm infections.

- Removes banner ads and pop-ups.

McAfee Firewall (see Figure 20.3)
www.mcafee.com

- Filters inbound and outbound communications between your computer and the outside world.

- Provides comprehensive Log and Tracking.

- Integrates smoothly and transparently with the existing desktop environment while monitoring your system for security threats.

- Filters all applications, system services, and protocols including file and printer shares (i.e., NetBIOS); IP protocols (i.e., TCP/IP, UDP/IP); service-based protocols (i.e., FTP, Telnet); ARP/RARP; and DHCP.

- Blocks IPX and NetBEUI on a per-device basis.

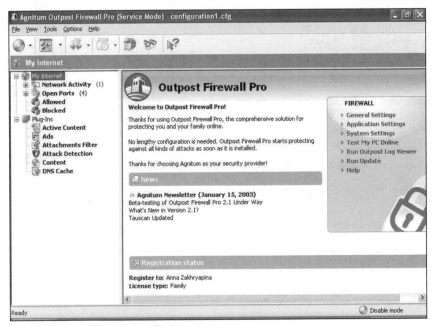

Figure 20.2 Outpost Firewall Pro

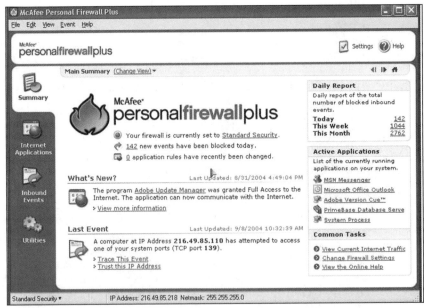

Figure 20.3 McAfee Firewall

ZoneAlarm (a free program; see Figure 20.4)
www.zonelabs.com

- Sends immediate alerts when there is any new activity, giving you the opportunity to stop it instantly.

- Uses simple "yes" or "no" options over which applications can access the Internet.

- Runs in stealth mode so hackers can't find your computer(s).

- Uses simple and easy displays and controls.

- Allows user to customize the firewall or run it preconfigured.

GRC NetFilter (see Figure 20.5)
grc.com/nf/netfilter.htm

- An "abuse aware" filter monitors all of the data flowing across Internet connections to "filter out" anything that should not be allowed.

- Monitors Internet activity to selectively block malicious and annoying content.

Putting a Spin on It

Some online users have taken matters into their own hands. Neil Schwartzman, founder of peteMOSS Publications at Petemoss.com, distributes a weekly e-newsletter about spam. How he got to that point is an interesting story.

"Pete Moss Productions was my record company in the 1980s when I was producing independent albums for local bands," Schwartzman says. "That line of work dried up and the company remained dormant for a while. In 1992, I went online after a mass murder at the university where I worked, mostly because of my morbid curiosity about postings the killer had made to Usenet."

Schwartzman saw how fast spam proliferated not only on newsgroups but also via e-mail. Although he doesn't consider himself a techie, he began to collate and post news clippings about spam to a mailing list he participated in called SPAM-L. Not everyone on the list liked his frequent postings, so he began his own mailing list in 1996 and called it Spam News.

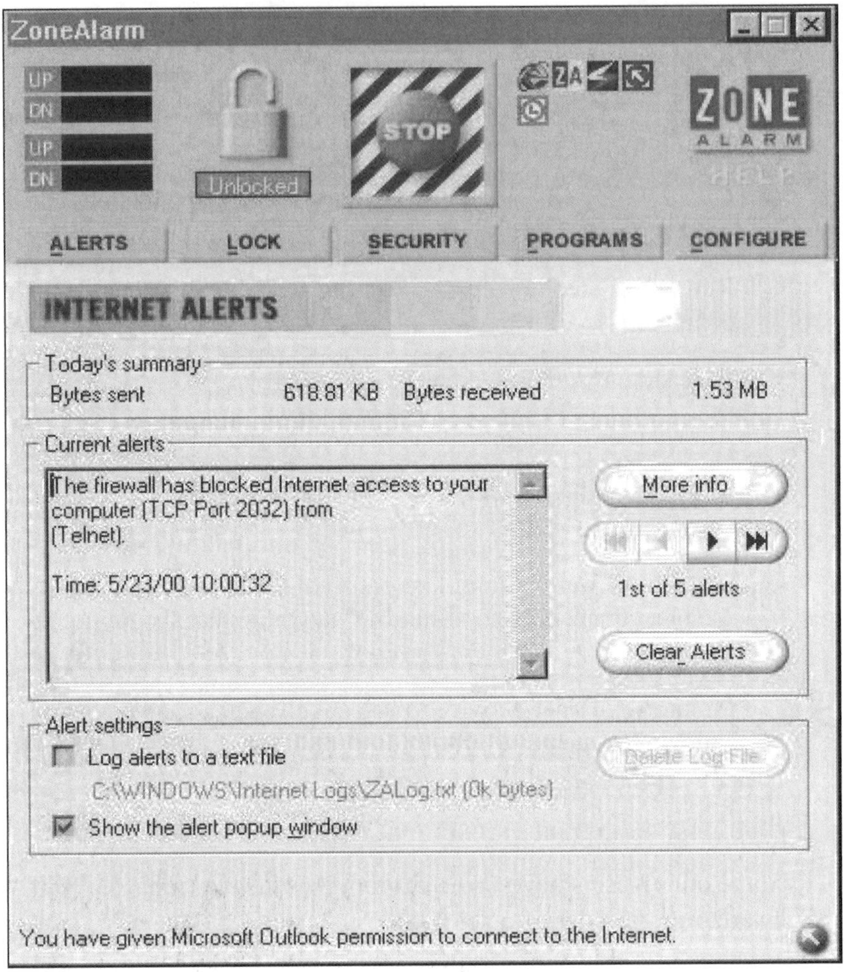

Figure 20.4   ZoneAlarm

"One day I realized that to gain a modicum of legitimacy I needed to have a company under whose aegis I would publish," Schwartzman says. "I chose petemoss.com, harkening back to my old record company. I never quit my day job, and did this as a hobby."

Petemoss.com has grown over the years, as has its subscriber list. Although Schwartzman has tried to launch other weekly e-newsletters, Spam News is the only one that remains. Its popularity has never waned, probably because press coverage of spam has expanded significantly as the problem has grown.

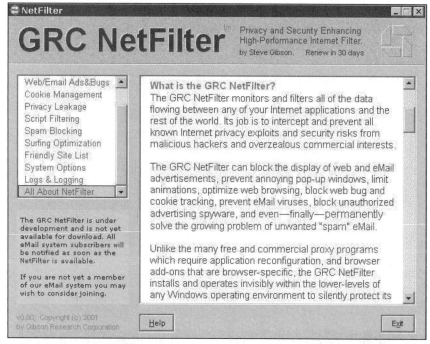

Figure 20.5 GRC NetFilter

As a result of his collating of news stories, Schwartzman has become something of a spam and security expert. He sees the potential for big problems for the future—and the present.

"Off-shore spammers and crackers, obviously operating not only outside the law, but oftentimes in places outside the reach of international law, are what we need to be aware of," Schwartzman says. "As hacktivism and cracking become more commonplace as methods of protesting government and business, crackers living in those regions will become freelance guns for hire. Indeed, this is happening to a certain extent now."

With the rise in online crimes, Schwartzman sees a future that many online users fear. It's what is commonly referred to as "Big Brother."

"I think we will see legislation eventually, with bilateral agreements to deal with such things as advertising or spam, security, and privacy, as lawmakers become more savvy to the fact that the Net is indeed borderless," Schwartzman says. "Thus, the only effective way to deal with such problems is in tandem with international partners. Perhaps we will see an Interpol computer division stake its claim."

Schwartzman doesn't see the Internet, as a whole, being regulated.

"I'm not sure we want to," he says. "Regulate some of the activities, sure—that's happening now. Legislators will remain in a reactive rather than a proactive stance, as millions of new ideas are played out on the Net."

Rhode Island's Lieutenant Governor Charles J. Fogarty agrees to a certain extent.

"In the early 1990s, most of us didn't know what the Internet was. Then you look at it today and you see the advances and changes. You know we'll see problems and challenges that our laws need to keep up with, whether on a state or federal level," Fogarty says. "The laws have to keep up with these changes in technology because people want the same basic protections they have in the rest of their lives. I can tell you that Rhode Island, for one state, is going to make sure we keep on top of this."

An aside: Rhode Island became the 31st state to pass a cyberstalking law, in June 2001. A first offense is a misdemeanor and/or a fine; a second offense is a felony.

Common Home Computer Intrusions

The most common intrusion is still a good old virus, although the two most common traditional hacking activities that home users with cable or DSL modems experience are port scans and Trojan Horse access attempts. Tom Powledge of Symantec's Norton Internet Security notes the more common intrusions:

- Ping Sweeps: Ping is a diagnostic function generally used for network troubleshooting that reports whether a computer is online. A hacker can use ping to determine if your computer can be accessed without your knowledge.

- Port Scans: The hacker makes connection requests to selected ports on your computer to see if any of the connection requests are accepted. If the port being scanned is not in use (no listening service), the computer typically refuses the connection. Although the connection is refused, the message indicates that there is a computer at that IP address, encouraging the hacker to probe further.

- Trojan Horse Programs: Remote Access Trojans (RATs) are small servers that are installed on your computer without your permission, typically with a benign or seemingly useful program. Once installed, RATs let the attacker take complete control of your computer. Examples are BackOrifice and NetBus.

- Fragmented Packets: A Denial of Service (DoS) attack sends incomplete or fragmented packets to your computer. These packets cause your computer to request a resend or to hold the packets, waiting for the rest of the information to arrive. Enough of these requests can overload your computer and cause it to quit responding.

- Zombies: Zombies are small programs installed on your computer without your knowledge. Once installed, they let the attacker use your computer to launch a coordinated DoS attack against a third party. These are called Distributed Denial of Service (DDoS) attacks. The attacks against Yahoo! in February 2000 are examples of this type of attack.

- File Sharing Over the Internet: One of the more common and potentially most dangerous ways your computer can be hacked is if you inadvertently turn on File and Print Sharing over TCP/IP, which many home users with networks and small businesses enable. However, if you then install a broadband[6] Internet connection such as a cable modem, your networks are exposed to neighbors—or everyone on the Internet.

Passwords

Passwords ensure that your online connection, credit card information, various accounts, and Web site registrations are for your eyes only. But if you don't choose a password that is truly unique, a hacker or someone who is Net-knowledgeable and wants to create havoc can easily take over your online life.

The most common mistake people make when creating a password is to use something they won't easily forget, usually a pet's name, birth date, an anniversary date, child's name, and so forth. If you won't forget it then it's likely that someone trying to break into your account will be able to guess your password.

The best way to create a password is to use a combination of letters and numerals, such as "1xp4u8m4." Yes, it will be harder to remember, but it's less likely to be guessed by someone else. If you insist on using something more familiar and easier to remember, then change your password once a month or more often. This keeps your private and confidential information a bit safer.

Tips to Help Keep Your Passwords Confidential

1. Secure pin numbers and passwords at all times. This means do not keep them in a file on your hard disk. If you want to keep them in a text file, save them to a diskette, ZIP disk, or CD-ROM and then keep that in a safe place. Or you can write or print out the pin numbers and passwords and put them away for safekeeping.

2. Write your password on something—such as the back of a picture on your wall—but don't include any explanation for what it is. The point here is to keep others from knowing what it is. Don't write it on a sticky note and put it on your monitor for everyone to see.

3. Don't share passwords or pin numbers with others or use someone else's password to log onto the Internet. This sounds like simple advice, but you'd be amazed how many people are too trusting. For an example of what could happen, let's say a friend is visiting and wants to send an e-mail. You give him or her the password to your AOL account, and a week later you find out someone is using your AOL account and running up a big bill.

4. If you have a lot of passwords and find them hard to remember, consider using password management software such as Robo Form (www.roboform.com) or EZ Password Manager (www.northwind-tech.com). These programs allow you to securely keep all your passwords in one place in case you forget them.

Several of the firewall/security programs mentioned offer alerts if confidential information is being accessed when you're online. You can input whatever confidential information you want to get alerts about, such as credit card numbers, your birth date, social security number, and so on. If someone tries to use that information, the program will let you know and you can avert an undesirable situation.

Cookies

Cookies are small text files created when you visit certain Web sites and stored on your hard drive. These files contain information about you and what you've done online. So the next time you visit the same Web site, the cookie tells that site what you did on your previous visit.

Some Web sites are just trying to keep track of how often you visit; others want to get as much information as possible, such as your buying habits at their online store, which photos or graphics you clicked on or saved to your hard drive, and your personal information — which they might share with others.

Sometimes cookies can be helpful, especially if you have to log onto a particular Web site often and would rather not have to fill in the same information every time. The cookie file will keep your logon information so that the next time you go to the site, you're already signed in.

Stephen Gibson, the founder of Gibson Research Corporation, makes this comment:

> Cookies are not inherently evil but they are prone to abuse. If cookies were *only* used to track a person around a single, local Web site — as they were intended — there would not be a problem. But cookies can be used to track individuals across the entire Internet, and that's a problem. When coupled with several insecurities in the way Web browsers accept input data through forms, comprehensive third-party databases can be created to assemble profiles of individual users.

The solution is not to simply kill all the cookies but to take proactive measures to tame the Web's browser cookies.

Do you have cookies?

How can you tell what cookies are on your computer and what information they have on you?

Usually, there is a file called cookies.txt in the same directory as the Web browser you use. Here's an example of what a cookie will look like:

```
audiobookclub.com    TRUE   /    FALSE
2051222359 SITESERVER
ID=3e0f44675cf50ea462eaf24adf12469e

tripod.com    TRUE   /    FALSE
1019405226    CookieStatus COOKIE_OK

network54.com   FALSE   /    FALSE
1145689162    Apache bac2010d844cd74261dbb-
dbb1bb5488c
```

Looks like a bunch of gobbledy-gook, right? Believe it or not, these files give the Web site information such as whether or not you've disabled cookies on your computer, which site you visited before theirs, and your username (encrypted, such as the one for network54.com shown in the example).

How can you get rid of the darned things? If you're worried about cookies, you should get one of the firewall/security programs mentioned in this chapter and follow the instructions to clean the cookies off your hard drive. You can also open the cookies.txt file in Notepad (or other word processing programs), select all the information, then delete it and save the file with no information in it. However, many experts warn against this, as it may cause problems when running your Web browser (although personally I've never had a problem with it).

Another option is to make your cookies.txt file a read-only document. This means you can view the document, but not make changes to it, which means cookies created by any new sites you visit won't be added to the file. To do this:

- Find the cookies.txt file for Microsoft Internet Explorer and/or Netscape Navigator/Communicator.

- Place the mouse cursor on the file and right-click (the right button on your mouse).

- Select Properties when a mini menu pops up.

- Click the Read-Only box under Attributes; then click OK.

If you don't feel comfortable going through these steps, you can reduce the number of cookies stored by turning cookies off in your Web browser. But, this does mean you'll be limited as to the number of Web sites you can visit. Many sites demand you keep your cookies turned on or you'll get a blank page or a "site not found" or similar error message. An alternative is to change the option to "allow cookies for originating Web site only."

To turn off change cookies preferences in your Web browser:

For Microsoft Internet Explorer 6.x (see Figure 20.6)

- From the top toolbar menu, select Tools, then Internet Options. A new window pops up.

- Select the Privacy tab.

- Click on Advanced. A new window pops up.

- Check the box next to "override automatic cookie handling," then select from:
    - Accept
    - Block
    - Prompt

First-Party Cookies:
- Accept (default)
- Block
- Prompt

Third-Party Cookies:
- Accept (default)
- Block (recommended)
- Prompt

If you select Prompt, be aware that you may be getting pop-up window alerts more often than you'd like. But give it a shot to try it out.

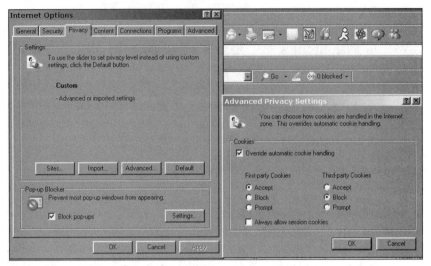

Figure 20.6   MSIE cookie

For Netscape Communicator/Navigator 7.2 (see Figure 20.7)

- From the top toolbar menu, click on Edit, then Preferences. A separate window pops up.

- Click on Privacy & Security, then Cookies, then select the option you want:

  - Block cookies

  - Allow cookies for the originating Web site only (recommended)

  - Allow cookies based on privacy settings

  - Allow cookies (the default)

There are other cookie options. Always check all the options available and select the ones you feel most comfortable with.

You can install software programs that kill or reduce the incidence of cookies. Some examples include:

Cookie Pal
www.kburra.com/cpal.html

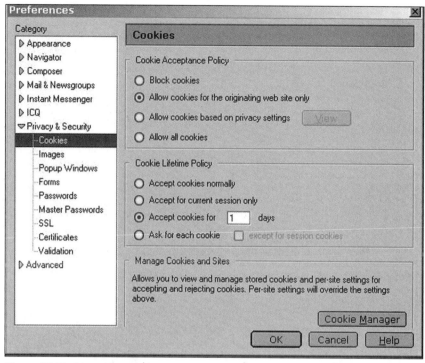

Figure 20.7   Netscape cookie

Smasher
www.popupstop.com

Cookie Crusher
www.thelimitsoft.com/cookie/

Cookie Jar
www.dittotech.com/Products/CookieEater/

Endnotes

1. LAN: Local Area Network; an internal network consisting of two or more computers "connected" to each other and accessible only from within that office or organization.
2. DdoS: Aka DoS Distributed Denial of Service or Denial of Service. To flood a network or ISP with unwanted traffic, trying to shut down that network.

3. Kbps: Kilobytes per second or the speed of a modem.

4. True Vector technology is patented by Zone Labs 5.

5. Packet: A unit of data sent between an origin and a destination online.

6. Broadband: A wide band of frequency used for telecommunications. Term is used when describing either DSL or cable connection to the Internet.

The Basics of Staying Safe Online: A Review

In this closing chapter, I'll review some of the most important steps you can take to stay safe online, first outlining some general guidelines and then recapping specific tips from various chapters. Use this chapter as a quick overview, but also be sure to read those chapters that are appropriate to your situation—they include a great deal of additional detail.

Basic Guidelines

Choose Your Username Carefully

Always select a gender-neutral username for the first part of your e-mail address or for chat or discussion forums. The majority of online victims are female, so if you're a woman, the first smart step you can take in avoiding trouble is to conceal your sex. Resist the impulse to pick something cute, sexy, or feminine, like misskitty@someisp.com (unless you're looking for trouble)—and be sure to explain this to children and young adults who may be choosing their own online identities.

Don't select something that identifies your physical location, such as dovernh, hollywood, or ImInIowa. There is no point in letting everyone know where you live, even in a general way, and it could come back to haunt you.

A random combination of letters and numerals as a username is a good bet for two reasons: It's less likely someone will have already taken such a username, and it effectively obscures your identity, including your gender, name, and location.

At the point in the set-up of your e-mail or newsgroup program where you must add your e-mail address, use your initials rather than your real name so that when you send a message, the FROM: line will read something like:

```
FROM: "JAH"  rtlm1359@hotmail.com
```

Alternatively, don't enter a name at all. If you leave the name fields blank only your e-mail address will show up in the FROM: line.

Keep Your Primary E-Mail Address Private and Get a Secondary E-Mail Account

Keep your primary e-mail address private and use it to communicate only with people you know and trust. This is both a safety and a convenience issue because it will reduce the amount of spam sent to your primary address.

Establish a secondary, free e-mail account and use it for all your "casual" online activity, including chatting, IM, newsgroups, forums, shopping, and communicating with people you don't really know. Again, select a gender-neutral username and make it something very different from your primary account username. There are many free e-mail providers, including Hotmail, Juno, Yahoo!, and Hushmail, and they have their unique advantages and disadvantages. Using your favorite search engine to search the phrase "free e-mail account" will result in hundreds of hits: Look over the first few result pages and choose a provider that appears to best suit your needs. Many free e-mail providers offer built-in filtering designed to send spam into a folder other than your inbox. However, no currently available service can claim to filter all the spam.

Don't Defend and Don't React

It's a natural impulse to defend yourself, and that's why it's the most common reaction when someone taunts you online. But a reaction from you is just what harassers want. When you reply, whether in a chat room, via IM, e-mail, newsgroup, message board, or anywhere online, you've taken the bait. No matter how difficult it is, ignore these people. When they realize they can't get you to react, they'll look for easier prey.

Lurk First

"Lurk" on—that is, watch and study—newsgroups, message boards, mailing lists, and chat rooms before posting any messages. This gives you a chance to evaluate a given forum before joining in. Go elsewhere if it's not just what you're looking for.

Read FAQs

Before joining a newsgroup, mailing list, message board, or forum, check to see if it has a Frequently Asked Questions (FAQ) page or file. Many do. Read the FAQ before asking questions or commenting. If you start asking questions that are covered in the FAQ, you may be told (in some cases rather rudely) to go read it.

Go to Moderated Forums

For most online users, moderated forums are preferable to non-moderated ones because there's someone working (to one extent or another) to weed out troublemakers—whether it's a troll going from forum to forum to start arguments or a run-of-the-mill loudmouth. Moderators will frequently ban such individuals from involvement in a group once they've shown their true colors.

Watch What You Say Online

Don't be overly brash, aggressive, revealing, or critical. A good rule of thumb is to write only the types of things you would be willing to say to someone's face. People tend to divulge things online they wouldn't dream of saying in person. This happens most frequently in chat rooms, where two chatters forget there are other people in the room who can read everything they're saying. If it's something very personal, it could be used against them—if not now, then sometime in the future. Remember that the other chatters may be as far away as another country, but can just as easily reside down the street. My advice is that if you wouldn't say it to a stranger in an elevator, don't say it online.

Use Brief Signature Files

Signature files are lines of identifying text that are appended (either automatically or by selection) to the end of your messages and posts. If you use a signature file, don't include your full name, address, and phone number. Keep it short and simple. I personally use:

J.A. Hitchcock
www.jahitchcock.com

If you must include an address and phone number in your signature file, consider the next piece of advice.

Get a Free Fax/Voicemail Number and Purchase a P.O. Box

If you need a contact phone number anywhere online—in your signature file or in your profile—get a free fax/voicemail number. Quite a few Web sites offer this service and, yes, it's really free. You register, get a free telephone number (not always in your area code, but you can pay a nominal monthly fee for that—usually as little as $4.95/month), and then you can post it on your Web site or put it in your signature file. Give this number, rather than your home or work number, to those you're not quite sure you trust. When someone calls the number, he or she will first hear a short ad for the service (that's why it's free) followed by a pre-recorded message stating that you're unavailable. Callers can then leave a voicemail message or send a fax, and you'll receive notification via e-mail that a communication has arrived. You can play the voicemail message on your computer (you'll need speakers and a sound card for this) or open and print the fax.

If you need a contact mailing address, spend the money and get a P.O. Box in your town or the next town over. It's better to be safe than sorry!

Get an Unlisted Telephone Number

If you currently have a telephone number that's listed in the White Pages, remember that means, in this Information Age, that it's available worldwide. If you don't believe me, go to The Ultimates (www.theultimates.com). Click on White Pages, input your information, and you'll see how many directories you're listed in. Try a reverse search, too: Input your telephone number and see what comes up. Google offers a similar phone number look-up through its main search box and other search engines are sure to follow.

If you want to have your contact information removed from these online directories and search engines, you can, but you'll have to go to each "offending" Web site and find and follow the appropriate instructions. An unlisted telephone number costs a bit more each month than a listed one, but depending on your privacy needs, that may be better than having your number and address available worldwide via a simple Web search.

Get Caller ID

If you decide to keep a listed phone number, then get Caller ID so that if someone harasses you, you can figure out who it is (much of the time, anyway). Also think about using *69 (reverse call) and *57 (phone trace), if these services are available in your area.

Use an Answering Machine

If you don't have an answering machine, get one. That, combined with Caller ID, will help you decide when to answer a phone call. If it's a number you don't recognize, or it comes up as Unknown, Private Caller, or something else, let the answering machine pick up. If the caller is someone who really wants to get in touch with you, he will leave a message. If you are present when the answering machine picks up and either recognize the voice or discern that it's a legitimate call, either pick up and apologize for not catching the phone before the machine answered (I do this all the time) or let the message record and return the call at a later time.

Don't Give Out Your Password

Never give your password to anyone, and be particularly alert to IMs (instant messages) and e-mail messages purporting to be from your ISP, asking you to verify it. Your ISP will never, ever ask you for your password via e-mail. In fact, I'd be surprised to hear of an ISP asking you for your password, period. If an ISP needs this information it should be available in its own records. If you call your ISP for tech support, there are a few—rather rare—instances in which the support person might ask you for your password, but there's no legitimate reason for anyone to contact you for it.

Don't Give Out Your Credit Card Number

Don't provide your credit card number or other identifying information as proof of your age, identity, and so on, to access or subscribe to a Web site run by a company you're unfamiliar with. For that matter, be wary of companies you *are* familiar with—there's a lot of spoofing going on these days and it can be very difficult to tell the real firms from the pretenders.

Monitor Your Children's Internet Use

You should monitor what your children are doing online, even if you feel you've trained them to be safe online and you trust their judgment. Remember: There's no software in the world that can replace the involvement of a concerned parent.

Also, explain to your children that they should never, ever give out personal information online—or offline—such as their name, address, or phone number without your permission.

Be Cautious About Posting Photos

Be very cautious about putting pictures of yourself or your children anywhere online, or allowing anyone else—well-meaning relatives, schools, dance academies, sports associations, and the like—to post such photos. Stalkers have been known to become obsessed with a person's photographic image, especially that of a woman or child. Having said that, there are a growing number of secure Web sites that allow you to safely post photos of your newborn, wedding, anniversary, and other special occasions. You're given a URL that you then send to people you want to view the photo(s) and they're given a password to access the photos.

Install Anti-Virus Software and a Firewall Program

Install an anti-virus program (such as one of those discussed in Chapter 20) on your computer, and remember to keep it updated so your computer is inoculated against new viruses that crop up.

A firewall program will protect your computer and Internet connection from hackers and Trojan viruses. Whether you have a regular modem or are using DSL or cable, everyone should have a firewall program installed. Be sure to keep it updated. If you don't, your computer won't be protected from new Trojans or emerging methods for hacking into a system.

Conduct Regular "Ego Surfs"

How much information is there online about you? How about your family members? If you want to get at least a sense of this, ego surf. Look yourself up online. A good place to start is a major search engine. Although no search engine indexes every Web page, many include hundreds of thousands of pages in their databases, and some of them may include information about you.

How does this happen? Programs called "bots" go out and search for new or updated pages, sometimes looking for specific keywords. If a page or site matches the keyword(s), it will be added to the search engine's directory.

Here's how to ego surf (we'll use Yahoo! for this example):

1. Go to www.yahoo.com and type your name in quote marks—as "John Smith," for instance—then click the Search button. Putting your name in quotes refines the search so that you weed out all the "Johns" and "Smiths" while retaining all the "John Smiths." The resulting listing will, for the most part, include Web pages where this name appears, and the more common your name, the more Web pages there will be. (With a name like "John Smith," you're in trouble—if you have a middle name, use it!) You can further refine your search by using Yahoo!'s "Advanced Search" option. Once you have your results, if you take the time to go through some of them you may be surprised to find numerous references that do, in fact, relate to you. Some of what you discover may not make you happy.

    For instance, if you signed a guestbook at a Web site, there's a good chance it has been picked up by a search engine. If you went to a message board located at the Web site of your favorite TV show and posted a message, it might show up in a search. If you purchased a home or property and your town or state has a Web site, it's likely your purchase is listed on the site. If your employer has a Web site, you may be listed as an employee. Local newspapers are putting their archives online, so if you won an award, got married, had a baby, got a divorce, got into a car accident, or were arrested for DUI, it just might be online.

    Besides finding legitimate listings of your name, if someone has put up a Web site about you or forged your name in newsgroups, forums, in personal ads, or somewhere else, there's a good chance you can catch it and get it taken down or removed before any damage is done. As each search engine will index different pages and at different times, it makes good sense to ego surf on more than one of them.

2. Go to a metasearch engine such as Metacrawler (www.metacrawler.com), Copernic (www.copernic.com), or DogPile (www.dogpile.com). Metasearch engines compile results from a number of different search engines to come up with a more compact list of results (this works some of the time). Type your name in quotes and click the Search button, and do the same with the names of your spouse, significant other, or children. Remember to put names in quotes to refine the search results.

Don't Fill Out Profiles

Don't fill out profiles or—if and when you must—try to provide as little information as possible. When subscribing to or signing up for e-mail accounts, chat rooms, IM programs, message boards, news services, zines, or Web sites, you don't need to divulge everything that's asked for. If the mandatory information isn't obvious on the form, it will be once you hit the Submit button. Be stingy with your personal data.

Use Preferences/Options on IM and Chat

Block or ignore unwanted users. Whether you are in a chat room or using IM, you should always check to see what options and preferences are available and take advantage of them.

Following are instructions for checking/changing preferences in some popular chat and IM programs.

AIM (AOL Instant Messenger)

You do not need to be an AOL member/customer to use AIM. It is probably the most popular IM program and can be downloaded from many Web sites, including www.aim.com.

1. Click on My AIM, Edit Options, then Edit Preferences (shortcut is the F3 key).

2. In the Category frame, click on Privacy (see Figure 12.1).

3. Under Who Can Contact Me, select Allow Only Users On My Buddy List.

4. Under Allow Users Who Know My E-mail Address ..., select Nothing About Me.

5. Go through the other categories to make sure all the default sections are what you really want.

6. Click on the OK button on the bottom before continuing so that the changes can take place.

MSN Messenger

As with AIM, it is not necessary to have MSN as your Internet service in order to use this IM program; it comes with the latest version of Windows or can be downloaded at messenger.msn.com.

1. Click on Tools in the toolbar, then Options. A separate window pops up with several tabs.

2. Click on the Privacy tab (see Figure 12.2). This is where you can add or block people.

3. Go through the other tabs to make sure the default sections are what you want.

4. Click on the OK button on the bottom before continuing so that the changes can take place.

Yahoo! Messenger

You will need to open a Yahoo! account to use this IM program.

1. Click on Login in the toolbar, then Privacy Settings. This brings up a separate window with Category selections on the left; Privacy will be pre-selected.

2. In the window on the right, select Ignore Anyone Who Is Not On My Messenger List (see Figure 12.3).

3. Select (check) Login As Invisible; this allows you to login without anyone knowing except users you decide to IM.

4. Under When People See My ID on Yahoo! Web Sites, select Do Not Allow Other Users to See Me Online and Contact Me.

5. Check the other options available in this Category.

6. Go through the other Categories to make sure the default selections are what you want.

7. Click on the OK button on the bottom before continuing so that the changes can take place.

ICQ (IM Program)

This IM program is available at www.icq.com.

1. Click on the Main graphic on the bottom, then Preferences and Security (see Figure 12.4).

2. Under Security on the left, select General.

3. Under Contact List Authorization, select My Authorization Is Required Before Users Add Me to Their Contact List.

4. Under Web Aware, deselect (uncheck) Allow Others to View My Online/Offline Status from the Web.

5. Under Security Level, select the Medium Level as recommended or select the one you are most comfortable with.

6. Click on Spam Control in the left panel.

7. Under Accepting Messages, select (check) Accept Messages Only From Those On My Contact List.

8. Unless you feel otherwise, deselect (uncheck) the World Wide Pager Messages and Email Express Messages selections.

9. Click on Ignore List in the left panel; this is where you can add users who are bothering you or ones with who you don't want to have contact.

10. Click the Apply button on the bottom before continuing so that the changes can take place.

Yahoo! Chat

1. When you go into the chat room of your choice, click on the pencil graphic in the toolbar just above the text box (see Figure 12.5).

2. Click on the Preferences you want. It's highly recommended to check the boxes next to Ignore Invitations to Join a Room and Ignore Private Messages from Strangers.

3. Go back to the main chat window and right-click on your username. A small window pops up.

4. Check the Preferences. If you filled out your profile, click on Edit Your Profile and change or delete any information that someone could use against you, such as your real name, your age, location, and personal Web page. If you clicked on female, change it to male to be safe.

5. If anyone bothers you in a chat room, right-click on their username, then click on Ignore Permanently so you will no longer see that chatter in the chat room, and/or check the box next to Ignore.

6. If someone continues to bother you by signing on under a different username, contact chat-abuse@yahoo.com or fill out Yahoo!'s feedback form at http://add.yahoo.com/fast/help/chat/cgi_abuse.

CompuServe Chat

1. Choose the chat room of your choice, then click on the Options tab, as shown in Figure 12.6. There are boxes that have been prechecked. Make sure the only ones checked are:

   • Accept incoming text styles.

   • Record room transcript. (Click on the Browse button to see which folder the log file is in for future reference.)

   • Record group transcript (same as previous bullet point).

   • Track member actions. (This brings up a separate window so that you can see who's going to what rooms; click this only if you're already being harassed and need to keep track of the harasser. This pop-up window stays up even when you leave chat, so it can become annoying.)

2. If anyone bothers you in a chat room, click on the Members tab, highlight the name, and click on Ignore so that chatter won't appear in any chat room you go into. You can also do the same thing once you enter a chat room.

3. Click on Enter or Eavesdrop. If you're new to the room or chatting in general, Eavesdrop is the best choice so that you can "lurk" and get to know the room before chatting.

ICQ Chat

1. Click on the System Notice button in the ICQ Window and select History & OutBox or double-click on System Notice, click on My ICQ and select History, then select History & OutBox.

2. Click the System tab to display a list of events received.

3. Click the OutBox tab to show the events that you sent (see Figure 12.7). Events are stored in the OutBox until you connect to an ICQ server and, if necessary, until the recipient goes online.

4. Double-click on a message to get a dialog to display the contents of that message.

5. Right-click on System Message for options regarding the selected message.

A Recap of Important Tips

Shopping and Banking Online

Make sure to read Chapter 5 for complete coverage on shopping and banking online, but in the meantime, here are some the most important rules of thumb for conducting financial transactions online:

• Use one credit card for all your online purchases or transactions and use it only for that purpose. Then, when you get your monthly statement, you can tell if it was used illegally. It's much easier to cancel one credit card instead of several.

- Use a service such as PayPal or Billpoint, which allow payment with a major credit card. Then, if something happens, you can dispute it through the bank issuing your credit card and file a complaint with PayPal or Billpoint. Many online merchants also use these services as a way to let you pay for items in their store if credit cards are not accepted directly.

- Don't give out financial information, such as your checking account and credit card numbers and especially your SSN to a Web site or anyone online unless you initiate the communication and know the person or organization.

- Protect your passwords and Personal Identification Numbers (PINs) for your ATM, credit cards, and online accounts.

- Be creative in selecting passwords and PINs for any ATM, credit card, or online account. Avoid using birth dates, part of your Social Security or driver's license numbers, address, or names of your children or spouse. Try using passwords that are at least eight characters in length and a mix of letters, numbers, and one special symbol, typically a punctuation mark.

- Find out where the online merchant is located. Does it have its own domain name or is it using a free Web site through someplace like Geocities? If the merchant is using a free Web site instead of its own, that could be a warning sign—the majority of legitimate merchants have their own domains or use a paid site, such as eBay Stores and Amazon.com Stores.

- Ask yourself if the Web site looks professional. If it doesn't, you might want to steer clear.

- If the merchant doesn't have physical contact information with the street address or telephone number, consider that a warning sign.

- Make sure the Web site has secure shopping. If it doesn't state so on the site and you go to the order page and your Web browser doesn't show it as being secure, don't shop there.

- If you're buying an expensive "I have to have it" item, and the merchant doesn't have secure shopping, ask if it will go through an escrow service, such as Tradenable (formerly iEscrow). If it won't, you don't have to have the item that badly.

- Find out what information the merchant collects and what it does with it; most sites have privacy policies clearly stated.

- Make sure you know everything about the product/offer—how much the item is, shipping and handling costs, taxes, insurance, guarantees or warranties, return and cancellation policies, and when and how fast will it be delivered. If you're still unsure, check with the Better Business Bureau (BBB) online or in the state where the merchant is located.

- Keep records of everything. Print your order form with payment information, product description, delivery information, privacy policy, warranties, and any confirmation notices that the seller sends you via e-mail.

- For online banking, make sure it's legitimate and that your deposits are FDIC-insured.

- Find out what fees are involved to switch to online banking; sometimes it's actually less expensive than keeping your regular checking account.

- Ask if there are fees to cancel the service and if there is a contract.

Online Auctions

Chapter 6 offers complete coverage on online auctions, but here are some ways that online bidders can be auction-savvy:

- Check the feedback or comments on the seller. Even if there are only a few negative comments, they can guide you toward making a safe decision. If need be, contact the people who left negative feedback via e-mail to find out why they were dissatisfied with the transaction.

- See what else the seller is currently selling. Check any past auctions by that seller. If you see more than one of the same item you want to bid on, be wary. If you see a large number of the item you want to bid on, DON'T bid on them.

- Look at other auction items of the same type and see if their descriptions match word for word. Many fraudulent sellers use several IDs or usernames to get as many of the same products out as possible.

- If you're having doubts, get the seller's user information, e-mail address, and mailing address and compare it to similar items up for sale. If more than one seller matches, you'd be wise not to bid on that item.

- If the seller has only a few feedback comments and you really want an item they have up for auction, see if they take credit cards, PayPal, BidPay, Billpoint, or some other form of online payment. If they don't and only accept money orders to be sent to a P.O. Box, be wary. Many fraudulent sellers will put "ghost" items up for auction, then disappear once the money is sent. If you use a credit card, make sure it's one that will allow you to dispute a charge in case the seller does turn out to be fraudulent.

- Read the description carefully. Make sure the item is really what you want before bidding on it or you may be stuck with a lemon (unless that's what you wanted, of course).

- Don't get caught up in the last-minute bidding of an auction. Some bidders feverishly try to outbid someone and then end up with an overpriced item.

- Don't be afraid to e-mail questions to the seller. If the seller responds curtly or negatively, then it might not be a good idea to bid on the item.

Phishing and Other Scams

Chapter 7 discusses increasingly popular phishing scams. Lest you fall for a phishing e-mail, which may appear to come from a legitimate person or company, consider the following advice from the Federal Trade Commission:

- If you get an e-mail or pop-up message that asks for personal or financial information, do not reply or click on the link in the message. Legitimate companies don't ask for this information via e-mail. If you are concerned about your account, contact the organization in the e-mail using a telephone number you know to be genuine or open a new Internet browser session and type in the company's correct Web address. In any case, don't cut and paste the link in the message.

- Don't e-mail personal or financial information. E-mail is not a secure method of transmitting personal information. If you initiate a transaction and want to provide your personal or financial information through an organization's Web site, look for indicators that the site is secure, such as a lock icon on the browser's status bar or a URL that begins "https"(the "s" stands for secure). Unfortunately, no indicator is foolproof; some phishers have forged security icons.

• Review credit card and bank account statements as soon as you receive them to determine whether there are any unauthorized charges. If your statement is late by more than a couple of days, call your credit card company or bank to confirm your billing address and account balances.

• Use anti-virus software and keep it up-to-date. Some phishing e-mails contain software that can harm your computer or track your activities on the Internet without your knowledge. Anti-virus software and a firewall can protect you from inadvertently accepting such unwanted files. Anti-virus software scans incoming communications for troublesome files. Look for anti-virus software that recognizes current viruses as well as older ones, can effectively reverse the damage, and can update automatically. A firewall helps make you invisible on the Internet and blocks all communications from unauthorized sources. It's especially important to run a firewall if you have a broadband connection. Your operating system (like Windows or Linux) may offer free software "patches" to close holes in the system that hackers or phishers could exploit.

• Be cautious about opening any attachment or downloading any files from e-mails you receive regardless of who sent them.

• Report suspicious activity to the FTC. If you get spam that is phishing for information, forward it to spam@uce.gov. If you believe you've been scammed, file your complaint at www.ftc.gov and then visit the FTC's Identity Theft Web site at www.consumer.gov/idtheft to learn how to minimize your risk of damage from ID theft. Visit www.ftc.gov/spam to learn other ways to avoid e-mail scams and deal with deceptive spam.

What to do ...

... if you took the bait and gave away your financial information:[1]

• Report it to the card issuer as quickly as possible: Many companies have toll-free numbers and 24-hour service to deal with such emergencies.

- Cancel your account and open a new one.

- Review your billing statements carefully after the loss: If they show any unauthorized charges, it's best to send a letter to the card issuer describing each questionable charge.

- Credit Card Loss or Fraudulent Charges (FCBA): Your maximum liability under federal law for unauthorized use of your credit card is $50. If the loss involves your credit card number, but not the card itself, you have no liability for unauthorized use.

- ATM or Debit Card Loss or Fraudulent Transfers (EFTA): Your liability under federal law for unauthorized use of your ATM or debit card depends on how quickly you report the loss. You risk unlimited loss if you fail to report an unauthorized transfer within 60 days after your bank statement containing unauthorized use is mailed to you.

… if someone is using your eBay account to bid, leave feedback, or list auctions without your permission:

- Contact eBay: Go to http://pages.ebay.com/help/confidence/isgw-account-theft-reporting.html and follow the instructions there.

- Attempt to sign in and change your password: If you are able to sign in, change your password and hint immediately, and begin to undo any damage done by the hackers; remove any bogus auctions, contact bidders and sellers, and so on.

- If you were unable to regain control of your own account, go to the http://pages.ebay.com/help/confidence/isgw-account-theft-reporting.html link (eBay will likely put your account on hold until it completes the investigation).

… if you gave out personal identifying information:

- Report the theft to the three major credit reporting agencies — Experian, Equifax, and TransUnion Corporation (see contact information in Appendix B: Resources or online at the book's supporting Web site) — and do the following: (1) request that they place a fraud alert and victim's statement in your file, (2) request a free copy of your credit report so that you can check to see if any accounts have been opened without your consent, and (3) request that they remove any inquiries and/or fraudulent accounts stemming from the theft.

- Notify your bank(s) and ask them to flag your accounts and contact you regarding any unusual activity: If bank accounts were set up without your consent, close them. If your ATM card was stolen, get a new card, account number, and PIN.

- Contact your local police department to file a criminal report.

- Contact the Social Security Administration's Fraud Hotline to report the unauthorized use of your personal identification information.

- Notify the Department of Motor Vehicles of your identity theft. Check to see whether an unauthorized license number has been issued in your name.

- Notify the passport office to watch out for anyone ordering a passport in your name.

- File a complaint with the Federal Trade Commission at www.ftc.gov/ftc/consumer.htm

- File a complaint with the Internet Fraud Complaint Center (IFCC) www.ifccfbi.gov/index.asp

- Document the names and phone numbers of everyone you speak to or contact regarding the incident. Follow up your phone calls with letters. Keep copies of all correspondence.

Online Adoptions

Chapter 8 covers the heart-wrenching topic of adoption fraud. Here's a quick run-down on the safest way to proceed:

- Go through an official agency or attorney.

- Don't give in to requests for immediate money.

- Be leery of e-mail messages or chat rooms. Don't reveal too much about what kind of adoption you're hoping for—scam artists love to sound like what you're looking for.

- Remove any time limits. You won't get a baby or child overnight.

- Ask for information about the birth mother and father, for example, social, psychological, and medical information.

- Network online with other adoptive parents and parents-to-be.

- Educate yourself before you adopt and while you're waiting. Adopting a child can take a while, but when you bring the child home, will you really be ready?

- Don't be rushed into a decision.

- If you have a Web site that includes contact information and a description of the kind of child you want to adopt, use a toll-free number or have calls go to your attorney or an adoption agency.

Online Dating/Personal Ads

Chapter 13 covers the subject of online dating. Here are some basic tips:

- If there's something in a profile that doesn't fit with what you're looking for, keep looking.

- Don't be in a hurry to meet once you've found a profile that appeals to you. Take your time e-mailing back and forth, and don't agree to get together until all your important questions have been fully answered.

- "Google" a potential date to find out as much as you can about him or her before meeting.

- Choose a public place for your initial meeting, and let a friend know the details.

- Trust your instincts. If something doesn't feel right, clear it up before pursuing any type of relationship with someone you've met online.

Staying safe online requires the equivalent of the efforts you make to stay safe offline. You use "street smarts" when you're driving, walking, shopping, banking, and playing offline—use "cyber street smarts" to stay safe online.

Endnote

1. Some tips from www.antiphishing.org

Afterword

After the first edition of this book was published in 2002 and I did book signings and lectures, I sometimes got the question, "Won't this book be outdated in a few months?" I was confident enough to reply with a "No" then and I still feel that way now.

When asked to do a second edition of the book, I found I had to change very little. Instead, I replaced some sample cases with more recent ones, added additional material to some chapters, got updated comments from the experts and victims, and wrote two brand new chapters—one about online dating and the other covering the various scams found online these days, particularly those pesky Nigerian scams.

I had a lot of fun going over the book again and adding the new items. It was refreshing to see that although more people have gone online since 2002, nothing major has changed in the ways that keep you best protected online. People still fall for scams, some even reply to spam they receive, and others don't know when to stop arguing online before it blows out of proportion ... and it usually does. I have come up with a new term for some of the scary situations that happen online between complete strangers—Internet Road Rage. Just like offline road rage, no one knows what the "trigger" is that causes a person to lose all control and harass and stalk someone online. Unfortunately, the trend isn't getting better. The more newbies that show up online, the more cases we see at WHOA, the organization of which I'm president.

I think what bothers me most is the hype that the media makes out of certain situations. One example happened in December of 2004: When a young pregnant woman, Bobbie Jo Stinnett, was found dead in her Missouri home, the baby she had been carrying for eight months ripped from her womb, the trail led to an online acquaintance, Lisa Montgomery, who desperately wanted a baby. First it was reported that these two women met in a chat room, then a message board, then via IM. It was finally revealed that Bobbie Jo had a Web site where she offered rat terriers for sale and one photo on the site showed her clearly pregnant. Lisa Montgomery inquired via e-mail about purchasing a dog, but used the name Darlene Fischer. A date and time was set up to meet.

Those e-mails are what did Montgomery in. FBI investigators were able to view the full headers, find the IP address, and trace it back to the originating ISP, who then provided the information as to who had the account associated with that IP address. This quick deduction probably saved the baby's life, now safe and sound and living with her father. I found only two articles written by an AP reporter that accurately explained how Montgomery was tracked down.

The media needs to cover these types of crimes more often—mainly to show that no one is truly anonymous online. You can change your name, your e-mail address, open up a free e-mail account, and so forth, but just about anything you do online can indeed be traced back to you.

I travel the country each year conducting cybercrime training for law enforcement and others, and all I see is an eagerness to learn. Those in law enforcement still have a long way to go—there are so many police departments that don't have the knowledge, and all it takes is less than a day of training to get them started. They are getting better and I predict that every police department will eventually have at least one person who will be able to properly handle online crimes, if not a department devoted to these crimes.

But what it truly takes is a knowledgeable public—individuals who know how to stay safe online, how to keep their computers virus and hacker-free, how to sensibly take part in auctions and shop, how to avoid fraud, and how to report spam. Most of all, you, dear reader, need to know when to step back from a situation before it escalates out of control. But if it does, never fear—just go to www.haltabuse.org and let WHOA help you.

In closing, the Internet is a truly wonderful place, but for now it's still the "wild, wild Web." If you keep this in mind, and act accordingly, you'll have the best possible chance of staying safe online.

Appendix A:
Where to Go for Help Online

Following is a partial list of the many online safety organizations available. These sites were mentioned throughout the book and are recapped here for your convenience. Do a search through your favorite search engine to see what other choices may be available.

WHOA

www.haltabuse.org

WHOA was created in February 1997 by Lynda Hinkle, a victim of cyberstalking. She initially called the organization Women Halting Online Abuse because the majority of online victims at that time were women. When I took over as president in June 1999, a vote from the Board of Directors changed the name to Working to Halt Online Abuse. More men were coming forward for help, so our new name described us better. WHOA works primarily with adults; we refer child-related cases to WHOA-KTD or other organizations.

Since its inception, WHOA has grown and so has its Web site. Included on the site is a page listing every state and whether it has a cyberstalking or related law on the books, with links to the pending or current law; instructions on how to show full headers in most e-mail and newsreader programs; and explicit instructions on what to do if you've been harassed.

All board members are volunteers, and most are former victims of cyberstalking and online harassment. Victims who come to WHOA for help won't be told, "Stay off your computer" or "I don't understand what a newsgroup is."

WHOA works with law enforcement agencies around the world. We not only help enforcement officers with cases but provide training as well. Although WHOA members aren't cybercops, we are able to resolve more than 80 percent of the cases without involving law enforcement officials.

WHOA-KTD (Kids/Teen Division)
www.haltabusektd.org

Established in September 2005 as an offshoot of WHOA, the KTD was designed to help kids and teens who are online victims of bullying, harassment, and stalking, in addition to educating them how to stay safer online. Parents, educators, and concerned adults will also find important information on the site, as well as the ability to get help for a kid or teen who is being bullied, harassed, or stalked online. Staffed by experienced members of WHOA, the KTD is headed up by Joan Welch, a librarian with more than a decade of experience, who worked for other online safety organizations before joining WHOA-KTD. Resources, research, and other helpful information is also available on the Web site.

Operation Blue Ridge Thunder
www.blueridgethunder.com

In 1998 the Bedford County Sheriff's Office (BCSO) in Virginia unveiled Operation Blue Ridge Thunder, the code name for the undercover cyberspace patrol that cracks down on child pornography distributed over the Internet and other computer-related crimes. Its successes have garnered the attention of local, national, and international media and of the U.S. Department of Justice, which in October 1998, awarded the BCSO a $200,000 grant to continue its efforts.

The people behind Operation Blue Ridge Thunder include a supervisor, two full-time investigators, an analyst, and a capable, comprehensive task force who blend their talents and resources to fight child exploitation on the Internet. They work diligently to apprehend perpetrators, protect potential victims, and educate parents, teachers, and children all over the country.

i-SAFE
www.isafe.org

The U.S. Congress designated i-SAFE America Inc., a nonprofit Internet safety foundation, to bring Internet safety education and awareness to the youth of this country. Founded in 1998, i-SAFE is a proactive prevention-oriented Internet safety awareness program. It provides Internet safety information and knowledge to students, parents, and everyone in the community in a variety of ways.

Cybersnitch
www.cybersnitch.net

Cybersnitch was developed in 1997 as a voluntary online crime-reporting system enabling the public to take action against all crimes that occur using computer technology and the Internet.

Reports go directly to members of the Cybersnitch Investigators Network. The Network consists of law enforcement officers and agencies and experts in high-tech criminal investigation.

CyberAngels
www.cyberangels.org

Recipient of a 1998 Presidential Service Award, CyberAngels was founded in 1995 as the first cyber-neighborhood watch and is one of the oldest in online safety education. Its mission is to function as a "virtual 411" safety destination and to address the concerns of parents, the needs of children, online abuse, and cybercrime, while supporting the right of free speech.

National Center for Missing and Exploited Children (NCMEC)
www.ncmec.org

NCMEC was created in 1984 as a public-private partnership and serves as the national clearinghouse for information on missing children and the prevention of child victimization online and offline. NCMEC works in partnership with the Office of Juvenile Justice and Delinquency Prevention of the Office of Justice programs at the U.S. Department of Justice. NCMEC's state-of-the-art Web site at www.missingkids.com brings images and information about missing children and a wealth of child protection information to a global audience.

National Center for Victims of Crime (NCVC) Stalking Resource Center
www.ncvc.org/src

The NCVC is the nation's leading resource and advocacy organization for crime victims. It is dedicated to forging a national commitment to help victims of crime rebuild their lives. The National Center's toll-free help line, 1-800-FYI-CALL, offers crime victims, criminal justice officials, attorneys, and concerned individuals practical information on appropriate community resources for crime victims. It also offers information on how to find supportive counseling and skilled advocacy in the criminal justice and social service systems.

The NCVC Stalking Resource Center at www.ncvc.org/src provides resources, training, and technical assistance to victim advocacy organizations and criminal justice professionals in an effort to promote a shared national understanding of stalking.

Appendix B:
Resources
www.netcrimes.net

Organized by chapter, here is a listing of Web resources mentioned in the book or relevant to chapter topics, along with some bonus sites. Because such resources come and go, I maintain a linked and periodically updated directory on the official *Net Crimes & Misdemeanors* Web site, www.netcrimes.net. For more information, see "About the Web Page" on page xxix of the book.

Chapter 1: Cyberstalking Happened to Me

Home Page of J. A. Hitchcock
www.jahitchcock.com

Abuse of Usenet
www.jahitchcock.com/cyberstalked

WHOA (Working to Halt Online Abuse)
www.haltabuse.org

U.S. Postal Inspection Service
www.usps.com/postalinspectors

Chapter 2: Words Can Hurt

"Shut the Door," online safety brochure by Taryn Pream
www.netcrimes.net/shutthedoor.html

What Are Full Headers?
www.haltabuse.org/help/header.shtml

How to Show Full Headers in E-mail/Newsreader Programs
www.haltabuse.org/help/headers

PestPatrol
www.pestpatrol.com

MailShield
www.mailshield.com

WHOIS
www.networksolutions.com/cgi-bin/whois/whois

WHOIS Lookup
www.whois.sc

SamSpade
www.samspade.org

IP Address Guide
www.ipaddressguide.com

Spiderhunter
www.spiderhunter.com/tools

State-by-State Online Harassment/Stalking Laws from WHOA
www.haltabuse.org/resources/laws

WHOA
www.haltabuse.org

Chapter 3: Spam Not in a Can

"On the Junk Mail Problem," by Jon Postel
www.ietf.org/rfc/rfc0706.txt

The Green Card Spam
http://en.wikipedia.org/wiki/Green_Card_spam

The Infamous "Green Card" Lawyers
http://agents.www.media.mit.edu/people/foner/Essays/
Civil-Liberties/Project/green-card-lawyers.html

Ray Everett-Church
www.everett.org

CAUCE (Coalition Against Unsolicited Commercial E-mail)
www.cauce.org

The Story of "Nadine"
www.honet.com/Nadine

SpamCop
www.spamcop.net

SpamCon
www.spamcon.org

SpamCannibal
www.spamcannibal.com

WHOA's Is It Harassment
www.haltabuse.org/help/isit.shtml

SamSpade
www.samspade.org

SPAM and the Internet
www.spam.com/ci/ci_in.htm

spamNEWS
www.petemoss.com

Fight Spam on the Internet!
http://spam.abuse.net

101 Things to Do with a Spammer
http://computeme.tripod.com/spammer.html

Vanquish Labs
www.vanquish.com

Spam Arrest
www.spamarrest.com

MailWasher
www.mailwasher.net

SpamLaws
www.spamlaws.com

Random Spam
http://dustman.net/andy/randomspam

In Defense of Spam
www.provider.com/framesbulke.htm

SatireWire's Annual Poetry Spam
www.satirewire.com/features/poetry_spam/poetryintro.shtml

How to Get Rid of Spam, Junk Mail, and Telemarketers
www.ecofuture.org/jnkmail.html

Getting Rid of Spam
www.spamprimer.com

Goodbye Spam
www.goodbyespam.com

Chapter 4: Urban Legends and Hoaxes: Can They Possibly Be True?

Snopes.com, Urban Legends Reference Pages
www.snopes.com

TruthOrFiction.com
www.truthorfiction.com

Don't Spread that Hoax!
www.nonprofit.net/hoax

The Urban Legend Combat Kit
www.netsquirrel.com/combatkit

HoaxBusters
http://hoaxbusters.ciac.org

Break the Chain
www.breakthechain.org

Purportal.com—Your B.S. Detection Kit
http://purportal.com

USPS Response to "E-mail Tax Bill"
www.usps.com/news/2002/press/emailrumor.htm

How Urban Legends Work
www.howstuffworks.com/urban-legend4.htm

Official CDC Hoaxes & Rumors Page
www.cdc.gov/hoax_rumors.htm

Chapter 5: Scams, Safe Shopping, and Online Banking

The FBI's Internet Fraud Complaint Center
www.ifccfbi.gov

National Fraud Information Center Internet Fraud Watch
www.fraud.org/internet/intset.htm
800-876-7060

Tips to Protect Yourself While Shopping Online
http://familyinternet.about.com/library/weekly/aa102899.htm

PayPal
www.paypal.com

Bidpay
www.bidpay.com

MasterCard International Security and Basics
www.mastercard.com/us/personal/en/securityandbasics/

American Express Fraud Protection Center
http://home3.americanexpress.com/corp/consumer_resources.asp

Discover Card Security Information
www.discovercard.com/discover/data/account/securityprivacy/
shopping.shtml

Visa Online Shopping Protection
www.usa.visa.com/personal/security/

Other Credit Card Companies, Fraud, and Identity Theft
www.yourcreditcardcompanies.com/forconsumers/fraud.asp

Privacy Foundation
www.privacyfoundation.org

U.S. Postal Inspection Service
www.usps.com/postalinspectors/

Banking and Investing Online Resources Group
www.bank-accounts-online.com

Quicken Online Banking
www.quicken.com/banking_and_credit

MS Money Online Banking Page
www.msmoney.com/mm/banking/onlinebk/onlinebk_intro.htm

Scams, Frauds, Hoaxes, Chain Letters: On the Net!
http://advocacy-net.com/scammks.htm

Crimes of Persuasion: Scams, Schemes & Hoaxes
www.crimes-of-persuasion.com

Scambusters
www.scambusters.com

WebAssured.com
www.webassured.com

Planet Feedback
www.planetfeedback.com

Epinions.com
www.epinions.com

BizRate.com
www.bizrate.com

ConsumerSearch
www.consumersearch.com

PriceWatch (comparison shopping)
www.pricewatch.com

Best Shopping
www.bestshoppingcenter.net

Internet Fraud: How to Avoid Internet Investment Scams
www.sec.gov/investor/pubs/cyberfraud.htm

BBB Online's Safe Shopping Site
www.bbbonline.org/consumer/

BBB (Better Business Bureau Online Complaint System)
www.bbb.org/complaint.asp

BBB Locator (for the office nearest you)
http://lookup.bbb.org

The National Consumers League
www.natlconsumersleague.org
202-835-3323

CCIPS (Computer Crime and Intellectual Property Section, USDOJ)
www.cybercrime.gov

FDIC Tips for Safe Banking Over the Internet
www.fdic.gov/bank/individual/online/safe.html

Chapter 6: Auction Caution

eBay Community Life (Online auctions advice)
http://pages.ebay.com/community/life

BBB Online Auctions
www.bbb.org/alerts/article.asp?ID=192

The WebStore Online Auctions Guide
www.thewebstoreguide.com/auctions.html

Online Auctions - Bidder Beware
http://csjava.occ.cccd.edu

Auction Watch
www.auctionwatch.com

Fraud Bureau
www.fraudbureau.com

Auction Essentials 4 U
www.auctionessentials4u.com

UACC (Universal Autograph Collectors Club)
www.uacc.org

PADA (Professional Autograph Dealers Association)
www.padaweb.org

Scamming the Scammer
http://p-p-p-powerbook.com

Chapter 7: Gone Phishing: Nigerian Scams and More

Yahoo! Groups, Nigerian Scam
http://groups.yahoo.com/group/Nigerian_Scam/

Ebola Monkey Man (caution: obscenities abound)
www.ebolamonkeyman.com

419eater
www.419eater.com

Nigeria—The 419 Coalition Website
http://home.rica.net/alphae/419coal/

Welcome to the Kisombe Correspondence
www.savannahsays.com/kizombe.htm

Having Fun with Those Nigerians
www.flooble.com/fun/reply.php

How the Nigerian Scam Works
www.quatloos.com/scams/nigerian.htm

Nigerian Scam News Articles
www.nigeriamasterweb.com/419NewsFrmes.html

Anti-Phishing Working Group
www.antiphishing.org

eBay Securing Your Account and Reporting Account Theft
http://pages.ebay.com/help/tp/isgw-account-theft-reporting.html

NetScalped
www.netscalped.com

Major Credit Reporting Agencies:

Equifax
P.O. Box 740241
Atlanta, GA 30374-0241
800-525-6285
www.equifax.com

Experian
P.O. Box 9530
Allen, TX 75013
888-EXPERIAN (397-3742)
800-972-0322
www.experian.com

TransUnion
Fraud Victim Assistance Division
P.O. Box 6790
Fullerton, CA 92634
800-680-7289
www.transunion.com

Federal Trade Commission and Other U.S. Government Resources:

FTC Complaint Center
www.ftc.gov/ftc/consumer.htm

IFCC Complaint Form
www.ifccfbi.gov/index.asp

FTC's Identity Theft Web Page
www.consumer.gov/idtheft

FTC Spam Scam Page
www.ftc.gov/spam

Chapter 8: Where the Heartache Is: Adoption Fraud

NCFA (National Council for Adoption)
www.ncfa-usa.org
202-328-1200

Adopting.com—Internet Adoption Resources
www.adopting.com

About Adoption/Foster Care
http://adoption.about.com

Adoption Resource Directory
www.adopt-usa.org

American Adoptions
www.americanadoptions.com

Internet Adoption: How Much Is That Baby in the Window?
http://gsulaw.gsu.edu/lawand/papers/su01/dutrow_wade/

Chapter 9: Cases of Stolen Identity

FTC (Federal Trade Commission)
www.ftc.gov/ftc/consumer.htm

SEC (U.S. Securities and Exchange Commission)
www.sec.gov

U.S. Secret Service
www.treas.gov/usss/index.html

FTC's Identity Theft Web Page
www.consumer.gov/idtheft

Identity Theft Resource Center
www.idtheftcenter.org

Cybersnitch
www.cybersnitch.net

Equifax Credit Information Services
Consumer Fraud Division
P.O. Box 105069
Atlanta, GA 30348-5496
800-525-6285
www.equifax.com

Experian
P.O. Box 9532
Allen, TX 75013-2104
888-EXPERIAN (397-3742)
www.experian.com

TransUnion Fraud Victim Assistance Dept.
P.O. Box 6790
Springfield, PA 19064-0390
800-680-7289
www.transunion.com

MasterCard International Security and Basics
www.mastercard.com/us/personal/ensecurityandbasics/

American Express Fraud Protection Center
http://home3.americanexpress.com/corp/consumer_resources.asp

Discover Card Security Information
www.discovercard.com/discover/data/account/securityprivacy/
shopping.shtml

Visa Online Shopping Protection
www.usa.visa.com/personal/security/

Chapter 10: Your Personal Life Exposed

WHOA
www.haltabuse.org

CyberAngels
www.cyberangels.org

The Stalkers Home Page
www.glr.com/stalk.html

SafePlace
www.austin-safeplace.org

U.S. Dept. of Justice Office for Victims of Crime
www.ojp.usdoj.gov/ovc
800-627-6872 (resource center number)

National Center for Victims of Crime Stalking Resource Center
www.ncvc.org/src/

Cyberstalking Statistics
www.haltabuse.org/resources/stats

Offline and Online Stalking
www.cotse.net/privacy/cyberstalking.htm

Stalkers Online
www.fridgemagnet.org.uk/stalkersonline/

Stay Safe Online
www.staysafeonline.info

The Terrifying Reality of Cyberstalking
www.itc.virginia.edu/virginia.edu/fall02/stalking/home.html

Chapter 11: Ugly Beasts Lurking Online

Searching for Safety Online: Managing "Trolling" in a Feminist
Forum
www.slis.indiana.edu/CSI/WP/WP02-03B.html

Flame Wars and Other Online Arguments
http://members.aol.com/intwg/flamewars.htm

Beware the Troll
www.teamtechnology.co.uk/troll.htm

Internet Trolls
http://members.aol.com/intwg/trolls.htm

Trolls—A Unique Social Movement?
www.io.com/~zikzak/troll_thesis.html

Google Groups
http://groups.google.com

Yahoo! Groups
http://groups.yahoo.com

Central Newsfeed
www.centralnewsfeed.com

CyberFiber Newsgroups
www.cyberfiber.com

Newsville
www.newsville.com/news/groups/

Forté Agent
www.forteinc.com/agent

Yahoo!
www.yahoo.com

AltaVista
www.altavista.com

Google
www.google.com

Metacrawler
www.metacrawler.com

Dogpile
www.dogpile.com

List of Online Harassment/Stalking Laws
www.haltabuse.org/resources/laws

Chapter 12: A Little Harmful Chat

Yahoo! Chat
http://chat.yahoo.com

Park Chat (easy-to-use interface)
www.the-park.com

TalkCity Chat
www.talkcity.com

Excite Chat
http://communicate.excite.com/chat.html

ParaChat (add a chat room to your Web site)
www.parachat.com

Active Chat Rooms
www.active-chat-rooms.biz

#1 Chat Avenue
www.chat-avenue.com

Just A Chat
www.justachat.com

The Center for Online Addiction
www.netaddiction.com

Chat Danger
www.chatdanger.com

Chat Room Advice for Dum Dums
www.webspawner.com/users/laurenshappyhour/chatadvicehaha.html

Chat Room Tips & Tricks
http://onlineinstitute.com/chat/tricks.html

Chat Etiquette
www.kidsturncentral.com/chat/chatnet.htm

Online Chatting Basics
http://familyeducation.com/article/0,1120,1-4358,00.html

Chat Safety
www.chatmag.com/help/safety.html

U.K. Chat Safety Advice
www.justchat.co.uk/chat/safety.htm

Tech Dictionary—Chat Acronyms
www.techdictionary.com/chat.html

AOL IM
www.aim.com

ICQ
www.icq.com

MSN Messenger
http://messenger.msn.com

Yahoo! Messenger
http://messenger.yahoo.com

Trillian (use several IM programs at once)
www.ceruleanstudios.com

GAIM (secure IM)
http://gaim.sourceforge.net

Jabber

www.jabber.org

Chapter 13: Lookin' for Love in All the Online Places

Yahoo! Online Dating/Personals

http://personals.yahoo.com

DateSeeker

www.dateseeker.net

Match.com

www.match.com

Cupid.com

www.cupid.com

eHarmony

www.eharmony.com

U.K. Date

http://uk.date.com

True.com

www.true.com

Senior FriendFinder

www.seniorfriendfinder.com

Date Safely!

www.datesafely.com

Chapter 14: Other Ways They Can Get You

Guestbook.de
http://two.guestbook.de

Dreambook
www.dreambook.com

Creation Center
www.creationcenter.com

Guestbook.nu
www.guestbook.nu

eFree Guestbooks
www.efreeguestbooks.com

HTML Gear
http://htmlgear.lycos.com

Guestbook Depot (free)
www.guestbookdepot.com

Yahoo! Games
http://games.yahoo.com

WebCam List (free)
www.webcam-list.com

CamCities
www.camcities.com

WebCam Central
www.camcentral.com

WebCamNow
www.webcamnow.com

iCamMaster
www.icammaster.com

Webcam Index
www.webcam-index.com

LiveJournal
www.livejournal.com

Blogger
www.blogger.com

DiaryLand
www.diaryland.com

Blurty
www.blurty.com

Dear Diary
www.deardiary.net

MySpace
www.myspace.com

Where All the Journals Are
www.justme.org/geographical.htm

Spybot Search & Destroy
http://security.kolla.de

Lavasoft AdAware
www.lavasoftusa.com

PestPatrol
www.pestpatrol.com

Anti-Spyware Guide
www.firewallguide.com/spyware.htm

Picturephoning.com
www.textually.org/picturephoning

TextAmerica
www.textamerica.com

Mobile Asses
www.mobileasses.com

Moblogs
www.moblogging.us/moblogs/

Your Safety Weblog
www.yoursafetyblog.com

Chapter 15: Protecting the Children

National Center for Missing & Exploited Children (NCMEC)
www.ncmec.org
800-843-5678

WHOA-KTD (Kids/Teen Division)
www.haltabusektd.org

Operation Blue Ridge Thunder
www.blueridgethunder.com

COPPA (Children's Online Privacy Protection Act)
www.coppa.org

CIPA (Children's Internet Protection Act)
www.ala.org/cipa

CCRC (Crimes Against Children Research Center)
www.unh.edu/ccrc/factsheet.html

DOJ's Child Exploitation and Obscenity Section
www.usdoj.gov/criminal/ceos/index.html

FTC's KidzPrivacy Site
www.ftc.gov/bcp/conline/edcams/kidzprivacy

DOJ's Justice for Kids & Youth
www.usdoj.gov/kidspage/index.html

FBI's For The Family Page
www.fbi.gov/fbikids.htm

Safe Kids
www.safekids.com

McGruff Safe Kids
www.mcgruff-safe-kids.com

Get Net Wise
www.getnetwise.org

Consumer Reports
www.consumerreports.org

PC Turnoff
www.pcturnoff.org

U.K. Guide to Online Safety for Kids and Parents
www.thinkuknow.co.uk

World Village
www.worldvillage.com

Safe Chat for Kids
www.girl.com.au/safechat.htm

KidChatters
www.kidchatters.com

Cyberbullying.ca
www.cyberbullying.ca

Bullying Online
www.bullying.co.uk

Be Safe Online—Bullying Online
www.besafeonline.org/English/bullying_online.htm

Online Bullying Help
www.bullying.newham.net

Cyberbullying
http://csriu.org/cyberbullying/

Filtering Software and Filtered Web Providers:

CyberSitter
www.solidoak.com/cysitter.htm

Net Nanny
www.netnanny.com

McAfee
www.mcafee.com

Norton AntiVirus and Internet Security 2005
www.symantec.com

CyberPatrol
www.cyberpatrol.com

EnoLogic NetFilter Home
www.enologic.com

iProtectYou Pro Web Filter
www.softforyou.com

Software Time
www.softwaretime.com

Safe Eyes Platinum
www.safeeyes.com

Family.net
www.family.net

Family Safe Web, the Family Friendly Internet Service Provider
www.familysafeweb.net

Mayberry USA
www.mbusa.net

Safe Access
www.safeaccess.com

Dnet/Internet Services
http://get.dnet.net

The List
http://thelist.internet.com (type "filtered" in the search text box)

Chapter 16: Office Know-How: Stay Safe in the Workplace

Title VII of the Civil Rights Act of 1964
www.eeoc.gov/policy/vii.html

TrueActive
www.winwhatwhere.com

PearlEcho Monitoring Software
www.pearlecho.com

How to Handle Online Corporate Harassment
www.bankrate.com/brm/news/biz/Biz_ops/20011029a.asp

Employment Law News: Online Harassment
www.winnebantalaw.com/news/10-00.htm

AMA (American Management Association)
www.amanet.org

Stroz Friedberg, LLC (computer crimes consulting firm)
www.strozllc.com

SurfControl
www.surfcontrol.com

Sample Acceptable Use Policy
www.efa.org.au/Publish/aup.html

Vault.com
www.vault.com

The Bureau of National Affairs: Online Guide to E-Mail and the
Internet in the Workplace, by Susan E. Gindin
www.info-law.com/guide.html

Creating an Online Privacy Policy
www.info-law.com/create.html

Technology and Online Harassment in the Workplace
www.westbuslaw.com/blt/internet_employment.html

Chapter 17: Police Duty: Our Nation's Finest Boot Up

Kennebunk, Maine, Police Department
http://kennebunkpolice.maine.org

Maine Computer Crimes Task Force
www.mcctf.org

Nashua, New Hampshire, Police Department
www.ci.nashua.nh.us/police

Massachusetts Attorney General's Office
www.ago.state.ma.us
617-727-2200

Massachusetts Attorney General's Office—Computer Crime
www.ago.state.ma.us/sp.cfm?pageid=1198

Alexandria, Virginia, Police Department
http://ci.alexandria.va.us/police

Somerset, Kentucky, Police Department
www.somersetpd.com

San Diego County District Attorney
www.sdcda.org

C.A.T.C.H. (Computer And Technology Crime High-Tech Response Team)
www.catchteam.org

NCVC (National Center for Victims of Crime)
www.ncvc.org
800-FYI-CALL (800-394-2255)

National Center for Victims of Crime Stalking Resource Center
www.ncvc.org/SRC.htm

Cybersnitch
www.cybersnitch.net

SamSpade
www.samspade.org

CCIPS (Computer Crime and Intellectual Property Section, USDOJ)
www.cybercrime.gov

Cops Online
www.copsonline.com

Officer.com
www.officer.com

International Association of Chiefs of Police
www.iacp.org

Chapter 18: Universities Catch Up with the Net

George Mason University
www.gmu.edu

George Mason University—Online Harassment (Cyberstalking)
www.gmu.edu/facstaff/sexual/online_telephone_harassment.html#
online

The Jake Baker Scandal
www.trincoll.edu/zines/tj/tj4.6.95/articles/baker.html

Center for Democracy and Technology (CDT)
www.cdt.org

University at Buffalo
www.buffalo.edu

Central Michigan University
www.cmich.edu

University of Maryland University College
www.umuc.edu

Campus Security (includes campus crime statistics links)
www.ed.gov/admins/lead/safety/campus.html

Security on Campus, Inc.
www.soconline.org

Report It
www.report-it.com

Ponzi Scheme
http://home.nycap.rr.com/useless/ponzi/

Chapter 19: Encryption Made Easy

CryptoRights Foundation
www.cryptorights.org

EFF (Electronic Frontier Foundation)
www.eff.org
415-436-9333

Philip Zimmermann
http://web.mit.edu/prz

Federal Electronic Signatures in Global and National Commerce
Act
http://thomas.loc.gov/cgi-bin/bdquery/z?d106:s.00761:

Consumers Union
www.consumersunion.org
914-378-2000

PGP Freeware
http://web.mit.edu/network/pgp.html

PGPi (recommended for Internet beginners)
www.pgpi.org

PGP FAQ
www.cam.ac.uk.pgp.net/pgpnet/pgp-faq

PGP Questions & Answers
www.mccune.cc/PGPpage2.htm

GNU Privacy Guard (free)
www.gnupg.org

Cryptography Resources
www.crypto.com

Computer Resource Security Center
http://csrc.ncsl.nist.gov

MIT PGP Public Key Server
http://pgpkeys.mit.edu

Online Privacy in Australis
www.efa.org.au/Issues/Privacy/

Privacy Rights Clearinghouse
www.privacyrights.org

CDT (Center for Democracy and Technology)
www.cdt.org
202-637-9800

EPIC (Electronic Privacy Information Center)
www.epic.org
202-483-1140

Privacy Foundation
www.privacyfoundation.org

Instructions on Adding an Electronic Signature in MS Outlook
www.nova.edu/techtrain/forms/Signature-OUTLOOK.doc
(Microsoft Word document)

Digital Signature Standard (DSS)
www.itl.nist.gov/fipspubs/fip186.htm

Chapter 20: Protect Your Computer!

Crimelabs Security Group
www.crimelabs.net

Norton AntiVirus and Internet Security 2005
www.symantec.com

Jammer
www.agnitum.com

Outpost Firewall Pro
www.agnitum.com/products/outpost/

Internet Security Systems — BlackICE Defender
www.iss.net

ZoneAlarm
www.zonelabs.com

McAfee Anti-Virus & Firewall
www.mcafee.com

GRC Net Filter
http://grc.com/nf/netfilter.htm

AVG Anti-Virus
www.free.grisoft.com

RoboForm
www.robo-form.com

EZ Password Manager
www.northwind-tech.com

Cookie Pal
www.kburra.com/cpal.html

AdSubtract
www.adsubtract.com

Cookie Crusher
www.thelimitsoft.com/cookie.html

PopUp Ad Smasher
www.popupstop.com

Freebie List
www.freebielist.com/antivirus.htm

Virus Bulletin
www.virusbtn.com/index

Joe Wells' Wild Virus List
www.virusbtn.com/WildLists

Computer Associates Virus Information Center
www.ca.com/virusinfo

CERT/CC Advisories
www.cert.org/advisories

Virus Myths
www.vmyths.com

Protect Your PC (free)
www.my-etrust.com

FAQ—Internet Firewalls
www.interhack.net/pubs/fwfaq/

Firewall Guide
www.firewallguide.com

Kaspersky Labs Anti-Virus
www.kaspersky.com

AdGone Popup Remover
www.adsgone.com

Reviews of Online Security/Anti-Virus Software
http://computeme.tripod.com

Chapter 21: The Basics of Staying Safe Online: A Review

Online Safety Tips
www.haltabuse.org/resources/online.shtml

FAQ Central
www.faq-central.net

Internet FAQ Archives
www.faqs.org/faqs

eFax.com (free fax)
www.efax.com

Jfax (free voicemail and fax)
www.j2.com

Free Voicemail/Fax Web Site Listings
www.fecg.net/voicemail.asp

The Ultimates White Pages Directory
www.theultimates.com/white

The Ultimates E-Mail Directory
www.theultimates.com/email

Web Shots
www.webshots.com

Club Photo
www.clubphoto.com

Off-line Safety Tips
www.haltabuse.org/resources/offline.shtml

Major Credit Reporting Agencies:

Equifax
P.O. Box 740241
Atlanta, GA 30374-0241

800-525-6285
www.equifax.com

Experian
P.O. Box 9530
Allen TX 75013
888-EXPERIAN (397-3742)
800-972-0322
www.experian.com

TransUnion
Fraud Victim Assistance Division
P.O. Box 6790
Fullerton, CA 92634
800-680-7289
www.transunion.com

Reader Bonus

Here are some additional useful sites, not listed elsewhere in the book, to keep you surfing safely!

Learn the Net
www.learnthenet.com
How to find information, download files, master the basics, and more. Soon you'll be surfing the Net like a pro!

Family Friendly Sites
www.familyfriendlysites.com
Offers a search engine with family-oriented results (no worries about pornography or obscene language here), online safety resources, and tips.

Family Internet at About.com
http://familyinternet.about.com
Find out everything you need to know about your computer, the Internet, and more.

Netiquette
www.albion.com/netiquette

Be polite online—this is the place to learn the "rules" of cyber-space. Follow these rules and you can stay safe.

Spyware

www.cexx.org/problem.htm

Are there programs hiding on your computer that shouldn't be there? Scan your computer and remove them by using a free software program called Ad Aware at www.lavasoftusa.com.

Whatis?.com

http://whatis.techtarget.com

Got questions about computers and the Internet? Whatis?.com is one of the best sites for the answers.

Freeware/Shareware

www.tucows.com

Want to get software for free or almost free? Tucows.com offers everything you can imagine, from anti-virus to firewall software, to games and screensavers, utility programs, cookie removers, and lots more.

TracerLock

www.tracerlock.com

One of the best ways to keep track of yourself online, see if some-one's impersonating you, or just for curiosity—and it's free! Submit your search parameters—your first and last name or your e-mail address—and TracerLock will e-mail you when it finds a match on a Web page/site, in newsgroups/forums/message boards, "for sale" and auction sites, employment listings, and personal ads.

Ask An Expert

www.askanexpert.com

Whether you have a question about something online or offline, Pitsco's Ask An Expert Web site has hundreds of "real world experts" who will answer your questions for free!

Looking For a New ISP?

www.isps.com

If you're looking for a new Internet Service Provider (ISP), look no further than this site. Search by area code, price, name, national, or toll-free ISPs.

The Internet Archive
www.archive.org
  The Internet Archive is building a digital library of Internet sites and other cultural artifacts in digital form. Like a paper library, it provides free access to researchers, historians, scholars, and the general public.

Online Tonight with David Lawrence
www.onlinetonight.com
  Nationally syndicated radio show (you can listen to the shows on the Web site as well) with a variety of computer and Internet-related subjects.

eBayers That Suck
www.ebayersthatsuck.com
  Lists eBayers (buyers and sellers) who have caused problems, whether as scammers or non-paying bidders or types who claim items are broken when they're not, and so forth. This Web site reads: "So next time you deal with a swindler and don't want to leave negative feedback for fear of retaliation, post it here. You will get the last laugh when they are officially branded with our puke green 'you suck' logo and the online auction world can see what a deadbeat they really are."

I can't make these up, folks! And, just for fun:

DVD Easter Eggs
www.dvdeastereggs.com
  Most DVDs have hidden content you can't get to from the main menu or other menu selections. This Web site helps you find any hidden content aka "Easter eggs" or if you find one, you can submit it to the site.

And just for the heck of it:

Stuff On My Cat
www.stuffonmycat.com
  Don't be drinking anything when you go to this site or it may come through your nose. Even if you don't like cats, you'll get a kick out of this Web site.

Glossary

Acceptable Usage Policy. Also known as an AUP. The majority of ISPs have these in place indicating its terms of use when you get an account and the conditions in which your account can be cancelled.

Address. The location of an Internet resource. An e-mail address usually looks like johnsmith@nowhere.com; a Web address looks like www.jahitchcock.com

AIM. Acronym for AOL Instant Messenger.

AOL. America OnLine, a popular Internet service provider.

Baud. Modem speeds are measured by their baud rate, which is the rate at which they send and receive information.

BBS. Bulletin Board System. Not used as often now, but was popular in the early days of the Internet. This was basically a virtual bulletin board. Users could post announcements, have discussions, and upload/download files.

Blog. Web log or online journal/diary, usually located on a central Web site (such as blogger.com or livejournal.com) or on a personal Web site.

Bookmark. Marking and saving a favorite Web site URL or location within your Web browser. Lets you easily return to it without having to search for the URL in a search engine or try to remember the URL off the top of your head.

Bounce. When an e-mail message you have sent is returned to you as being undeliverable or due to another error, indicating there is a problem with the recipient's account.

Broadband. A wide band of frequency used for telecommunications. Term is used when describing either DSL or cable connection to the Internet.

Browser. A program used to view sites/pages on the World Wide Web. Popular browsers are Netscape Communicator, Microsoft Internet Explorer, and Mosaic.

Cable. High-speed Internet access through your cable service line.

Cache. A folder/area on your hard drive where frequently accessed data is stored, such as the Web sites and pages you've visited plus the cookies and graphics associated with those sites. The info in your cache allows your Web browser to access a Web site faster if you have visited it in the past, unless you have deleted the cache.

Carders. People who get credit card numbers by phishing or scamming or even purchasing them from other scammers online. Carders then use the stolen credit cards to purchase items online or resell the numbers for a profit. Most of the time, Phishers, Scammers and Carders are all one and the same.

Chat. Real-time or live conversation online. This occurs in an online forum where anywhere from a few people to a hundred or more congregate; or the conversation can take place one-on-one in what is called a "private room." People chat about anything and everything, whether or not it has to do with the name of the chat room. Names of chat rooms range from "The TV Room" to "Adults 30+" to "Los Angeles Teens."

Client. A program—like a Web browser—that connects to and requests information from a server.

Communities. Many Web hosts, such as Geocities, AOL, and Excite, have communities that contain Web pages created by users registered with that ISP or Web site. These users can interact with each other within their "community" via chat rooms, discussion boards, or forums.

Cookies. Information files stored on your hard drive by your Web browser when you visit certain Web sites. This information is then used to keep track of, for example, the last time you visited that Web site, what you ordered, or where it was mailed. Each cookie is different. Some may have basic information, such as your last visit, while others may have a lot more information, including what kind of computer you use, the name of your ISP, and your full name, address, and telephone number. Not all Web sites "set" cookies (save them to your hard drive). Most firewall/security programs allow you to delete these cookies if you wish.

Cracker. Usually more destructive than a hacker, this is a person who breaks into a Web site or system to sabotage, damage, or alter the site or system.

Cross-post. Post a message to several newsgroups at one time. This is actually considered a big no-no, especially when you post the same message to more than two newsgroups at once.

Cyberbully/cyberbullying. When offline bullying heads to the Internet, mainly via IM and cell phone text messaging, primarily targeted at school age children, literally giving them nowhere to hide from their bullies.

Cyberspace. Coined by author William Gibson in his novel *Neuromancer*, it refers to the Internet or World Wide Web as we know it and the culture that has spawned from it.

Cyberstalker/cyberstalking. People who track another person or persons' online activities. Cyberstalking sometimes leads to physical stalking.

DdoS. Aka DoS, Distributed Denial of Service or Denial of Service. To flood a network or ISP with unwanted traffic, trying to shut down that network.

Dial-Up Service. A way to connect to the Internet through a modem and telephone line if you don't have DSL or cable. The modem dials into your Internet Service Provider (ISP) and connects you to the Web.

Digital Signature. Also called a digital ID or certificate, a secure way of identifying individuals on the Internet; often used to authenticate each user in a digital transaction. VeriSign is one provider of digital certification.

Discussion Group. Also called newsgroup or forum, where people can post and reply to messages on a variety of topics.

DNS. Domain Name System. A database system that translates a domain name into an IP address. For example, a domain name such as www.comset.net converts to the numeric address 213.172. 9.119.

Domain. The Internet is divided into smaller sets known as domains, including .com (business), .gov (government), .edu (educational), .mil (military), .org (nonprofit organizations), .net (miscellaneous organizations), and more to come in the future.

Domain Name. This identifies the Web site and consists of two parts: the first is the registered name of the site and the second is the sub-domain or category. Take, for example, the Web site address usmc.mil. The "usmc" is the United States Marine Corps Web site and ".mil" is the military category. Put together, they form the domain name.

DSL. Digital Subscriber Line. Available through the telephone company, it allows high-speed access to the Internet through your telephone line.

Ego Surf. To perform a search online for yourself as a safety precaution to make sure there isn't more information out there about you than you want. The best way to ego-surf is to put your name in quotes in a search engine, such as "jayne hitchcock," then check the results to see which sites/pages you may be listed on.

Electronic Signature. A form of encryption that allows online users to sign documents, pay bills, bank, and shop online with an electronic or digital signature unique to only them.

E-Mail. An e-mail address consists of the user name, then the "@" (called an "at" sign), the name of the Internet service provider (ISP), and the domain, or what designation the ISP has been assigned. In the e-mail address "Janice@hotmail.com," "Janice" is the user name, "hotmail" is the ISP, and ".com" is the domain category of companies.

E-Mail Bomb. When hundreds of e-mail messages are sent to one e-mail address in an effort to overload the account and shut down that e-mail inbox.

E-Mail Threats. Threats and/or harassment sent via e-mail.

Emoticon. A combination of characters that form a facial expression, of sorts, when looked at sideways. For example, the characters :) make a smile or, in Web terms, a smiley. Often used in e-mail and newsgroup messages, as well as chat rooms.

Encryption. Scrambling messages so that they are unreadable by anyone except the sender and the recipient. One of the most popular encryption programs is Pretty Good Privacy (PGP).

FAQ. Frequently Asked Questions. A collection of the most frequently asked questions and answers on a particular subject or about a newsgroup or Web site.

Feedback. Found mostly in online auctions, the seller and winning bidder can leave feedback or comments for each other when an auction sale is completed. Feedback allows you to see if the seller or bidder has had positive, neutral, or negative feedback before you bid on an item.

Filtering. See Kill Filter.

Finger. A program that reports the name associated with an e-mail address and may also show the most recent logon information or even whether the person is currently connected to the Internet.

Firewall. Protection for computer systems and networks from attacks by hackers, viruses, Trojans, and more, in either hardware or software form.

Flame. A public response to a message or posting on a newsgroup, mailing list, or chat room that goes beyond polite disagreement, belittling the author's point of view and frequently insulting him personally. If the author responds just as nastily to the flame, a "flame war" often ensues. On moderated lists, flaming can frequently be stopped before it gets out of control.

FOAF. Acronym for Friend of a Friend, a term often used in urban legends.

Forged. A term used when someone uses an e-mail address that is obviously a fake.

Forum. Can also be called a discussion group, message board, or newsgroup.

Full Headers. Technical information in the header of e-mail and newsgroup messages; the information is hidden when you receive/send mail.

Gateway. Hardware or software set up to translate between two protocols that are not similar. AOL, for example, is a gateway to the Internet. You must use its software to connect to AOL first and then use its interface to access Web sites, chat, e-mail, etc., which are outside of its system.

Geocities: An online "homestead" where people can get free Web page space, free e-mail, and other online extras. Located at www.geocities.com.

Guestbook. Much like a guestbook at weddings, this is on a person's Web page/site so that a visitor can add a comment about the Web page/site.

Guidelines: Many Web sites also call these their Terms of Service (TOS).

Hackers/Hacking. You've seen them in the movies and on TV. Most hackers are people who want to test a Web site or Internet connection just to see if they can break in, sometimes for the fun of it, sometimes at the owner's request. Some are called "crackers," people who are out to cause trouble and possibly fraud by doing something such as breaking into the computer systems of banks to transfer money to hidden bank accounts in their names. They are also known to wreak havoc at a former employer's Web site or LAN, steal someone's Internet account to spam or harass someone, copy files from hard drives, wipe a computer hard drive clean, and more. See Cracker.

Harassment. Badgering, annoying, worrying, or tormenting another person, often through repeated unwelcome contact. Online harassment typically occurs when someone begins sending nasty messages via e-mail, chat, IM, or newsgroups. If not stopped at this stage, it could lead to cyberstalking.

Header. What you usually see in an e-mail message or Usenet post: the TO:, FROM:, DATE:, and SUBJECT: lines. See Full Headers.

History: Text file that lists all the Web sites you visited with your Web browser.

Hoaxes. Similar to urban legends, hoaxes are the messages and posts that try to convince people they can get something for nothing, or that a bad virus is coming their way, or some other nonsense. P. T. Barnum supposedly said, "There's a sucker born every minute"—online, there's no shortage of hoaxes aimed at proving that point.

Home Page. The first page of a Web site, or the Web page/site that automatically loads each time you launch your browser.

Host. The name of a specific machine within a larger domain.

HTML. HyperText Markup Language. What Web pages are really made of. Tags that make what you see look "pretty." Example: I am here would make those words show up in bold type: **I am here**. If you're not familiar with HTML, go to a Web site/page, right-click your mouse, click on "View Source," and you'll see what looks like a different language. Anything in "arrows" is the HTML code.

HTTP. HyperText Transfer Protocol. Seen at the beginning of a URL, this is basically a set of instructions for communication between a server and a site.

HTTPS. This means you've gone to a Web site that is secure, allowing for safe online transactions, whether it's shopping, banking, or a protected site that only certain people can access.

Identity Theft. When someone steals your identity online, impersonates you, and wreaks havoc in your name; many times the thief charges money to credit cards you never received, takes out loans, and orders items, among other damaging activities.

IM: Instant message. Similar to chat except the conversation is one-on-one instead of in a room with many other people; popular IM programs include AIM (AOL Instant Messenger), ICQ, and Yahoo! Messenger.

Internet. A worldwide set of computers using TCP/IP; the World Wide Web is a subset of these computers.

Intranet. Similar to a local area network (LAN). An internal Internet available only to those within that company or building.

IP. Internet Protocol. How data is sent from one computer (aka a "host") to another on the Internet. This is the most popular of protocols on which the Internet is based. Each host has at least one IP address that uniquely identifies it from all other hosts on the Internet. See IP Address.

IP Address. Internet Protocol Address. A set of four numbers that identify where you are located on the Internet. Every computer/server has a unique number, so if you use a dial-up ISP, you may have a different IP address each time you dial in to the Internet, as ISPs run more than one server to accommodate their customers. The larger the ISP, the more servers, thus the more IP addresses. So one day you may log in to an IP address of 204.52.190.0, the next day you might log in to an IP address of 204.52.191.2.

IRC. Internet Relay Chat. Similar to chat, a system that allows you to have text-based communication with one or more people, but without all the "pretty" graphics.

ISP. Internet Service Provider. Also called an IAP (Internet Access Provider), a company that provides access to the Internet.

IT. Acronym for Information Technology.

Kbps. Kilobits per second, or the speed of a modem.

Keystroke Loggers. Software programs and/or hardware devices that record every key you strike on a computer keyboard, usually installed without the user's knowledge.

Kill Filter. Many e-mail programs offer this feature so that the e-mail program can automatically delete any e-mail the user doesn't want. Most people use this for spam.

LAN (Local Area Network). Sometimes known as an intranet, an internal "Internet" for a company; only employees and those within the company can access it. LANs are not available to the general public; some large corporations have an intranet/LAN accessible by a branch of that corporation, whether it is across the U.S. or on the other side of the world.

Lurker. Someone who goes to a newsgroup or chat room and reads what's going on but does not participate in the discussion. This is called "lurking."

Mailing List. Similar to a newsgroup, but all messages (new ones and replies) are sent to your e-mail inbox. If the mailing list is especially active, this could be as many as 100 messages or more in your e-mail inbox daily.

Message Board. Similar to a newsgroup, but located on a Web site; usually message boards are not moderated, which opens the door for trolls and spoofers.

Metasearch. Conducting a search on the Web by using several search engines at once, with the results compiled and given to you so that there are no repeats.

Mirror Site. A Web site set up as an alternate to a busy site, with copies of all the files stored at the primary location.

Moblog. Mobile phone (cell phone) blog (see Blog), except with photos instead of text.

Modem. It's usually inside your computer (some people like to use external modems). A modem helps connect you to the Internet, whether you're using an older dial-up modem, cable, or DSL.

Mung. As in "munging an e-mail address." To add numerals, letters, or characters to your e-mail address so that spammers can't harvest your e-mail address to send you spam. Example: Instead of using anotherwriter@hotmail.com, change the preferences and reply-to settings in your e-mail program to read "another-NOT-writer@ hotmail.com."

Netiquette. To be polite online. Basically it's Internet etiquette.

Netizens. Common nickname for online users.

Network. A system of connected computers exchanging information with each other. A LAN is a smaller form of a network. The Internet is a fantastically huge worldwide network of computers.

Newbie. Someone new to the Internet.

Newsgroup. Also known as Usenet, a newsgroup is similar to a message board. It is topic-specific, such as misc.writing for writers, alt.beer for beer lovers, or alt.fan.harrison-ford for fans of the actor. A message is posted on a newsgroup usually about a particular subject that is already being discussed. Others can reply to that post or start a new subject. Anyone who visits the newsgroup can read the messages and replies without posting anything (see Lurker). There are thousands of newsgroups on the Net, with the number growing every day.

Newsreader. A software program that allows you to access and keep track of available newsgroups through your ISP (alphabetically) and which ones you subscribe to; it also helps organize the messages and replies received from any newsgroups you're subscribed to. Many people like to use a separate newsreader program, such as Forté Agent, instead of using the newsreader that comes with their Web browser or a Web-based newsgroup search engine, such as Google Groups or Newsone.net.

Nigerian Spam. Common spam from someone claiming to have inherited or suddenly come into millions of dollars and who needs your help to transfer the money to the U.S. (or wherever you live). The catch? You need to open up a bank account in your name or use your current bank account and give the sender all your account information. If you do this, then it goes from being spam to scam.

NSLookup. A software program in which you enter a host name (for example, "disney.com") and see what the corresponding IP address is. NSLookup also does reverse name lookup to find the host name for an IP address you specify.

Online. When you connect to your ISP, whether it's AOL, CompuServe, Netcom, Earthlink, or a local bulletin board system, you are online. Anything you do related to this is considered being online, whether it's sending e-mail, surfing Web sites, chatting, or reading newsgroups.

Online Auction Fraud. When a seller offers something that is not what was claimed, such as forged autographs or memorabilia; pirated software, videos, or music; and any prize that is not as initially described.

Online Banking. Doing all of your banking online, including paying bills.

Online Scams. The same as scams offline, in which an offer is just too good to be true but some people still fall for it.

Online Shopping. Shopping from the comfort of your home or office via the Internet.

Packet. A unit of data sent between an origin and a destination online. Example: When any file (e-mail message, graphic/photo, HTML file, Web site URL request) is sent from one place to another online, it's divided into packets so that these smaller "chunks" are easier to send. Each packet has its own unique number, which includes the Internet address of its destination. These packets may take different routes from each other, but they all arrive at the same destination where they are reassembled back into the original file that was sent.

PDA. Personal Digital Assistant, such as a Palm Pilot or other handheld "mini-computer" used for keeping track of appointments, to store phone numbers, and more.

PGP. Pretty Good Privacy. A form of encryption, it scrambles messages so they are unreadable by anyone except the sender and the recipient. This is one of the most popular encryption programs available.

Phishing. A play on the word "fishing," when scammers try to get you to reply or take them up on an offer to make money, or they claim your account needs to be verified by reconfirming everything from your user ID and password, to credit, banking, and other information.

Ping Sweeps. A diagnostic function generally used for network troubleshooting that reports whether a computer is online.

Port Scans. Making connection requests to selected ports on a computer to see if any of the connection requests are accepted. Typically used by hackers.

Post. To send a message to a mailing list, newsgroup, or other online forum. You use links or click on graphical buttons that read something like "Post a new message/subject" or "Reply to this topic/subject." Each list, group, and forum has a different way to post.

Preference Settings (Options). Where you can select which options you want in your browser, e-mail, newsreader, and IM programs.

Profile. All about you, depending on how much information you input. Popular with chat programs and some ISPs, such as AOL. Remember, the less information you provide, the less likely you'll become an online victim. Don't give away too much.

RATs. Remote Access Trojans. Small servers installed on a computer without permission, typically with a benign or seemingly useful program. Once installed, RATs let the attacker take complete control of a computer.

Remailer. An online service that allows you to send e-mail messages through its Web site instead of through your e-mail program so that you retain a bit of anonymity.

Scammers. People who are out to illegally make a buck by running fraudulent schemes online.

Screen Name. See Username.

Scroll. When on a Web site, place your mouse cursor on the bar on the far right or bottom of the screen and move the bar down or up to go to a different part of a Web page; the page up/page down or a scroll button on a mouse can be used to do this as well.

Search Engine. A tool for searching for information on the Internet by topic. Popular search engines include Yahoo!, Google, Ask Jeeves, and Excite. You type in your search query using one or more words.

Server. A computer connected to the Internet that stores and/or provides information, such as Web pages, e-mail messages, and newsgroup posts.

Shill Bidding. Found on auction Web sites, this refers to sellers with more than one User ID. These sellers use one ID for selling the item(s), then the other(s) to bid on the item(s) to drive the bid up, unbeknownst to legitimate bidders.

Signature File. A line or two of words, usually a user's name and contact information or favorite Web site URL, automatically added to the end of every e-mail or Usenet message sent out.

Site. A single page or collection of related Web pages at one domain.

Smiley. See Emoticons.

Snail Mail. The U.S. Postal Service delivers this to your house six days a week.

Sock Puppet. An e-mail address that goes nowhere when someone tries to send a message to it.

Spam. Unsolicited electronic junk mail, usually advertisements or offers, and, more often than not, unwanted by the receiver; sometimes used as a revenge tactic by pretending to be someone, then spamming messages to hundreds, sometimes thousands of people.

Spamming. When someone posts a message to more than 20 newsgroups at a time.

Spoofer. Someone who impersonates another person online. A spoofer will sometimes open several e-mail accounts in the victim's name, then use those accounts to post messages on Web sites; send offensive e-mail messages to others (typically employers, family, and friends of the victim); pose as the victim in chat rooms, newsgroups, and mailing lists; sign guestbooks; and commit various online transgressions in the name of the victim; a form of identity theft.

Spyware. An independent, executable program on a computer, usually put there without the computer user's knowledge.

SSL. Secure Socket Layer; also known as Secure Server. A form of encryption that scrambles your credit card and other information, allowing for safe transmission of the transaction.

Subscribe. To become a member of a mailing list, newsgroup, or other online service.

Surf. Common term for going from site to site or page to page on the Web.

Techie. Someone who is a computer and/or Internet expert.

Texting. Also known as Text Messaging, mostly associated with cell phones. Similar to IMs, messages can be sent from your cell phone to another person's cell phone or to someone's IM account.

Thread. A group of messages that are replies to a subject or topic being discussed in an online forum, newsgroup, or message board.

TOS. Terms of Service. Basically the rules and regulations an ISP, Web site host, forum, etc. implements; its users must abide by the rules or risk being kicked off or denied access to the service. See Guidelines.

Trash. Usually a function in e-mail programs that allows the user to delete unwanted e-mail, thus putting it in the trash; usually the trash empties when the user exits or ends use of the e-mail program.

Trojan. Much like the fabled Trojan horse the Greeks built to gain entrance into the city of Troy, a Trojan in computerese is a program designed to perform functions on a computer without the computer user knowing it's there.

Troll. Someone who visits a chat room, newsgroup, message board, or other online forum and writes messages meant to get the other people online upset. The action is called trolling.

UCE. Unsolicited Commercial E-mail. More commonly known as electronic junk mail or spam.

UDP. Usenet Death Penalty. When an ISP is "shut off" from newsgroups and other forums because of the lack of response to complaints about spammers using their service. A UDP means no one using that ISP can read or post messages to newsgroups and other forums until the ISP takes appropriate action against the spammers and revises its policies and/or terms to prohibit spammers from using them in the future.

UNIX. An operating system favored by many computer users. An operating system is the program that tells your computer what to do and how to interact with the keyboard, mouse, printer, and other peripherals. Other operating systems include Windows, LINUX, and DOS.

Urban Legends. Online, they're much like the ones you've heard offline—stories so incredibly unreal they're, well, unreal. Online legends keep popping up in e-mail, on Web sites, in newsgroups, and in chat rooms even after they've been debunked.

URL. Uniform Resource Locator. A Web site address, such as www.disney.com.

Usenet. Short for "User's Network," a list of thousands of discussions on just about any topic you can imagine. Broken down into several categories, you'll find everything from alt.sex.fetish to comp.microsoft to rec.bicycling to misc.writing.

Username. Also user ID or screen name. What you select or are given to use as your ID online. Example: anotherwriter@hotmail.com—"anotherwriter" is my username/user ID for my Hotmail account. It's always good to select a gender-neutral username.

Virtual. Objects, activities, etc. that exist or are carried on in cyberspace. For example, you can shop at a virtual store on the Web.

Virus. A program that "infects" your computer. Some computer viruses are a mere nuisance (snow or dancing animals may appear on your screen for a few minutes, then disappear), but others can cause serious damage, such as corrupting or deleting computer files. Some—like the Melissa virus, which appeared on computers worldwide in 1999—can wipe a hard drive clean.

Web Host. A site that allows users to join/subscribe and receive a host of services, such as personal Web page space, e-mail accounts, chat, message boards, and more, usually for free. Web hosts are available to people who already have online access through an ISP.

Web Wreckers. People who put up harassing Web pages about another person or persons.

Webcam. A camera attached to your computer used to transmit images over the Internet to others who have a Webcam or are in Webcam chat rooms.

WHOIS. An Internet database that provides information on who owns a certain domain.

Worm. A type of virus. See Virus.

WWW. World Wide Web, or simply, the Web.

Zombies. Small programs installed on a computer without your knowledge. They allow an attacker to use your computer to launch a coordinated DoS attack against a third party.

About the Author

Jayne A. Hitchcock is a nationally recognized Internet crime and security expert. She has helped pass laws related to online harassment in many states, including Maryland, Minnesota, Michigan, Maine, Rhode Island, and New Hampshire. As president of Working to Halt Online Abuse (WHOA, www.haltabuse. org) and WHOA-KTD (Kids/Teens Division, www.haltabus ektd.org), Jayne helps victims of various Internet crimes fight back. She has taken her online harassment expertise to the lecture circuit throughout the world, providing messages of hope to victims and training workshops for law enforcement and security personnel. She also volunteers her time as a consultant on Internet crime cases for police departments worldwide, the U.S. Department of Justice Victims of Crime, and the National Center for Victims of Crime.

Jayne also provides lectures to educators, librarians, corporations, students, and the public. She contributes articles and columns to several magazines, including Link-Up (a former print magazine that is now available at www.infotoday.com/linkup/ and as a section in *Information Today* magazine), *Cinescape*, *Naval History*, *Pipes & Tobaccos*, and *Intranet Professional*, and is frequently quoted in media coverage of cyberstalking and related topics. She has been featured in *Time*, *Los Angeles Times*, *Boston Globe*, *Ladies Home Journal*, *Glamour*, *Family Circle*'s "The Web Made Easy," and on the

Associated Press newswire. She has appeared on *Primetime Thursday*, *48 Hours*, A&E's *Investigative Reports, Inside Edition, Good Morning America*, and the *Montel Williams Show*.

Jayne is currently a teaching assistant at the University of Maryland University College for basic and advanced Internet courses, which are conducted online. She lives in New England with her husband, Christopher, and their two Shiba dogs, Bandit and Guin. For more information about Jayne, visit her Web site: www.jahitchcock.com.

Index

I

N

More Great Books from Information Today, Inc.

The Visible Employee

Using Workplace Monitoring and Surveillance to Protect Information Assets—Without Compromising Employee Privacy or Trust

By Jeffrey M. Stanton and Kathryn R. Stam

The misuse of information systems by employees can result in leaked and corrupted data, crippled networks, lost productivity, legal problems, public embarassment, and more. Organizations are increasingly monitoring employee usage of network resources including the Web—but how well are they doing? Based on an extensive four-year research project, *The Visible Employee* reports on a range of security solutions and the attitudes of employees toward workplace surveillance. A must-read for managers, IT staff, and employees with privacy concerns.

376 pp/softbound/ISBN 0-910965-74-9 $24.95

Naked in Cyberspace, 2nd Edition

How to Find Personal Information Online

By Carole A. Lane
Foreword by Beth Givens

In this fully revised and updated second edition of her bestselling guide, author Carole A. Lane surveys the types of personal records that are available on the Internet and online services. Lane explains how researchers find and use personal data, identifies the most useful sources of information about people, and offers advice for readers with privacy concerns. You'll learn how to use online tools and databases to gain competitive intelligence, locate and investigate people, access public records, identify experts, find new customers, recruit employees, search for assets, uncover criminal records, conduct genealogical research, and much more.

586 pp/softbound/ISBN 0-910965-50-1 $29.95

Super Searchers Make It on Their Own

Top Independent Information Professionals Share Their
Secrets for Starting and Running a Research Business

By Suzanne Sabroski
Edited by Reva Basch

If you want to start and run a succesful
Information Age business, read this book. Here,
for the first time anywhere, 11 of the world's top
research entrepreneurs share their strategies for
starting a business, developing a niche, finding
clients, doing the research, networking with peers,
and staying up-to-date with Web resources and
technologies. You'll learn how these super searchers
use the Internet to find, organize, analyze, and
package information for their clients. Most importantly, you'll discover
their secrets for building a profitable research business.

336 pp/softbound/ISBN 0-910965-59-5 $24.95

Teach Beyond Your Reach

An Instructor's Guide to Developing and Running Successful
Distance Learning Classes, Workshops, Training Sessions
and More

By Robin Neidorf

Distance learning is enabling individuals to earn
college and graduate degrees, professional
certificates, and a wide range of skills and
credentials. In addition to the rapidly expanding
role of distance learning in higher education, all
types of organizations now offer Web-based
training courses and teleseminars to employees,
clients, and other associates. In *Teach Beyond Your
Reach*, teacher and author Robin Neidorf takes a
practical, curriculum-focused approach designed to
help new and experienced distance educators develop and deliver quality
courses and training sessions. She shares best practices and examples,
surveys the tools of the trade, and covers key issues, including
instructional design, course craft, adult learning styles, student-teacher
interaction, strategies for building a community of learners, and much more.

248 pp/softbound/ISBN 0-910965-73-0 $29.95

Web of Deception

Misinformation on the Internet

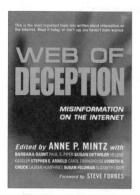

Edited by Anne P. Mintz
Foreword by Steve Forbes

Intentionally misleading or erroneous information on the Web can wreak havoc on your health, privacy, investments, business decisions, online purchases, legal affairs, and more. Until now, the breadth and significance of this growing problem for Internet users have yet to be fully explored. In _Web of Deception_, Anne P. Mintz (Director of Knowledge Management at Forbes, Inc.) brings together 10 information industry gurus to illuminate the issues and help you recognize and deal with the flood of deception and misinformation in a range of critical subject areas. A must-read for any Internet searcher who needs to evaluate online information sources and avoid Web traps.

304 pp/softbound/ISBN 0-910965-60-9 $24.95

Yahoo! to the Max

An Extreme Searcher Guide

By Randolph Hock
Foreword by Mary Ellen Bates

With its many and diverse features, it's not easy for any individual to keep up with all that Yahoo! has to offer. Fortunately, Randolph (Ran) Hock—"The Extreme Searcher"—has created a reader-friendly guide to his favorite Yahoo! tools for online research, communication, investment, e-commerce, and a range of other useful activities. In _Yahoo! to the Max_, Ran provides background, content knowledge, techniques, and tips designed to help Web users take advantage of many of Yahoo!'s most valuable offerings—from its portal features, to Yahoo! Groups, to unique tools some users have yet to discover. The author's regularly updated Web page helps readers stay current on the new and improved Yahoo! features he recommends.

256 pp/softbound/ISBN 0-910965-69-2 $24.95

Business Statistics on the Web
Find Them Fast—At Little or No Cost

By Paula Berinstein

Statistics are a critical component of business and marketing plans, press releases, surveys, economic analyses, presentations, proposals, and more—yet good statistics are notoriously hard to find. This practical book by statistics guru Paula Berinstein shows readers how to use the Internet to find statistics about companies, markets, and industries, how to organize and present statistics, and how to evaluate them for reliability. Organized by topic, both general and specific, and by country/region, this helpful reference features easy-to-use tips and techniques for finding and using statistics when the pressure is on. In addition, dozens of extended and short case studies demonstrate the ins and outs of searching for specific numbers and maneuvering around obstacles to find the data you need.

280 pp/softbound/ISBN 0-910965-65-X $29.95

Building & Running a Successful Research Business
A Guide for the Independent Information Professional

By Mary Ellen Bates
Edited by Reva Basch

This is the handbook every aspiring independent information professional needs to launch, manage, and build a research business. Organized into four sections, "Getting Started," "Running the Business," "Marketing," and "Researching," the book walks you through every step of the process. Author and long-time independent researcher Mary Ellen Bates covers everything from "is this right for you?" to closing the sale, managing clients, promoting your business, and tapping into powerful information sources.

488 pp/softbound/ISBN 0-910965-62-5 $29.95

The Extreme Searcher's Internet Handbook

By Randolph Hock

The Extreme Searcher's Internet Handbook is the essential guide for anyone who uses the Internet for research—librarians, teachers, students, writers, business professionals, and others who need to search the Web proficiently. Award-winning writer and Internet trainer Randolph "Ran" Hock covers strategies and tools (including search engines, directories, and portals) for all major areas of Internet content.

There's something here for every Internet searcher. Readers with little to moderate searching experience will appreciate the helpful, easy-to-follow advice, while experienced searchers will discover a wealth of new ideas, techniques, and resources. Anyone who teaches the Internet will find this book indispensable.

296 pp/softbound/ISBN 0-910965-68-4 $24.95

Cashing In With Content

How Innovative Marketers Use Digital Information to Turn Browsers into Buyers

By David Meerman Scott

In failing to provide visitors with great information content, most of today's Web sites are missing a golden opportunity to create loyal customers—and leaving a fortune in new and repeat business on the table. According to Web marketing expert David Meerman Scott, too many marketers focus on style over substance. While a site may win awards for graphic design, Scott demonstrates that the key to Web marketing success is compelling content, delivered in new and surprising ways. In *Cashing In With Content*, he interviews 20 of today's most innovative Web marketers, sharing their secrets for using content to turn browsers into buyers, to encourage repeat business, and to unleash the amazing power of viral marketing. The book features a diverse range of content-savvy organizations from the worlds of e-commerce, business-to-business, and government/nonprofit.

280 pp/softbound/ISBN 0-910965-71-4 $24.95

The Accidental Webmaster

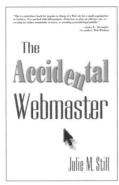

By Julie M. Still

Here is a lifeline for the individual who has not been trained as a Webmaster, but who—whether by choice or under duress—has become one nonetheless. While most Webmastering books focus on programming and related technical issues, *The Accidental Webmaster* helps readers deal with the full range of challenges they face on the job. Author, librarian, and accidental Webmaster Julie Still offers advice on getting started, setting policies, working with ISPs, designing home pages, selecting content, drawing site traffic, gaining user feedback, fundraising, avoiding copyright problems, and much more.

208 pp/softbound/ISBN 1-57387-164-8 $29.50

Electronic Democracy, 2nd Edition
Using the Internet to Transform American Politics

By Graeme Browning
Foreword by Adam Clayton Powell III

In this new edition of *Electronic Democracy*, award-winning journalist and author Graeme Browning details the colorful history of politics and the Net, decribes key Web-based sources of political information, offers practical techniques for influencing legislation online, and provides a fascinating, realistic vision of the future.

200 pp/softbound/ISBN 0-910965-49-8 $19.95